Understanding Criminal Behaviour

Understanding Criminal Behaviour

Psychosocial approaches to criminality

David W. Jones

WILLAN
PUBLISHING

Published by

Willan Publishing
Culmcott House
Mill Street, Uffculme
Cullompton, Devon
EX15 3AT, UK
Tel: +44(0)1884 840337
Fax: +44(0)1884 840251
e-mail: info@willanpublishing.co.uk
website: www.willanpublishing.co.uk

Published simultaneously in the USA and Canada by

Willan Publishing
c/o ISBS, 920 NE 58th Ave, Suite 300
Portland, Oregon 97213-3786, USA
Tel: +001(0)503 287 3093
Fax: +001(0)503 280 8832
e-mail: info@isbs.com
website: www.isbs.com

First published 2008

Reprinted 2009

ISBN 978-1-84392-303-9 paperback
        978-1-84392-304-6 hardback

British Library Cataloguing-in-Publication Data

A catalogue record for this book is available from the British Library.

FSC
Mixed Sources
Product group from well-managed
forests and other controlled sources
Cert no. SGS-COC-2482
www.fsc.org
© 1996 Forest Stewardship Council

Project managed by Deer Park Productions, Tavistock, Devon
Typeset by GCS, Leighton Buzzard, Bedfordshire
Printed and bound by T.J. International Ltd, Padstow, Cornwall

Contents

Acknowledgements

I must thank Brian Willan for the encouragement of the project in the first place and then for patience while waiting for the book to be finished. Thanks are due to the University of East London for continuing to support cross-disciplinary academic work, and for a semester-long sabbatical that has allowed this book to be finished. In particular, thanks are due to colleagues involved in psychosocial studies, most especially Candy Yates for the supportive reading of drafts.

This book emerges from several years of teaching students. I am grateful for their interest, thoughtful responses and provoking questions.

Thanks to Helen, Izzie and Ben for putting up with it all again.

Thanks ultimately to my parents and particularly the memory of my mother (1930–2002), who would have been pleased to see Wordsworth in a criminology book, and my children who probably agree with the sentiment:

Enough of Science and of Art;
Close up those barren leaves;
Come forth, and bring with you a heart
That watches and receives.

'The Tables Turned' (William Wordsworth, 1798)

Preface

This book presents an argument for the invigoration of criminological thought by putting the case for the proper integration of psychological theorising within mainstream criminological theory. Our understanding of criminal behaviour and its causes has been too long damaged by the failure to integrate fully the emotional, psychological, social and cultural influences on people's behaviour. This book therefore proposes a psychosocial model of the understanding of criminal behaviour.

As it developed during the latter half of the twentieth century, criminology became a discipline that was dominated by sociological thinking that has emphasised socially structured inequalities as the chief causes of crime. The rejection of the psychological dimension was part of this political viewpoint. Meanwhile, much academic psychology did little to construct dialogue. Psychology's focus on the individual often appeared to consist of a circular exercise of blaming criminals for their own criminal propensities. Few psychologists engaged with criminological theory, and the discipline of psychology was dominated by methodological concern to mimic the success of the natural sciences and study people by experimental methods. Questions about the messy lives of those who end up on the wrong side of the law, and how they got there, do not lend themselves well to the methods of experiment and the laboratory.

This disciplinary schism is no longer tenable. Criminology without the tools to grasp the significance of the internal and emotional worlds of individuals has reached a dead end. In contemporary social conditions, understanding the way that individuals construct their selves and moralities has become ever more pressing. To understand the impact of social structure on people's lives, we often have to understand the relationships that they have with others and the histories of those relationships. This book is proposing a model for understanding criminal behaviour in terms of a better grasp of the link between emotions, morality and culture. It will be argued that crime can often be viewed as emerging from disordered social relationships. In order to understand the roots of those disorders, we need to be able to explore the emotional worlds of those individuals and how morality, crime and violence are hewn from feelings of anger, shame and guilt that develop in relation to others.

Introduction: psychological perspectives on criminal behaviour

The original motivation for writing this book came from teaching psychological perspectives on criminal behaviour to students, and feeling frustration about the role of psychology in criminological study. Although I believed that psychology did have something to say about criminality, much of the important work was fragmented within academic psychology and quite marginalised within academic criminology. For some time now, I have been struck by a series of paradoxes concerning the relationship between psychology and the study of criminal behaviour, the central paradox being that while many people are asking very psychological questions about crime, notably those concerning individual motivation (*why did they do it?*), there seem to be relatively few academic psychologists who are interested in engaging with those questions.

The marginalisation of criminal behaviour within academic psychology

One very obvious paradox (and the chief inspiration for this book) seemed to be the increasing numbers of students at the beginning of the twenty-first century volunteering to study courses that offer the combination of psychology and criminology who wanted to know more about the minds, the motivations of the criminal – 'What makes people do wrong?', 'Are people who commit crime different from anyone else?' Meanwhile, the vast majority of the growing number of books concerned with psychology and crime have been covering topics within the areas of *forensic and legal psychology* (such as eyewitness testimony, interviewing and other investigative techniques) rather than *criminological psychology* (the study of criminal behaviour; Farrington 2004). Indeed, the decision in 1999 by the British Psychological Society's 'Division of Criminological and Legal Psychology to rename itself the 'Division of Forensic Psychology' is highly symbolic of this shift within academic psychology away from criminological and behavioural issues. No doubt, there are various influences leading to this shift, but I would argue this is symptomatic of a reliance on a narrow range of methodological techniques. In short, academic psychology has become overly dependent on experimental methods. As David Farrington explained in the introduction to the collection of papers on 'Psychological Explanations of Crime' (Farrington 1994: xiii),

> Generally psychologists are committed to the scientific study of human behaviour with its emphasis on theories that can be tested and falsified using empirical, quantitative data, controlled experiments, systematic observation, valid and reliable measures, replications of empirical results and so on.

Such methods are the hallmark of positivistic approaches that came to be rejected within sociology. These methods undoubtedly have their strengths, as Farrington's own work (which will be discussed in some detail in Chapter 3) so effectively demonstrates. Unfortunately, the application of experimental techniques is limited to those situations where it is practicable and appropriate to assign people to control and experimental groups, and where the crucial variables are objectively measurable. It seems ironic that notable areas where experimental methods are difficult to apply are those concerned with such deeply psychological issues as 'Why do we do what we do?' and 'How do we become the sort of people we are?' Born of the desire for methodological purity, much of academic psychology has turned away from analysing the meaning of human experience and has turned instead, within the arena of criminality, to the instrumental questions of how to catch people or tell whether people are lying, or how better to close down the opportunities for the commission of crime (Pease 2002). It often seems as though the people carrying out those acts, with their diverse, complex motivations and emotions, are often quite studiously avoided.

The marginalisation of psychology within criminology

The second edition (1997) of *The Oxford Handbook of Criminology* (Maguire *et al.* 1997) contained 32 chapters, only one of which (David Farrington's chapter, on 'Human Development and Criminal Careers') can be described as taking a broadly psychological perspective and one other that, although not primarily psychological in perspective, takes a distinctly psychological turn (Tony Jefferson's chapter, 'Masculinities and Crimes').[1] Yet, in the same volume, in discussing the history of criminology, Garland (1997) emphasises the 'medico-legal' roots of the discipline. Up until the middle decades of the twentieth century, those who, with hindsight, might be identified as pursuing 'criminology' were often of a distinctly medical orientation, looking at criminals as though they might be categorisable as deviant medical 'types'. This apparent paradox can be cleared up, as Garland explains:

> The irony is that, in Britain at least, criminology came to be recognised as an accredited scientific specialism only when it began to rid itself of the notion of the distinctive 'criminal type' – the very entity which had originally grounded the claim that a special science of the criminal was justified.
>
> (1997: 37)

Thus, those academics who came to identify themselves as primarily criminologists were quite consciously rejecting what they saw as the unduly positivistic and reductionist approaches taken by psychiatrists and psychologists interested in crime. The schism between the sociological and psychological approaches will be returned to, particularly in Chapter 1.

The problem of crime: what needs to be explained?

Any studies of the phenomena of crime need to grapple with the question, what is crime? The difficulty is that any answer to that question has to be understood as being shaped by certain social and political assumptions. As will be discussed in some more detail in Chapter 1, highly influential ideas within criminology in the second half of the twentieth century took a political and critical stance on the study of crime, questioning seemingly common-sense notions concerning its nature. Up until this time, the prevailing definition of crime was that a criminal was someone who committed criminal acts, and these occurred when someone broke the law. The difficulty for this faultlessly logical definition occurs when the law itself is questioned. Who decides what is a law, and when it has been broken? The social critics pointed out that 'the law' was largely defined by those with money and power. It was they who created laws that defended their interests. Therefore, the argument goes, the law has been created by the ruling classes and is predisposed to criminalising the activities of ordinary, working-class people, and biased against criminalising the activities of the rich and powerful. In concrete terms, the law is more concerned with minor property crimes or crimes of disorder, committed by those who have little, than it is with major theft and fraud perpetrated by the already rich and powerful (Taylor *et al.* 1973). To this school of thinking, the major structures of the criminal justice system – the prisons, the courts and the police services – are really about controlling the behaviour of the masses and maintaining the social status quo (with all its inequalities of wealth). Rather different theories such as labelling, radical and conflict theories (to be discussed in Chapter 1) come under this category.

Another front in this debate has been opened up through the investigation of 'white-collar crime' (Nelken 2002). These are the crimes committed by the middle classes (rather than the blue-collar working classes). The crimes range from petty theft in the office (such as using the work telephone or the photocopier for personal matters) to large-scale fraud and embezzlement involving massive amounts of money. It has been argued that all these crimes remain largely hidden because the criminal justice system has effectively been set up to protect the interests of the middle and upper classes – not to police their activities. Anxieties about crime are thus 'socially constructed' and encouraged in order to excuse the increasing surveillance and supervision of the working classes.

More recently, there has been a move to rather different types of 'realist' perspectives (Williams 1991: ch. 16). The central tenet of realist perspectives is that crime is a *real* problem and that society does need to seek to reduce it. Right realism has been highly evident in government policy and rhetoric – notably from conservative governments in the UK and the USA. Right-wing governments on both sides of the Atlantic through the 1980s (notably those of Thatcher in the UK and Reagan in the USA) professed the desire to get tough on crime, to roll back what they saw as liberal policies that, they argued, had been soft on criminals and had thus encouraged the growth in criminality (Wilson 1975). More police, and longer, tougher sentences (and in the USA the increasing use of the death penalty) were seen as key in bearing down on crime rates. Left realism has been championed by British criminologists. They have taken the view that crime is indeed a real phenomenon that affects people's lives – and that it has its greatest negative consequences for the poor (Young and Mathews 1992). Using evidence from surveys of people's experiences of crime, they emphasise how it is the poor, the powerless and the marginalised (the elderly, women and ethnic minorities) who are most likely to be victims of crime, who are most likely to have their lives dominated by anxiety (and actual experiences of crime). Reducing crime is thus a legitimate progressive goal, and the means of achieving such a goal are viewed as complex. To the left realists, issues such as policing and control have their place, alongside addressing the underlying causes of crime (that might well be to do with social inequality and poverty).

Measuring crime

In seeking to study and understand the causes of criminal behaviour, we need some working notion of what it is that must be studied. There are various means of measuring crime.

Official statistics

Essentially, official statistics are made by collecting statistics on:

1 the number of offences reported to the police
2 the number of crimes recorded and/or investigated by the police
3 those arrested, cautioned or convicted of committing offences.

It has been argued for many years that all these official measures are inadequate. For various reasons, it has been assumed that official statistics underestimate the true extent of crime. It seems likely that many crimes go unreported and are not investigated by the police. The obvious problem with relying on conviction rates is that this depends on the police being able to apprehend the offender and then for the offender to be successfully prosecuted. All this depends upon, among other things, such issues as resources and policy decisions about what crime should be pursued. The number of reported offences might be assumed to give the largest estimate, since the police are obliged to record all offences that are reported (regardless of whether they follow these up in any way). The difficulty here is that there are good reasons to suppose that far from all crime is reported to the police. It may be that many crimes have no obvious victims to report them (a lot of white-collar crime might fit into this category). It may be that the victims feel that there would be little point in reporting a crime (a victim of theft who sees little hope of the crime being investigated); the victims might be unwilling to report a crime (due to fear or feelings of loyalty if they know the perpetrator); or the victims may themselves feel alienated from police authorities. The mass of officially unrecognised crime has been called the 'dark figure of crime'.

Crime surveys

One attempt to gauge the 'dark figure' has been through the use of 'crime surveys'. A good example of these have been the various British Crime Surveys (BCS) which began in 1983 and have been carried out annually since then. These are essentially surveys of the general population, asking representative samples of the population about their own experiences of crime in the past 12 months. These are thought to give a good picture of certain crimes that affect individuals, such as petty theft, vandalism, verbal abuse and minor assault. They do not pick up data on more substantial crimes such as murder and serious assault, as these are relatively rare and so are unlikely to occur within the sample surveyed in any given year. They will also not pick up crime that does not feature an individual victim (crimes committed against corporations, or indeed committed by corporations: white-collar crime such as fraud and tax evasion). There are various other possible difficulties (Williams 1991), such as the dependence on the fallible memories of the interviewees. In general the crime surveys are thought to present an important addition to the picture of crime in society. As expected, the BCS suggested much higher levels of crime than in the official statistics of recorded crime.

Self-reports of criminal activity

There is a third method of collecting data on crime and that is by asking people what crimes they have committed. Clearly, this is highly problematic, as it is unlikely that people will volunteer potentially incriminating information. This is a method that has been used, however, with some impact, particularly in the area of youth crime and relatively minor offences. As Chapter 5 'Youth Crime' will discuss in some depth, this method has seemed to demonstrate the high levels of petty delinquency among young people.

Crime: what needs to be explained?

Clearly, any studies of crime could be detained for a great deal of time in these debates about the definitions of, and measurement of, crime. For the sake of this book, the following assumptions are made. In agreement with the principles of left realism, crime is a phenomenon that affects greatly, and negatively, the lives of many ordinary people. There are certain facts of crime that seem to stand up to scrutiny and that are worthy of further investigation. Examples of these facts are the following:

1 The vast majority of crime is committed by young people (although a great deal of this is of a relatively minor nature).
2 Men commit far more crime than women, and they commit more crime that is of a serious nature.
3 Crime rates do vary quite markedly in different social contexts.

The investigation of this book will be empirically informed. It will be argued that a great deal of light can be thrown on various aspects of criminal behaviour through the development of a psychosocial approach.

Contemporary criminology

Important strands in criminological thinking will be described in Chapter 1. The phrase 'aetiological crisis' was used by Jock Young, a now eminent British criminologist, to describe the impasse that mainstream criminological theory had reached (Young 1986). Many of its core assumptions revolved around the idea that poverty creates crime. The harsh fact that during the post-World War II years general wealth increased at the same time that the crime rate rocketed cast doubt on those assumptions.

More recently, there has been a renewed interest in grand theory and the causes of crime (Hayward and Young 2004). Links are being made to the changes being wrought by the large-scale social and economic shifts that have been termed variously post, late or high modernity. The globalisation of capital and labour on a mass scale has led to the disappearance of many of the apparent certainties of former years (Giddens 1991). Many communities in the West have witnessed the disappearance of 'traditional' industries of mass employment. We have shifted from a society organised around the 'production' of goods to one organised around the consumption of goods and the provision of services. These changes, Young has argued, have led to new and more vicious forms of 'social exclusion' (Young 1999). Crime may now have little to do with the feelings of groups of relatively deprived people, but more to do with the dynamic set-up between the apparent winners and losers of this post-traditional order.

Hayward and Young (2004) have recently proposed another new criminological school – that of 'cultural criminology', one that is able to engage with these contemporary social conditions. While this is a self-avowedly multidisciplinary movement (Hayward 2004), theorisation has thus far not strayed onto psychological territory. These issues of criminological theory will be returned to in the conclusion. Meanwhile, this book presents the case for the inclusion of psychological theorisation within mainstream criminology to form a psychosocial approach.

Psychosocial perspectives on criminal behaviour

This book does not present a critical analysis of psychology, nor of criminology. Instead the book presents a constructive view of how psychology already does contribute, but might have more to contribute, to the debate about the problem of crime. It draws together a diverse range of material. Some of the work has been carried out by psychologists using conventional methodologies and by those using some less conventional methodologies, sometimes working in clinical contexts. There is also useful work by non-psychologists that has psychological implications. I am arguing for psychological perspectives on crime that are methodologically eclectic, where narrow adherence to methodological techniques has been stripped away. By doing this, we can begin to understand individuals as agents with interior worlds who are themselves *inextricably* linked to society, to culture, to biology and to their own histories and aspirations.

A consistent thread through the book is that the world of the emotions has often been ignored by mainstream criminology, or when emotions are taken into account, they have not been well theorised. Mainstream psychology has also not always engaged well with the study of the world of emotions either. The emotions belong so firmly to the subjective worlds of inner experience that they have not lent themselves very well to the experimental methods that have been favoured by mainstream psychology.

Overview

Chapter 1 will chart the relationship between psychological and criminological ideas about crime. It will be argued that much of academic criminology developed through the latter half of the twentieth century as an essentially sociological discipline. In large part, this was due to the aversion of academic psychologists, influenced first by behaviourism and then cognitivism, to the messy business of studying real lives in all their intricate contexts. It must be understood, however, that there are different kinds of psychologies. Those psychologists working in the clinical world, much more affected by psychoanalytic thought, were influential during the first half of the twentieth century on criminological thought (not just within the academic world, but also within government and health and social services, as Garland [1997] emphasises). Sociological criminology meanwhile came to reject these clinical perspectives, accusing them of focusing on disordered individuals rather than the social structures that were producing the disorder.

Chapter 2 ('Mental disorder: madness, personality disorder and criminal responsibility') directly examines the relationship between notions of mental health and crime. The chapter is concerned with a fundamental philosophical question concerning the extent of individual responsibility for crime. For many centuries, it has been assumed that being 'insane' could be regarded as a significant excuse for criminal behaviour. This issue has become increasingly pertinent, as it is recognised that large numbers of people in prison are suffering from mental disorders of some kind. Should people who are diagnosed as suffering from mental illness be excused from punishment if they break the law? Should they be dealt with by the criminal justice system or by the health services? The chapter looks at the history of, and some of the problems presented by, the 'insanity defence'. Particular attention will be given to the topic of psychopathy, or 'antisocial personality disorder', as it is being referred to more recently. In this category are people who seem not to suffer from delusions or hallucination; their thinking seems quite clear and their perceptions seem 'normal'. However, their actions are often severely 'abnormal' and so cruel that they suggest highly disturbed emotional responses. Either they seem to enjoy hurting others, or they are at least not inhibited by the pain that they inflict on others. Despite being clearly abnormal in terms of their behaviour to others, they have not generally been viewed as insane. It can be argued that the legal definitions of insanity have favoured the view that only disorders of rational thought might be deserving of sympathy, while those who seem to suffer from disordered emotional responses have not been seen as legally insane. The arguments around antisocial personality disorder in many ways encapsulate the debates about the nature of criminality. Can people whose behaviour seems so far beyond the normal be understood in terms of their individual psychopathology? Are they victims of their own genes? Or are there some people whose behaviour is simply bad? The answers to these questions are not easily forthcoming. At present, the conceptual difficulties in defining a psychopath or someone deemed to be suffering from antisocial personality disorder remain unresolved. The debates within psychology about the nature of these 'disorders' are good examples of the splits within the discipline between those who see such behaviour as stemming from emotional distress and those who view it as resulting from brain disorders or failures of cognition.

There is evidence that those with the diagnosis of antisocial personality disorder do often share life histories marked by familial and social deprivation. Chapter 3 ('The contribution of criminal career research') examines the evidence about links between adult criminality and childhood behaviour and circumstances. It will begin by reviewing evidence from a number of longitudinal studies that have investigated the lives of children and then followed those children into adulthood to see which of them acquire criminal records. Such a methodology allows us to look back and try to determine whether there are factors in childhood that might be associated with later criminality. One of the most important issues that emerged from this research is that it is possible to see that there are different types of offender. There are, first, the large numbers of people who commit some kind of offence, usually during their teenage years, and who then stop (as we shall explore further in Chapter 5, there may be grounds for arguing that a certain amount of lawbreaking in the teenage years is statistically and psychologically 'normal'). Second, there are the smaller numbers of offenders who start getting into trouble at a younger age, who commit more serious offences, and who carry on offending into adulthood. The evidence from these studies suggests that it is very likely that these two groups need to be understood as being psychologically and socially distinct. An important finding that emerged from these longitudinal studies is that the more serious and persistent offenders seem to be those who had more severe problems in their childhood. They were getting into serious trouble in school (perhaps being excluded or expelled); they were more likely to leave school with few or no qualifications; their family backgrounds were more likely to be marked by difficulties. The question is, of course, how are we to understand these links? The various competing explanations will be considered in this chapter. Are these children simply victims of poor social circumstances – living in areas of social deprivation where expectations of behaviour, and of school, are low? Are they being labelled early in their lives in such a way that they are on a pathway to delinquency, via school exclusion and failure? Perhaps society has little to do with it, and their behaviour is shaped by their genes? Or is their behaviour shaped by more developmental processes: are their personalities being shaped by poor early experiences in their families; are they learning difficult behaviour from their peers? There has been an accumulation of evidence that family background is significant in determining later delinquency and criminality.

This issue will be examined in detail in Chapter 4 ('Familial and parental influences'), in which competing theories will be compared. Are different parenting styles and practices to blame? Are children who are subject to very harsh discipline or to too little discipline vulnerable to later delinquency? Is it important that children feel loved and develop strong emotional attachments to their parents? Is it damaging, as some have suggested, for children to grow up with just one parent? A great many assumptions are commonly made about the significance of the role of parents in shaping the personalities and behaviour of their children. All these assumptions face two rather different challenges. The first is that when we witness apparently poor parenting practices – are we often actually seeing 'ordinary parents' struggling with 'difficult children'? The children's behaviour may be difficult because of biology – their own genetic predispositions, some biochemical or neurological fault, or perhaps even poor diet. The other challenge is more sociological – are these parents themselves being blamed for factors beyond their control? Perhaps the parents themselves are economically and socially deprived, and are bringing up their children in less than ideal environments, and sending them to overburdened and under-resourced schools where they meet and mix with large numbers of similarly disadvantaged children? Perhaps there are more important social mechanisms of control that operate through extended families and wider communities? It will be argued that despite the power of these challenges, psychological explanations do still have something to offer. There is promising work that examines the development of the so-called moral emotions, notably shame and guilt. It can be argued that the capacity to experience and process emotions, including the moral emotions, develops within the context of early family relationships.

Chapters 5 ('Youth crime') and 6 ('Gender and crime') will look at what can be said about two crucial facts of offending that seem reasonably consistent across different cultures: most offending is carried out by young people and by males. While the facts of these circumstances seem to be fairly well accepted, explanations are highly contested. On the one hand, some people seek to explain these facts in terms of individual biology. It is perhaps young men's genetic programme; they are driven by hormones pushing them to be more aggressive and more risk taking. On the other hand, some observers claim that both 'youth' and 'masculinity' are socially derived constructs. It will be argued that neither extreme view is tenable in the light of the evidence. People must be understood as amalgamations of biology, development and culture. Young people, and men in particular, cannot be understood in isolation from their own struggles to forge identity and meaning from the material provided by their own bodies, their relationships with others, and the surrounding cultural ideals of gender, including the construction of gender in the family, and within schools and the workplace. The further development of the moral emotions can be traced through adolescence. The ability to think and feel in moral ways can be argued to be a developmental achievement that occurs through adolescence and into adulthood. It is a development that takes place within the context of relationships with family, peers and the wider social network.

The analysis of gender as a variable is carried into the next chapters, which focus on serious violent offending; this involves crimes that are overwhelmingly associated with men. Chapter 7 ('Understanding violence: learning from studies of homicide') looks more closely at acts of violence. The argument will be made that some of the most useful work has emphasised a better understanding of the immediate circumstances of acts of violence. The point can be made that much violence can be construed as 'social psychological' acts in which people's individual behaviour can be understood only as a highly 'emotional' response to threats to their identity that occur in a group or some imagined group or hierarchy. This identity is itself a product of an individual's history and the social and cultural context within which that has developed. Moreover, although such acts may be importantly 'social', they are also linked to issues of identity, and are often rooted in the relatively intimate world of emotion (notably shame). The significance of violence that occurs within intimate relationships is explored further in Chapter 8. Intimate violence and sexual crime have taken two very different views. On the one hand, 'clinical' perspectives have sought to identify and classify forms of individual deviancy that can lead men to sexual assault, rape and paedophilia. On the other hand, research connected to more cognitive models has emphasised that attitudes that might be thought of as encouraging the general derogation, and ultimately rape, of women are to be found plentifully in the whole of the 'normal' male population (this work finds resonance in feminist sociological analyses of patriarchy). A review of the evidence suggests that neither of these different views can be discounted, and both need to be integrated. There are people whose behaviour is best understood as frankly deviant, yet their acts are also shaped by the cultural expectations around them.

Chapter 9 ('Conclusions') moves on to look at some of the implications of the previous chapters in terms of both criminological theory and policy interventions. It is argued that there is sufficient evidence gathered here to suggest that the theoretical impasse that criminology has reached can be resolved by integrating these psychosocial perspectives.

Note

1 The 2002 edition removed this chapter, but did include a more general chapter on 'Psychology and Crime' by Clive Hollin.

Chapter 1

The relationship of psychology and sociology in the study of crime

Introduction

It will be argued in this chapter that the study of criminal behaviour has suffered from a schism in the human sciences, particularly between sociological and psychological perspectives. This chapter will provide a brief and schematic history of criminological approaches to understanding criminal behaviour. Despite its youth as a subject area, the history of criminology is controversial (Garland 1997). As criminology matured into a fully fledged discipline during the latter half of the twentieth century, it identified itself as being largely informed by sociological perspectives that stood in opposition to psychological theories. In some respects this is rather odd, since as Garland (1997) highlights, those who can now be seen as laying the foundations of criminology frequently took distinctly psychological 'clinical' perspectives, often working as psychiatrists, for example, in the fields of treatment and rehabilitation. I suggest that two factors led to the parting of the ways between criminology and psychology that began during the first half of the twentieth century and ended in divorce in the second half of the century. First, the post-war sociological turn of much of the nascent criminology was heavily influenced by the rejection of positivism and associated methodological techniques (which pivoted on the idea that the human world may be understood in similar terms as the physical one), and the dismissal of the belief that social difficulties may be addressed by recourse to individualistic explanations. Second, during the early decades of the twentieth century, academic psychology itself took a turn *toward* highly the positivistic assumptions and methodologies that were beginning to be rejected in sociology and criminology. Academic psychology was dominated first by learning theories and then cognitive models. Both paradigms have been reliant on experimental methods which valued laboratory studies and the measurement of behaviour. This not only alienated the sociologists who were interested in crime, but also hindered psychology's involvement in studies of criminal behaviour. Criminal behaviour, after all, is simply not a subject that lends itself to easy study in the laboratory.

The premise of this book is that there is much to be gained by seeking the integration of psychological approaches within mainstream criminology in order to create a psychosocial perspective. Theories on either side of the disciplinary divide have often foundered as they fail to account for the complexities of the reality encountered by those trying to understand crime. Soothill *et al.* (2002c) suggest that there are two fundamental roots of criminological thought; first the classical school and second nineteenth-century positivism. Both of these will briefly be described since they provide the foundations of the discipline of criminology as it emerged during the twentieth century. It is possible to see the beginnings of a divide that opened up between criminology and psychology as they developed during the latter half of the twentieth century.

As will be described below, the first recognisable school of criminological thought, 'the classical school' (well represented by the work of Beccaria), provides an example of the difficulties that follow an attempt to ignore the psychological realities of individuals that exist within the broader social nexus. The vision of the classical school was that the problem of crime could be immensely reduced if only the rules and punishments associated with crime were made transparent. The model of the individual was that of an entirely rational creature who would simply perceive the negative consequences of lawbreaking and would therefore desist. It will be argued instead that people's motivations for crime are complex. Following a brief description of Beccaria's work, nineteenth-century developments of criminological thinking will be described. Here the split between sociological and psychological schools becomes clear. Sociological thought is effectively represented by the 'cartographic' school, which examined patterns of offending by geographical area, and in which, clearly, matters of individual agency were ignored. Lombroso is usually taken as representative of biological/psychological positivism at this time, in which crime is explained entirely in terms of individual characteristics while the social context is ignored. The twentieth century witnessed the development of modern criminology. As will be illustrated, however, the various strands of sociological thought, although opposed to the methodologies chosen by mainstream psychology, do show increasing awareness of the significance of more psychological issues (such as emotion and agency). During the twentieth century, the story within psychology itself was one of methodological schism. Mainstream psychology came to be dominated by the laboratory and experimental methods that limited psychology's involvement in many criminal issues (most of which could not be studied in the laboratory). Meanwhile, there were those working clinically with offenders who did influence early criminological thought but came to be rather marginal within later criminological debate.

Beccaria and the study of crime

Beccaria (1738–1794) was an Italian thinker who wrote a pamphlet called *An Essay on Crimes and Punishments* (originally published in 1764). He was a member of a widely spread group of theorists who were writing in the emerging tradition of Enlightenment thinking that emphasised the power of reason to solve problems (as opposed to the appeal to divine forces). Beccaria's work is taken as a milestone in the development of criminological thought (Monachesi 1955; Mannheim 1960), with good reason. It is a short pamphlet but it is a distinctly passionate appeal for a systematic approach to understanding the problem of crime.

Beccaria was influenced by ideas that were emerging from French revolutionary thought and British utilitarianism, and he wrote a prescription for how societies should try to understand and respond to crime. Beccaria's pamphlet in turn is thought to have had considerable influence on the development of utilitarianism, post-revolutionary thought in France, the US Constitution and indeed on legal thought throughout the world. Until around this point in European history, responses to crime appeared quite random and very often barbaric. Perusal of court records from the seventeenth and eighteenth centuries illustrates the brutality. For example, from the proceedings of the Old Bailey, 20 May 1681, we learn that a Francis Russell, of 'about 8 years of age' was condemned to death 'for picking eleven Guineas, and seven shillings in silver out of a Gentlewoman's Pocket near St. Dunstans Church, and Convicted of the same by his own Confession' (Old Bailey Session Papers, 1681).

Even by the time Beccaria was writing in the second half of the eighteenth century, branding, whipping, and death were common sentences for what seem to be minor offences to modern eyes. On 11 January 1775, Lyon Elcan was sentenced to death at the Old Bailey for forging a receipt to the value of £160 (Old Bailey Session Papers, 1775). However, the chances of actually being caught and prosecuted appeared to be remote for most people (Weisser 1982). Beccaria argued that society's responses to crime should be much more rational and controlled. At the heart of Beccaria's plan was a vision of the individual as a rational agent, capable of acting under free will. If society could organise itself so that individuals were faced with a system that had certain expectations of conduct, and sanctions for behaviour that transgressed the law, then they would, in general, Beccaria argued, choose not to commit crime:

> If mathematical calculation could be applied to the obscure and infinite combinations of human actions, there might be a corresponding scale of punishments, descending from the greatest to the least; but it will be sufficient that the wise legislator mark the principal divisions, without disturbing the order, lest to crimes of the first degree be assigned punishments of the last.
>
> (Beccaria, ch. 6, 'Of the Obscurity between crimes and punishment')

Beccaria had many remarkable suggestions, including the principles of 'egalitarianism' (that all should be equal before the law), 'proportionality' (the punishment should fit the crime), 'legality' (the law should be used to define what is illegal – if an act was not against the law when it was committed, it could not be punished), and 'humanitarianism' (the least severe punishments should be used to achieve the goal of deterrence). In Chapter 11 (Of Crimes Which Disturb the Public Tranquillity), he marks out a vision of the future territory of criminology by suggesting a series of questions:

> What are, in general, the proper punishments for crimes? Is the punishment of death really useful, or necessary for the safety or good order of society? Are tortures and torments consistent with *justice*, or do they answer the end proposed by the laws? Which is the best method of preventing crimes? Are the same punishments equally useful at all times? What influence have they on manners? These problems should be solved with that

geometrical precision, which the mist of sophistry, the seduction of eloquence, and the timidity of doubt, are unable to resist.

Besides marking out the territory of criminology, Beccaria was prescient in another crucial respect; he was highly political. He overtly advocated greater democratic involvement in the law, notably celebrating the printing press, 'which alone makes the public, and not a few individuals, the guardians and defenders of the law'. He was scathing about the way the law has been used by tyrants to oppress the people, and also celebrated the loosening of religion's hold on law and morality, scornfully noting 'ministers of the gospel of Christ bathing their hands in blood in the name of God of all mercy' (ch. 5, 'Of the Obscurity of Law').

Despite many of these notable elements, the important philosophical stance that is often drawn out of Beccaria's work is his assumption that individuals are rational creatures who decide how to behave by calculating the possible benefits versus the potential negatives. If people committed crimes, Beccaria assumed it was because they had simply chosen to do so. The way of controlling crime was to make sure that people understood that they would receive a particular punishment if they committed a specific crime. The level of punishment should be set so that it would be sufficient to make it clear that there would be significant disadvantage to those who commit the offence.

There is no doubt that Beccaria's ideas influenced those who were formulating policies on crime and punishment in many parts of the world in the nineteenth century. They were notably apparent in the penal code emerging after the French Revolution, for example (Hopkins Burke 2005: 27). Those charged with putting such ideas into practice, however, ran into difficulties of implementation. The courts and other authorities that were dispensing justice found it very hard to concentrate just on the criminal act that had been committed and then simply read off the proposed punishment. It was difficult, in reality, to avoid considering the individual circumstances of the offenders themselves. To many people, the presence of mitigating circumstances, or histories of previous wrongdoing, or, indeed, the fact that individuals did not comprehend the charges they faced were significant factors that had to be taken into account. It was these considerations that led to the neoclassical school, which included such authors as Rossi, Garaud and Joly. Certain important principles, such as that the very young and those perceived as insane or feeble-minded should not be judged as fully responsible for their actions, were already well in place (see Chapter 2 for discussion of the legal provisions surrounding mental disorder). According to Taylor *et al.* (1973: 9), the thinking of neoclassicism has been very influential:

> The neo-classicists took the solitary rational man of classicist criminology and gave him a past and a future, with an eye to the influence of factors which might determine the commission of a criminal act and the notion of human volition. They merely sketched in the structures which might blur or marginally affect the exercise of voluntarism. It is this model – with minor corrections – which remains the major model of human behaviour held by agencies of social control in all advanced industrial societies.

The idea that retribution for illegal acts had to be tempered by knowledge of individual weakness in terms of will and understanding ultimately opened the door to armies of experts and theorists whose role it was to assess individuals and make recommendations for individual punishment or treatment. Indeed, during the nineteenth century, another group of thinkers were shifting their attention entirely in this direction. They were seeking explanations for crime within the differences between individuals, whether in terms of circumstances or character. Under the general banner of 'positivism', there were a number of schools of thought that sought to understand society and crime by methods rather like those of the natural sciences.

Nineteenth-century positivism

As Enlightenment ideals spread and developed throughout the Western world, many people became interested in the idea that there might be a set of underlying forces propelling individuals and groups of people to act in certain ways. Just as the movements of the planets, or of apples falling from trees could be understood in terms of underlying forces (such as gravity), perhaps there were also underlying forces that were causing crime. Their job as they saw it was to uncover and describe these forces. The various thinkers and researchers in these categories are called positivists (and indeed referred to themselves as positivists). They were interested in studying crime as a thing in itself, and believed that the principles that were being successfully employed to observe systematically and explain the natural world could be used to understand the human social world. The important distinguishing feature of the various schools of positivism was that they put far less emphasis than the classical school on the free will of individuals, as they were interested in the underlying forces that might drive people to criminality. Rawson (1839: 316) put the case for the statistical analysis of crime in the early nineteenth century by arguing that science could be used to examine 'moral phenomena':

> Undeserved ridicule has been cast upon some attempts which have been made to show that moral phenomena are subject to established and general laws ... Science has taught, and daily experience proves, that the universe is regulated upon a uniform and immutable system; that the several parts coexist and are kept together by means of fixed laws. ... Mankind is not exempt from these laws. ... Neither can it be denied that the mind is subject to such laws.

There were, however, two distinct versions of positivism that had very different views about the location of those forces. First, there were the more sociological schools that looked to the social forces that were propelling people toward criminality. Second, there were schools of thought that took a more individualistic or 'psychological' perspective in assuming that the seeds of criminality could be found in the make-up of individuals. Some people, they suggested, are simply born with physical and psychological characteristics that made crime much more likely.

A notable form of early sociological investigation that used maps to trace the incidences of crimes in different locations will first be discussed. In many ways, the findings prefigured many sociological concerns with the influence of poverty on crime. Second, nineteenth-century biological criminology will be discussed. This work was also influential in rather a different way, as the rather crude, and exaggerated, claims of the significance of an individual's physical characteristics helped to marginalise those fields of enquiry that assumed that the individual ought be the focus of research.

Early sociological work: the cartographic school

A great deal of early sociological work emphasised the social conditions that might lead to crime. The first tool in to be used in this task was that of 'mapping'. There was considerable interest in the statistics of crime particularly in the late nineteenth century, most particularly in the geography of crime. A lot of this work took place on the back of anxiety about the rapidity of social change and the threats posed by these transformations to social order. Cities were developing at a great pace, being populated by a growing proletariat who were working in the newly emerging industries. These new urban areas were seen by the middle and upper classes as dangerous places, full of vice and crime.

André Michel Guerry was a French lawyer who wrote an *Essay on the Moral Statistics of France* in 1833, and Adolphe Quetelet was a Belgian mathematician who wrote about 'the social system and the laws that govern it' in 1842. They both produced very similar work based on analyses of contemporary crime figures, and their work informed Rawson's statistical analysis of crime in England. All of them made a number of observations about crime rates that are still made consistently today:

- Men commit more crime and more serious crime then women.
- Younger adults commit more crime.
- There is a notable seasonal variation in rates of crime (the summer months seeing more crimes against the person).

Both Guerry and Quetelet also observed that a number of areas of France with higher poverty rates had lower rates of crime. Such findings were taken to contradict 'common-sense' ideas of the relationship between poverty and crime, and they foreshadowed debates in the twentieth century on the influence of poverty. At the heart of this cartographic work lay the belief that individuals were relatively passive objects, being pushed around by the larger social forces that surrounded them. As Quetelet, himself put it,

> Society prepares crimes and the criminal is only the instrument that executes them. … the criminal is then, in a way, the scapegoat of society … Society contains the germs of all crimes that will be committed … as well as the necessary facilities of their commission.
> (Quetelet, *Physique Sociale*, book IV, quoted in Fattah 1997: 211)

In England, work catalogueing day-to-day social conditions, such as Henry Mayhew's studies of London (*c.* 1861) and Charles Booth's[1] ambitious work on mapping social phenomena in England, mirrored this interest in the impact of social conditions on people's lives.

Nineteenth-century biological criminology

During the same historical period, there was a version of positivism that shifted the focus of attention to the individual. Cesare Lombroso (1835–1909) is the name most associated with the shift toward understanding criminality in terms of the pathological make-up of individuals. He was an Italian physician who came to be regarded as a leading member of the so-called Italian school of positivism. It is arguable that Lombroso's work fulfils an important rhetorical function in the history of criminology. His theories were shaped by ideas about evolution and inherited degeneracy. He was certainly influenced by the French doctor Morel (1809–1873), who published a *Treatise on Degeneracy* in 1857 that described how bad breeding could, in a number of generations, lead to insanity. Lombroso was also directly influenced by the work of Charles Darwin himself. A number of scientists (including Gall and Spurzheim) at this time were attempting to make firm links between physiognomy (of the skull in particular) and psychological characteristics (Wolfgang 1961).

According to Lombroso, a significant proportion of criminality can be understood in terms of *atavism*, and *degeneracy*. Atavism is the notion that some individuals are born with features of more primitive forms of humanity. They are genetic throwbacks to earlier forms of organism that have featured during the evolution of human beings. These genetic throwbacks were said to be less suited to human civilisation; they are more prone to aggression, and have less self-control than truly 'modern men'. In a similar way, 'degeneracy' was referred to as a process whereby serious problems emerge in individuals born of parents suffering from diseases such as syphilis, disorders such as epilepsy, and the ravages of alcohol abuse and immoral living (this notion of degeneracy came clearly from Morel's earlier work). There is a striking, and often-quoted paragraph (Wolfgang 1961: 369) taken from Lombroso's description of how he came to his insights from the post-mortem examination of a particularly notorious criminal:

> This was not merely an idea, but a revelation. At the sight of that skull, I seemed to see all of a sudden, lighted up as a vast plain under a flaming sky, the problem of the nature of the criminal – an atavistic being who reproduces in his person the ferocious instincts of primitive humanity and the inferior animals. Thus were explained anatomically the enormous jaws, high cheek-bones, prominent superciliary arches, solitary lines in the palms, extreme size of the orbits, handle-shaped or sessile ears found

9

in criminals, savages, and apes, insensibility to pain, extremely acute sight, tattooing, excessive idleness, love of orgies, and the irresistible craving for evil for its own sake, the desire not only to extinguish life in the victim, but to mutilate the corpse, tear its flesh, and drink its blood.

The language used here is helpful in explaining both the popular appeal of Lombroso's work and its ultimate discrediting in the eyes of those who were more soberly poring over the theory and statistics of crime. As Lombroso's many critics have pointed out, despite his own profession of scientific method, he actually went far beyond the bounds of direct observation and instead elaborated rather wildly in describing the criminal deviousness and evil of those he studied. Many of his claims were simply not sustainable when the evidence was reviewed (as Goring did with some impact in 1913). It is arguable that Lombroso's consistent appearance in criminology textbooks suggests that he is often used as something of a 'straw man' in the debates on the nature of criminology (e.g. Fattah 1997: 228).

Correspondingly, Lombroso's name does not even appear in the index of Ronald Blackburn's otherwise comprehensive *The Psychology of Criminal Conduct*. To the advocates of psychological approaches (such as Blackburn), Lombroso has become something of an embarrassment, but to the critics of psychological approaches his work is a useful stick. Undoubtedly, Lombroso's work ran into treacherous waters. Links between Lombrosian theories, eugenics and the Nazi ideologies that saw those with mental and physical disabilities (among many others) being put to death for the good of the purity of the Ayran race are easily made. By the middle of the twentieth century, criminology had begun to establish itself as an independent field of enquiry. Perhaps in part because of the ideological watershed of the World War II, criminology came to be largely dominated by various sociological schools by the latter half of the twentieth century.

Twentieth-century sociological criminology

A sociologically inclined criminology began to emerge, mainly in the USA, during the early decades of the twentieth century. The sociological schools of criminology came to power during times of optimism about the direction and power of social change, and stood in opposition to those ideas that could be labelled biological determinism and so smacked of the defeated Nazi ideologies.

Reviews of the work of these schools of thought can be found in a large number of criminology textbooks (Williams 1991; Hopkins Burke 2005). For the purposes of this book, it worth noting two features of this work, both of which have served to separate these sociological schools from psychological thinking. First, there has been a strong assumption that social conditions, rather than the characteristics of individuals, are a significant cause of crime. Second, there has been a more theoretically led, radical critique of conventional definitions about crime which have argued that societies' definitions of crime have been biased toward the control of ordinary working people.

Social conditions and crime

Perhaps the earliest recognisable school of thought in the twentieth century was the Chicago school. The central concern was to link crime to social conditions. Shaw and McKay's (1942) work echoed the earlier European work of Guerry and Quetelet. They used official statistics to study how different parts of the city produced different numbers of juvenile offenders. They associated these variations with the social characteristics of the neighbourhood: in particular the level of social disorganisation in an area. The idea that some environments encourage delinquency was taken up in more detail by Edwin Sutherland, in particular through the notion of *differential association* (e.g. Sutherland 1947). The focus here was on the normal learning processes though which people develop what become their everyday attitudes and behaviours. It is not that delinquency emerges through a lack of social training, but that it emerges from social training within environments that encourage delinquency. Sutherland generally argued strongly that it is the social conditions in which an individual grows up that are the key influence, despite the possible influence of 'personal traits' (Sutherland 1947: 25).

Other notable strands in sociological criminology that have emphasised social conditions as causing crime have been the 'strain' and 'subcultural' theories that have been particularly concerned to understand the phenomena of deviant groups and gangs. Merton (1938, 1957) argued that deviance is encouraged within a group of people who experience 'strain', as they feel that they have, because of class and economic obstacles, little way of becoming successful in mainstream society. The only way they can achieve the markers of success is by illegitimate means. Merton was sharply critical of American consumerist society, in which the only symbols of success were material goods. He argued that American society was creating crime, as it was becoming free of community and cultural values that provide any alternative frameworks: '"The-end-justifies-the-means" doctrine becomes a guiding tenet for action when the cultural structure unduly exalts the end and the social organization unduly limits possible recourse to approved means' (Merton 1938: 681).

Merton argued that it was these social conditions that create the 'rational man' that the utilitarian philosophers (following Beccaria's arguments on crime) assumed was normal. It was only in conditions of anomie where people feel disconnected from each other and not linked to values that they would be left to make individual calculations about cost and benefits to themselves of various actions.

Cloward and Ohlin (1960) were also interested in the strains suffered by particular subcultural groups, such as delinquent gangs. They argued that such groups could effectively write their own rules of behaviour within the group and become successful within their own parameters. Cloward and Ohlin, Katz argues, 'hit perhaps the pinnacle of academic and political success in the history of criminology, winning professional awards and finding their work adopted by the Kennedy administration as part of the intellectual foundations of what later became the War on Poverty' (Katz 1988: 314). Despite interest in the transmission of subcultural attitudes, Cloward and Ohlin argued that 'delinquency is not in the final analysis, a property of individuals or even of subcultures; it is a property of the social systems in which individuals and groups are enmeshed' (1960: 211). Matza (1964) was another American criminologist who engaged with the notion of subcultures. He was critical of earlier theorists (such as Cloward and Ohlin) for ignoring the fact that subcultural groups are not so self-contained and that they are themselves, as Merton had argued, subject to values and norms of the wider society. The individuals within the subcultures are aware they are violating those norms but they can 'drift' free of those norms within the subculture when various conditions are met – including the anxiety of the individual to seek approval and belonging within the group, where certain delinquent ideologies might be strong. Given the interest in the individual acting within the group and the attention to the will of individuals, there was the potential for a shift toward a more psychological perspective in Matza's work. Matza was, however, scathing about much psychological theorising, on the one hand because of its apparently circular determinism: delinquents are delinquent because they have delinquency within them; 'even if one changes, it is because he had it in him to change. If he does not change it is because he was unlucky' (1964: 93). On the other hand, Matza was critical because psychological theory and the professionals who used it, he argued, simply provided excuses and reasons for the delinquent to break the rules.

Radical critiques

Other schools of sociological criminology became even more overtly political and critical, and attempted to subvert common-sense notions about crime and criminals. They have taken the view that the criminal is, very often, actually 'the victim' (Hopkins Burke 2005). Howard Becker (1963), for example, argued that any apparently 'criminal' act carries that meaning only because society defines and labels that act as criminal (see also Lemert 1951). The person who carries out that act becomes therefore a 'criminal'. Once someone is so labelled, this has great implications for that person's life. On the one hand, these effects can be regarded as 'external'. That is, once people are perceived by others as 'criminal', they will have fewer opportunities in mainstream society; fewer legitimate employment opportunities, for example. On the other hand, they may also internalise the deviant values that they experience as being assigned to them. They then become the criminal person as identified by the label. The difficulty with the account is that it does little to explain why some individuals or even groups of people are prone to these processes of labelling.

Even more radical analyses argued that our very definitions and understanding about what is a crime are being skewed by social forces (e.g. Quinney 1970). Simply put, street crime and property crime are a 'problem' for those classes who have property to lose. These powerful classes therefore created the criminal justice systems to enforce their definition of what constitutes a crime. These definitions were mainly concerned with property and general order rather than with the harm that might be done through the activities of industry (through pollution, environmental damage or the harm done to individual workers in carrying out their work) or of government (through its economic policies and waging of war). William Bonger (1969), in a rather similar argument to Merton, argued that capitalism itself was the cause of crime through its encouragement of 'egoism' – that is individualism and selfishness at the expense of a more social orientation and altruism. Another element of radical critique has been to draw attention to the significance of 'white-collar crime' (see Nelken 2002, for review). Definitions are problematic but the phrase is generally used to cover middle-class, occupationally based crime. Most of the criminologists who have turned their attention to white-collar crime are interested in demonstrating, on the one hand, the volume and seriousness of this crime, and, on the other hand, the hidden nature of this crime. This, they argue, emphasises how biased the criminal justice system is against the visible but relatively minor crimes of the proletariat. Overall, the theorising of much of the radical critique has clear roots in the work of Marx and Engels (Taylor *et al.* 1973). Solutions lay in social change and the overthrow of the capitalist system and the advancement of socialism.

Both of these important strands in sociological criminology, those that looked to the social conditions that create crime and the radical critique of definitions of crime, have been highly influential on the discipline and have meant that a great deal of psychological thinking – that puts stress on individual factors – has not been taken seriously. These powerful strands in sociological criminological thought were subject to what was described by Jock Young as the 'aetiological crisis':

> In the post-1945 period, official crime rates continued to rise remorselessly, year by year, even accelerating as we entered the affluent sixties. Real incomes became the highest in history, slums were demolished one by one, educational attainment rose, physical fitness improved dramatically, social services expanded in order to provide extensive welfare provisions and safety nets, and yet the crime rate continued to doggedly rise! All of the factors which should have led to a drop in delinquency if mainstream criminology were even half correct, were being ameliorated and yet precisely the opposite effect was occurring.
>
> (Young 1986: 5)

Over the post-war decades in the West, just as the incomes of most ordinary people soared, their health improved, and their opportunities for education and social mobility increased, so did the crime rate. The difficulty has been that this crisis has not resolved (Nelken 1994; Young 1999; Hayward and Young 2004). It can be argued that the beginning of the twenty-first century has witnessed further abandonment of theories that have attempted to understand the causes of crime, and the rise of 'administrative' criminology (the effort simply to measure crime rates and compare methods of control) (Young 1986).

It will be argued that it is the reluctance of mainstream criminology to engage with the psychological worlds of individuals that has led to this impasse. Neither the schools that have assumed that social conditions create crime, nor those that were more radical and argued that crime is largely a social construction have seriously considered the individual agent. Two further areas of criminology that did seem to steer the analysis toward the individual agent will be briefly described; 'control theories' and the phenomenological approach of Jack Katz. Both assume that a great deal of crime gives pleasure to those that commit it. Control theories have sought to explain the factors that inhibit people from doing what is otherwise pleasurable. Katz has been meanwhile more interested in exploring the sensual pleasures evoked in the commission of crime. It will be argued that lines of thought in both of these offer the promise of a richer exploration of crime. In both cases, these hopes have not quite been realised, in part due to the lack of full engagement with psychological theorisation.

Control theories

A whole group of theories were given shape by Travis Hirschi in his book *Causes of Delinquency* published in 1969. He argued that far too much criminological thought had become caught up in the question of what forces propel people toward delinquency. To Hirschi, the real question was *'Why don't we do it?'* (1969: 34). Crime, after all, can be profitable and fun, so why do not more of us do it, more of the time? Hirschi's own answer in 1969 was to say that we need to understand the attachments that people have for others and the social institutions that are in place to prevent us from committing crime, most of the time. Children, for example, spend much of their waking hours being supervised by parents and teachers. Later in life, people may be held in check by the responsibilities they have. For most adults, the job that pays the mortgage and the car loan would be imperilled by being caught robbing the local bank. Their family relationships and their ties and status among their peers and neighbours would also be threatened. Those at risk of deviancy are those not well 'held' by community attachments or the bonds of responsibility around them: they are people who simply have less to lose. Adolescence, for example, could be argued to be an unusual time of relative freedom from parental supervision, and adolescents are not burdened by having too many responsibilities, and so it is a time in which people may indulge their impulses. While the question, 'What stops us committing crime?', was original, the emphasis on institutions and community bonds clearly linked with much earlier ideas from the Chicago School (Shaw and McKay 1942) and Mertonian anomie (Merton 1938). John Braithwaite (1989) has produced what might be argued to be a variant of control theory by arguing for the social significance of shame in reducing crime. He argues that the experience of shame is an extremely powerful inhibiting effect on individuals' propensities to commit antisocial acts. Cultures that are good at stimulating and using shame to inhibit antisocial tendencies have had, he suggests, relatively low crime rates. As will be argued later in the book, shame is certainly an important concept that does link the social and psychological domains in important ways. Concepts of shame have remained relatively unexplored at a psychological level in the criminological literature, despite acknowledgement that shame has been 'under-theorised' (Ahmed *et al.* 2002: 41).

Hirschi and Gottfredson (1990) updated control theory and gave it a much more psychological emphasis two decades after the original control theory (Taylor (2001) traces some of the theoretical journey). While institutional controls still had their place, far more emphasis was put on the importance of individual self-control. Some people were simply better at self-control than others, and it was family upbringing that was usually responsible. Hirschi and Gottfredson (1990: 97) argued that '[t]he major "cause" of low self-control thus appears to be ineffective children rearing'. Here was a mainstream criminological theory that began to foreground psychological issues. The difficulty that control theories have had is that it can be argued that they have done little more than describe the relative lack of engagement and attachment of delinquent individuals with conventional relationships and social institutions. The nature of those attachments is left unexplored and under-theorised. What is the nature of the attachment between individuals and their parents, and to their schools and their peers? Hirschi himself identified that even his version of control theory was still leaving the individual out of the analysis: 'failure to incorporate some notions of what delinquency does for the adolescent probably accounts for the failure of theory in these areas' (Hirschi 1969). The difficulty with Hirschi and Gottfredson's (1990: 97) later argument, that it is the rearing of children in families that creates the problem, is that their analysis remained at a descriptive level of there being a number of associations between familial supervision and the control of delinquency. As they put it themselves, 'In order to teach the child self-control, someone must (1) monitor the child's behaviour; (2) recognise deviant behaviour when it occurs; and (3) punish such behaviour.' Nearly all the evidence they point to really concerns the level of surveillance in the household. They argued that larger families cannot supervise individuals as well as smaller families, that single parents cannot supply the same levels of supervision as two parents and that mothers who work out of the home cannot supervise like a 'stay-at-home mother'. While such suggestions have attracted the criticism of social conservatism (see Taylor 2001, for comment on this issue), what is more striking is the psychological model of child development that is being applied here. This is really the rational actor of classical theory drawn down into the household. The assumption is that if children are supervised and punished for wrongdoing, they will learn not to do it. Hirschi and Gottfredson (1990) do also point to the more general concepts of 'attachment' and 'parenting styles' – but these concepts are not theorised at all. It is suggested that it is beneficial to have 'strong' or 'good' attachments between parents and children. But the nature of these attachments is not explored. Equally, what are the 'parenting styles' that really make a difference? Hirschi and Gottfredson's analysis stops at the surface of the interactions between people, and there is no attempt to understand the emotional worlds of the individuals or their relationships.

There is one very notable attempt within criminology to tackle the significance of individual agency, and this is Jack Katz's work that will be discussed next.

The Seductions of Crime: *the phenomenological approach*

Jack Katz (1988) argued that criminology had become overly concerned with the search for the background causes of crime and needed to be more interested in the actual experience, the thoughts and feelings of people as they commit crime. It was not that background factors were irrelevant, but in understanding crime we had to understand the moment of the act of crime, for

> Although his [the assailant's] economic status, peer group relations, Oedipal conflicts, genetic makeup, internalized history of child abuse, and the like remain the same, he must suddenly become propelled to commit the crime. Thus, the central problem is to understand the emergence of distinctive sensual dynamics.
>
> (1988: 4)

Katz used a mixture of autobiographical depictions, published academic reports and ethnographic work by students to build up phenomenological accounts of the commission of crime. Some of this work is compelling, and the motivations for violence resonate with other work described in Chapters 7 and 8 of this book. People committing acts of violence, Katz argues, are often warding off their own feelings of humiliation. Links are made with such feelings to issues of social class, gender and ethnicity. Despite the richness of the data, and largely favourable reviews, Katz' work seems to have had little influence on subsequent criminological theory (although there has been some interest in recent years, as will be discussed briefly below and in the conclusion of this book). A difficulty with Katz' work is that the psychological aspects of those experiences, which appear to be so important, are not theorised. The case for the significance of feelings is well made, and the links with social factors is suggestive. The difficulty is that the emotions and motivations themselves are taken for granted. For example, Katz accuses mainstream criminology of having a 'sentimental' attachment to the idea that poverty somehow leads to crime. Katz argues that crime is not really about the acquisition of goods at all, and he quotes the US writer John Edgar Wideman on what his brother Robby Wideman (who was convicted of committing murder during a robbery) had told him:

> Straight people don't understand. I mean they think dudes is after the things straight people got. It ain't that at all. People in the life ain't looking for no home and grass in the yard and shit like that. We the show people. The glamour people. Come on the set with the finest car, the finest woman, the finest vines. Hear people talk about you. Hear the bar go quiet when you walk in the door. Throw down a yard [$100] and tell everybody drink up.
>
> (Katz 1988: 315)

Robby Wideman claims he was not after the money as such but was after 'glamour', and chiefly *respect* from others. However, Katz's analysis stops at this point. It is apparently self-evident that someone like Robby Wideman is motivated to transcend everyday concerns and desires and become one of 'the show people'. But why? What is the allure of this 'glamour', and why should only some individuals be motivated by it, and not others? The failure to try to answer these questions is not surprising. While Katz gives little space to formal methodological concerns, the philosophical roots of his work, as Hagan (1990) points out, are clear enough. He was working in distinctly sociological traditions of the phenomenology of Alfred Schutz (1967) and particularly symbolic interactionism, which had already been influential within sociology and criminology (notably the work of Becker and Goffman). Here was the commitment to understand the world of the social actor from the inside, with no attempt to apply psychological theory to what is found there.

Katz' work has been revisited by criminologists interested in exploring the experience of crime (O'Malley and Mugford 1994; Hayward 2004; Lyng 2004). Lyng (2004) links the motivation for criminal behaviour with enthusiasm for other exciting, risk-taking pursuits such as rock climbing, skydiving and downhill skiing. Lyng suggests that people are exploring the edges of their own limits ('edge work'), asserting a sense of selfhood in circumstances in which they are more routinely subject to considerable social constraint. While Lyng (1990) acknowledges that the great majority of the people he was observing were young men, neither gender nor youth is a part of his analysis or theorisation. As this book will argue, there are very good reasons to analyse a great deal of youthful criminality in rather different ways from offences carried out by others. Masculinity itself as a factor in criminality also needs to be explored in some detail. This book argues that links can be made with the observations that Katz was making and more psychological work that examines the experiences of individuals. It needs to be acknowledged that the links are not easily made, however; there has been so little cross-disciplinary dialogue that could help us to understand these issues.

When we review the development of sociological approaches, it is clear that many of the approaches contain an ambivalence. There is an avoidance of psychological methodologies and language, alongside the repeated emergence of psychological issues. Whether we contemplate the mechanisms of labelling, strain, control or sensual pleasure, the significance of individual factors constantly emerges and yet remains undeveloped. By the end of the twentieth century, the consideration of psychological issues was becoming more pressing. Control theories had shifted toward understanding how individuals are able to control their own behaviour, while other important ideas such as those concerning 'shame' and the significance of social bonds were also becoming prominent. Meanwhile, however, psychological approaches to crime were developing in isolation from these criminological theories.

The next section of the chapter will review psychological approaches to crime as they developed through the twentieth century. This is a much smaller body of work, and the chief difficulty of much of the work is that it has tended to work within fairly narrow theoretical frameworks and has not engaged well with either criminological theories or issues.

Twentieth-century psychological approaches to crime

In considering the development of psychological approaches to criminality, it is important to emphasise the differences between the experimental and clinical traditions. Both traditions take individuals to be the focus of their concerns, but they have very different methodologies. Academic psychology has been committed to the experimental method. Ideally, this involves studying people in conditions where particular variables can be manipulated under controlled laboratory conditions. While there are real strengths to this approach, it has also, perhaps, hindered psychology's involvement in the study of criminal behaviour (which is hard to replicate in the laboratory). Meanwhile, the clinical disciplines have relied on case studies, and they have not engaged with much academic debate and have thus suffered from a lack of credibility through a time when quantitative methods have predominated in psychology (Nemeth 1995).

This section of the chapter will introduce the major categories of psychological approach to understanding criminal behaviour. The aim is to provide a brief guide to non-psychologists that will also serve to emphasise that there are a range of very different psychological approaches. The following categories will be described: psychology and biological differences, learning theories, cognitive theories and psychoanalytic ideas.

Psychology and biological differences

The notion that individual inherited differences account for criminality has been a consistent strand in positivistic thinking since the nineteenth century. The idea that genetics can predispose to crime is still strongly held, despite the difficulties that have been encountered in providing evidence, or for pinning down the mechanisms for the transmission of criminal behaviour through genetics. In more recent years, evolutionary ideas have been used by psychologists to explain the propensity of some groups and individuals to crime.

Genetics and crime

It has long been a common observation that 'crime runs in families'. As Raine (1993: 245) put it, 'The question of whether having criminal parents predisposes to crime is not in dispute.' However, as will be explored further in Chapter 4, there are many competing explanations for this. This could be evidence for the importance of parenting, it could be evidence of a genetic component of criminality, or, indeed, it could simply be a rather spurious correlation, as the causal mechanisms might have more to do with the social conditions that surround both parent and child. The possibility of direct genetic causes of crime has stimulated a great deal of research. Lombroso, as discussed earlier, had strong ideas on the links between genetically endowed characteristics and criminality. The search for the personality characteristics of individuals who might be particularly prone to criminality has been a popular path for many psychologists to take.

Therefore, attempts have been made to tease out particular genetic effects that may be operating. The common methodologies used to do this are studies involving twins and adoption (people with similar, if not identical, genetic material being brought up in different environments). Studies of criminality among adopted cohorts and twin studies have been used as evidence of a genetic link (Cloninger and Gottesman 1987; Mednick *et al.* 1987), although, when those studies are examined (see Chapter 4, p. 123–6), the evidence is not as strong as the claims that are frequently made.

Psychobiology

As Lombroso's work demonstrates, interest in the links between psychobiological and behavioural characteristics is perhaps the oldest recognisable psychological approach. It was assumed that the personal characteristics associated with criminal behaviour are determined by physiological and hereditary factors. Within psychology, there remains a strong interest in biological explanations of behaviour. For example, there has been some interest in the potential role of 'male' hormones in explaining gender and age differences in offending. This is partly due to awareness of the fact of the predominance of men in the crime figures and an assumption that it is to do with male hormones. This issue will be discussed further when we look at gender and crime (Chapter 6) and also in relation to youth and crime (Chapter 5), since teenage boys have large increases in testosterone levels, a fact that has been used to explain the prominence of adolescent males in the crime figures. Mental deficiency and low intelligence have also been suggested as causes of crime. The possible interaction of intelligence differences will be discussed in Chapter 3. There has also been some interest in the possibility of neurological or biochemical causes of such difficulties as conduct disorder or attention deficit disorder, also discussed in Chapter 3. Deficiencies in diet have also been identified as potentially playing a role in delinquency through decreasing powers of concentration and increasing impulsivity (Schoenthaler and Bier 2000).

Evolutionary psychology

As already discussed, Lombroso was very interested in the idea that serious criminality can be explained in evolutionary terms; that some people's genes are effectively throwbacks to more primitive forms of humanity. The association with eugenics and 'final solutions', and the clear exaggeration of the case by Lombroso and some of his followers rendered this mode of thought very unpopular for decades. In recent years, there has been a growth in interest in evolutionary psychology and criminality (Daly and Wilson 1988; Ellis and Walsh 1997). There are three different aspects of evolutionary theory as it applies to crime:

1 It is argued that deception and cheating may be a strategy that some people are genetically selected for. In addition, a certain amount of egotistic selfishness might help enhance an individual's reproductive success. In other words, selfish individuals who takes resources for themselves may increase the likelihood of their offspring surviving (and thus their genetic material being passed down the generations).

2 Specific types of crime might be explicable in evolutionary terms. It has been argued that crimes such as rape make sense from an evolutionary point of view and from the male point of view, as by rape men may be successfully disseminating their own genetic material (Thornhill and Palmer 2001).

3 There are also ideas about the evolution of the male of the species that will be covered in more detail later in the book. As will become clearer (Chapter 6), crime is very much a male-dominated occupation. Perhaps there is something about the evolved roles of men and women that explains crime. In very general terms, it is argued that because men can have lots of children, while women can have relatively few, it makes sense for women to be more responsible for those children, and hence more responsible

generally. Women evolved to be more caring and nurturing. Men, on the other hand, can generally be adventure seeking, irresponsible and non-nurturing. They may also be more interested in material success and status. Males with higher status find it easier to obtain sexual partners, as they may be better placed to provide for their partners and offspring. These factors may add up to a propensity to crime.

While a great deal of evolutionary theory is open to the criticisms that were made of Lombroso, that the ideas are untestable and unduly deterministic, there are elements of more sophisticated thinking, linking evolutionary ideas to social behaviour (Archer 1994; Cohen *et al.* 2002), that have been used to explore relationships between masculinity and crime. Some of these will be taken up further in Chapter 6 on gender and crime.

By the 1930s, academic psychology had become much more interested in how the environment shapes behaviour, in particular how organisms, including human beings, learn to modify their behaviour in response to their experience of the environment.

Learning theory, conditioning, and crime

Learning theory dominated thinking in academic psychology from the 1930s well into the 1970s. The impetus for this work came originally from Pavlov's experiments with dogs. In his most famous experiment, he was able to teach dogs to salivate at the sound of a bell. The laboratory dogs were already salivating at the sight and smell of a plate of meat (the *unconditioned stimulus*), and would not normally salivate at the sound of a bell. However, if the bell was rung repeatedly when the dogs where being presented with their meat, they would learn to associate the bell with being fed and so would learn eventually to salivate at the sound of a bell (the *conditioned stimulus*). Many psychologists who followed and worked in the tradition of this work believed that such mechanisms for learning could be used to understand more complex behaviours. They stood in opposition to those who believed that psychology had to be based on either the introspection of Wundt or the interpretive speculation of psychoanalysis. They believed that there was little point in trying to study what was actually going on inside people's heads, since such things were not open to the objective observation and measurement that are necessary if psychology is to be a 'real science' like chemistry or biology.

Learning theory offered the hope that we could understand how people come to behave as they do by studying the impact that external inputs (the stimuli) have on behaviour (the responses). Human beings, it was believed, can be understood as bundles of learnt responses. Although the methods of experimentation were new, the model of humanity that was being presented here was not. The person was being presented as essentially hedonistic (pleasure seeking) and pain avoiding. In other words, those behaviours that lead to pleasant experiences would be more likely to be repeated, and those behaviours that lead to pain would be less likely to be repeated. As far as this relates to criminal behaviour, it is strikingly similar to the classical view of Beccaria (discussed earlier in this chapter).

In this tradition, effort has been made to link associative learning mechanisms to the development of conscience (Lykken 2000). People who had been punished in some way for doing wrong would learn that certain behaviours lead to pain, and their conscience would remind them of this before they do the act. Despite having a remarkable hold over mainstream academic psychology (certainly in the USA and the UK) for some decades, behaviourism and learning theory eventually fell out of favour. Too much of what was interesting about people could not be studied with these methods. Behaviourism was eventually overrun by the cognitive revolution (Neisser 1976), which will be discussed later. Despite largely falling out of fashion in terms of theory, learning theories have informed many efforts at behavioural therapies for a range of unwanted or 'deviant' behaviours (Murdoch and Barker 1991).

Developments of learning theory have been used to understand criminal behaviour, however. First, they were used by social learning theorists who moved on from the very simple models of behaviour shaped by punishment and reward to include the idea that people can learn from observing others' behaviour in their environment. Second, they were used by Hans Eysenck, who attempted to link learning theory with inherited personality factors (discussed in some detail below).

Social learning theory

There has been considerable interest in social learning theory as an account of the acquisition of criminal behaviour, notably Bandura's work on the acquisition of violent conduct. Bandura's 'bobo doll' experiment (Bandura *et al.* 1961) is often quoted as evidence of the importance of social learning in the acquisition of violence. Small groups of boys and girls aged 37–69 months were exposed to either a man or a woman who was verbally aggressive to a large, plastic doll. When observed afterwards, those children were generally more aggressive than a control group of children who were exposed to an adult behaving non-aggressively.

Social learning theories have obvious links to more sociologically orientated work, and Sutherland's (1947) theory of differential association might be seen as fitting into this category. Sutherland proposed that individuals learn delinquency from those around them.

Eysenck: learning, crime and personality

A body of psychological work has tried to link criminal tendencies with certain personality types (Blackburn 1993). Work with detailed personality inventories such as the MMPI (Minnesota Multiphasic Personality Inventory) does clearly show strong correlations between offending and a 'high' score on such scales as the psychopathic deviate scale of the MMPI. The difficulty is that it would be tautologous to suggest that the personality traits were causing the offending (Farrington 1994: xvi). In other words, it is perhaps not surprising that someone who fills in a questionnaire admitting that they care little for the feelings of others, that they enjoying harming others and that they enjoy taking risks might be more likely than others to be involved in criminal behaviour.

Hans Eysenck's (1987) work on crime and personality is worth discussing, in that it offers a comprehensive theory of crime. He took two important principles that were dominating academic psychological thought at this time: (1) learning theory, the idea that behaviour can be understood as a consequence of the patterns of reward and punishment that individuals are exposed to; and (2) the idea that individuals have different personalities that affect their ability to learn from experience.

Eysenck argued that people are born with certain personality characteristics that remain constant throughout their lives and that the key characteristics for understanding the development of crime are extroversion, neuroticism and psychoticism. Extroversion refers to the degree that someone is outgoing and excitement seeking. Neuroticism refers to the degree of natural anxiety that someone has. Someone who is seen as high on psychoticism is likely to be uncaring, troublesome, cruel, insensitive, hostile, sensation and risk seeking (Eysenck 1987: 198). People could be categorised according to Eysenck's theory depending on how they respond to questionnaire items (in the Eysenck Personality Questionnaire (EPQ) (Eysenck and Eysenck 1970), for example).

Eysenck was able to associate the extroversion and neuroticism variables with physiological differences. People high on extroversion, Eysenck argued, have lower levels of cortical arousal. Put simply, their brains are naturally under-stimulated; hence, they have a low boredom threshold and are motivated to seek stimulation and excitement. Those high on neuroticism are seen as having more labile autonomic nervous systems, and they are therefore more prone to mood swings and experiences of negative emotions (depression, anxiety, poor self-esteem) for no particular reason. Eysenck predicted that those most disposed to criminality would be likely to be high on extroversion (attracted to excitement and danger) and high on neuroticism (such people who have difficulty learning from experience; since they are prone to uncomfortable feelings in many situations, they do not learn to discriminate between those events that have led to pleasure and those that have led to pain). There has generally been only very weak support for these variables relating to criminality. It would be reasonable to conclude that there is no consistent relationship between extroversion or neuroticism and criminality. Psychoticism, however, does seem to relate more strongly. There is a major conceptual difficulty here, however. In many ways, the description of the person who scores high on psychoticism is indeed a description of someone who is likely to offend. It could be argued that there is an entirely circular argument here. Those who are happy to admit to such antisocial activities as enjoying hurting others, and that they like people to be afraid of them (as on the on the P-scale of EPQ), are also perhaps likely to enjoy fairly antisocial pursuits.

There is still interest among some psychologists in linking personality characteristics with greater or lesser propensities to crime. To an extent, the same criticism can be levelled at them – they are describing the characteristics of those who indulge in crime without necessarily providing an explanation of where those propensities come from or what interventions might be most effective. The notion that some individuals might have disordered personalities that lead them toward serious criminality has been of interest to government in recent years, and it is discussed in some detail in Chapter 2.

Cognitive theory

Psychologists interested in studying thought processes have formed an important tradition, usually looking at how thinking develops in children. Piaget is undoubtedly the most significant name in this field. His work was concerned with understanding the development of thinking in children, and he argued that it needed to be understood as taking place in a series of stages. A similar model has been used to understand the development of moral development. Lawrence Kohlberg suggested that moral thinking can be understood as taking place through a series of stages, in particular that of adolescence (discussed in Chapter 5, 'Youth Crime').

Perhaps it was partly due to the increasing availability of Piaget's work in English (Piaget was Swiss) during the 1960s that learning theories began to be superseded in academic psychology by cognitive theories. Cognitive ideas became popular partly because of the increasing disillusion with learning theory. There was simply too much that was not begun to be explained by learning theories about the way that many animals behaved, never mind human beings. Much of the cognitive work has been based on an 'information-processing model' – inspired by the belief that the human mind can be understood as though it functions like a computer (or an information processor). As Ulric Neisser explained, 'The activities of the computer itself seemed akin to cognitive processes. Computers accept information, manipulate symbols, store items in "memory" and retrieve them again, classify inputs, recognise patterns, and so on' (Neisser 1976: 5). Models were built, using experiments and observations, of the way the mind might function. Cognitive psychology did indeed represent a revolution in academic psychology, shifting attention back toward what might be going on in people's heads. In terms of its methodology, however, the continuity with behaviourism was very clear. There was a strong reliance on laboratory experiments featuring directly observable tasks and behaviours. As Neisser implies, it is a very rational model of human thinking that is being assumed here. Much of the academic work in cognition has remained at the level of investigating mental processes such as those to do with memory, perception and language, and has not been so concerned with behaviour such as deviancy and criminality. There have, however, been three direct contributions to criminological thought: first, through the development in the 1980s of theories of crime, notably 'rational choice theory' (Clarke and Cornish 1985), which was itself clearly similar to Cohen and Felson's (1979), 'routine activities theory'; second, through theories that supposed that individuals may have different cognitive styles and abilities that would lead to differences in behaviour (including criminal behaviour); and third, through the development of cognitive and cognitive-behavioural therapies, which have begun to be used with offenders. Each of these will be briefly described.

Rational choice theory

Cognitive theory has featured as a central component of a more general theory of crime: 'rational choice theory' (Clarke and Cornish 1985). As Fattah (1997: 264) points out, rational choice theory represents a significant return to older classical thinking in criminology. It contrasts strongly with much positivistic thinking in that it does not see individuals as being 'dupes' of hidden forces (whether those forces are understood to be rooted in sociology, psychology or physiology). Here the individual is viewed as coming to make a rational decision to offend. It is assumed that individuals have free will; they make choices based on the information available to them. People's decision to commit burglary is based on their assessment of what the rewards might be (whether in terms of financial reward, esteem in the eyes of their peers, or the immediate enjoyment), what the chances of getting caught are, and awareness of what the consequences might be if they did get caught. If they judge that the benefits outweigh either the chances of getting caught or the negative consequences that would follow, then they will commit the crime. It is worth noting that Clarke and Cornish (1985) saw their theory as being able to bring together other criminological theories and observations. They point out that many sociological theorists have dwelt on the fact that offenders seek to 'rationalise' their behaviour (notably Matza (1969), as discussed above). Their theory could also incorporate social factors such as poverty (or perceived poverty) and the significance of the group culture (which an individual could decide to be consistent with). Psychological models that take into account that some people make poor judgements and are not rational in their decision-making could also be included. The fact that rational choice theory can be extremely inclusive and that very complex models can be built around an individual offender gives rise to the very potent criticism that can be made of this theory – does it really do any more than describe a whole range of potential factors that might affect an individual's behaviour? Does it have any way of discriminating between factors? Is it possible to make useful predictions from this model? In other words, is it really a theory of crime – or simply a descriptive model of people's behaviour and circumstances? Rational choice theory (and the related 'routine activities theory') has been used as an argument to support the benefits of a shift of attention from understanding the causes of crime to understanding the importance of the immediate circumstances and therefore to develop strategies that make crime more difficult to commit (Pease 2002). Decker *et al.* (1993), for example, provided evidence that potential burglars are more likely to be deterred by an increased threat of arrest than by more severe punishment. The study also found that those with criminal histories are more likely to make pro-criminal decisions, pointing to the importance of individual differences. Other theories of cognition have evolved that look much more closely at individual differences.

Individual differences and cognition

Hollin (2002) describes some of the ways that cognitive ideas have been marshalled as explanations for individual differences in offending.

Lack of self control. Ross and Fabiano (1985) suggested that individuals vary in the degree to which they are able to pause and reflect before having an impulse to act and acting on that impulse. This is a complicated concept that has been the subject of a great deal of speculation. As discussed previously in this chapter, Hirschi and Gottfredson (1990) proposed that this is the significant variable that can explain differential rates of offending. As will be discussed in Chapter 2, the idea that crime-prone individuals have problems in controlling their impulses in one way or another has been an alluring one.

Lack of empathy, difficulties with perspective taking. A number of authors have suggested that some people have a higher propensity to commit crime and do harm to others either because they are poor at empathising at an emotional level with the victim, or they struggle to see the perspective of others. These ideas have been used to explain the behaviour of very antisocial individuals who can act seemingly with no regard for others. They are often labelled as psychopaths or as suffering from antisocial personality disorder. More recently, there have been efforts to identify the possibly very specific cognitive deficits of 'psychopaths'. Blair (1995) has suggested, for example, that they have deficits in a 'violence-inhibitor module' that make them more likely to indulge in extreme violence. These issues are discussed further in Chapter 2 in relation to theories of the causes of the 'personality disorders'.

Moral reasoning ability. Some criminological work has developed from Lawrence Kohlberg's extension of Piagetian thinking on stages of cognitive development (Palmer 2003). Paralleling Piaget's work on the development of thinking, Kohlberg suggested that the development of moral thought can also be traced to stages of development in cognitive functioning. The suggestion is that the forms of thinking necessary for people truly to appreciate the perspective of others and to be able to apply moral concepts such as justice require quite advanced levels of cognitive ability that develop only through the late teenage years and early adulthood (and do not develop fully in some individuals). These ideas are dealt with more thoroughly in Chapter 5 ('Youth Crime'), since they might explain why so many young people commit offences (that is, many teenagers are not sufficiently morally developed to appreciate why offending might be wrong).

Social problem solving. Another group of researchers have tried to argue that offenders are less well equipped to deal with and solve complex problems, particularly social problems. While 'normal' people develop a whole range of strategies to deal with the complex problems thrown up by life – such as how to get along with people we do not like, and how to balance material desires with limited means – it is argued that some people do not develop sophisticated strategies but rely on simple solutions such as 'If I begin to lose an argument with someone, I will hit them', or 'If I need more money, I can steal somebody else's money'. This idea was used most prominently in relation to sex offenders, with the assumption that perpetrators of sexual assaults perhaps lack the social skills to make and develop relationships with others as a precursor to consensual sexual activity. Little evidence has emerged to support this view (as discussed in Chapter 8).

Cognitive therapies

Cognitive theory began increasingly to be used in the clinical field from the late 1970s. One key development was Aaron Beck's work on depression (Beck 1967). Beck argued that people suffering from depression have developed maladaptive thought processes. They have acquired thought patterns that consistently portray the world and themselves in a negative light. They underestimate their own abilities and assume that others view them very negatively. This notion of aberrant thought patterns has been applied to many psychological conditions, including anxiety, psychosis and anorexia (e.g. Hawton 1989). Since the 1980s, increasing attention has been paid to the idea that such thinking can be applied to offenders. Much of the early work was carried out in the high-profile area of sexual offending, which is explored further in Chapter 8 (Marshall *et al.* 1999).

Yochelson and Samenow's (1976) work was an early effort to apply cognitive ideas to criminality, as they sought to analyse the minds of serious offenders. There has also been interest in the idea that biased cognitive functioning predisposes people to criminality (Dodge and Schwartz 1997), and there has also been great interest in what cognitive (and cognitive-behavioural) approaches might offer in terms of treatment/rehabilitation (e.g. Hollin 1990).

While cognitive theories have consistently emphasised the importance of understanding behaviour in terms of rational conscious thought, another school of psychological thought has emphasised the importance of understanding behaviour in terms of irrational factors and emotions.

Psychoanalysis and the clinical tradition

Whereas academic psychology was dominated by learning theory and subsequently cognitive theory, the professionally related disciplines of psychiatry, clinical psychology and social work were much more strongly influenced by psychoanalytic psychology (which stemmed from the writings of Sigmund Freud). The fundamental points of psychoanalysis are that early childhood experiences are highly formative of adult character and personality, and that many of those influences operate at an unconscious level. The concept of the unconscious, which lies at the heart of psychoanalysis, is that there are memories, thoughts and, most crucially, feelings that, although they may significantly shape people's behaviour, are not available to observation or even to the self-report of the individual subject. The only way that their existence can be deduced is through interpretation of the subjects' overt behaviour or speech (Freud, for example, put much emphasis on the analysis of dreams, or the free associated speech of his patients). This latter point is the defining feature of psychoanalytic thought and is also the position that has led to its almost total banishment from the academic discipline of psychology, which has come to define itself by studying observable behaviour.

Although they have not been highly regarded within academic psychology, Garland (1997) points out that psychoanalytic ideas were influential in the development of British criminology. Certainly, Edward Glover, a psychoanalyst, and Emanuel Miller, a psychoanalytically inclined psychiatrist, were founder editors of the

British Journal of Delinquency in 1950 (later renamed *British Journal of Criminology* in 1960 (Rustin 2000; Garland 2002). During this period, as Garland (2002: 38) puts it, 'if British criminology can be said to have developed radical analyses during this period, they were inspired by Sigmund Freud rather than by Karl Marx.'

Garland plots the history in detail (see also Valiér 1998), but it is interesting to note that the enthusiasm for psychoanalysis alongside hostility to official penal policy among the founders in 1931 of the Institute for the Scientific Study of Delinquency led to its being ignored by the Home Office when they chose Cambridge to host an 'Institute of Criminology'. As the academic discipline of criminology began to take shape during the middle of the twentieth century, the British Society of Criminology was formed, and it split off from those who had more of a clinical perspective. The clinicians were seen as being too entwined with the institutions of control (such as the prison and psychiatric services), and their interest in individuals was taken to be unhelpful, as they seemed simply to blame individuals rather than examine the social processes that were influencing them. In the latter half of the twentieth century, psychoanalysis, marginalised from mainstream academic criminology and psychology, has been a distinctly muted voice on crime.

Freud himself did not directly study the development of criminality, although August Aichorn (1925), a disciple of Freud, did. The overarching theoretical framework is set by the traditional Freudian model of the infant being born to seek immediate pleasure, but then learning through processes of development and interaction with the environment that desires cannot always be immediately gratified. The inner life of people can, according to the theory, be divided into three areas – the id (representing the instinctual drives toward nourishment and sexual gratification, for example), the ego (representing the selfhood of the child which develops as the child learns that gratification of its instinctual desires is not possible without interaction and negotiation with the outside world), and the superego (the conscience of the self). Children develop their ego as they learn that attempts at immediate gratification of wishes can lead to painful experiences. The ego can negotiate between the need for pleasure and the reality of the world where such needs cannot easily be met or harm may be done to the self or others. The aspect of the ego that is particularly responsible for the control and inhibition of drives is the superego. It was portrayed as developing through an identification with the father (as the figure of authority and discipline). The superego acts throughout life as a sort of conscience, keeping the demands and desires of the id in check.

Delinquency would occur through disturbances in the development of the ego, and superego in particular. Perhaps encounters with reality were too harsh or too early, or there were insufficient encounters with reality. Children who were not said 'no' to, who were spoilt, would, according to this account, have problems in dealing later with the demands of reality. Children brought up with unrelenting cruelty may identify with their harsh, demanding, physically abusive parents and so see only one way of striving to have needs met – by acting in a similar fashion. Aichorn is at pains to point out that individual cases must be understood in their own right, however. His account of working with 'wayward youth' (those committing relatively minor offences) illustrates various applications of psychoanalytic theory whereby the delinquency is seen as representing a symptom of some unresolved unconscious conflict. In one case study, a young man is stealing from his father. Eventually, this is understood by Aichorn as an unconscious acting out of the jealousy and rivalry the subject felt toward his father for marrying his stepmother, for whom the subject had developed unconscious sexual feelings. Aichorn also gave accounts of working with more seriously disturbed boys (he referred to them as 'the aggressive group'). These boys were described as having backgrounds marked by emotional deprivation and physical abuse. The treatment here would be the presentation of unconditional love that might allow for the development of positive identifications with authority figures (that might be internalised in the form of a superego).

Psychoanalysis, with a methodology so contrary to those fashionable in academic psychology, has been consistently scorned by the latter. Meanwhile, psychoanalysis has been used by psychiatrists and social workers working with offenders. These professionals were, however, identified as being too much associated with the politics of control, and became unfashionable as the more sociologically orientated, nascent criminology took a distinctly political turn from the middle of the twentieth century. At the beginning of the twenty-first century, there is renewed interest in aspects of psychoanalytic thought as concern to find explanations of the role of masculinity in crime has grown (e.g. Jefferson 1997; Gadd 2000; Gilligan 2003), and in more general terms as evidence appears to accumulate that early family experiences may well be highly significant (to be explored quite thoroughly in Chapter 4).

Overall, the study of the psychology of criminal behaviour has not developed a strong body of theory or evidence. The core theories of psychology have been applied to crime, but have not provided great leaps in understanding. They have engaged well neither with the background social factors that have been emphasised by sociological criminology nor with the phenomenology of crime that has been described so powerfully by Katz (1998).

Conclusion: psychology and criminology – a psychosocial perspective

The premise of this book is that integration of psychological approaches within mainstream criminology is now an important task. The classical school, perhaps the first recognisable school of criminological thought, foundered when it became difficult to enforce simple principles in the face of the reality of individual differences and circumstances. The nineteenth century witnessed a division between sociological and psychological positivistic schools as they searched for the underlying causes of crime. This schism continued and grew within the twentieth century. The commitment of academic psychology to experimental methods and biological determinism, coupled with the ideological opposition within sociology to anything that smacked too much of biological determinism, or explanations that located the origins of crime within individuals, drove a wedge between sociological and psychological criminology.

In this brief survey of theoretical approaches, several instances have emerged in which fertile lines of enquiry ran into sterile ground due to the lack of sufficient cross-disciplinary theorising. Ironically, questions of the significance of individual agency keep arising in criminology. Taylor *et al.* (1973) asked that the individual agent (albeit it one in a particular political context) be more central to criminological concerns. Similarly, Katz (1988) argued that criminology had ignored the very direct sensual pleasure and satisfactions that are gained by people actually committing crime. Writing at the beginning of the twenty-first century, Hayward and Young (2004) argue that sociological criminology has come to be dominated by rational choice theory (which assumes an entirely rational actor) and versions of positivism that, while acknowledging the significance of social conditions, still offer a 'desperately thin narrative, where intensity of motivation, feelings of humiliation, anger and rage – as well as love and solidarity – are all foresworn' (2004: 264). The problem is that Hayward and Young, in putting forward 'cultural criminology', still do not seem to be allowing psychological theorisation into the framework. This book aims to do that by offering a psychosocial formulation. Human beings are active agents who act upon and shape the world in which they live. But they are active agents who are shaped themselves by the culture, history and biology that they are born into. The disciplinary schisms in the human sciences (most notably between psychology and sociology) mean that this concern about the gap between the individual and the social needs to be drawn attention to again. This book represents an attempt to link the psychological back into sociological criminology.

In particular, it will be argued that there is much to be gained by examining the significance of the world of emotion and crime. Karstedt (2002) observed that there appears to be turning to the emotions in the criminal justice system in two areas; first, in 'the emotionalization of public discourse about crime', and, second, in 'the implementation of sanctions in the criminal justice system that are explicitly based on – or designed to arouse – emotions' (Karstedt 2002: 301). The first point refers to various moral panics, such as that surrounding paedophilia (often led by the popular press), and the second to interest in using shame in 'restorative justice'. Karstedt (2002) is largely sceptical about both aspects of this shift, arguing that it has little to do with the reality of the difficulties faced by criminal justice systems and simply reflects popular and academic fashion. In contrast to this view, I would argue that we are indeed witnessing an upturn in interest in the emotions, but that this is not simply academic fashion but has appeared because emotions have perhaps become more relevant to understanding criminal behaviour. The increasing social significance of emotion will be returned to in the concluding chapter.

The topic addressed in the next chapter is that of mental disorder, in which the significance of psychological issues has long been apparent. It can be argued that theorisation about mentally disordered offenders represents a prehistory of criminology (Rafter 2004), in that debate about what to do with those who did not seem to be in their right minds, or, indeed, the question of who should be considered 'insane' has been going on for many years. Debate and argument between legal understandings of madness and those of psychiatrists and other experts have taken place for many years. Analysis of the history of these debates reveals a particular problem with people whose perceptions or understanding of the world around them seems to be sound, but whose behaviour suggests that they have deficits either in their moral senses or in controlling their emotions. Such individuals would often, at various times over the last 200 years, attract the medical diagnoses of 'moral imbecility', 'psychopathy', or 'personality disorder'. These are highly controversial medical categories that are used to refer to people who seem to have disorders of their emotional and relational worlds. Contemporary surveys of the mental health of prison populations suggest that large numbers of people in prison can be argued to suffer from 'personality disorders', and this, in turn, suggests that the validity of the diagnosis requires further analysis.

Note

1 This work is described and can be reviewed on the library pages of the London School of Economics: http://booth.lse.ac.uk/.

Chapter 2

Mental disorder: madness, personality disorder and criminal responsibility

Introduction

The subject of mental disorder and crime is usually to be found as an autonomous and rather isolated topic in criminology textbooks and courses. It often appears as though the subject is quite separate from the main concerns of criminological theorising. Questions are raised about the particular problems caused by those apparently unusual individuals who suffer from mental disorders and also commit crime. It will be argued here, like Peay (1997), that the topic needs to be integrated within mainstream criminology, as it raises issues of quite fundamental importance. Two important matters can be considered:

- First, the complex question of how individual responsibility for criminal acts can be judged can be traced in debates about what mental disorders should be recognised as being likely to lead to criminal behaviour (and the individual be treated with some 'leniency').

- Second, the increasingly commonly used diagnosis of 'personality disorder' (despite its controversial status) serves as a useful lens through which to study some of the debates surrounding ideas about the causes of criminal behaviour.

Despite some of the ambivalence toward psychology evident within criminology (described in the previous chapter), the criminal justice system itself often finds that it is being asked to make judgements on issues that are distinctly psychological in nature. In making judgements of guilt or innocence, the legal system will often attach great importance to understanding the mental state of an individual. In court, the crucial question can be, did this particular accused person *know* what he was doing when *acting* in this criminal manner? The term 'mental state' is used when we try to describe and summarise the moods and thoughts that an individual experiences at a particular time. In trying to understand this, we are trying to understand the mind of another.

When the mental states of offenders are considered, a number of significant philosophical issues that have practical implications for the criminal justice system are raised. When an accused person is facing trial for an offence, the prosecution needs to establish the following two things: (1) the *actus reus* – that is, that a criminal offence has been committed and this particular defendant carried out that act; and (2) the *mens rea* – that is, that the defendant's mental state was consistent with the act and the defendant had some intention to carry out that act (Molan and Douglas 2004: particularly ch. 2). It is possible to raise some difficult philosophical questions concerning the nature of free will at this point. It may be asked when any of us are truly, knowingly, responsible for our actions? Are we simply acting out a destiny that is really determined by the will of the gods; or are our actions simply the product of the random chemical exchanges in our brains, or are we impelled to act by social forces that we cannot resist? For the most part, however, the criminal justice system avoids these tricky questions and simply assumes a model of individual responsibility. When people are found guilty of a criminal act, it is assumed that they knew what they were doing and that what they have done is wrong. Hence, if a man is caught leaving a shop with a book that has not been paid for hidden under his coat, it is assumed that he understands that one is supposed to pay for things in a shop and that leaving without paying is theft. There are, however, two conditions in which this convenience fails. The first involves child offenders and the second involves those who are viewed as mentally disordered.

The question concerning at what age we are right to assume that children understand the world enough to be responsible for their criminal acts is controversial. Clearly nobody would seriously accuse of theft a 3-year-old who grabbed a book and walked out of a shop. It would not be reasonable to expect such a young child to understand the significance of money and the value of objects. At what age, however, do we expect children to understand what they are doing? The legal systems in different countries hold very different beliefs about the age at which children can be assumed to be fully responsible for their actions. This issue is taken up in Chapter 5 'Youth Crime'.

The second condition in which the convenience of assuming that people are responsible for their actions becomes strained arises when mental illnesses or mental disorders are suspected. This condition is the topic of this chapter. As will be discussed below, people have assumed for many centuries that those who are suffering from some kind of mental disorder should not necessarily be seen as culpable for their wrongdoings. Simply put, being seen as 'mad' rather than 'bad' has been widely recognised as a legitimate excuse for criminal behaviour. However, there are complexities here. There is also the fact that significant numbers of people who come to be prosecuted and convicted for offences have histories of mental illness. Surveys of prison populations suggest that rates of diagnosable mental illnesses in prisons are high (Fazel and Danesh 2002; O'Brien *et al.* 2003).

Rates of mental disorder in prison

Many observers have noted the seemingly large numbers of people in prison who suffer with mental health problems. Such observations have been confirmed by formal surveys of the mental health status of prison inmates. Fazel and Danesh (2002) reviewed a total of 62 surveys of prison populations that sought to measure the incidence of serious mental illness. They found that serious mental disorders were widespread, but that the most common were personality disorders, with 65 per cent of the male prisoners surveyed being so diagnosed (see Table 2.1). These figures clearly suggest that there is significant overlap between the concerns of the criminal justice system and our categories of mental disorder.

Of course, such figures tell us only that there is some relationship between mental disorder and prison. It might be that the association can be explained in very different ways:

1 It may be that people suffering from mental disorder are not more criminally prone than the rest of the population, but that they are caught more often.
2 It may be that the stress of being in prison has an adverse effect on the mental health of those imprisoned.
3 It may be that people with mental disorders are more likely to commit offences.

Table 2.1 Results of the meta-analysis of surveys of prison populations: percentages of samples with particular diagnosis (from Fazel and Denesh 2002)

Men	Per cent diagnosed with disorder	95% confidence interval
Psychosis	3.7	3.3–4.1
Depression (major)	10	9–11
Personality disorder	65	61–68
Antisocial personality disorder	47	46–48

Women		
Psychosis	4	3.2–4.5
Depression (major)	12	11–14
Personality disorder	42	38–45
Antisocial personality disorder	21	19–23

We will see in the following chapters that the relationship between mental health and crime is complex. Table 2.1 shows the diagnosis most strongly associated with criminality is 'personality disorder'. Broadly speaking, the term 'personality disorder' refers to individuals who appear to have highly abnormal emotional lives and relationships. There is real controversy about whether these should be seen as medical disorders (Pilgrim 2001), and the issue will be discussed in more detail later in this chapter. The association between other forms of mental disorder (such as schizophrenia) and crime is much less clear, despite there having been a number of high-profile incidents such as the killing of Jonathan Zito in 1992 on Finsbury Park Station, London. Zito was killed in a seemingly random attack by a man who had been treated for schizophrenia for many years (Ritchie *et al.* 1994). Despite this kind of dramatic incident, evidence suggests that people with such diagnoses as schizophrenia are no more likely than others to be involved in serious violence (Walsh *et al.* 2002).

The controversy over the medical and legal status of personality disorder draws attention to a long-running debate over what forms of mental abnormalities can be deemed to be acceptable 'excuses' for criminal behaviour. A case can fairly easily be made that criminal justice systems have tended to deem disorders of 'reason' as deserving of consideration as 'excuses' for criminal acts. For example, someone who appears to be insane and kills his next-door neighbour because he *believed* the neighbour was the devil who was about to steal his soul would very likely to be treated with some leniency by the courts (the defendant would at least be viewed as having only *diminished responsibility* for the crime, as described in more detail below). What might be seen as disorders of emotions, rather than of reason, have, however, not been seen in such a light. This might not be surprising, since it can be argued that one of the chief purposes of the criminal justice system is to assert the value of reason over emotion; no matter how justifiably angry people are, if they act on that anger and harm another they will often be guilty of an offence. For example, the man who is angry with his neighbour who has vandalised his car, may well have good reason to be angry. If he acts on that anger and hits his neighbour, he is still very likely to be seen as guilty of assault in the eyes of the law. It may well be, however, that those whose emotional responses are in some way disordered do present difficulties to the criminal justice system. One such group of people whose reason appears to be intact, yet whose emotional lives often seem to be disordered, are sometimes diagnosed as suffering from 'personality disorders'.

A particular group like this are those who have been variously described as psychopaths, as sociopaths, or as suffering from 'antisocial personality disorder' (APD). They have caused considerable deliberation among lawmakers. While the medical status of the personality disorders themselves remains contested, they are often found in conjunction with less controvertible diagnoses and difficulties such as drug abuse, homelessness, self-harm (Haw *et al.* 2006) depression and psychotic illnesses (Blackburn *et al.* 2003). As a group, those diagnosed with personality disorders can often be distinguished through their socially and emotionally deprived backgrounds. These latter issues will be pursued more fully in the following chapters. This rest of the chapter will consist of the following three sections.

The first section will present a brief history of the notion of criminal responsibility as it relates to mental disorder. The idea that the presence of insanity presents a legal defence has a long history, certainly far longer than our modern psychiatric notions of mental illness. Despite the long history, there are still fundamental disagreements about the nature of insanity. It is possible to trace some debate between those who have argued that insanity can be understood only in terms of impairment to cognitive and rational thought processes and those who have argued that the concept should also include disorders of emotions. It can be argued that the model that emerged from the nineteenth century was one that privileged a cognitive understanding of insanity. Difficulties in operationalising the insanity defence, however, led to the introduction of the option that someone might be found guilty of taking the life of another but with 'diminished responsibility' for the act due to the presence of some kind of mental disorder. The accused would then be convicted not of murder but of the lesser charge of manslaughter.

The second section will explore the medical and legal definitions of insanity and *diminished responsibility* for taking the life of others that were ushered in by the 1959 Mental Health Act in England and Wales. It will be argued that despite the apparent turn to medical expertise, the legal system remains highly ambivalent about the status of these experts and their categories. Recent debates over the revision of the Mental Health Act in England and Wales reflect some of these considerable difficulties.

The third section will explore further the most controversial category of mental disorder; that of 'psychopathy', or the 'antisocial personality disorders'. These are the most significant disorders in relation to crime. These categories most starkly reveal the conflict between ideas of insanity that have focused on deficits in cognitive processes and the disorders of emotions.

A brief history of criminal responsibility and mental disorder

The idea that people who are somehow 'not in their right minds' should be treated differently from those who are considered sane when they committed a criminal offence has a long history (Walker 1968; Reznek 1997). Haji (1998) begins discussion of criminal culpability with a discussion of Aristotle's writing on the conditions whereby people may not be seen as blameworthy for their actions (these conditions were roughly, if they were either ignorant or compelled to act in a certain way). There is a long history of special provision being made for insanity in English law. The earliest authority that Croty (1924) could find was from around AD 680 with the then Archbishop of Canterbury, Theodoric, proclaiming that it was lawful to say Mass for suicide victims but only if they were insane. Walker quotes from a document that is assumed to have reflected some jurisdiction in at least part of pre-Norman Britain (over 1000 years ago):

If a man fall out of his senses or wits, and it come to pass that he kill someone, let his kinsmen pay for the victim, and preserve the slayer against aught else of that kind. If anyone kill him before it is made known whether his friends are willing to intercede for him, those who kill him must pay for him to his kin.

(Walker 1968: 15)

The emphasis on the payment of compensation rather than punishment was consistent with the manner in which many cases of murder would be dealt with. The assumption that the offender who is 'out of his senses or wits' is deemed not to be responsible for the payment of that compensation is notable. As recognisable criminal law began to take shape during the eleventh century, the principle of leniency toward the mentally disordered becomes clearer:

If a person be deaf and dumb, so that he cannot put or answer questions, let his father pay his forfeitures. Insane persons and evil doers of a like sort should be guarded and treated leniently by their parents.

(Walker 1968: 17; *Laws of Henry the First*, probably operating through the twelfth century in at least part of England and France)

This historical perspective draws attention to the fact that centuries before societies began to develop systematic or 'scientific' understandings of mental illness, the notion that people who are insane should be treated as though they are not necessarily responsible for their acts was strongly rooted. This is important since, as we will see, despite the increasingly formal definitions of insanity being produced by psychiatrists over the last 200 years or so, we still see lawyers in court making appeal to 'common-sense' notions of sanity and responsibility that focus on the individual's capacity for rational thought. These common-sense notions have often won over juries despite the best efforts of expert psychiatric witnesses (Reznek 1997). An important landmark in the effort to formalise the management of mental disorder within the criminal justice system was the trial of Daniel M'Naghten in Victorian England (Walker 1968; Reznick 1997) which will be discussed in some detail. First, however, the very particular case of infanticide will be discussed.

Infanticide

The Infanticide Act 1922 was introduced to English law and allowed special provision to be made for women who killed their newly born babies when 'they had not fully recovered from the effect of giving birth to such child, and by reason thereof the balance of her mind was then disturbed' (Ward 1999: 163). If the defendant was found guilty of infanticide, the charge was reduced to manslaughter, rather than murder, and thus the mandatory death sentence was avoided. This was updated by the 1938 Act, which extended this partial defence to up to 12 months after the birth.

The reason that such special provision was made under the law has been the subject of considerable debate in social and legal studies. For many years, the acceptance of this special case of infanticide has been argued to be a result of the medicalisation of the law (Zedner 1991); that is, that legal definitions came to be strongly influenced by medical ideas. Ward (1999), however, argues that the infanticide provision was not brought in through the influence of doctors, but instead came about because of pressure within the legal system. Courts were having to deal with relatively large numbers of desperate, poverty-stricken women who killed their own babies. They evoked sympathy and courts were reluctant to convict for murder, as this would result in the death penalty. The use of medical evidence and terms during the promotion of the Act was simply a convenience (see also Kramar and Watson 2006). The 1938 Act remains in place today.

Daniel M'Naghten and the insanity defence

A much wider framework for a legal defence against a charge of murder was set by the 'M'Naghten rules'. The failure of an English court to convict M'Naghten of murder, despite his having undeniably shot dead the prime minister's secretary, led to a legal review (Walker 1968). Daniel M'Naghten was the son of a Glaswegian woodturner. From the descriptions of his life and mental state, there seems little doubt that he would today have received a diagnosis of 'paranoid schizophrenia'. For at least 5 or 6 years before the trial, he had developed fairly eccentric interests and behaviour. He also lived for periods in France and then London and became involved in radical Scottish nationalism. He developed the strong idea that he was personally being persecuted for anti-Tory, anti-English political views by the then British prime minister, Sir Robert Peel. He drew some attention to himself for loitering around Whitehall near the prime minster's office. As this was a time before photographs of politicians were available in newspapers, M'Naghten developed the idea that Peel's private secretary Drummond was in fact the prime minister himself. On 20 January 1843, he followed Drummond up Whitehall and shot him in the back. M'Naghten was immediately seized by a nearby constable (before he could fire a second shot). Drummond died 5 days later. At the trial, medical testimony and evidence from those who had known M'Naghten before the event were sufficient to convince the jury that he should be found not guilty by reason of insanity. M'Naghten was therefore, instead of being hanged, transferred first to Bethlem Lunatic Asylum and then, 20 years later, to Broadmoor (where he died of tuberculosis in 1865). While the precedence for this outcome was already well established, the high profile and political impact of the case drew a great deal of attention to the verdict. The subsequent public outcry (fuelled in part, perhaps, by Queen Victoria's apparent dismay at the verdict) about the apparent leniency of this outcome led to substantial debate and review of the law in regard to insanity (Walker 1968).

The result of this review was the so-called M'Naghten rules, which aimed to spell out what conditions had to be met for defendants to have their behaviour excused by reason of insanity. For the insanity defence to be applicable, it became established that

> at the time of the committing of the act, the party accused was labouring under such a defect of reason, from disease of the mind, as not to know the nature and quality of the act he was doing; or if he did know it, that he did not know he was doing what was wrong.
>
> (Walker 1968: 100)

When these fairly dense phrases are unpacked, they actually set strict criteria for the acceptance of the insanity defence. The defence has to prove that the accused is suffering from a *'disease of mind'* (that is, a medically recognised illness of some kind) that led to a *'defect of reason'* (the illness has to be shown to be affecting the ability to think). The defence then has to show that this *defect of reason* means that the defendant either *'did not know what he did was wrong'*, or did not *'know the nature or quality of the act'*. For the latter point, it would have to be shown that the defendant was entirely deluded at the time and did not know he was committing the act of which he is accused. For example, if he was so deluded and hallucinating that he genuinely believed he was firing a gun at, say a target rather then a person, a court might accept the defence. If he shot someone because he was following the orders of voices in his head telling him to shoot, such a defence *on its own* would be unlikely to be accepted (he still knew the he was killing someone). The former point about not knowing that the act is wrong, is, again, hard to prove in reality – although a court might in principle accept a defence if the defendant could prove that he genuinely believed, for example, that he was saving the planet from imminent destruction by shooting someone he *believed* to be about to carry out an heinous act. It can be argued that the M'Naghten rules helped establish legal definitions of insanity in a highly rational and cognitive way. As the American Psychiatric Association (APA) reflected:

> M'Naghten quickly became the prevailing approach to the insanity defense in England and in the United States, even though this formulation was criticized often because of its emphasis on the defendant's lack of intellectual or cognitive understanding of what he was doing as the sole justification for legal insanity.
>
> (APA 1982: 2)

Other ways of seeing insanity, as being a product of disorders of the emotions, for example were thoroughly marginalised by this definition (Rafter 2004). This debate between those who argue that legal insanity can be understood only in cognitive and rational terms and those who argue that emotions can also be disordered has resurfaced in more recent discussions about the nature of personality disorder. The issue of personality disorders and their relationship to offending behaviour will be discussed in the final section of this chapter.

Diminished responsibility

The difficulty of establishing that the M'Naghten criteria have been fulfilled, coupled with the all-or-nothing nature of this defence (the offender was either wholly sane and therefore completely guilty or 'not guilty on the grounds of insanity'), meant that the insanity defence was difficult to operate (particularly at a time when the death penalty was still used and juries were making life-and-death decisions). This difficulty was addressed in English law by the Homicide Act, 1957 which introduced the important notion of 'diminished responsibility' (being largely imported from Scottish law, where it was first introduced) (Walker 1968). If diminished responsibility was agreed, it would lead to someone being convicted of the lesser charge of manslaughter rather than murder. The capital sentence (or life sentence) was no longer mandatory, and the court could recommend that the defendant be sent to a hospital rather than prison (Walker 1968).

The difference between murder and manslaughter comes down to matters of intent. To convict a defendant of murder in an English court, the prosecution must show that the accused meant to do significant harm. So if you hit someone over the head with a very heavy piece of lead piping and he dies, that is likely to be considered murder since even if you claimed you did not mean to kill – the prosecution would certainly argue that you meant to do serious harm. On the other hand, if you are arguing with someone and you push him, and he falls over, hits his head and dies, the defence would certainly argue that the act could only be manslaughter, since you did not set out to cause serious harm. For the diminished responsibility defence on the grounds of mental abnormality to be accepted, it must be established that:

> Where a person kills or is party to the killing of another, he shall not be convicted of murder if he was suffering from such an abnormality of mind (whether arising from a condition of arrested or retarded development of mind or any inherent causes or induced by disease or injury) as substantially impaired his mental responsibility for his acts or omissions in doing or being a party to the killing.
>
> (Homicide Act 1957)

The central points of that ruling remain today. The Act seemed to remove the tight cognitive criteria of the M'Naghten rules (Reznek 1997) and instead required that the defence demonstrate the presence of a pathological condition (arrested, retarded development, inherent causes, disease or injury). Full recognition of the fact that a medical model of diminished responsibility was being propounded was given in the Mental Health Act (MHA) 1959, which, theoretically at least, put the decision about whether someone was suffering from an abnormality of mind into the hands of doctors. That is, a defendant would have to have medical witnesses testify as to the presence of an abnormality of mind, or the defence would fail. However, even where medical evidence is put forward, it would still be up to the court to decide whether to accept that defence. The conflict remains between popular understandings of 'responsibility' and attempts by psychiatrists and others to draw boundaries around certain behaviours and apply medical labels.

It is interesting to observe that there was a public debate over the appropriateness of the cognitive definition of insanity in the USA following the trial of John Hinckley in 1981. Hinckley was accused of stalking the actress Jodie Foster and of trying to assassinate the then US president, Reagan. As part of what seemed to be a bizarre scheme to gain the attention and love of the Hollywood actress, Hinckley fired six shots at President Reagan, almost killing him, and seriously injuring a police officer, a Secret Service agent and a political aide. The controversy over the eventual verdict of 'not guilty by reason of insanity', following weeks of detailed evidence about Hinckley's mental state, led to review of the use of the insanity defence and a tightening of the criteria (APA 1983). Many states in the USA had moved to slightly looser criteria in adopting the so-called ALI (American Law Institute) guidelines on insanity. The ALI guidelines differed in the following three ways from the M'Naghten rules:

> First, ALI substitutes the concept of 'appreciation' for that of cognitive understanding in the definition of insanity, thus apparently introducing an affective, more emotional, more personalized approach for evaluating the nature of a defendant's knowledge or understanding. Second, the ALI definition for insanity does not insist upon a defendant's total lack of appreciation (knowledge) of the nature of his conduct but instead that he only 'lacks substantial capacity.' Finally, ALI, like the 'irresistible impulse' test, incorporates a so-called volitional approach to insanity, thus adding as an independent criterion for insanity the defendant's ability (or inability) to control his actions.
>
> (APA 1983)

The review of the insanity defence that followed the Hinckley trial led to a return to the tighter criteria that focused on the cognitive criteria of insanity that have held sway in the UK, and away from the looser guidelines provided by ALI.

Diminished responsibility and medical definitions

Although the MHA 1959 in England and Wales was historically significant in formally acknowledging the role of medical experts in identifying the presence of mental abnormality, there is no need to dwell on the detail of the MHA 1959 since it was superseded by the 1983 Mental Health Act (that itself has been subject to review).

Mental Health Act 1983: four categories of mental disorder

The MHA attempts to define a number of important relationships between notions of mental illness and the legal system. Sections of the MHA allow for the involuntary detention of people considered to be suffering from mental disorder. They may be detained in a hospital for assessment or treatment if it is deemed necessary for the health or safety of the patient, *or for the protection of other persons*. In order that someone be detained for treatment, it must also be argued that such treatment could not be provided unless they were detained in hospital. The inclusion of the notion that people can be detained for the protection of others clearly brings the MHA into the ambit of the criminal justice system.

In addition, the MHA stipulates conditions under which someone can be treated with greater apparent leniency if judged to have only *diminished responsibility* for the committed crime owing to the presence of mental abnormality. In order to be considered under the MHA 1983, an individual must fit into one of four categories of mental disorder (these categories building on those mentioned in the Homicide Act 1959):

- *arrested or incomplete development of mind*: This category refers to forms of mental handicap or learning difficulties.

- *mental illness*: Definitions of mental illness are not actually given in the MHA, and it is left instead to medical experts to decide. In reality, recognised psychiatric definitions of illnesses, such as schizophrenia, are used.

- *psychopathy*: This is defined by the MHA as 'a persistent disorder or disability of mind (whether or not including subnormality of intelligence) which results in abnormally aggressive or seriously irresponsible conduct'.

- *any other disorder of the mind.*

While each of these can be discussed briefly in turn, it can be noted that the UK government has been trying to amend the MHA and replace these categories with a single definition (DOH 2006).

Arrested or incomplete development of mind

This category refers to those who suffer from mental impairments arising out of what has been termed 'mental retardation' or

49

'mental handicap'. More modern terms are 'learning disabled' or 'intellectually impaired or disabled'. People in this category would be expected to be functioning at a low level of general intelligence. In addition to these cognitive impairments, it is usually assumed there is also some impairment in people's social abilities and that this has usually been present from birth. There is no proper legal definition of these impairments. A clinical 'rule of thumb' would suggest that people who score less then 70 in a standard IQ test (where around 100 would be considered to be average, and above 120 to be much above average) would be considered to be 'borderline mental handicap'. Definitions of social impairment are so problematic that often intellectual impairment is in reality the sole criterion. Even definitions of intellectual impairment are contested, however. Sometimes the group are defined by having IQs lower than 50; sometimes by their educational history, attendance at special schools, for example (Lindsay 2002).

The relationship between intellectual impairment and crime is a politically controversial area. As Holland *et al.* (2002) point out, it was assumed for many years that the relationship between intellectual incapacity and antisocial behaviour is strong. As discussed in Chapter 1, Lombroso's work achieved high and controversial profile within criminology. Although Lombroso's work was largely discredited, the link between mental deficiency and antisocial behaviour was strong enough in the mind of policymakers under the influence of the eugenics movement to have a bearing on the development of mental handicap hospitals that sought the segregation of the mentally impaired from the rest of society (Holland *et al.* 2002). Statements about the relative rates of offending among people with intellectual impairments are contested. Simpson and Hogg (2001), Lindsay (2002) and McBrien (2003) carried out systematic reviews of the evidence in this area. They emphasise the many difficulties of finding reliable data. The difficulties of defining who should be considered in this category, already mentioned, are then compounded by the difficulties of defining criminal involvement. It may well be that many in this category are protected from the law by relatively informal processes within families and by attitudes of authorities (Holland *et al.* 2002).

People falling in this category are likely to be involved in the criminal justice system as witnesses (Kebbell and Davies 2003). Particular attention needs to be paid to the interviewing methods used so that such witnesses are not led to give particular answers (Hayes 1996). Concerns have been raised about the vulnerability of this group to interrogation, leading to 'false confessions' (Gudjonsson 2003).

Mental illness

Mental illness was not defined by the MHA, but instead diagnoses used by psychiatrists can be applied. Psychiatric diagnoses that are quite commonly used in this way are depression and schizophrenia. The latter is the closest to a stereotypical view of madness. It is quite likely that Daniel M'Naghten, whose crimes led to the M'Naghten rules on the insanity defence, would today have received a diagnosis of schizophrenia. As the figures from Fazel and Danesh (2002) suggest, rates of mental illnesses among offenders are relatively high. Questions can still be asked about the significance of those figures, however. Is it that people with mental health problems are more likely to become involved in criminal activity or is it that contact with the criminal justice system is more likely to lead to mental disturbance? A study by Wallace (1989) suggested that the majority of offenders with a mental disorder committed their first offence before having contact with psychiatry. A study by Belfrage (1998) found that 28 per cent of a group of 893 people discharged from Stockholm mental hospitals with diagnoses of schizophrenia, affective psychosis or paranoia who were followed up 10 years later had criminal records (compared to an expected rate of around 9 per cent for people aged 15–69). Forty-seven per cent of those who had committed crimes had committed violent offences (murder/manslaughter, assault, illegal threat and violence against officers). Eleven people had been convicted of murder or manslaughter or attempted murder. However, most offences were far more minor. They were crimes that Belfrage (1998) describes as 'social drop-out criminality' (1998: 151), that is, minor offences such as petty theft and drink- and drug-related offences. The often suggested link between violent crime and schizophrenia seems to be not real – despite the publicity given to a number of high-profile cases (Walsh *et al.* 2002).

Mental illness on trial: successful use of diminished responsibility

A straightforward example of the plea of diminished responsibility being used in a murder trial occurred in May 2005. A man named Glaister Butler appeared in Birmingham Crown Court accused of killing a police officer a year earlier. Police had been called to investigate the threatening behaviour of the man. When challenged, Butler had run away and was then pursued by Detective Constable Michael Swindells. When the officer caught up, Butler stabbed him to death with a 12-inch knife, killing him instantly. After 2 weeks of the trial proceedings, the prosecution announced that they accepted that the evidence was 'all one way' in clearly pointing to a verdict of diminished responsibility, on the grounds that Butler was suffering from an abnormality of mind. He had a 20-year psychiatric history, having been diagnosed as suffering from paranoid schizophrenia. He was ordered to be detained indefinitely under the MHA (The *Guardian*, 20 May 2005).

Unsuccessful use of the diminished responsibility:
Peter Sutcliffe (the Yorkshire Ripper)

A more notorious and controversial case where the defence of diminished responsibility, on the grounds of mental illness, was used was the trial of the 'Yorkshire Ripper', who had murdered and terrorised women in northern England for a number of years in the 1970s (Burn (1984), provides one of several accounts of the life of this man). Peter Sutcliffe was arrested and confessed to the crimes. He was charged in 1981 with the murder of 13 women and the attempted murder of seven women. He pleaded not guilty of murder, but guilty of manslaughter on the grounds of diminished responsibility. There was agreement by all the psychiatrists who had interviewed Sutcliffe that he was suffering from mental illness – paranoid schizophrenia. At the outset of the trial, the prosecution was prepared to go along with this and agreed that the lesser charge of manslaughter could be accepted. The judge, however, refused to accept this and insisted that the jury should decide. Sutcliffe therefore stood trial for murder, but entered his plea that he was guilty only of manslaughter on the grounds of diminished responsibility owing to mental disorder. The real business of the trial therefore became about Sutcliffe's mental state at the time of the killings.

The defence argued that Sutcliffe was suffering from paranoid schizophrenia. He claimed that he had begun hearing voices and had become deluded years before, but the main symptoms had remained 'encapsulated'; that is, he was able to function fairly normally while his delusions remained as only one aspect of his mind. As described by the defence, it was in 1967, while working in a cemetery, that Sutcliffe claimed he first heard the voice of God (from transcript of trial):

Mr Sutcliffe: 'I was digging and I just paused for a minute. It was very hard ground. I just heard something – it sounded like a voice similar to a human voice – like an echo. I looked round to see if there was anyone there, but there was no one in sight. I was in the grave with my feet about five feet below the surface.

There was no one in sight when I looked round from where I was. Then I got out of the grave. The voice was not very clear. I got out and walked – the ground rose up. It was quite a steep slope. I walked to the top, but there was no one there at all. I heard again the same sound. It was like a voice saying something, but the words were all imposed on top of each other. I could not make them out, it was like echoes. The voices were coming directly in front of me from the top of a gravestone [which was Polish. I remember the name on the grave to this day. It was a man called Zipolski. Stanislaw Zipolski. ... It had a terrific impact on me. I went down the slope after standing there for a while. It was starting to rain.]. I remember going to the top of the slope overlooking the valley and I felt as though I had just experienced something fantastic. I looked across the valley and all around and thought of heaven and earth and how insignificant we all are. But I felt so important at the moment.

He claimed that he later felt compelled to carry out a mission to rid the world of prostitutes. The acts were never something he enjoyed. He described himself as often feeling that he was in 'turmoil', but he still felt that he was doing the right thing. For example, from the transcripts of the trial, here are his responses to questioning (by his defence barrister, Mr Chadwin) about the first time he killed someone:

When asked why he set out that night to kill a prostitute, Mr Sutcliffe replied: 'The same reason as before. I was reminded it was my mission. It had to be done, so I went.'
Mr Chadwin: This time you did kill.
Mr Sutcliffe: Yes.
Mr Chadwin: Did you enjoy striking the blows you struck?
Mr Sutcliffe: No.
Mr Chadwin: How did you feel about the physical act of striking those blows?
Mr Sutcliffe: I found it very difficult, and I couldn't restrain myself. I could not do anything to stop myself.
Mr Chadwin: Why could you not stop yourself?
Mr Sutcliffe: Because it was God who was controlling me.
Mr Chadwin: How was he doing that?
Mr Sutcliffe: Before doing it, I had to go through a terrible stage each time. I was in absolute turmoil, I was doing everything I could do to fight it off, and asked why it should be me, until I eventually reached the stage where it was as if I was primed to do it.

53

> Mr Chadwin: Did you ever look forward to killing anyone with pleasure?
> Mr Sutcliffe: No, certainly not.

It can be seen in this exchange that the defence is suggesting that Sutcliffe felt that he was being controlled by God, that he was not acting under his own will, and that he certainly experienced no enjoyment. The last two lines of the exchange above are perhaps crucial. The defence knew that if it could be shown that Sutcliffe took pleasure in killing, he was dammed. It is clear that to enjoy murdering someone is not a sign of insanity.

The prosecution, however, argued that Sutcliffe's defence was simply a fabrication. They suggested that he was pretending to be guided by the voice of God, pretending that he 'could not restrain himself' so that he could plead for the lesser charge of diminished responsibility and spend time in a hospital rather than prison. They pointed to the facts that he did not immediately reveal his 'mission' when arrested by the police, and that his wife Sonia had earlier experienced a mental breakdown and so he might well be familiar with the symptoms of serious mental illness.

The jury agreed with the prosecution and found Sutcliffe guilty of murder, and he was sent to prison. However, in 1984, after he was injured by another prisoner, he was transferred to Broadmoor Special Hospital, where he has remained, and debate still continues as to whether he should best be considered mad or bad.

Clearly, there are important differences between the Sutcliffe case and that of Glaister Butler. The latter had a long, well-documented history as a patient diagnosed as suffering from schizophrenia. He had previously been involved in episodes of violence that were fuelled by delusions. He had formerly been detained under the MHA, and had been released as a community care patient. He lived in a series of dilapidated flats, at one point living without electricity for two years. The attack on the policeman was consistent with his delusions that he was being persecuted. Everything in this story fits with the popular view of 'madness'. Sutcliffe, however, had never been so diagnosed. He lived an otherwise normal life; he was married, had friends and worked as a lorry driver. He seemed to perceive and understand the world in an ordinary rational manner. The delusions that he claimed at his trial to have experienced had been entirely hidden; no one else knew about them. It was relatively easy for the prosecution to argue that he was feigning mental illness. The prosecution case was that the killings were sexually motivated, and carried out for pleasure.

And yet, even if were true that Sutcliffe was not suffering from schizophrenia, the question remains – how 'sane' is someone who commits so many appalling acts of violence?

While perhaps there are elements of the Sutcliffe case that are unusual, there are more commonly cases in which defendants do not claim to be *mentally ill*, but their behaviour so defies our expectations of normality that questions are raised about their mental state. These cases might be included in the category of psychopathy, to be discussed next.

The problem of psychopathy and personality disorder

While the Sutcliffe case and others have drawn attention to the difficulties of establishing the presence and significance of 'mental illness' in criminal cases, the even more problematic category is that of 'psychopathy', which featured as a category of mental disorder in the MHAs 1959 and 1983. According to the Act, the term refers to 'a persistent disorder or disability of mind (whether or not including sub-normality of intelligence) which results in abnormally aggressive or seriously irresponsible conduct' (MHA 1983, Section 1 (2)).

This has been a most challenging category for psychiatry and for those in the criminal justice system concerned with mental disorder (Glannon 1997). Rafter (2004) argues that debates about this category of offenders represent the prehistory of criminology (see Chapter 1). A number of influential clinicians during the nineteenth century in different countries began to concern themselves with people who seemed not to have totally lost their reason but could act in very antisocial and often aggressive ways. Working in the asylums of Paris, Pinel (1806) is credited with the first formal written account of 'mania without delirium'. According to Pinel, this could be an intermittent or continuous state, notable for there being 'no sensible change in the functions of the understanding; but perversion of the active faculties, marked by abstract and sanguinary fury, with a blind propensity to acts of violence' (Pinel 1806: 156). While Pinel's characterisation is similar to the notion of dangerous psychopaths, the English physician Prichard's descriptions of 'moral insanity' are taken to be the first published definitions of more general personality disorders (Elliott and Gillet 1992: 53). Prichard was describing people who seemed to have normal intellectual functioning; like Pinel's patients, they were not suffering from delusions or disorders of perception, but their behaviour was clearly abnormally antisocial. Their behaviour suggested that while they appeared to perceive and comprehend events around themselves in a 'normal' manner, they acted with so little regard for the welfare of others that it was concluded that they suffered some defect either in feeling, or in the ability to think in moral terms. In a famous and often-quoted passage, Prichard (1835) described 'moral insanity' in the following terms:

> A form of mental derangement in which the intellectual faculties appear to have sustained little or no injury, while the disorder is manifested principally or alone, in the state of the feelings, temper, or habits. In cases of this description the moral and active principles of the mind are strangely perverted and depraved; the power of self government is lost or greatly impaired; and the individual is found to be incapable, not of talking or reasoning upon any subject proposed to him, for this he will often do with great shrewdness and volubility, but of conducting himself with decency and propriety in the business of life. His wishes and inclinations, his attachments, his likings and dislikings have all undergone a morbid change, and this change appears to be the originating cause, or to lie at the foundation of any disturbance.
>
> (Prichard, *A Treatise on Insanity*, 1835: 4)

In making the distinction between disorders where the intellectual faculties appear to be malfunctioning (such as delusional states) and those that seem to involve no such deficits but where people's feelings and conduct toward others are distorted, Prichard is often credited with sowing the seed of the modern diagnosis of 'psychopathy' (Augstein 1996). Prichard's choices of examples have sometimes caused confusion as to whether he should be credited with describing the violent and cruel offender that has become identified with the term (Rafter 2004). Prichard was at times concerned with disorders of the relatively wealthy who had become eccentric, selfish and unconcerned with the welfare of those around them (Augstein 1996). In view of some of his case descriptions, it may well be that some of his patients would nowadays receive diagnoses such as bipolar affective disorder. Nonetheless, the issues being highlighted by Prichard are quite consistent with some of the cases of personality disorders described 100 years later who might be quite successful, but ruthless, in their careers (Cleckley (1941), and Hare (1993), for example, write about 'psychopaths in everyday life', some of whom might be successful as doctors or business people).

Prichard (1835) argued that it was possible for people's thinking to be intact, but for their moral and emotional understanding to be so disordered that they deserved to be treated as insane. Such offenders, Prichard argued, should be sent to asylums rather than prison or the gallows. In the USA, Isaac Ray was directly concerned with the legal definitions of insanity, writing *A Treatise on the Medical Jurisprudence of Insanity* in 1838, in which he argued that cases of 'moral mania' and 'partial moral mania' should be recognised. This latter category supposed that 'the derangement is confined to one or a few of the affective faculties' (1838: 186). Types of partial moral mania included compulsive stealing, lying, erotomania, and destructiveness, as well as 'homicidal insanity', whereby '[t]he criminal act ... is the result of a strong and sudden impulse opposed to his natural habits and generally preceded or followed by some derangement of the healthy actions of the brain or other organ' (Ray 1838: 264).

Ramon (1986) argued that the interest in 'moral insanity' was in keeping with the more general tendency to try to distinguish, and therefore segregate, other forms of 'antisocial' behaviour. The nineteenth century witnessed the birth of psychiatry and the mushrooming of asylums for the insane (Jones 1972; Scull 1979). However, the notion of 'moral insanity' did not become accepted like other psychiatric diagnoses, such as that of 'schizophrenia' (initially called 'dementia praecox'). Instead ideas about moral insanity have remained controversial. This is perhaps because they draw attention to fundamental philosophical debate about the nature of humanity – are we better defined by our capacity to experience emotion or our capacity for rational thought? On the one hand, there is the clear line of argument, visible through the rise of the Enlightenment, that privileged rational thought. According to this argument, it was the ability to think rationally that was the hallmark of humanity. Human beings could rise *above* emotion, could decide what to do, what was right and what was wrong, by reference to laws and values. Feelings, it was thought, were more primitive and should be subservient to reason. People might be excused if there could be shown to be an impairment in their ability to perceive or understand the world in a rational way (the cognitive view of insanity, as forcefully put by Robinson (1999), for example). On the other hand, there was the belief (best exemplified by the various 'Romantic' schools in art, music and literature) that it was our capacity to *feel* that raised us above other species. To feel love and to act upon feelings of care, altruism or even hatred, or imagination were the truly important human capacities (Eichner 1982). Within this framework of understanding, exemplified by Prichard's ideas on 'moral insanity', it was possible to imagine that someone might suffer deficits in these higher emotional capacities. Such deficits might lead people to behave irresponsibly.

Debates were taking place in courts about the status of partial insanity or moral insanity. Eigen (1991) uses nineteenth-century court records to plot some of the arguments between lawyers and medical witnesses about insanity. However, although there was no great public debate about the status of moral insanity (Rafter 2004), by the end of the nineteenth century it seemed to be clear that moral insanity had no real legal status. The M'Naghten rules had bolstered the cognitive view of insanity, while ideas of moral insanity had meanwhile been incorporated into Lombrosian arguments (see Chapter 1) about degeneration and descriptions of those suffering from mental handicap. Those individuals were taken to be 'throwbacks' to more primitive forms of humanity. It is notable that the Mental Deficiency Act 1913 included the category of 'moral defective' (Ramon 1986). Deficits in emotional responses were seen as necessarily being connected with disorders of relatively primitive functions. As discussed in Chapter 1, Lombroso's ideas with their rather inflated and unsubstantiated claims concerning the significance of physiognomy were largely abandoned as explanations of criminal behaviour.

Interest in issues such as 'moral insanity' began to re-emerge as debates about 'psychopathy' in the middle of the twentieth century. Ramon (1986) argues that there are good reasons to believe that World War II itself represented a milestone in the 'recognition' of psychopathy, and she suggests that a number of factors were involved. First, through the study of battle stress, there was full recognition that otherwise healthy individuals of sound mind could be turned 'insane' through trauma. Second, there was also interest in explaining atrocities carried out by Allied soldiers (since they were on the 'good side', their behaviour had to be explained through notions of individual psychopathology rather than sick ideals or ideology). Third, there was interest among military psychiatrists in experimenting with ideas about therapeutic communities (which combined psychoanalytic ideas with theories from industrial psychology and group therapy). In Britain, two military therapeutic communities were set up (Northfield and Mill Hill) (Walker and McCabe 1973; Ramon 1986). In addition, David Henderson's (1939) psychoanalytic descriptions of *psychopathic states* was influential on psychiatry in Britain. Meanwhile, there was considerable interest in the idea of 'psychopathy' in the United States. Harvey Cleckley's book *The Mask of Insanity* (1941) brought wider attention to the issue of psychopathy, and the term 'psychopath' began to be taken seriously, certainly in the clinical literature in Britain and the USA. Cleckely's Psychopathy Checklist provides a useful description of the type of people who were being considered under this category (Table 2.2).

When used to create a psychopathy rating, each factor in Table 2.2 receives a score between 0 and 2, where 0 suggests that the individual does not exhibit the behaviour, 1 suggests the description applies 'somewhat', and 2 suggests that the description 'definitely' applies. Subjects thus receive a score of between 0 and 40. There is no definite cut-off score, although studies typically assume that a score of above 25 or 30 indicates the presence of psychopathy (Walters 2004). A number of difficulties emerge when this list is examined. First, how many people could be categorised in this way, at least at some point in their lives? Walters (2004) argues that high rates of 'false-positives' (that is, people who do not seem to have serious problems coming out with scores that suggest they should) are common. Second, most of the characteristics are *extremely* subjective. Definitions have always been problematic; as Ramon (1986: 216) explains, 'the *definition* of psychopathy has changed little from 1835. However, available

Table 2.2 Cleckley's Revised Psychopathy Checklist (PCL-R) (Hare 1991)

1. Glibness/superficial charm
2. Grandiose sense of self-worth
3. Need for stimulation/proneness to boredom
4. Pathological lying
5. Cunning/manipulative
6. Lack of remorse or guilt
7. Shallow affect
8. Callous/lack of empathy
9. Parasitic lifestyle
10. Poor behavioural control
11. Promiscuous sexual behavior
12. Early behaviour problems
13. Lack of realistic, long-term goals
14. Impulsivity
15. Irresponsibility
16. Failure to accept responsibility for own actions
17. Many short-term marital relationships
18. Juvenile delinquency
19. Revocation of conditional release
20. Criminal versatility

definitions have been recognised as unsatisfactory; so much so that as late as 1944 Curran and Mallinson entitled their chapter on psychopathy "I can't define an elephant but I know one when I see one".' The definitional problem has given ammunition to the critics of the concept for a long time (Pilgrim 2001), yet, despite this, it seems that the 'elephant' has not gone away. Psychopathy appeared as a category of mental disorder in the Mental Health Act 1959, and despite constant criticism it has remained and indeed has achieved new levels of government interest into the twenty-first century.

Psychopathy and the MHA

Although the argument for such a thing as 'moral insanity' seemed to have been lost during the nineteenth century, and despite the difficulties of definition and the misgivings of many psychiatrists the category of 'psychopath' was included in the MHA 1959 in England and Wales. Ramon (1986) argues that there were a number of reasons for the government to be interested in provision for this group at this time. Through the 1950s, more liberal 'open-door' policies took hold in the by now very overcrowded asylums. This led to larger numbers of people with mental disorders living outside asylums. Some overtly antisocial individuals, like those falling in the category of psychopath, were still presenting as a problem. One option might have been to criminalise them and lock them up in prison, yet there was reluctance to do this. The prison populations were already large and there was recognition that prisons were not successful in rehabilitating people (Carlen 1986). There was also increasing acceptance of psychological modes of thought in understanding antisocial behaviour (Rose 1989), and, of course, these were individuals who had often not actually committed offences of sufficient seriousness to allow long-term imprisonment. With lobbying from a minority of psychiatrists (notably David Henderson) who were working in this field (Ramon 1986), the term 'psychopath' was included in the MHA. It identified psychopathy as 'a persistent disorder or disability of mind ... which results in abnormally aggressive or seriously irresponsible conduct, and requires or is susceptible to medical treatment'. So psychopathy, clearly a version of moral insanity, was recognised as a mental disorder, and yet was still seen as distinct from 'mental illness'. Despite this attempt to bring psychopathy within the realm of professional medical expertise, the issue of whether psychopaths should be regarded as criminals or psychiatric patients was still not resolved. So while the inclusion of 'psychopathy' received widespread support among politicians as a step that could lead to greater control over the group, many mental health professionals remained distinctly ambivalent about this group and tended to avoid admitting those so labelled to hospital (Ramon 1986).

As time went on, the term 'psychopath' itself began to be seen as unhelpfully vague and stigmatising, and so, instead, the term 'personality disorder' began to become popular. Its use was recommended by the Butler Report in 1975 (DSS 1975; McCallum 2001). Yet despite the increasing use of the term 'personality disorder' in the 1970s, it became clear that the ambiguities of the definition had not gone away. Consultation on the redrafting of the MHA in the early 1980s again recommended dropping of the category 'psychopath' and the use of 'personality disorder' as an alternative. Neither took place and the Mental Health Act 1983 still included the category 'psychopath'.

The continuing social problem of personality disorder

By the end of the twentieth century, in the UK at least, interest in psychopathy was again considerable. One particular crime served as a catalyst to government action. On 9 July 1996, Lin Russell and her 6- and 9-year-old daughters were walking home along a country lane in Kent, England. They were savagely attacked and their heads battered with an object that was never found, but might well have been a hammer. Lin and her younger daughter were killed. Nine-year-old Josie was so badly injured that it was certain that she had been 'left for dead'. Her head injuries were such that her subsequent recovery was widely seen as miraculous, with the extent of the injuries leaving no doubt that this was an utterly brutal attack where the intention had been to kill all three. There appeared to be no real motive for the attack, beyond minor robbery perhaps. The callousness of the assault on two young girls and their mother in broad daylight not only caused considerable public disquiet and outrage, but also eventually prompted the government to consider what it could do to prevent violence such as this being carried out by people suffering from personality disorder. The government was directed in this way because the man, Michael Stone, who was eventually convicted of the crimes was well known to psychiatric services and was considered to be suffering from a personality disorder. Although he had contact with psychiatric services, Michael Stone has never been considered to be mentally ill. He has never claimed that he was possessed by the devil, or that he has was told how to behave by the voice of God. Two years earlier, in 1994, he had been committed to hospital under the Mental Health Act, but since he was not *mentally ill* and was not treatable, it had been decided that he could not be detained.[1]

His prosecution was not straightforward, however. The police in the case had few leads even 12 months after the crimes. At this point, after a television appeal for witnesses, Michael Stone was arrested. He was tried and convicted twice, first in October 1998, but this conviction was quashed in February 2001, mainly due to a prosecution witness confessing to having lied. Stone was retried in September 2001 and again found guilty of two counts of murder and one of attempted murder. He was given three life sentences. No forensic evidence associated Stone with the crimes, and he has always maintained his innocence. While the conviction remains controversial, it may be that part of the difficulty with such a prosecution is the apparent lack of motive and reason for the attacks. Wagenaar *et al.* (1993) argue that courts often reach verdicts on the basis of the strength of the competing narratives presented by defence and prosecution. Those crimes, where good forensic or witness evidence is lacking, and that appear to be without motive, may well be very difficult to prosecute in the absence of a clear narrative that would include the criminal's motivation.

Despite the difficulties over the prosecution of this particular case, the brutality and senselessness of the attack crystallised concern in this highly controversial area. What can be done about people who do terrible things, without any apparent reason, but who are seemingly otherwise sane? After Stone's initial conviction in 1997, the then home secretary Jack Straw stated in the House of Commons that the government intended to explore the possibility of introducing legislation that would enable people deemed to be suffering from dangerous forms of personality disorder to be detained on 'indeterminate' sentences. The UK government then struggled for a number of years to introduce a new mental health act that would enable this to happen. The government set up an initiative called the DSPD (Dangerous People with Severe Personality Disorder) programme that brought together elements of the Home Office, the Department of Health and the Prison Service.

The UK government appears to be convinced that personality disorders represent a significant health issue, and has become interested in how 'personality disorders' in general are being dealt with in the health service. This concern has led to a series of initiatives that aimed to promote the treatment of personality disorder, notably the document *Personality Disorder: No Longer a Diagnosis of Exclusion* (DOH 2003). The aim of this document would seem to be to encourage the National Health Service to take greater care of those judged to be suffering from personality disorders. It remains a highly controversial topic, however, many still arguing that personality disorders do not exist (Pilgrim 2001). Despite the criticisms, personality disorders have received worldwide attention, and they are now defined by both DSM-IV (*Diagnostic and Statistical Manual of Mental Disorders*, 4th Edition) (APA 1994) and ICD-10 (*International Classification of Disease*, 10th Revision) (WHO 1992) systems of classification. They are defined in similar terms in both systems (DOH 2003) as follows:

- **ICD-10**: 'a severe disturbance in the characterological condition and behavioural tendencies of the individual, usually involving several areas of the personality, and nearly always associated with considerable personal and social disruption'

- **DSM-IV**: 'an enduring pattern of inner experience and behaviour that deviates markedly from the expectations of the individual's culture, is pervasive and inflexible, has an onset in adolescence or early childhood, is stable over time, and leads to distress or impairment'.

DSM-IV describes three clusters of personality disorder

- **Cluster A** (the 'odd or eccentric' types): paranoid, schizoid and schizotypal personality disorder

- **Cluster B** (the 'dramatic, emotional or erratic' types): histrionic, narcissistic, antisocial and borderline personality disorders

- **Cluster C** (the 'anxious and fearful' types): obsessive-compulsive, avoidant and dependent

---

Clearly, Cluster B is of most relevance to issues of criminality, in particular antisocial personality disorder (APD). People diagnosed as suffering from narcissistic and borderline personality disorders have also been associated with antisocial behaviour (Conrad and Morrow 2000; Wilkins and Warner 2001; Leichsenring *et al.* 2003).

In what is thought to have been a legal first, a young man who was charged in June 2005 with killing his parents pleaded not guilty to murder, but guilty to manslaughter instead on the grounds that he was suffering from 'narcissistic personality disorder' (a Cluster B personality disorder according to the DSM-IV categories). The judge on the case, held at Liverpool Crown Court, instructed the court to accept this plea, and Brian Blackwell was found guilty only of manslaughter. The decision was controversial. Blackwell had been sent to private school, and he had done just well enough there to obtain a place at medical school. He had, however, developed a fantasy life, which he used to attract the attentions of the young woman who became his girlfriend. In this fantasy life, he was a successful young tennis player with lucrative sponsorship deals. The fantasy was supported by his misuse of his parents' money. The prosecution case was that it was his parents trying to stop him spending their money, and thus exposing the fantasy, that led him to batter them both to death. Blackwell's defence team argued that the fantasy life was symptomatic of his narcissistic personality, which demanded the attention and adoration of others. Exposure of the fantasy risked unleashing a violent response (see Chapter 7, pages 188–90). The use of the defence of personality disorder in this way may well have important implications if it does set a precedent (Cohen 2005).

Antisocial personality disorder?

The difficulties in the definition of personality disorder have not gone away and remain problematic. Indeed, basic issues of terminology can be confusing. The word 'sociopath' has at times been used fairly interchangeably with 'psychopath' (Blackburn 2000). More recently, labels such as APD and borderline personality disorder (BPD) are commonly used in relation to disturbed and disturbing behaviour. Undoubtedly, there are differences in the definitions, but they are often quite subtle. It could certainly be argued that the existence of these various terms, with their overlapping definitions, strengthens the case of those that suggest that these are simply labels that we put on people that are bad whom we do not otherwise know what to do with (Pilgrim 2001).

The box below gives the DSM-IV definition of APD. The difficulties that were apparent in Cleckley's checklist for 'psychopathy' are still with us. The criteria are highly subjective and could potentially be used to describe large numbers of people. Indeed, by DSM-IV criteria, estimates of the prevalence of personality disorder within the general population suggest that as many 10–13 per cent of the population could be diagnosed as suffering from some kind of personality disorder. While the overall rates of men and women are estimated to be similar, men are far more likely to be judged 'antisocial', and women more likely to be seen as 'borderline'. APD is estimated to exist at a level of between 1 and 3 per cent in the general population

The DSM-IV criteria for antisocial personality disorder (APD)

According to DSM IV, the criteria for APD are that an individual:

1 shows a pervasive disregard for the rights of others, as indicated by at least three of:
  • repeated illegal behaviour
  • repeated lying and cheating for profit or pleasure
  • impulsivity
  • aggressiveness (fights/assaults)
  • disregard for safety of others
  • irresponsibility (work, financial)
  • lack of remorse
2 is over 18 years old
3 shows evidence of conduct disorder before 15 years of age

(Moran 1999; Moran and Hagell 2001). The rates within prison are considerably higher (as the figures from Fazel and Danesh (2002), make clear). While various efforts to refine and adapt definitions and measurement scales have been made (Blackburn 2000), the difficulty remains: is this really just a description of someone that no one likes and society does not know what to do with? To some, the notion of 'personality' should simply not be a health matter (Pilgrim 2001). Indeed, despite efforts, as described above, to define moral insanity nearly 200 years ago, the idea that seemingly rational people can suffer from disorders of their morals or emotions has lost ground, certainly as far as the criminal justice system was concerned. So although 'psychopathy' is a category recognised by the MHA, according to legal definitions, insanity can really be understood only as failure of cognition; as disorder of perception and rational thought. Yet, the problem of what to do with people who are intellectually intact, but whose behaviour suggests considerable abnormality, has not gone away. The police and courts seem to be confronted with many individuals whose behaviour seems to fit the descriptions of APD and similar disorders. The dilemma of whether to criminalise them or to try to treat them remains. Therefore, it is still useful to ask whether there are causes of their actions. Is it possible that there are identifiable reasons for their behaviour, whether in terms of their personality, constitution, life experiences, or social context?

Theories of the cause of psychopathy/APD

Moran and Hagell (2001) reviewed evidence about the causes of APD and argued that there is a broad range of identifiable risk factors. They mention genetic influences and temperamental factors (such as the presence of early aggression). There is evidence that such difficulties will have been long-standing ones in the individual's life, and that such persons come from families marked by difficulties. There may well be other mental health problems (notably substance abuse, anxiety, depression, self-harm and suicide attempts). As the next two chapters will explore further, there is certainly evidence that adults whose behaviour is consistent with the presence of APD do often have histories of difficulties going back to their childhood (e.g. Vitelli 1998). Yet, large questions remain as to whether this signifies that those difficulties are being caused by some features of the individuals themselves or whether they are being created by the circumstances in which the people have developed. Indeed, there has been quite a long history of debate over whether the difficulties arise from some physiological defect or from flaws in the personality of the individual deriving from their personal histories (Ramon 1986). Clearly, there may well be overlap between these two positions.

A number of efforts have been made to identify specific causes of psychopathy as if it were a precise disorder. First, theories that assume there is some defect in neurocognitive functioning will be examined and then theories that assume there are defects in character or personality.

Causes of APD: neurocognitive theories
Blair and Frith (2000) argue that APD might be the product of certain 'malfunctions' in how the brain processes information. It is arguable that these theories fall into two fundamental categories, which in some respects echo those earlier debates about the status of 'moral insanity'. Can personality disorders be understood simply as failure of people to assert control over their emotions in a rational manner, or do they stem from more fundamental abnormalities in the emotional world of the individual? Both of these theories will be considered.

First, some theories assume that such disorders are caused by a deficit in the ability of people fully to control their actions. That is, they are unable to plan their actions and inhibit undesirable behaviour. Such difficulties are referred to as deficits in executive control. In neurological terms, this might represent a lesion in the prefrontal cortex of the brain (Dinn and Harris 2000). There are certainly cases where damage to those areas of the brain has led to increased likelihood of antisocial behaviour (Damasio 1994; Grafman 1996); however, people with APD or psychopathy have not been found to have poorer general executive control than 'normals' (Damasio 1994; Blair and Frith 2000).

Second, it may be that the difficulties stem primarily from deficits in emotional processing. In other words, perhaps the individual has specific difficulties in identifying emotionally significant stimuli and incorporating that emotional information in plans for behaviour. Possible links with difficulties of understanding the minds of others have been proposed (e.g. Kegan 1986). It has been found that those with such diagnoses of APD or psychopathy do not have impairments on 'theory of mind tests' (Dolan and Fullam 2004). Damasio (1994) has suggested that people exhibiting antisocial behaviour may have difficulty in taking into account information that includes a 'somatic marker'. That is, it is assumed that we learn through life to take particular notice of certain kinds of information when it is marked as being emotionally significant (it is 'somatically marked'). Perhaps people are failing in some way to take account of information in these somatic markers. Blair and Frith (2000) assert that evidence to support this has not been forthcoming, and they argue instead that there is a more fundamental problem with the ability to process emotional information (Lösel and Schmuker 2004). Current evidence seems to suggest that the difficulties of those with APD do lie in the emotional realm. Greene and Haidt (2002) argue that there is good evidence from brain studies that what they refer to as personal moral thinking is driven by emotions, while impersonal moral decisions can be made by reason alone. That is, when people are making moral decisions that involve other people, parts of the brain that are known to be associated with emotional responses are active. This is potentially very important, suggesting that the notion that moral behaviour stems from abstract rational thought is wrong.

While the neurological basis of personality disorders remains unresolved, it is becoming clearer that there is a strong association with environmental factors – in particular, those factors that involve emotional trauma or deprivation. It is certainly striking that Blair and Frith (2000), in their review of neurocognitive theories, are moved to point out:

> It seems to be without a doubt that for an individual to present with the full-blown syndrome of psychopathy he/she

needs to have a socially, though not necessarily economically, disadvantaged social childhood environment.

(Blair and Frith 2000: s77)

There is, indeed, now growing evidence that personality disorders are associated with negative life events (Pagano *et al.* 2004) and deprived childhoods in particular (Bandelow *et al.* 2005). Hodges (2003) argues that BPD might better be understood in terms of post-traumatic stress, given the likelihood that the individual's difficulties have been created by trauma. Graybar and Boutilier (2002) do point out, however, that not all people seen as suffering from such difficulties have traumatic childhoods.

Causes of APD: social causes

There is now a growing body of evidence that there are links between personality disorders and childhood histories marked by episodes of emotional deprivation and deficits in the individual's ability to process emotional information. Perhaps further study in this area will lead to rapprochement between the cognitive views of insanity and those that encompass more emotional understandings. It is also useful to consider evidence about the overlaps between other categories of personality disorder, APD and violence. In particular, there are powerful reasons to believe that there are overlaps between BPD and antisocial behaviour (Conrad and Morrow 2000; Leichsenring *et al.* 2003), and also with the group of offenders identified as 'life-course-persistent' offenders (who will be discussed in detail in Chapter 4).

Failures of emotional representation

Clinicians, often informed by psychoanalytic theory, have worked with personality disorders for many years (Kernberg 1992). Fonagy *et al.* (2003) put forward a theory that sought the developmental roots of BPD. Not surprisingly, given the psychoanalytic perspective of these theorists, they found those roots in early experiences, particularly experiences of disordered attachments to significant carers. Their theory is interesting in that it at least resonates with those neurocognitive theories that point to some kind of deficit in the ability to process emotionally significant information. It is also consistent with debates that go back at least 200 years about the nature of 'moral insanity' and the suggestion by Prichard and others that the central difficulty is one of emotional or moral understanding (Rafter 2004).

Fonagy *et al.* (2003, 2004) argue that one of the reasons that a good relationship with at least one parental figure is essential for psychological development in the early years of life is that it is through constant interaction and feedback that we develop an understanding of ourselves as individuals with our own internal world and emotions. People develop the ability to 'mentalise' – that is, they build an internal model of themselves and are thus able to think about how they feel and how they appear in the world. Fonagy *et al.* argue that we are not born with the ability to be aware of our own emotion states, but that the ability to develop an internal representation of our own mental states is a developmental achievement. Children build up a representation of their own emotional states by having their emotions mirrored back to them by a reasonably sensitive and empathic caregiver. For example, if the caregiver sees that the baby is sad, and mimics an exaggeratedly sad face, the baby gets an idea of what sadness looks like and so learns to associate its own feelings with a representation of those emotions. This, Fonagy *et al.* (2004) argue, is a crucial step in individuals building up a sense of themselves as individuals who can contemplate and act with agency on the world. Fonagy *et al.* (2003) argue that children who do not experience such a close empathic relationship may fail to develop an internal representation of their own emotional states. This leaves individuals unable to think about their feelings. They still experience those feelings, and act on them – but cannot stop and think about how they are feeling. This, they argue, explains the impulsivity, insecure sense of self and ultimately, in some case, the subsequent propensity to violence.

Lansky (2003) argued that Fonagy *et al.* were wrong to stress the mother–child dyad, arguing instead that there are at least theoretical grounds for supposing that the influence of other relationships may also be key in understanding how children might learn to be able to reflect on their own selves. Lansky also questioned the explanatory power of the notion of there being a general failure of representational capacity. He argued that Fonagy *et al.* had overlooked the particular significance of shame, and that impulsive behaviour (that may include violence, for example) might better be explained by individuals feeling as though they were being 'flooded with shame that is felt to be unbearable', rather than indicating that they face a basic deficiency in the ability to mentalise emotional states (2003: 470). In a rather similar vein, Crowe (2004: 330–1) argued that the concept of BPD itself might be explained as 'an overwhelming shame response linked to an impairment in the development of those interpersonal skills necessary to integrate the shame affect into their self image'. The emotion of shame emerges as a significant issue in a number of places throughout this book. It is arguably one of the important 'moral emotions' whose development during childhood might be a significant factor in the development or inhibition of delinquent behaviour (Chapter 4). It also emerges as possibly important trigger of violence (Chapters 7 and 8). Whether the emphasis should be on shame or on more general emotions, there is still a coherent theoretical framework here that suggests that people's ability to process and reflect on emotion is essential if they are to experience themselves as having a coherent self that can act with agency.

One of the difficulties that face those that are drawing up a consistent response to the problems posed by personality disorder is the question of treatability. At the request of the UK government (Home Office and DOH), Warren and colleagues provided, a comprehensive review of the evidence on the 'treatability' of severe personality disorder, with particular reference to issues of dangerousness. The review describes a paucity of reliable evidence about treatments that work, but does reveal some relatively optimistic findings concerning the effectiveness of therapeutic efforts such as therapeutic communities. It would seem that government concern with personality disorder continues to grow (see Cabinet Office (2006); and the discussion in the conclusion to this book).

Conclusion

The topic of mental disorder is an important one that introduces a number of significant themes. The figures on the proportions of prison inmates with mental disorders certainly suggest that there are some important links between mental disorder and crime. Further inspection of those figures reveals that it is the category of 'personality disorder' and particularly APD, that is the most significant. The category of APD, which has become the focus of so much anxiety, while perhaps questionable as a distinct category in its own right, also points us to consideration of a number of more general mental health issues. While it is possible to dispute the status of 'personality disorder', as a medical syndrome, we do know that the personality disorders can overlap considerably with more general mental-health issues (Blackburn et al. 2003) and other social difficulties, including drug abuse, self-harm and homelessness (Campbell 2006; Haw et al. 2006).

There is also evidence that there are important continuities between childhood circumstances and behaviour that is consistent with a diagnosis of APD. The next chapter (Chapter 3) will begin to explore the significance of life history and the links between childhood factors and criminality. Strong theoretical reasons and evidence from clinical literature seem to suggest that there might be connections between severe personality problems of the kind that might well be associated with serious criminality and deprived childhoods. Chapter 3 will examine studies that have traced the influence of various childhood circumstances on later offending behaviour. Chapter 4 will take this analysis further in looking in more detail at the evidence that seems to implicate family background as a significant cause of crime.

The other important issue here is how ideas about mental disorder might influence how responsibility might be assigned to the actions of those who carry out serious offences. Reflection on the history of the insanity defence, and of moral insanity in particular, suggests that a cognitive view of insanity triumphed over the view that would allow disorders of the emotions to be seen as categories that carried some weight of mitigation. It could be argued that this sits uneasily with some of the evidence about the significance of emotional disorders and antisocial behaviour.

Note

1 See *Joint Agencies' Response to the Recommendations of the Independent Inquiry Report into the Care and Treatment of Michael Stone.* South East Coast Strategic Health Authority, Kent County Council, Kent Probation Area, Medway Primary Care Trust, Kent and Medway NHS and Social Care Partnership Trust, Medway Council.

Chapter 3

The contribution of criminal career research

Introduction

This chapter will examine an influential body of research seeking to answer the question of whether we can understand the causes of criminality in terms of the histories of the offenders. Many assumptions have been popularly made about the backgrounds of those who commit crime. These assumptions have been clearly present in psychoanalytic work (e.g. Aichorn 1925) in which people who commit crime were seen as responding to emotionally deprived backgrounds. The assumption that crime occurs through neglect and poverty was a strong theme in more sociologically orientated work from the end of the nineteenth century (as discussed in Chapter 1). Such views have been subject to criticism, however, three particular observations being made. First, the anecdotal observation was made that many people emerged from backgrounds of deprivation and poverty *without* turning to crime. Second, it can be argued that those working with offenders had a biased perspective. They were learning about the past lives of the offenders from the offenders themselves. The offenders clearly had a vested interest in presenting their lives as ones marked by difficulties (in order to explain away their behaviour). Third, the more general observation could be made that although average income and general wealth among the masses of people rose enormously in the West in the second half of the twentieth century, crime rates also increased greatly. As discussed in Chapter 1, this observation cast doubt on there being any simple relationship between social deprivation and crime.

A number of important pieces of research have been carried out to examine whether early experiences of difficulties increase the likelihood of someone's becoming an offender later in life. There are two distinct methods of studying the impact of an individual's history on offending. First, there are *prospective, longitudinal* approaches, which involve the collection of data on groups of young children and then following up those children over the years into adulthood. One can then see which of them have gone on to have criminal records, and look back at the data collected earlier and ask whether there are certain features of the offenders' lives that mark them out as significantly different from those who did not become offenders. This is a very powerful methodology. A great deal of accurate data can be collected through time on the lives of individuals. It is, however, extremely expensive to collect this kind of detailed information on individuals and to track them through their lives, and so sample sizes have been limited. This has meant that the rarer and more serious offenders are not necessarily likely to be included in these studies.

Second, *retrospective, cross-sectional* designs can be used. This involves surveying large numbers of adults and collecting information about their criminal history and also gathering data retrospectively about their childhoods, families and schooling. This method can be relatively inexpensive, as it does not involve keeping track of and in touch with individuals, and collecting data at different points in time. This means much larger sample sizes can be used. The weakness of this method is that the information gathered is much less detailed and is more prone to inaccuracy (some will be dependent on the abilities of individuals to recall aspects of their own past). Indeed, there is evidence those who are more seriously antisocial are more likely to be particularly poor informants (Moffitt *et al.* 2002: 192).

Data using longitudinal methodologies will be the focus of this chapter. In particular, one influential classic study, of a group of boys who grew up in London in the 1960s, will be examined in detail. Several points will be extracted from this study. First, we are drawn very firmly toward awareness of the heterogeneity of offenders. That is, there are very different types of offender, and it is misleading to base studies of criminality on a crude distinction between offenders and non-offenders. Second, the longitudinal studies can tell us a great deal about the life circumstances of those who do go on to develop serious criminal lifestyles. Third, they point us toward the potential value of understanding criminal behaviour in terms of the pattern of offending over time – in other words, the 'criminal career' of the offender.

The London Longitudinal Study

In 1960, a group of researchers based at the Institute of Criminology at Cambridge (hence it is sometimes referred to as 'the Cambridge Study') identified a sample of 411 8–9-year-old boys living in an inner London district. They included all the boys in that age group at six different primary schools. They chose an area that they described as being largely white (just 12 of the sample were black, being of Caribbean origin). West describes the area as a 'typically working class, residential area, where families were inclined to stay put for long periods, most of them housed in local authority accommodation. The area was not prosperous, but not especially impoverished' (West 1982: 7). They collected data at different points in the boys' lives (interviews with the boys typically occurring at the ages of 8–9, 10–11 and 14–16, and then into adulthood at ages 18–19 and 21, 25 and 32). A number of sources of data were used:

- Interviews were carried out with the boys themselves.
- Parents were interviewed separately.
- Home background was assessed by social workers according to income, maternal attitude and parental vigilance.
- School records of progress and achievement were included.

Many reports have now been made on this study (Farrington 2002). In order to give a good impression of the methodology and the central empirical issues, the following review is based mainly on the substantial report on the study by West (1982).

Age on first conviction

The study group had access to centrally held records on criminal convictions. These did not include motoring offences. Table 3.1 shows the age categories in which the boys received their first conviction.

The first thing to note in Table 3.1 is the age distribution of these first offences. The most common age to be convicted was 13–14 (there were 34 boys in this category). Overall, roughly 20 per cent had acquired an official record by the time they were 17 (84 of the 411 in the whole sample), and 25 per cent by age 18 (103/411), and then by 25 years, 33 per cent of the total group had at least one conviction (136/411). Using data from larger samples, Farrington (1981) calculated that the chances of a man being convicted for a non-motoring offence by the

Table 3.1 Age at which boys had their first criminal conviction

Age	Number of boys receiving their first conviction	% ($n = 136$)	Cumulative % of total ($n = 411$)
10–12	20	14.7	4.9
13–14	34	25.0	13.1
15–16	30	22.1	20.4
17–18	27	19.8	27.0
19–20	17	12.5	31.1
21–24	8	5.9	33.1
Total	136	100	33.1

age of 25 was 26.6 per cent. This suggests that the study group were slightly more likely to commit offences than a more general sample. This is consistent with the fact that the boys in the London study lived in an urban area where rates of delinquency would probably be relatively high. These figures are consistent with many studies of the relationship between age and offending.

Seriousness of offences
When we consider how serious these offences are, we find that the great majority of them were minor. If the severity of sentence can be taken as a proxy measure of the seriousness of the crime, then, of the 131 whom they were able to follow-up properly (from the 136 who had committed some kind of offence), it was found that only a small minority received any kind of custodial sentence:

* 13 sent to borstal
* 14 to detention centre
* 12 to prison (including five who had been in borstal or detention centre).

There were 257 offences committed by juveniles. The majority of offences (89.1 per cent) were for dishonesty. Only seven of the 131 offenders (who had offences and still lived in Britain) were thought to be still active or dangerous. There were another 14 who continued to sustain convictions but only of a minor nature.

Repeat offending

A similar pattern emerges from examination of the figures on the numbers of offences committed (Table 3.2), in that most offenders had a small number of convictions. Of the 136 people who were known to have at least one conviction, five could not be followed up properly as they had left the country. Over half of those with convictions had only one or two convictions.

As Table 3.2 shows, 38.2 per cent of the 131 offenders followed up had just one conviction. Smaller numbers had two and three convictions. However, a larger number (31.3 per cent) had more than three convictions. In fact, 30 of the offenders were responsible for 56.6 per cent of all the recorded convictions. This pattern of a small minority of offenders committing a large proportion of the total has been confirmed many times now and will be discussed in more detail in this chapter.

Do official records reflect reality?

As discussed in the Introduction, there is considerable scepticism within criminology that official records give a true picture of criminal activity. It may be that studies that look at actual convictions and sentences are ignoring the great number of offences that occur but go undetected – the notorious dark figure of crime. Fortunately, the Cambridge study did not rely only on official records of crime. It also included information gathered confidentially from the boys and young men themselves about their activities. A card-sort technique was used to gather this information. The boys were given a series of cards with various offences on them and were asked to sort the cards into different piles depending on whether they had been involved in that activity 'never', 'one or twice', 'sometimes', or 'frequently'. This technique is considered useful in circumstances where people might be reluctant to discuss their behaviour. Investigations using

Table 3.2 Repeat offending

No. of offences	No. of offenders	%
1	50	38.2
2	21	16.0
3	19	14.5
>3	41	31.3
	(n = 131)	

this were carried out at ages 14 and 16. Perhaps not surprisingly, it was found that the official conviction rates were indeed but a pale reflection of the rates of criminal activity reported by the boys themselves. However, the vast majority of the offences admitted were minor; letting fireworks off in the street (87 per cent) and 'buying or accepting something that is thought to be stolen' (57 per cent) for example.

West *et al.* also found that those who were self-reporting high levels of activity, including more serious offending, were also those that had official criminal records. So it seemed in this sample that the presence of a criminal record was indicative of slightly more serious offending. This is reassuring for the many studies of criminal activity that rely on official measures, and the broad picture emerging here, that self-report studies reveal a great deal more crime than official records, but that those self-reporting more serious crime tend to be those with criminal records, has been generally confirmed (Farrington 2002: 704). Nevertheless, when self-report measures are used, we find that some kind of criminal activity is very common. Indeed, West (1982: 21) commented sardonically, 'The exceptional few who claimed always to have behaved with near perfect conformity to law were, at least in a statistical sense, a highly deviant group.' The question of why so many young people (and particularly young men and boys) have some engagement with criminality will be engaged with fully in Chapter 5.

Identifying the risk factors for criminality

The great strength of longitudinal data is that we can look at who the problem offenders are in their mid-twenties and look back to see whether there were aspects of their childhoods, their upbringing, or their schooling which might suggest that they had been set on a pathway to offending. Did they have difficult childhoods; were they from poorer backgrounds or broken homes? When the data from this London study are examined, we find almost an embarrassment of riches. As West (1982: 72) puts it, 'Virtually without exception it was the adverse points of any rating that were associated with future delinquency. It was the boys from broken homes rather than intact homes, those from poor homes rather than affluent homes, those with unhealthy rather than healthy mothers, and those born illegitimate[1] rather than those born to married parents who were more likely to become juvenile delinquents.' The following are some examples of factors associated with delinquency.

Individual cognitive ability

The main measure used in the study was of IQ score as measured by Raven's Matrices (a test of intelligence relying on non-verbal reasoning) taken at age ages 8 and 10 (with the average of the two scores being used in analyses). It was found that the juvenile delinquents had an IQ score of 95 compared to 101 for the rest of the group. Low IQ has since been found to be a reliably associated with delinquency (Hirschi and Hindelgang 1977, Rutter *et al.* 1998), although, as Emler and Reicher (1995) emphasise, the relationship is small. The association is seen to remain intact even when social class is taken into account (Moffitt *et al.* 1994). The explanation for the relationship is open to dispute (Donnellan *et al.* 2000). It could be argued that intellectually less able people are not necessarily more delinquent, but they are more likely to get caught. However, data from the London study showed that the association was there even when self-report offences were taken into account. Perhaps low IQ leads to educational failure and therefore disaffection in school and later unemployment. On the other hand, it may be that certain behavioural traits lead to less engagement with education, which, in turn, leads to lower IQ scores. Indeed, it may be the interactions are more complicated than this. Perhaps lower intellectual capacity inhibits the development of social skills and problem solving, leading older children and adults to resort to aggression and overt deviance to get what they want.

Financial status and housing

Family income and status were judged partly by social worker estimates and dependence on welfare benefits. The less wealthy families were more likely to produce delinquents. An abundance of research on the impact of poverty and disadvantage confirms that these factors do 'constitute reasonably robust (although not always strong) indications of an increased risk of delinquency' (Rutter *et al.* 1998: 199). As Rutter *et al.* (1998) argue, it is clear that poverty is not a direct cause of delinquency, but interacts with other factors. Such thinking is broadly in keeping with the range of sociological theorising discussed in Chapter 1. It may be, for example, that, as Merton (1957) argued, crime results from the strain that occurrs as people feel that the social limits around them are dashing their material aspirations.

Child rearing

Various factors, such as maternal attitude, maternal discipline, parental attitude, paternal discipline, marital disharmony and parental inconsistency, were rated by social workers doing the original assessments. All of these seemed to correlate with delinquency. The more negative the assessment of the child rearing, the greater was the likelihood of delinquency. This has become a highly contested area, and the evidence of the impact of family factors and parenting practices will be dealt with in detail in Chapter 4.

Are there key factors that cause delinquency?

Given the volume of variables that correlated in some way with delinquency, it was clearly necessary to try to identify what might be the most important factors. The many variables that had been collected were put through a series of factor analyses to isolate the following five factors that seemed particularly powerful in explaining the eventual outcomes.

Coming from a low-income family
Of 93 boys so identified by social work assessment, 33 per cent became juvenile delinquents.

Coming from a large family
This was defined as having four or more surviving siblings born to the boy's mother before his tenth birthday. There were 99 such boys, and 32.3 per cent of them became juvenile delinquents.

'Unsatisfactory' child rearing
These were the families that were given an overall 'unsatisfactory' rating by the social workers who did the initial assessments. Some 103 boys were identified as experiencing unsatisfactory child-rearing practices. Of these, 32.3 per cent later came to have criminal records, compared to 15.9 per cent of the rest of the sample.

Below-average intelligence
A group of 103 boys were defined as having an IQ of less than 90 on Raven's Matrices. Of this group, 31.1 per cent had acquired a criminal record, compared to 15.9 per cent of the rest of the sample.

Having a parent with a criminal record
The definition used was that one parent (almost invariably the father) acquired a criminal record before the boy's tenth birthday. There were 103 such boys, of whom 37.9 per cent had criminal records, compared to 14.6 per cent of the rest.

There was significant overlap between all of these five factors, some families having several of the factors.

How well do these factors predict offending?

All five of these factors were associated with criminality. There seemed, however, to be a limit to the power of these factors to be predictive. That is, not all those who had a number of these risk factors acquired criminal records. The research team found that of the group of 63 who had several of these adverse factors, 31 had a criminal record while 32 did not. There were also another 53 who had criminal records but did *not* belong to the high-risk group. Therefore the question might be asked, how useful is it to think in terms of 'risk factors', if such a proportion who have these risk factors are able to avoid criminality? Further analysis of the data threw more light on this puzzle. West *et al.* discriminated between different types of 'criminal career'. They drew up a typology simply based on the numbers of known offences and at what age they were committed. They found that this analysis was particularly enlightening. They discovered strong associations between the categories so produced and degrees of seriousness of criminality. They used this analysis to suggest the following four categories of offenders who could be argued to have very different types of 'criminal careers'. The careers of the more serious and frequent offenders were much more strongly associated with the negative social and familial variables.

Juvenile one-time offenders (n=37)

These people had just one recorded offence while still juveniles. The people in this group were just about indistinguishable from non-offenders in terms of their background and behaviour. When the different variables were examined, it was found that this group had similar educational records and achievements, and similar family disadvantages to the non-offenders. As adults, they were just as likely to be in good jobs, and as likely to be married. It seemed that they were largely the same as the non-offending group, accept for the fact that they had been caught for a (probably petty) offence. Many studies have confirmed this finding that people who commit perhaps a single minor offence are largely indistinguishable from non-offenders (Moffitt 1993).

Latecomers to crime (n=33)

These were people whose first offence was after the age of 18. These may also be one-time offenders. When their backgrounds were examined, they were found to have been in a bit more trouble in school than the non-offending group. They were slightly more 'deviant' than the ones who committed a juvenile offence, but they generally had unremarkable backgrounds. Since then, other studies have suggested that this group is very small (Rutter *et al.* 1998: 104).

Temporary recidivists (n=25)
These were offenders with at least two offences up until the age of 18 but who then tailed off in their offending. They tended to come from relatively deprived backgrounds and to have been troublesome as schoolboys. Here is a typical example, described by West:

Case 852 (a temporary recidivist)

This was an intelligent boy from a materially satisfactory but emotionally fraught home background. The school authorities were concerned about his progress, but unable to prevail upon his parents to come to discuss the problem. He was a repeated offender as a juvenile. For an offence of housebreaking, committed while truanting, he was put on probation at the age of 12. Later he spent 18 months in approved school following conviction for another housebreaking, in which a flat was completely ransacked and a considerable amount of valuables was taken.

According to his mother he was branded as a troublemaker and a ring leader from the moment he started junior school at age 7. From then until he was committed to approved school at age 14 he was continually in trouble, cheeky, defiant, getting into fights and constantly truanting. A probation report quoted his headmaster as saying he was 'amoral and subversive'.

The parents refused, at first, to cooperate with the study. The boy himself complained that they were not interested in him and spent all their time out drinking, leaving him to be looked after by his elder sister. Interviewed at age 18, when he was still living in his parents' home, he commented about his father: 'He's never really cared for me … I'm getting my own back at me father and mother now for what they done to me … Whereas before they used to shout at me and all that, they can't now because I'm a bit bigger … I swear at my father and tell him where to go and all this if he tells me to do anything or says anything to me.'

In spite of a continuing aggressive attitude, he claimed (at 18) to have given up delinquency and given up the friends with whom he used to commit offences. … He had got engaged and thought this was the main reason for 'going straight' , but he thought that if this relationship were to break up he would go back to his old ways and his old mates.

He did not go back. Seen for the last time at 25, he was married with two children, working in a job he enjoyed, and living in a privately rented house. He had now given up his fighting proclivities as well as his delinquency. The interviewer commented, 'He seems to have settled down to a quiet existence. He goes out drinking, but generally takes his wife with him.'

(West 1982: 84–5)

It is interesting to note that the subject himself identified having a girlfriend and getting engaged as being significant in changing his behaviour. As we will discuss later, there are those that believe that occurrences such as these are themselves significant turning points in people's lives (e.g. Laub and Sampson 1993).

Persistent recidivists (n=36)

The people in this group started their criminal careers early, and, as the name suggests, they continued to commit crime well into adulthood. They very clearly came from the most deprived group. Twelve of them (33.3 per cent) came from a group that had four of the five adverse factors (only 5 per cent of the whole sample had this many factors). They differed quite sharply from the temporary recidivists. From interviews at age 22, there seemed to be a whole catalogue of behaviour and circumstances, including being involved in fights, living in temporary accommodation, being separated from offspring, not using contraception, and being likely to be unemployed. The description of Case 941 exemplifies the issues:

Case 941

This man came from a large, conflict-ridden family living in impoverished circumstances in very dilapidated housing which the occupants were struggling to maintain in habitable condition. Father and siblings had a criminal record. The father's work took him from home a lot, and when interviewed at 16 the parents were said to be separated.

He performed badly at school and was taken to court for persistent truancy. The probation officer found his mother cold and less than cooperative over the issue of school attendance. At school he was said to be 'indifferent to teachers, overbearing to other children and indulging in cruel bullying'.

On leaving school at the earliest permitted age, he worked off and on as an unskilled labourer, but with numerous job changes and periods of unemployment. When seen at age 18 he was talkative and slightly drunk. He admitted to having got into trouble on various occasions for drunken driving while disqualified and without insurance. He complained of heavy debts from unpaid fines. He was living with a girl whom he had made pregnant, but mentioned other sexual adventures 'on the side'. He said he had been 'a bit of a skinhead' and reported a recent head injury from fighting.

His conviction history began with a finding of guilt at age 15. He had threatened another boy with a stick and robbed him of £1. He had earlier been arrested for keeping lookout for another boy who was trying to break into a telephone box ... but was released for lack of evidence. His many convictions for traffic offences started at age 16. At 18 he was convicted for minor theft, although he admitted at interview he had been involved in numerous delinquencies around that time. Re-interviewed at 21, he claimed to be a re-formed character and was apparently embarked on a successful work career. However, at age 22 he was reconvicted for taking a car. ...

Marriage to the girl he had been living with brought only a worsening of his behaviour. His drinking began to get out of control, he began to take prohibited drugs and he was spending all his time away from home with delinquent companions in pubs and clubs. He gave up his job in order to join an 'organisation' involved in robberies. Eventually he received a long sentence for participating in a serious robbery and possessing a firearm. The incident concerned an old couple who had been tricked into letting the thieves into the house, overpowered and tied up, and robbed of a substantial amount of cash and jewels.

When interviewed ... at age 25 he was in prison, where he was in trouble again for fighting.

(West 1982: 88)

This significance and broad characteristics of this category of 'persistent recidivists' have been confirmed in many studies. For example,

Moffitt's influential typology, which will be discussed in more detail, uses the term 'life-course-persistent offenders' to describe offenders that are clearly analogous to this group. Generally, there appears to be an important hierarchy that emerges through the typology used in this London study. The risk factors are weakly associated with trivial involvement in crime, but as those risk factors accumulate in the lives of individuals, they become much more strongly associated with persistent and serious offending. As the lives of the more serious and persistent offenders are examined, factors of social and familial deprivation emerge more strongly.

Deprived non-delinquents: resilience?

An important objection can be raised to the claims about the practical importance of the finding of multiple deprivations being strongly associated with criminal outcomes. It is argued that not all people who come from deprived social and familial backgrounds go on to become offenders. Are there people who emerge from backgrounds of severe deprivation and do not turn to crime? In order to look at this issue more closely, the cases of 54 boys who had come from a criminal family and had at least two other risk factors in their backgrounds were examined. These risk factors were being born out of wedlock; coming from a family supported by welfare; experience of a period living in the care of the local authority; coming from a home where the parents separated permanently before the boy reached the age of 15; having lived in slum conditions; and coming from a family with a large number of children. Statistically speaking, this group would be highly vulnerable to delinquency. Indeed, it was found that 36 of them did have criminal records, and 17 of these fell into the category of 'persistent recidivist'. This latter figure seems to confirm the significance of the risk factors. There were 18 (33 per cent) of the 54, however, who had no conviction at all. What might be said about this group of 18? What had become of them? Might it be that there were factors that had given them resilience? In order to answer these questions an attempt was made to interview all 18 when they were 23–34 years of age. The researchers were not able to track down three of this group. They compared the remaining 15 to a control group who did not have these factors that suggest vulnerability. The following points emerged from this analysis:

- Of the deprived group, six admitted to an offence (compared to only one in a control group). Five had been involved in a fight in the past 18 months.

- Two of the deprived group acquired criminal records soon after their twenty-second birthday.

What was most striking, however, was the fact that all the men in the 'deprived but not criminal' group were not 'doing well'. As West (1982: 92) put it, 'The most prominent characteristic of the group of 18 deprived men . . . was their social failure, manifest in unemployment, poor living conditions and social isolation.'

- Seven were chronically unemployed. Of the employed, most were in low-status, low-pay jobs.
- Five lived in damp, dirty, cramped conditions.

The following case gives a feel of the difficulties being experienced by this group of deprived yet not delinquent men:

Case 011

This man's childhood was marred by impoverished conditions and extreme conflict between his parents. His father, who was chronically unemployed, was described as something of a hermit, hardly communicating even with his wife. He was 11 when his father died. His mother was an aggressive, quarrelsome woman with a long history of psychiatric disorder, diagnosed as 'paranoid psychosis with depressive features in a woman of low intelligence'. She made a number of suicide attempts.

At school he was no disciplinary problem, but was a poor attender and was taken before a juvenile court on that account. He was thought to be under his mother's domination. She would excuse his absences by complaining falsely that his classmates were picking on him. His mother and two of his siblings sustained criminal convictions.

He declined to be interviewed at 18, his mother writing on his behalf. ... When he was 20 the social services became involved with the household because his mother had attacked him with a knife. He was noted to be an unemployed labourer who rarely went out in the evening.

At age 23 he did agree to an interview. He was still living with his now aged mother, but his siblings had all left and he no longer saw them. The home was in a very neglected state with the living room floor partly eaten away by rats, the banisters and several doors fallen off and the sink almost permanently blocked. He had been continuously unemployed for 18 months. ... He had no outside human contacts apart from repairmen and council officials. Asked about offences, he replied pathetically: 'I can't get into trouble, I never go out.'

(West 1982: 95-6)

While this study was based on small numbers of individuals, other studies (such as the Dunedin study) also point to the numbers of children who score highly on risk factors for crime and exhibit antisocial behaviour, but who do not go on to develop serious offending careers. This group have been described as the 'childhood limited' or 'recovery group'; however, later follow-up suggested that this was over-optimistic and that they did continue to have problems, and they were perhaps better seen as 'low-level chronic offenders' (Moffitt *et al.* 2002).

Summary of the findings of the London study

The significant findings of this piece of longitudinal research were as follows:

- There seemed to be very important distinctions to be made between the more persistent, serious offenders and the much greater numbers of boys who committed minor offences during their juvenile years. Subsequent research has confirmed this analysis. There seems to be particular value in the distinction between 'life-course-persistent' (LCP) and 'adolescent-limited' (AL) offenders (Moffitt 1993), and this will be discussed further below.

- There were strong associations between 'life-course-persistent' offending and adverse background factors (individual, family and social circumstances). A very important suggestion of the longitudinal research is that the 'life-course-persistent' offenders may be identifiable very early.

These two points will be used to inform the discussion of the rest of the chapter.

Heterogeneity of offenders: AL versus LCP offenders

The finding of the heterogeneity of the offending population and the categorisation of the subgroups has been followed up and repeated by a number of significant studies. Perhaps the most consistent and potentially useful distinction is that made between groups analogous to the 'one-time juvenile offenders' and the 'persistent recidivists' described by West (1982). Particularly strong support for something like these groups has come from researchers using the Dunedin longitudinal study (Moffitt 1993), who distinguished between LCP and AL offenders.

The Dunedin Multidisciplinary Health and Development Study (DMHDS) is another influential longitudinal study. It consists of a continuing longitudinal study of 1037 babies born in Dunedin, New Zealand, between April 1972 and March 1973. The sample consisted of a full socio-economic range, and was 52 per cent male. The study has involved intensive study of the subjects, looking at a vast range of health, behavioural, educational and social measures. The subjects have been followed up regularly (every other year through childhood), and the intention is to study the group throughout adulthood. While the relative ethnic homogeneity of the group means that some questions about the interactions between ethnicity and all factors studied cannot be answered (93 per cent being identified as 'white' and the remainder Maori or Pacific Islanders), the data produced from the study have been heavily used by those interested in the causal pathways of delinquent behaviour (among other issues). The Dunedin study has been used to carry further the work of the London study that began to investigate differences between distinct groups of offenders. Terri Moffitt (1993) argues that the Dunedin data support the idea that an important distinction can be made between the LCP offenders and the AL group.

Moffitt (1993) argued that around 7 per cent of the Dunedin sample could be considered LCP, and around 26 per cent AL. The LCP would typically manifest antisocial behaviour relatively early in childhood, and this would have developed into criminal offending before the end of childhood. They would then tend to be involved in frequent and serious offending, which would continue into adulthood. The AL group would, as their name suggests, be most likely to embark on their criminal careers in adolescence and would not continue their offending into adulthood. The offending would be likely to be less frequent and less serious than that of the LCP group. In addition, in terms of background factors, the LCP could be statistically distinguished. In keeping with findings from the London study, those with greater numbers of risk factors in their backgrounds were more likely to be among the LCP offenders. In contrast, Moffitt *et al.* (2002: 180) argued that the AL group can be characterised as 'common, relatively temporary and near normative'. They suggest that delinquency in this group emerges:

> alongside puberty, when otherwise healthy youngsters experience dysphoria during the relatively roleless years between their biological maturation and their access to mature privileges and responsibilities, a period called the maturity gap. Whilst adolescents are in this gap it is virtually normative for them to find the LCP youths' delinquent style appealing and mimic it as a way to demonstrate autonomy from parents, win affiliation with peers, and hasten social maturation.
>
> (Moffitt *et al.* 2002: 180)

Sankey and Huon (1999) argued that criminologists and policymakers must be more aware of the distinction between these groups when studying or making provision for youth offenders.

We will explore further why delinquency seems to be such an attractive option for so many adolescents in Chapter 4 'Youth Crime'. The key issue for the time being is that those attracted to delinquency for the first time during adolescence seem to be very different from the LCP group, who present various forms of antisocial behaviour from early childhood; according to Moffitt, this includes 'biting and hitting at age 4, shoplifting and truancy at age 10, selling drugs and stealing cars at age 16' (Moffitt 1993: 679). As children, this group are distinguished by 'difficult temperament, neurological abnormalities, low intellectual ability, reading difficulties, hyperactivity, poor scores on neurospsychological tests' (Moffitt *et al.* 2002: 181). LCP groups have been found to have higher rates of poverty, neglect, and abuse than non-offenders and AL groups (Raine *et al.* 2005; using data from the Pittsburgh Youth Study). In terms of background childhood factors, the AL group, on the other hand, tended to 'have backgrounds that were normative or sometimes better than the average Dunedin child's' (Moffitt *et al.* 2002: 181).

During adolescence, the LCP group commit more frequent and more serious offences than the AL group. Early findings (e.g. Moffitt 1993) suggested that the AL group tend to cease offending as they move into adulthood. Further work (Moffitt *et al.* 2002) has found that at follow-up at age 26 the AL group were carrying on offending into their twenties. This was relatively infrequent, but was persistent. Moffitt *et al.* suggest that this might be evidence of the group (like many of their contemporaries in modern societies) living out an extended adolescence due to the combination of late marriage and the lack of early career opportunities or stability.

Further investigation also suggests that identification of additional groups might well be helpful. One group that has warranted some interest are the 'recoveries' (Moffitt *et al.* 1996) or 'childhood limited' (Raine *et al.* 2005), and this might offer some hope in identifying resilience (as discussed on p. 84). These were individuals who exhibited a number of antisocial features during childhood, but who seemed not to go on to offend in the style of the LCP group. For a number of years, there has been interest in exploration of 'resilience' factors (Rutter *et al.* 1998). Is it possible to learn from examining the lives of those who might well appear to be on track for lives marked by serious antisocial behaviour, but whose lives turn out very differently? The presence of a substantial group (Moffitt *et al.* (2002), estimated that 8 per cent of the male Dunedin sample fitted this description) of individuals exhibiting major problems in childhood, but who take a less antisocial path later, caused some interest. Moffitt *et al.* (2002) suggest that the initial optimism was not necessarily warranted, however. At follow-up at age 26, a clear picture of the deficits of the group had emerged. For one thing, it seemed that around one-quarter of them were offending as adults. The pattern of offending better fitted the description, 'low-level chronic offenders' (Moffitt *et al.* 2002: 196). Those who were not offending as adults, were not doing well in other ways. They suffered from uniquely high levels of internalising forms of psychopathology (such as depression and anxiety) and indeed were rated as being the most depressed and anxious men in the cohort. If they were protected from delinquency, it was perhaps because they were socially isolated. This is consistent with the investigation of a similar group in the London study who had committed fewer offences than predicted judging by their disadvantageous backgrounds (Farrington *et al.* 1988).

The LCP group, when followed up at age 26 (Moffitt 2002), appear to be a seriously disadvantaged and problematic group. The LCP group suffered (according to informants) from a range of mental health problems, being significantly more likely than the AL (or any other group) to suffer from drug-related problems, paranoid symptoms, symptoms of depression, and post-traumatic stress disorder. Interestingly, they were significantly more likely to have symptoms of antisocial personality disorder. This suggests an important link between themes raised in Chapter 2 'Mental Disorder: Madness, Personality Disorder and Criminal Responsibility', where the presence of personality disorder among the prison population pointed to the possible criminological significance of this group. Indeed, Moran and Hagell (2001), in reviewing the evidence about the possible causes of antisocial personality disorder, refer to the work on LCP offenders from the Dunedin study and acknowledge that at least some of the LCP group 'with enduring patterns of antisocial behaviour will be diagnosed in adulthood ... as having personality disorders, one of which is anti-social personality disorder' (2001: 1). Raine *et al*. (2005) report on the possible neurocognitive impairments that might underlie the behaviour of the LCP group. They scored significantly lower on IQ tests than AL groups; showed significant impairments in spatial memory, but not verbal memory; and showed significantly poor performance on tests of spatial ability. Raine *et al*. (2002) suggest that the group showed signs of poor right cerebral hemisphere function at age 3. They speculate that since this is the area of the brain that is typically responsible for non-verbal communication and the processing of emotion, the child might have difficulties in processing emotional information, so that making good bonds with parents would be difficult. All this is consistent with the work of clinicians discussed in Chapter 2 (pp. 68–70) who describe the particular difficulties of some individuals as being connected to 'failures of emotional representation' (Fonagy *et al*. 2003, 2004). Shore (1994) argues that failure of parents to attune to the mental states of their children in the early months and years of their lives can result in faults in the development of the psychoneurological structures within the right hemisphere that support the regulation of, and the ability to reflect upon, emotional experience. Morrell and Murray (2003: 500) use their detailed longitudinal studies of the development of the ability to process affective responses in very young babies to criticise Moffitt *et al*.'s conclusion that a psychoneurological fault underlies the difficulties of the LCP group: 'It is evident that what is being measured in these studies is not 'pure' temperament, but the result of the interaction between inherent characteristics and earlier environmental influences.'

Certainly, as adults, the relationships of LCP individuals with others seemed to be marked by conflict. They were unhappier in relationships than non-offenders, but were not unhappier in their relationships than the AL group, and were not more likely than the AL group to be involved in general abuse of partners. The LCP group were, however, likely to commit more serious abuse (11 per cent of the LCP men had a conviction for violence against women). The LCP men had proportionately fathered more children than anyone else, but they were the least likely to be living with those children. In some respect, this latter point might be seen as no bad thing, as they also 'were uniquely likely to hit a child in anger' (Moffitt *et al.* 2002: 194).

The LCP group had fewer qualifications than any other group (more than half left school with no 'high school' qualifications). When they were in legitimate employment, it was more likely to be of low status. They had longer periods of unemployment and reported difficulties in keeping jobs, often due to conflict with others. While the earnings in the LCP group were similar to those of other groups, this was significantly more likely to be made up of illegal income and welfare payments (Moffitt *et al.* 2002).

The longevity of the difficulties exhibited by the LCP group is striking. Data from the Dunedin study suggest that detectable differences are found between very young children who later go on to develop the more serious behaviour problems as adolescents and adults. White *et al.* (1990) used data from the Dunedin study to show that good predictors of delinquency problems at ages 11 and 13 were descriptions of the children as 'difficult to manage' at age 3 and as exhibiting behaviour problems at age 5. In reviewing the evidence from longitudinal studies, Farrington concludes:

> It seems that offending is part of a larger syndrome of antisocial behaviour that arises in childhood and tends to persist into adulthood ... there is significant continuity over time, since the antisocial child tends to become the anti-social teenager and then the antisocial adult.
>
> (Farrington 2000: 658)

While the evidence for the continuity between childhood difficulties is great, many more questions can be asked about the explanation for this link. The following section will address the question of what might explain the continuity.

Explaining the links between childhood antisocial behaviour and adult offending

The conspicuous findings of a number of studies have been the apparent continuities between childhood behavioural problems and later delinquency. Vizard *et al.* (2004) have argued that the evidence of associations between childhood antisocial behaviour problems and antisocial behaviour in adolescents and adults is now so convincing that a developmental syndrome of 'severe personality disorder emerging childhood' ought to be recognised. Such recognition of these difficulties would facilitate better intervention strategies with individuals. That argument supposes that we are witnessing some kind of psychopathology within the individual. There are, however, actually a number of different ways of understanding the continuity between childhood behaviour problems and later delinquency. Comparison and evaluation can be made of these three competing broad explanations:

- sociological explanations
- individual explanations: physiological variables
- individual explanations: psychological variables.

Sociological explanations

Sociological explanations point to the significance of either labelling or social disadvantage. Both perspectives assume that the continuity between childhood behaviour and the adult should be understood not in terms of the individual but by reference to the social environment surrounding the individual.

Labelling

Labelling theories have played prominent roles in sociological explanations of deviance (as discussed in Chapter 1). The thinking here is that if people are labelled as having certain characteristics, those around them will respond to them as though they do indeed manifest those characteristics. The behaviour and perhaps the very identity of the labelled individual will then be shaped by the expectations of others. In the particular case of delinquency, if young children are identified as being 'difficult' or 'naughty' early in their schooling, they will begin to be treated differently in the classroom, perhaps attracting negative attention from teachers more swiftly than other children. In the face of such negative feedback, their school work and behaviour will deteriorate. Thus, a vicious circle is set up that may lead the children to disaffection within, and ultimately exclusion from, school. This would set them firmly upon a 'pathway to delinquency'.

It certainly has been shown that labels themselves can powerfully affect the way people are perceived by others. Rosenhan's classic study of what happened to a group of people who had themselves admitted to various psychiatric institutions is a powerful example of what labelling can do. Even when they stopped pretending to have symptoms of mental illness, their ordinary behaviour was interpreted by staff as being pathological (Rosenhan 1973). Given this evidence, it would seem reasonable to suggest that labelling processes might play a part in at least maintaining someone on a criminal pathway. Labelling theory has faced two chief criticisms. First, labelling theory has been criticised for disregarding the powerful and complex social forces that might underlie those labelling process (Taylor *et al.* 1973). Second, it is has been argued that it is difficult to show that labelling itself is a significant cause of criminality in the absence of other factors (Williams 1991: 442). So, in relation to the issue being considered here, it is highly plausible that labelling helps maintain someone in stigmatised and marginalised circumstances, but it is difficult to show that a particular incidence of labelling alone can set someone on a 'delinquent pathway'.

Social deprivation

The other major sociological explanation of the continuities between childhood difficulties and later delinquency is that they can be explained in terms of the social conditions that surround people at different points during their life, rather than in terms of the individual. Perhaps some children grow up in poor areas, in overcrowded homes with stressed parents. They attend under-resourced schools, where the teaching staff are demoralised and so do not motivate the children. The same children live in neighbourhoods where the local peer groups are delinquent, and where their families are bringing them up in very far from ideal circumstances. It is all these factors that lead to those children manifesting disruptive behaviour from an early age. These children grow up in these disadvantaged circumstances, gain few qualifications or skills, and live as adults in areas of high unemployment. It is these factors of poverty, unemployment and the lack of opportunities that lead them as adults to careers of offending. So, according to this theory, the continuity between the disruptive childhood and later offending is simply a manifestation of the adverse environment affecting the same individual. If we put the same individual in different circumstances, the continuity would disappear. There is some evidence in favour of this theory in that immediate environmental factors can be argued to be significant factors in explaining someone's deviance. Notable among these factors are schools, peer groups, and 'opportunity' factors. Each of these factors is considered below.

School factors

It is well established that different schools have very different rates of delinquency associated with them (Rutter *et al.* 1998: 232). Indeed, schools with high rates of delinquency have been found to share characteristics such as 'high levels of distrust between teachers and students, low commitment to school by students, and unclear and inconsistently enforced rules' (Rutter 1997; Farrington 2002: 677). It is difficult to make the case, however, that it is the school environment that is the crucial factor in turning its pupils into delinquents. Another, entirely plausible explanation for the same data is that different schools have very different sets of problems to deal with in terms of the communities that they serve and the pupils who attend the schools. This latter explanation was confirmed, for example, in the London study, in which it was clear that the secondary schools with higher rates of delinquency had a greater proportion of their intake made up of boys who were already seen as 'troublesome' in their primary school careers (West 1982: 98). It is important to note that such selection effects can operate in quite subtle ways. Some studies (Reynolds 1976; cited in Blackburn 1993: 174) have confirmed the different delinquency rates between schools, but noted that these did not correlate with the social characteristics of the catchment populations. It would be wrong, however, to suggest that this indicates the influence of the school on delinquency, since this would involve ignoring the way that parents use schools quite selectively. Schools that are perceived to be good schools (even if they happen to be situated in poorer neighbourhoods) draw parents who are motivated and interested in the education of their children. The same parents manoeuvre to avoid sending their children to schools that are perceived as weak. Hence, schools perceived to be weaker fill up with the children of families less interested in their child's education (and who also are more likely to carry the disadvantages discussed in the first part of this chapter). While this selection effect is undoubtedly a powerful explanation of the very large differences in rates of delinquency within schools, Rutter *et al.* (1998: 230–5) argue that schools themselves can have an influence. Changes in regime and leadership in schools that have been seen as 'failing' can have a relatively large impact on pupil behaviour and achievement in a relatively short period of time (DfES 2001). However, controversy remains, as it has been claimed that schools can improve their performance by manipulating their intakes (Pennell *et al.* 2006). Despite evidence that some schools can do better than others at overcoming the adverse social conditions around them, the overwhelming evidence is that schools that have a high proportions of pupils who already carry the kind of social and familial disadvantages previously discussed will find it very difficult to counter those negative factors.

Peer groups

One obvious way that certain schools might exert a negative influence on individuals is through the fact that they may bring them into contact with delinquent peer groups. Some influential schools of criminological thought have emphasised the impact of peer groups, or subcultural groups (Cloward and Ohlin 1960; Cohen 1965) (as discussed in Chapter 1) for some time. Certainly, the presence of delinquent friends within an individual's social network is highly predictive of delinquent activity (Vitaro and Wanner 2005). If a teenage boy has a good friend involved in delinquent activities, there is a very good chance that he too will be involved in delinquency. It is, of course more difficult to demonstrate that the causal factor is the delinquent peer. It could also be that those with delinquent tendencies are drawn to each other. This argument has been given some support from data that suggest that the presence of a delinquent sibling does not have as strong a link to delinquency as the presence of a delinquent peer (Sampson and Laub 1993: 117). If it were simply that delinquent behaviour is learnt through close proximity to someone with delinquency, we would expect siblings to have a strong impact. This is not the case, suggesting that there is a more complex selection effect – perhaps those with delinquent inclinations are attracted to similarly minded people. It is also apparent that many teenage misdemeanours are committed in the company of others. Emler and Reicher (1995) argue that this is an important clue in explaining a great deal of youth offending. They suggest that many delinquent acts carried out by young people are very public statements of identification with their peer group. Why peer groups might be so influential on young people is discussed further in Chapter 5 'Youth Crime'.

Opportunity factors

A number of criminologists have consistently made the point that the immediate environment is usually the strongest determining factor in whether a particular crime is committed (Pease 2002). Therefore, those who live in areas where there are many opportunities for committing crime are themselves more likely to be offenders.

Overall, the idea that the immediate environment is the overwhelming factor is relatively easily refuted by reference to the apparent intractability of the difficulties that some individuals demonstrate even in the face of fresh circumstances. This issue is, of course, touching on a major issue in criminology – that of rehabilitation and what factors do change individuals from 'offenders' to 'non-offenders'.

The accumulation of disadvantage

A slightly 'softer' version of the sociological perspective on the links between childhood difficulties and later delinquency has been advocated by Laub and Sampson (1993), who refer to the notion of *cumulative continuity*. In discussing the careers of the LCP group, Moffitt (1993) also refers to this idea: 'The idea of cumulative continuity posits that delinquency incrementally mortgages the future by generating negative consequences for the life chances for stigmatized and institutionalised youths' (Moffitt 1993: 306). For example, exclusion from school will probably lead to the failure to achieve qualifications, a failure that will close many employment opportunities. This may leave crime as an option – subsequent arrest and conviction may further restrict future employment opportunities, making further criminal activity even more likely (see also Patterson *et al.* 1989; Simons *et al.* 1998). The corollary of such a model is that a particularly positive change in people's lives may be significant in shifting them to a very different pathway by opening up other opportunities.

Turning points in criminal careers

Sampson and Laub (1993) argue that people can indeed experience turning points in their lives, and they use the notion of 'social capital' (Coleman 1988) as part of their explanatory framework. They suggest that those with strong bonds of interdependence with others will be less prone to deviate from social roles and expectations. Those with loose social bonds – occurring through such things as weak family ties and insecure employment – will find it easier to deviate. Their behaviour will be less governed by those around them, and they will have less to lose if convicted. In this, their theory is very similar to Hirschi's (1969) version of control theory, discussed in Chapter 1. In Laub and Sampson's words: 'Adult social ties are important insofar as they create interdependent systems of obligation and restraint that impose significant costs for translating criminal propensities into action' (Laub and Sampson 1993: 311). Farrall and Bowling (1999) argue that more attention needs to be paid to studying desistance. They suggest that there is good reason to believe that interactions between individual agency and the social circumstances and structures around individuals are significant. Sampson and Laub (1993) argue that positive events in people's lives such as getting married or finding long-term employment can act as a 'turning point', allowing an individual to have access to a different life. They give the example of 'Charlie' (1993: 313), whose first arrest had been at the age of 8. He had a number of convictions following this for larceny and burglary, and was incarcerated on three separate occasions. At age 18, things changed. He obtained a job in the US Maritime Service and began a relationship with a woman who would become his wife. These changes led Charlie to a stable, law-abiding life. At follow-up at ages 25 and 32, he was happily married and securely employed. Warr (1998) also focused on desistance and used longitudinal data to argue that marriage was itself a very significant factor in leading an offender to desist. He argued that the shift to spending time with family and not so much with peers is the really significant factor. The difficulty that these analyses have is that they are not necessarily able to demonstrate that Charlie, for example, despite the criminal activity, was not also perhaps relatively psychologically 'healthy'. Did he already have the social and psychological resources that enabled him to become involved in a long-term relationship and engage with his job? A number of theories, which will now be discussed suggest that understanding the development of the individual is important.

Individual explanations: physiology or psychology

A number of related theories take the perspective that the continuity between childhood difficulties and later criminality can be explained in terms of the characteristics of the particular individual. There are two important variants of this explanation. First, there are a range of theories that take a physiological and genetic approach: they assume that the child is, in some sense, 'born difficult'. The child can perhaps be viewed as suffering from a 'disorder' that manifests early as behavioural problems. As the individual develops, these difficulties do not disappear but instead take on an adult form. Second, other theories do not see children as being born with particular propensities to crime, but see them as being significantly shaped by early experiences, so that negative experiences in childhood are very likely to generate a teenager and adult with significant problems.

Do biological childhood disorders lead to delinquency?

The continuity between childhood and adult antisocial behaviour might be explained by the presence of some underlying biological factor. One factor that has been studied regularly is impulsivity. The evidence suggesting that impulsivity is strongly associated with criminality is strong. Farrington (2002: 666) refers to it as 'the most crucial personality dimension that predicts offending'. Other personality factors have also been associated with criminality (extensively reviewed by Blackburn 1993: ch. 8). The attribution of most of these can be criticised for being largely tautological (Rutter *et al.* 1998: 145). That is, they are describing the presence of behaviour or attitudes that are themselves clearly antisocial (see the discussion of Eysenck's construct of 'psychoticism' in Chapter 1). This criticism could indeed be levelled at impulsivity also, since it can also be used to describe people who have acted antisocially as they have seemingly been unable to control themselves. What makes impulsivity a little more interesting is that it can be argued to be present in young children whose behaviour does not have the same social meaning. A number of theories have attempted to explain why impulsivity might be a fundamental physiological variable, although it has been difficult thus far entirely to disentangle environmental effects from physiological correlates (Lee and Coccaro 2001).

The idea that some individuals are naturally predisposed to crime is an old one (as discussed in Chapter 1). The broad evidence that has often been used to point to a genetic explanation of criminal tendencies is reviewed in Chapter 5. The case is made (e.g. Mednick *et al.* 1987) that disproportionate numbers of men whose biological fathers have criminal records are likely to acquire criminal records themselves (see pp. 123–5). The point is made in Chapter 5 that the difficulties of controlling for environmental effects mean that it is hard to accept the strong conclusions that are sometimes made about the influence of genetics on crime.

There is also the possibility that some children have particular biological disorders that manifest very early in their lives. These disorders might manifest as problem behaviour in very young children (such as angry, defiant behaviour and tantrums), then as disruptive behaviour in school and similar settings, and later as delinquency. Moffitt (1993) argued that LCP offenders are likely to be predisposed to delinquency through 'subtle dysfunctions of the nervous system' (1993: 685). These dysfunctions do not, she was careful to say, simply determine delinquency but do predispose to it and interact with adverse environmental influences to produce the difficulties manifesting in the LCP group. A number of 'disorders' have been identified that might be relevant to understanding the roots of delinquency. Some children are identified as suffering from conduct disorder (CD), sometimes referred to as CP (conduct problems). This label is used to describe a child who is overtly naughty – defiant, lying, cheating and fighting, for example. DSM-IV distinguishes between CD with childhood and adolescence onset. Childhood CD is typically preceded by ODD (oppositional defiant disorder), which is marked by defiance and irritability in infants. Attention-deficit hyperactivity disorder (ADHD) is a label applied to children with inappropriately low levels of concentration for their age, alongside impulsiveness and hyperactivity. Children with ADHD may not be able to finish a task without getting distracted (poor concentration), they may indulge in quite dangerous play with little apparent fear of the consequences (impulsivity) or they may be constantly fidgety and on the move (hyperactivity). A number of early follow-up studies of children diagnosed as 'hyperactive' suggested there were links with later delinquency. These studies were reviewed by Farrington *et al.* (1990), who also used data collected as part of the London study described in the first part of this chapter to assign retrospectively the children to categories of CP and HIA (hyperactivity-impulsivity-attention deficit). They found that despite the considerable overlap between the two categories (around 60 per cent of the boys falling in one of the categories, also fell in the other), the presence both of HIA and CP did predict juvenile delinquency. Farrington *et al.* (1990) argued that HIA is particularly predictive of more chronic offending. Since HIA is often diagnosable very early, certainly well before the age of 5, they argue that it could be a useful target for early interventions. Rutter *et al.*'s (1998) extensive review also emphasised the robustness of the association of hyperactivity with antisocial behaviour (see also Kratzer and Hodgins 1997; Holmes *et al.* 2001).

There is now a great deal of evidence to suggest that there is considerable continuity between observations of CD, ADHD in childhood and difficulties associated with antisocial personality disorder in adulthood (Vitelli 1998). The difficulty is that there is great debate as to the causes of CD and ADHD in children. On the one side of the argument stand those who argue that these are physiological disorders that include a largely inherited component (e.g. Levy 2002; Smalley *et al.* 2002). On the other side stand those who argue that such disorders are themselves social constructs (Timimi 2004), and that perhaps children's hyperactive behaviour is a response to stressful circumstances (Singh (2002), provides quite a balanced review). Thus far, consideration of ADHD and HIA does not necessarily take us any further in teasing out the causal pathways.

Theories of psychological development

A number of psychological theories emphasise the importance of early experience as essential in shaping the personality of the adult. Unsatisfactory nurturing experiences are very likely to lead to adulthood lives marked by difficulties. Such outcomes would be predicted by psychoanalytic theory and various models of child development that privilege the family as the most important agent in the socialisation of children (attachment theory, social learning, for example). It is here that important links can be made between psychological theories of development and contemporary debates within criminology about the importance of the internalisation of control (Gottfredson and Hirschi 1990) and of the significance of social bonds (Sampson and Laub 1993) and shaming experiences (Braithwaite 1989). Many studies have now pointed to family factors as being of huge developmental significance. The next chapter is devoted to looking at the influence of family factors on delinquency and offending.

The problem of white-collar crime and criminal careers

A potentially important criticism of the assumptions of the findings of some of the longitudinal studies has been made by a number of criminologists (e.g. Weisburd *et al.* 2001; Piquero and Benson 2004). They argue that the pattern of offending characteristic of white-collar crime is very different from those crimes more typically captured by the longitudinal studies (which might be referred to as 'street crime'). White-collar crime tends to be committed by those who first offend well into adulthood, and who are likely to be middle class and relatively well educated. Weisburd *et al.* (2001) suggest that this is a major problem for criminal career theorists. There are a couple of objections to this analysis. First, the empirical evidence on the childhood and family backgrounds of white-collar criminals has not been gathered. It is possible that the lives of such offenders have been marked by antisocial behaviour and possibly family deprivation before adulthood. Second, it may be that some similarity with patterns of 'street crime' does emerge when the distinction is made between chronic and one-off offenders. In their study of convicted offenders, Walters and Geyer (2004) found that those who had only ever been convicted of white-collar offences 'were less inclined to endorse criminal thoughts, identify with other criminals, and exhibit signs of a criminal lifestyle' (2004: 276) than either non-white-collar offenders or white-collar offenders with other convictions. They also found that 60 per cent of the white-collar criminals fell into the 'white-collar-only' category. This lack of versatility suggests that they are indeed a very different group from other serious offenders, that an understanding of their behaviour requires a different analysis, and that the findings of the longitudinal studies do not need complete overhaul. However, Weisburd *et al.* (2001: 90) found that chronic white-collar offenders did not seem so different from more serious general offenders: 'Deviance in the lives of these offenders is not restricted to criminality, but often appears to be a central part of their childhood development and adult histories. Such offenders are well described by common crime samples.'

Conclusion

The evidence reviewed in this chapter suggests that:

- In studying the causes of crime, it is important to recognise the heterogeneity of criminal careers. The distinction made between AL and LCP offenders seems to be particularly useful.

- Accumulations of social and familial disadvantage do correlate very strongly with criminal activity – particularly more serious offending (such as might be found among LCP offenders).

- There seems to be evidence of continuities between children who have behavioural difficulties very early in life and later delinquency and offending.

The consistent finding of considerable continuity of antisocial behaviour linking childhood, adolescence and adulthood is a powerful finding that has considerable implications for understanding the causes of crime. As Simons *et al.* (1998: 235) put it, 'The more popular criminological theories have failed to come to grips with the fact that the best predictor of chronic offending during adolescence and early adulthood is age of onset.' Difficulties remain in fully teasing out the causes of this continuity. The continuity has led to speculation that it might be some physiological factor (something like ADHD) within the child that is the cause of the difficulties. One major problem that such explanations face is that they do not explain changing crime rates. As discussed in Chapter 1, crime rates grew enormously during the second half of the twentieth century, and any theories based on inherited characteristics would need to explain this. As also discussed in Chapter 1, these facts are troubling for theories that look simply to social disadvantage; they have presented an 'aetiological crisis', in Jock Young's words (Young 1986). There have been many strong ideas about the role that families might play in this continuity. These same decades witnessed considerable changes in the patterns of family life. Divorce rates increased, as did the rates of single parenthood and children born out of marriage. The idea that families are a significant cause of crime is particularly controversial, and this will be the subject of the next chapter.

Despite the strength of longitudinal studies, one of their weaknesses needs to be acknowledged. It is a labour intensive and therefore expensive methodology. Relatively small populations are subsequently studied. Some important categories of serious offender have thus not necessarily been captured in the samples. One obvious group that tends not to be in such longitudinal samples are those who kill others. Retrospective studies of juvenile killers tend to confirm the picture of continuity, however. Dolan and Smith (2001: 327) conclude their retrospective study of juvenile homicide offenders by describing them as coming from 'disturbed and chaotic family backgrounds with high rates of paternal psychopathology'. The group would fit well in descriptions of the LCP offenders. Brame *et al.* (2001) looked specifically at violence in adolescence and before adolescence and found that it was children who had been physically aggressive before adolescence that went on to become the more seriously aggressive teenagers. Those who showed low levels of physical aggression before their teens were very unlikely to become highly aggressive teenagers. Loeber and Hay (1997) reviewed literature in relation to evidence about the development of violence and also concluded that highly aggressive teenagers were also those who had manifest problems earlier in childhood. Of course, there may be other offenders who did not fit such a pattern, and one group of these may be those who do not come from backgrounds that would suggest that offending is likely, nor do they have criminal records, but they do commit an offence of violence – perhaps in a state of 'rage'. Such individuals will be returned to later in the book.

The longitudinal studies have been very largely concerned with boys. The Dunedin study has included girls, but found that levels of offending are low among girls. Hipwell *et al.* (2002) report on the

Pittsburgh longitudinal study in relation to girls, and the findings suggest a similar association, in that girls who were very disruptive as young children tended to come from the most deprived backgrounds. The issue of the relationship between gender and crime is explored in Chapter 6.

Note

1 This study was carried out when fewer children were born outside marriage – illegitimacy would certainly have carried greater stigma then.

Chapter 4

Familial and parental influences

Introduction

Two consistent findings have emerged from longitudinal studies, such as those reviewed in the previous chapter. Firstly, there is the simple fact that crime appears to run in families (Farrington 2002). Secondly, there is the continuity in antisocial behaviour between childhood and adulthood witnessed in the more seriously antisocial individuals.

Strong evidence from across the world seems to implicate family background in criminality (Kolvin *et al*. 1988 – Newcastle, UK; Kjelsberg 1999 – Norway; Livaditis *et al*. 2000 – Greece; Sauvola *et al*. 2002 – Finland; Christoffersen *et al*. 2003 – Danish longitudinal study; Fergusson *et al*. 2004 – New Zealand longitudinal study). The other notable finding was that the more serious offenders had often been exhibiting antisocial behaviour in childhood. Analysing data from the London study (as discussed in some detail in the previous chapter), Farrington (2002) comments that children who were already causing notable problems in primary school were those that there getting into more serious trouble by the time they were in their teens, and were the same people who had serious criminal records later. The appearance of such behavioural features in young children has reinforced the impression that there is something about the family background that shapes the development of the child into the adult. In addition, evidence points to the significance of detrimental family experiences in the background of those who might be deemed to suffer from personality disorders. Work reviewed in Chapter 2 emphasised the prevalence in the prison system of people (Fazel and Danesh

2002) whose behaviour and characteristics seem to be consistent with the criteria for personality disorder (antisocial personality disorder in particular).

Despite the assertive conclusions of many such as Lykken (2000: 559), who argues that the increase in crime in the USA is caused by 'normal children whose failure of socialization was due to their being domiciled with an immature, overburdened, unsocialized, or otherwise incompetent parent or parents', other explanations might also explain the correlations between family factors and delinquency. This chapter will provide an analysis of the competing ways of understanding familial influences on crime. The rival explanations for the apparent relationship between family and crime can roughly be divided between the 'sociological' and the 'psychological'. The 'psychological' explanation is that families are responsible for shaping the mind and personality of the individual. According to these theories, a delinquent is the product of poor parenting or some otherwise unfavourable aspect of the family environment. There are also various sociological explanations. The 'strong' sociological explanation of the relationship between family and crime emphasises social deprivation. This theory suggests that the relationship between family background and crime is more apparent than real. The true causes of crime are the poverty and social disadvantage (Rich Harris 2000) within which the family happens to live. There is good evidence to suggest that this view is probably too simplistic (e.g. Wilson 1980; Fergusson *et al.* 2004), in that there are many people who grow up in poor social conditions and do not become antisocial. It would seem there is evidence that the family does have a role, at the very least as a factor that interacts with other variables (O'Connor 2002). This chapter will therefore review evidence in relation to three aspects of family characteristics.

Family structure

Early criminological work highlighted the over-representation of children of single parents among those with criminal records, thus inviting speculation about the significance of absent fathers (e.g. Neubauer 1960). This finding has been repeated over the past decades in different contexts. Sauvola *et al.* (2002), for example, found that single parenthood was significantly associated with increased risk of violent offending among males in Finland.

Parenting styles and early experience

There now seems to be significant evidence that different styles of parenting and particular disciplinary strategies are, at least, *associated* with different outcomes in terms of delinquency. Gottfredson and Hirschi (1990) argued that the crucial variable in determining offending rates is low self-control and that 'the major "cause" of low self-control ... appears to be ineffective child-rearing' (1990: 97). Child rearing has been examined in terms of discipline strategies, but there has also been more recent interest in the quality of the early relationship, particularly the quality of the emotional engagement between parent and child.

Genetics/child effects

There has also been interest in 'child effects'. That is, perhaps it is difficult children who make parenting difficult, and that explains the association between 'poor parenting' and deviant behaviour. While there has been interest in the presence of physiologically based disorders such as hyperactivity and ADHD, as discussed in the previous chapter, there is still only a limited literature on the impact that such difficulties might have on parents.

Family structure and delinquency

The term 'family structure' is used to refer to the individuals that make up a household – usually the interest is in the distinction between families with one or two parents. A great deal of controversy surrounds the relationship between crime and family structure. In particular, it has often been claimed that children brought up in single-parent homes or who have been affected by divorce and separation might be more likely to grow up to commit crime. Western societies have been witnessing some apparently important shifts in family life. Divorce has become very much more common in the past few decades. The number of children being born outside marriage, and the number of single-parent households have been increasing greatly during the post-war period (Silva and Smart 1999). Roughly speaking, this is the period that has witnessed an increasing crime rate. Many have therefore pointed the finger at these changes in family life for being a significant cause of delinquency (e.g. Lykken 2000).

Data from the early and middle part of the twentieth century seemed to show quite clearly that people who had grown up in single-parent households were over-represented in offender and prison populations. Slawson (1923) found higher rates of single-parent families in the backgrounds of New York City boys in a state reformatory. Burt (1925) found high rates among delinquent youth in London, and in a later study, Wadsworth *et al.* (1985) found that in the UK a higher proportion of 5-year-olds with one parent appeared to be 'antisocial'. The fact that the majority of these single-parent households were missing the fathers was of interest to psychoanalytically inclined theorists. Freud had suggested that the father's influence on a boy's moral development was particularly important (Freud 1925; see Minsky 1998). Psychoanalytic ideas about the significance of fathers, and some of the difficulties of these views, are discussed in Chapter 6.

The conclusions concerning the significance of the absence of fathers have since then been disputed (Juby and Farrington 2001). While the correlation between single parenthood and delinquency appears to be real, it may be that the problem that leads to the delinquency is poverty rather than the absence of one parent. Single-parent households are more likely to be poor, and it is, perhaps, the economic deprivation that leads to the difficulties.

A useful analysis of data from another longitudinal study was carried out by Joan McCord (1979). This important longitudinal study was carried out in Massachusetts, and Minnesota in the USA. Detailed information was collected on a group of 253 boys aged of 5–13 who were selected to take part in a delinquency prevention programme between 1939 and 1945. Some years later, it was realised that this information would provide a good basis for a longitudinal study, and the boys were followed up into adulthood, with particular attention being paid to criminal behaviour (McCord 1979).

Using the Massachusetts study to understand the influence of family structure

McCord (1990) looked for evidence of the influence of household structure. McCord reports on the use of data from 14 variables that concerned family structure to create three categories of household (Table 4.1).

A great deal of information had been collected on the families, including data on such things as family conflict, the relationship between parents, the disciplining style of the parents, the aggressiveness of the parents, and the demands on and expectation of children. By statistical analysis these variables were condensed to

Table 4.1 Categories of household

	$n = 231$
Intact: *still living with both parents at his 17th birthday*	130
Mother alone: *boy's father absent from the home for minimum of 6 months prior to the boy's 17th birthday*	60
Broken: *mother was absent or stepfather was present*	42
	(29 lacked father, 30 lacked mother, and 17 lacked both)

three factors: *mother's competence, father's interaction* and *family control*. Each of these three was constructed in the following way:

1 **mother's competence**, a category made up of the following factors:
   - mother's consistency
   - mother's self-confidence
   - mother's affection
   - mother's role: is the mother in charge or the child?

2 **father's interaction**, a category made up of the following factors:
   - mother's esteem for father
   - father's esteem for mother
   - parental conflict
   - father's affection for son
   - father's aggressiveness.

3 **family control**
   - mother's restrictiveness
   - supervision
   - demands.

The impact of these groupings of family characteristic on delinquency was compared with the impact of the categories of household structure. Table 4.2 shows some of the results of this comparison, demonstrating how the rates of various delinquent outcomes differed among the different combinations of household structure and 'parental competence'. It shows, for example, that 60 per cent of boys who grew up in a 'broken home', in which the mother was rated as being of 'low competence', received a conviction before the age of 18 (categorised as 'juvenile delinquent').

Table 4.2 clearly shows that the measure 'mother's competence' is a far more significant variable than the family structure variables. For example, 'broken homes' produced delinquents in only 18 per cent of cases when 'mother's competence' was high, but in 60 per cent of cases when 'mother's competence' was low. No significant differences in the rates of delinquency were produced by 'intact' or 'mother-alone' households, so long as 'mother's competence' was rated as high.

Table 4.2 Showing the percentage outcome in various family characteristics groups.

Outcome	Juvenile delinquent	Juvenile deviant	Criminal	Alcoholic	Occupational achievement
Mother's competence: *low*					
Broken (*n=20*)	60**	70**	50*	40	26
Intact (*n=59*)	34*	44**	39*	31	26
Mother alone (*n=30*)	53**	60*	57**	37	21
Mother's competence: *high*					
Broken (*n=22*)	18	27	18	23	43
Intact (*n=71*)	15	21	23	25	41
Mother alone (*n=30*)	20	30	23	37	40

Significant differences related to family structure, controlled for child-rearing variable, chi-square, df=2, $P<0.05$.
*Significant differences related to child rearing, controlled for type of family structure, chi-square, df=1, $P<0.05$.
**chi square, df=1, $P<0.01$.
***chi square df=1, $P<0.001$.
****chi square df=1, $P<.0001$.
Outcome definitions used in the table:
juvenile delinquency: conviction any time before 18 (*n=50* serious offences, *n=19* minor)
juvenile deviance: not convicted for crime but had delinquent peer groups or heavy smoker (*n=19*).
Criminal: men who had at least one conviction for more serious street crimes (*n=48*)
Alcoholic: as assessed by interview as having a problem with alcohol (*n=71*)
Occupational achievement: (*n=75*, achieved white-collar status).
Unsurprisingly, they found that all these negative factors were predictive of later offending.

Table 4.3 gives more detail about how family factors interact with the family structure variables. Family-type combinations toward the top of the table had the most favourable outcomes in terms of delinquency.

The worst consequences, in terms of criminal outcomes, were for boys who came from mother-alone households in which the mother was rated as having 'low competence'. On the other hand, the lowest rates of criminal outcome were associated with 'broken home' with a mother judged to be 'highly competent'. The next most favourable outcomes were the intact homes with good father interaction. The two permutations with the highest rates of delinquency were those with mothers judged as demonstrating low rates of competence in broken or mother-alone households.

Table 4.4 completes the picture of the interactions by examining the interaction of 'mother's competence' with 'father's interaction'.

If we assume that the measure 'father interaction' is some indication of the father's competence, then the greater the number of 'competent' parents children had, the less likely they were to be

Table 4.3 The impact of family structure and family discipline/interaction on rates of criminal outcome

Percentage with criminal outcome	n	Family structure	Family discipline/interaction
18	22	Broken home	High mother's competence
21	90	Intact home	Good father interaction
21	78	Intact home	Strong family control
23	71	Intact home	High mother competence
23	30	Mother alone	High mother competence
25	16	Broken	Good father interaction
26	19	Broken	Strong family control
32	28	Mother alone	Strong family control
35	17	Mother alone	Good father interaction
38	26	Broken	Bad father interaction
39	59	Intact	Low mother competence
39	23	Broken	Weak family control
42	43	Mother alone	Bad father interaction
44	52	Intact	Weak family control
47	32	Mother alone	Weak family control
50	40	Intact	Bad father interaction
50	20	Broken	Low mother competence
57	30	Mother alone	Low mother competence

Table 4.4 The interaction of mother's competence and father's interaction in the criminal outcome of son

% Criminal outcome	Mother competence	Father interaction
16	High	Good
33	High	Bad
37	Low	Good
52	Low	Bad

delinquent. Having two competent parents provided slightly more protection than one competent parent, but if children did not have at least one competent parent, they were very significantly more vulnerable to delinquency and criminality.

The analysis of these longitudinal data seems to throw some light on consistent findings on family structure: single-parent households are more likely to be associated with delinquency since they are less likely than two-parent households to contain one 'competent' parent. Yet, of course, there are very many single-parent families that are not associated with delinquency. There is nothing necessarily problematic about single-parent households, so long as that parent is 'competent'. These findings do suggest an explanation for the association between single parenthood and delinquency, as children with only one parent do have less chance of that parent being 'competent'.

These findings on the significance of competency might explain the correlations between teenage parenthood and delinquency that have been reported for some years (e.g. Conseur *et al.* 1997). It would seem that these associations can be explained by other mediating family factors rather than simply being the result of having a youthful parent. As Fergusson and Woodward (1999: 488) put it, 'Poorer outcomes of children born to teenage mothers may not reflect the youth of the mother, but rather arise from a selective process in which those women least equipped for child-rearing tend to give birth at a younger age.' Using longitudinal data from New Zealand, Fergusson and Woodward (1999) show that teenage parents are significantly more likely to be associated with a whole host of adverse factors such as having few qualifications, having records of offending, being involved in drug use, having mental health problems, and having poor relationships with their own parents, while their own mothers are less likely to have qualifications.

Since the data clearly point us away from seeing structural variables such as single parenthood or teenage parenthood as *the* causal factors themselves, greater attention can be paid to exploring the characteristics of parents or of parenting that are associated with differential outcomes.

Parenting styles and early family experience

It seems clear from the preceding consideration of the impact of family structure on delinquency that it is not the structure of the family itself that influences delinquency, but it may well be the behaviour of the parents in the household that is significant. In the Massachusetts study, families where the mother was rated as 'competent' and the father interacted well were those least likely to be associated with delinquency. Indeed, it is now well established that a range of parenting styles are more *associated* with delinquency than others (Farrington 2002). A number of questions can still be asked, however; is it the parenting behaviour itself that leads to delinquency, or is the parenting simply symptomatic of some other external difficulty that the family is facing (such as poverty, unemployment or housing difficulties) and that might lead to delinquent behaviour? The following sections will review the evidence that parenting itself can have an impact. First, there are studies of the long-term effects of abuse and neglect, which still leave some questions as to the mechanism through which abuse and neglect might operate. The subsequent sections will examine theories and evidence of the importance of supervision, of punishment and discipline styles, and of the significance of the emotional relationship between parents and children.

Abuse and neglect

Widom's (1989) prospective (longitudinal) study of the impact of childhood abuse and neglect is often cited as providing evidence of the significance of the long-term impact of abuse on children. The study begins with a review of the literature, in which Widom points out that, although it has been assumed that in families where children are exposed to violence, the maxim 'violence begets violence' is appropriate (Widom 1989: 160), there was little good empirical evidence to back those claims at that stage. Widom describes a study that recorded all cases of the neglect, or sexual or physical abuse of children under the age of 11 that were recognised by the courts in an urban area of the Midwest of the USA between 1967 and 1971. The court files were used to collect information on the family backgrounds of the victims, and juvenile court records and adult court records were used to determine the known offending histories of the same abused/neglected group alongside a matched control group. The abused/neglected group comprised 908 victims and the control group 667. The data reported by Widom suggested that the experience of abuse and neglect was associated with higher rates of violent offending. Table 4.5 compares the frequency of arrest for violent offences among people who had been exposed to various experiences of abuse and neglect as children with a control group.

Table 4.5 suggests that the experience of physical abuse on its own seems to make the victim about twice as likely to have a violent criminal outcome as the control group. The experience of neglect also seems to predispose to violent conviction. Sexual abuse and combinations of physical abuse and neglect seemed not to be associated with later violent convictions, however. It is possible that Widom's reliance on official records of crime is a weakness here. More recent work by Swanston *et al.* (2003) that did not rely on official convictions suggests that the experience of sexual abuse is an independent risk factor for delinquency. A review by Cerezo (1997) found that children subject to abuse or maltreatment are particularly likely to evidence higher levels of deviant, and lower levels of pro-social, behaviour.

As Raine (1993: 248–9) notes, although Widom's study is important, as it has been so influential and widely cited, it certainly cannot be regarded as conclusive. In many ways, it raises more questions than it answers. It is not clear why the combination of physical abuse and neglect (Table 4.5) should not be associated with more violence than the control group. Some hint of explanation for these findings comes from closer analysis. Ethnicity is one factor that might suggest

Table 4.5 The experience of childhood abuse and subsequent arrest for violent offence

Abuse group	n	Arrest for violent offence (%)
Physical only	76	15.8
Neglect	609	12.5
Physical and neglect	70	7.1
Sexual and other abuse	28	7.1
Sexual only	125	5.6
Control group	667	7.9

important social interactions. Those abused and neglected who were classed as 'white' were not significantly more likely to have violent outcomes, whereas those abused and neglected classified as 'black' were significantly more likely to have a conviction for violence. Gender is also perhaps a powerful variable. Females who were abused and neglected were also not significantly more likely have convictions for violence than the controls. As Raine observes, these particular findings might well be explained by the lower rates of violence generally among the 'white' and female groups. This certainly draws attention to the interaction of family factors with other variables. Gender itself is clearly an extremely important variable in crime (discussed fully in Chapter 6); the influence of ethnicity perhaps signals the influence of wider social variables (discrimination, poverty and social support, among other factors). Lang *et al.* (2002) found that data from a Swedish longitudinal study suggested that although poor adult adjustment, including the presence of 'psychopathy', was associated with the experience of violence as a child, this effect was 'mediated by psychosocial components' (2002: 98).

Nevertheless, findings that poor parenting practices are associated with children with poorer adjustment and greater propensity to delinquency have been repeated many times (Haapasalo and Pokela 1998; O'Connor 2002). The difficulty remains that, despite the statistical association, there is still a great deal of conceptual confusion about what really matters; as O'Connor (2002: 567) puts it, 'We still lack a *grand unifying theory* of parenting and its effects.' In order to explore the influence of parenting itself, a number of particular parenting variables will now be considered under the following three headings: supervision; punishment and discipline style; and relationship, emotion and communication.

Supervision

It has consistently been found that children who are not closely supervised are more likely to indulge in delinquent behaviour than those who are supervised (McCord 1979; Wilson 1980; Sampson and Laub 1993; and Chapter 3 of this book). Findings on supervision might be explained in two ways. On a simple behavioural level, it is likely that parents who do not know what their children are doing, will be unable to intervene and stop them behaving badly. Alternatively, it may be that low levels of supervision are themselves symptomatic of relatively uninvolved, unaffectionate relationships. There are a number of theories, as will be discussed, that suggest that a lack of emotional involvement may have developmental significance.

Farrington and Hawkins (1991) use data from the London study to argue that the involvement of fathers in leisure activities with their sons appeared to be a highly significant protective factor against delinquency. Not only did the involvement of fathers in shared leisure activities before the age of 10 predict significantly lower levels of early-onset delinquency at age 10, but, perhaps more startlingly, it also predicted lower levels of persistent delinquency at ages 21–32. Raine (1993: 261) notes the power of this factor and wonders whether the absence of shared leisure activities is symptomatic of a number of important family characteristics, including 'negative affect, family conflict, lack of support, time spent with delinquent peers, parental absence and criminality, neglect and lack of early attachment'. In other words, parents and children's ability to take part in shared activities, is a sign that the relationships between them are good, and the time spent in shared activities means that levels of supervision and communication are likely to be high and time spent with delinquent peers correspondingly reduced. Robertson (1999) also argues that shared leisure activities between parents and adolescent boys worked to reduce involvement in delinquency. Another consistent finding from longitudinal studies was that families with larger numbers of children tended to be more at risk of delinquency (West 1982). While different interpretations might be made (such as poverty), it is certainly plausible that the difficulty of supervising the individual children might well be the key issue.

Punishment and discipline style

Harsh parenting and physical punishment were noted to be associated with delinquency in a number of early studies (Glueck and Glueck 1968; Farrington 2002). Since then, the emphasis of a number of studies has shifted attention to the 'inconsistency' of discipline practices. The observation has been made that it was not necessarily the presence of physical punishment itself that is the significant factor but that frequent physical punishment by parents is associated with low levels of involvement in their children's activities, alongside a harsh and erratic approach to punishment. This has led to interest in work on discipline style. An influential distinction was suggested by Baumrind (1971), who characterised three prominent styles of parenting: *authoritative*; *authoritarian* and *permissive*. The distinction between authoritative and authoritarian parenting has made regular appearances in the criminological literature. Authoritative parenting involves a warm, affectionate relationship, in which boundaries are consistently and firmly held, and emphasis is given to the encouragement and reward of pro-social behaviour (rather than simply punishment of undesirable behaviour). Authoritarian parenting, on the other hand, is associated with cold, distant relationships, lower levels of involvement and subsequently erratic (yet often harsh) punishment. The child is told off for misbehaving but with no explanation or rationale. Permissive parenting, as the label suggests, means that few boundaries are set for children. Better outcomes have consistently been found for children who are subject to authoritative parenting (Baumrind 1971, 1978; Kochanska 1990). The better outcomes might be the result of the clear boundaries, or of the closer and warmer relationships that are implied by the definition of authoritative parenting. A strong tradition of psychological research has assumed that it is the quality of the relationship between the parents that is of most significance in determining children's developmental trajectories. This area will be reviewed next as we look at the significance of the emotional relationships within families and how they might facilitate the internalisation of control.

Relationship, emotion and communication: the internalisation of control
A number of very different theories have assumed that the internalisation of control, or self-discipline, is an essential ingredient in the development of civilised behaviour. The notion that children must learn to internalise control is one that has even achieved the status of a theory of crime, Gottfredson and Hirschi (1990) arguing that individuals are naturally propelled toward offences unless they develop the ability to control themselves. They argued that it was the family that nurtured this capacity of self-control. A range of psychological theories have proposed mechanisms for this internalisation. Freud argued that the developing child (the boy in particular) internalised the sense of anxiety at the threat of punishment from father figures for the transgression of social rules ('castration anxiety' is discussed in Chapter 6). From a learning theory perspective, Hans Eysenck argued that repeated experience of punishment following transgressive acts leads to an internalisation of that aversive feeling (Eysenck 1987).

Efforts to pin down the mechanism of this internalisation have more recently focused on the development of the 'moral emotions' of *shame, guilt* and *empathy* (Eisenberg 2000). Particular attention may be paid to guilt and shame, as these feelings are elicited in people when they have carried out acts that may meet with disapproval. There is still notable debate between those that point to shame as being the more important emotion in controlling antisocial behaviour (such as Braithwaite 1989) and those that argue that guilt is the most significant emotion (e.g. Fabricius 2004). A number of theoretical attempts have been made to distinguish shame from guilt (reviewed by Pattison 2000; Harris 2003). One long-running distinction (e.g. Benedict 1946) is that guilt is the feeling experienced when rules that have been internalised are violated, while shame is the feeling induced by disapproval (or imagined disapproval) by others. The observation that people experience shame in the absence of an audience has meant that this distinction has been hard to sustain. A more enduring theory is that guilt is associated with negative feelings about particular acts that we have carried out, while shame emerges from a negative evaluation of the 'self' (Piers and Singer 1954). This is certainly helpful, but the difficulty with this distinction is that it could be argued to be one of degree only. That is, if you commit an act that you feel bad enough about, you may well feel negatively about yourself and therefore 'ashamed' (Olthof *et al.* 2000).

Harris (2001, 2003) reports a study of shame and guilt reactions to court cases involving drink-driving offences in Australia that is helpful in articulating a distinction between shame and guilt. The offenders were interviewed, and their own reports of experiences of various emotions were subjected to factor analysis. Overall, the investigators found little support for a simple distinction between shame and guilt. They found that those who felt bad about what they had done and hurting others (guilt) also experienced shame and anger directed at themselves, and they thus seemed to experience 'shame-guilt'.

Harris argues that two other important, shame-related emotions emerged from the data – 'unresolved shame' and 'embarrassment-exposure'. 'Unresolved shame' was characterised as being 'bothered by thoughts that one was unfairly judged, and an inability to decide whether what one had done was wrong' (2003: 464). A third factor was 'embarrassment-exposure', in which feelings of embarrassment and humiliation were dominant. Harris found important distinctions in the interactions of the various emotions. He found that 'shame-guilt' seemed to have quite different effects from both 'unresolved shame' and 'embarrassment-exposure'. The existence of shame-guilt seemed to be associated with feelings of empathy and lower feelings of anger/hostility. In other words, people felt sorry for the harm they had done and had thoughts about how to make things better. In contrast, feelings of 'unresolved shame' and 'embarrassment-exposure', when not linked with 'shame-guilt', were not associated with feelings of empathy and reparation but were instead correlated with greater feelings of anger and hostility. Harris suggests that this is similar to the 'bypassed shame' described by Helen Lewis (1987), for example, where shame seems to be clearly present and affecting people's behaviour, but they are not able to talk about and reflect on it. This suggests there may be something important about our ability to process and reflect on feelings of shame. Perhaps those who cannot process shame – that is, they experience the feeling but are unable to reflect on it and make sense of it, are likely instead simply to try to discharge the feeling. This is certainly consistent with work that will be reviewed in Chapter 7 that suggests that the experience of shame, far from working to inhibit antisocial behaviour, can be a powerful trigger to violent action. Guilt, it might be argued, is the result of reflection and processing, as Fabricius (2004: 314) suggests: 'Indispensable parts of the guilt mechanism are perception of one's contribution to the event, and history of the relationship. ... Acknowledgment of guilt is the result of such reflection.'

Tangney *et al.* (1996) utilised a questionnaire methodology to study the relationship of guilt and shame proneness to anger responses of people in a range of age groups. They found that shame-prone individuals tend to react to conflict with more destructive aggressive responses – involving either active aggression or withdrawal. Both responses were unlikely to have constructive outcomes. The guilt prone were more likely to react proactively to anger and to behave constructively. Tangney *et al.* (1996: 806) noted a difference in the kinds of situations that caused anger in the two groups: the guilt prone were more likely to be angered by 'reality based violations and infractions committed by others' while the shame prone were more likely to experience 'shame based anger as a desperate attempt to rescue a devalued self mired in shame'. In other words, those prone to shame were vulnerable to threats to their identities, which would elicit angry responses. These threats might not be based in 'reality', however. As we will see in the later chapters that examine violence, shame does appear to be a significant trigger to violence. On this evidence, guilt seems to result in the more 'moral' behaviour, but the experience of shame appears to be a fundamental ingredient as a powerful signal of social disapproval. Therefore, perhaps, the key issue is how an individual develops the capacity to experience and process feelings of shame, as a signal of disapproval, into feelings of guilt (when appropriate). There is increasing evidence from observational study of infants and study of brain development that infants in the first months of life are capable of emotional interactions with their caregivers and that these interactions are crucial to psychological development (Stern 1985; Trevarthen 2001). There is evidence that interactions involving shame are detectable in the early months of life. Schore (1994: 240) argues that the 'socialization of shame is an essential task of socioemotional development, since this affect uniquely promotes sociability by acting as a restraint on self-centredness and egotism.'

The important question to be answered here is, are there circumstances within families that can lead to different capacities to process emotion? Schore (1998) uses observational and neurological studies of child development to argue that the ability to process shame is itself a crucial developmental task. Perhaps the failure to develop this ability to process the emotion of shame can lead to people being less able to experience guilt (an experience that can lead to more positive social behaviour). Schore (1994, 1998) argues that feelings of shame enter a child's life around the beginning of the second year. Until then, the vast majority of social interaction between parents and child will have been usually very positive – smiling, laughing, tickling – all leading to increasingly positive affect. After the beginning of the second year, as the child becomes more mobile and capable of a range of autonomous behaviour, the parents will begin necessarily to disapprove of some behaviour (as the child puts itself in potentially dangerous situations or breaks things, for example). Schore uses refined observation of parent–child interactions and describes in detail how the child typically responds as it begins to receive negative feedback for its behaviour from parents. This 'triggers a sudden shock induced deflation of positive affect, and the infant is thus propelled into a state which he or she cannot yet autoregulate. Shame represents this rapid state transition from a pre-existing positive state to a negative state' (Schore 1998: 65). Schore argues that it is important that a parent help the child cope with these highly unpleasant feelings:

> The child's facial display, postural collapse and gaze aversion act as non-verbal signals of his or her internal distress state. If the caregiver is sensitive, responsive, and emotionally approachable, especially if she re-initiates and re-enters into mutual gaze visual affect regulating transaction … shame is metabolized and regulated, and the attachment bond is re-established.

Schore suggests that is through relationship with others that the child learns to tolerate and process the feeling of shame. If the child is not helped to develop this ability to metabolise and cope with feelings of shame, it may, Schore argues, be prone to shame-rage cycles. Lyons-Ruth (1996: 70) presents evidence that 'maternal hostile-intrusive behaviours predicting aggressive behaviour disorders are observable as early as the sixth month of infancy'. While Lyons-Ruth does not write directly about shame, she does give examples of the lack of maternal responsiveness and affective communications particularly associated with disorganised attachment styles (themselves associated with early aggressive behaviour). These include confusing cues (for example, the carer extends arms towards the infant while backing away) or not responding appropriately to clear infant cues (for example, the carer laughs while the infant is distressed). The latter seems to be particularly evocative of a potentially shame-inducing experience.

Studies of slightly older children point directly to the effect of parenting styles on shame responses. Mills (2003) found that girls with both parents who were authoritarian in their parenting style at the age of 3, were more likely to show discernible shame responses at age 5 (and internalising behaviour and responses). When at least one of the parents was authoritative, used praise, and expressed positive feelings toward the children, shame responses were less discernible. Spinard et al. (1999) carried out a laboratory study of children (around 6 years of age) in potentially stressful situations (being asked to complete a difficult puzzle) with their parents. They found, as they predicted, that the parents who were more supportive and warm with their children in the potentially stressful situation had children who were more focused on others' needs and emotions, and were less likely to cheat. Kochanska et al. (2005) report studies of the significance of mutual responsiveness orientation (that is, the combination of mutual responsiveness and positive emotional involvement between parents and children) in the development of empathy and conscience. They report positive long-term effects – children with relatively mutually responsive relationships with their mothers were more likely to show pro-social behaviour.

Such findings on the significance of an ability to process emotions are consistent with theories of 'mental representation'. As described in Chapter 3 on mental disorder, Fonagy et al. (2003) have developed a theory of personality disorder that implies that good emotional relationships between parents and children are essential if children are to develop the capacity to think about their own emotional worlds. If the caregiver is emotionally attuned with the young child and can reflect back their emotional state to them, they will be able to build a symbolic representation of themselves and their own emotional worlds. Fonagy *et al.* suggest that such an internalised representation is essential for people to be able to think about their feelings rather than simply acting on them.

Laible and Thompson (2000) found that 4-year-olds who were observed to have conversations with their mothers that referred to feelings and moral evaluations were more likely to express guilt after wrongdoing. Mother–child relationships that appeared to be more secure were more likely to have these conversations about emotional matters. As they concede themselves, their data are cross-sectional and so do not necessarily tease out the causal relationships. Their findings are, however, certainly consistent with the theory that parents who engage with their children about emotional matters are helping them to process and make sense of emotions. An important emotion seems to be that of shame, an affect that signals disapproval. In this, it is very powerful feeling; what seems to be crucial is the ability to process and reflect on feelings of shame.

To summarise the evidence about the influence of parents, there is compelling evidence that there are strong associations between more involved parenting practices, including emotionally closer relationships, authoritative discipline strategies and discussion of emotional matters, and better outcomes in terms of delinquency. There is also a developing literature that suggests that the ability to regulate and process emotions, particularly the 'moral emotions' of shame and guilt, is an important developmental achievement on which parents can have considerable impact. The difficultly remains that although the associations are strong, and suggest that parental behaviour can be a significant cause of children's behaviour difficulties, the case is not yet proven. As the next section will explore, it may be that the associations we are witnessing are, at least in part, a result of the children themselves having difficulties that make them difficult to parent.

Child effects

This section will examine the possibility that a number of the difficulties that seem to be apparent in some families (and that seem to be associated with delinquency and criminality) might actually be the result of the family having to cope with a child whose behaviour can be challenging and disruptive. For a long time, when poor parenting was observed within the same family in which children's behavioural problems were apparent, it was assumed that the parents were causing the child's behaviour. In other words, the effects were viewed as being all in one direction. On the face of it, this is an unwarranted assumption – it might be that it is the difficult children that cause the bad parenting. There have been a number of studies since the mid-1990s that have attempted to resolve this (Rutter *et al.* 1998; Stern and Smith 1999).

Kandel and Wu (1995) carried out a longitudinal study that involved taking measures of parent's and children's behaviour at ages 3–11 (time (T)1) and then following up 6 years later (T2). They looked for relationships between parenting at T1 and child behaviour at T2, and between child behaviour at T1 and parenting at T2 (carrying out statistical procedures, called cross-lagged correlations). They concluded that the influences were running in two directions. Harsh parenting at T1 seemed to predispose the children to behave more disruptively at T2. But also aggressive children at T1 seemed to make it more likely that their mothers would emotionally withdraw, supervise less well and discipline more harshly. So there seems to be a reciprocal relationship.

Jaffee *et al.* (2004) investigated whether children who are difficult are more likely to elicit physical punishment and maltreatment from their parents (itself associated with delinquent outcomes). They concluded that 'genetic factors played a significant role in explaining why some children were more likely than others to experience normative physical disciplinary practices like spanking' (Jaffee *et al.* 2004: 1054), but they found no such evidence that genetic factors elicited *maltreatment*. In other words, if the child is particularly difficult, it would be more likely to face physical punishment, but this did not extend to maltreatment. The reasons for maltreatment seemed to lie squarely within the family environment.

O'Connor (2002: 563) reviewed findings in this area and concluded that there was good evidence that parenting styles do have an impact on children's development and behaviour, but there is evidence that 'there may be groups of children who may be less susceptible to parental influence or circumstances that inhibit parenting effects'. In relation to findings concerning the significance of traumatic family histories and personality disorder, Graybar and Boutilier (2002) caution researchers and clinicians against ignoring the fact that although there is good evidence that many people with diagnoses of 'personality disorder' do have such histories, there are others that do not. It may be, they suggest, that some individuals are predisposed to such difficulties.

Observational studies of young children and their parents suggest that there are important interactions between parents and their children. Daniel Stern's (1985) observational investigations of young babies and their parents have made this point very well. He observed that although some mothers seem to be initially poorly attuned to their babies' feelings, there is usually a process of accommodation whereby mother and baby adjust and become attuned.

Genetic explanations

The idea that some individuals may simply be genetically predisposed to behave in more deviant or aggressive ways than others has been around for many years (note the discussion on Lombrosian ideas in criminology in Chapter 1). Such speculation has been carried forward in more formal studies of genetic links and criminality. One particular study deserves some consideration, as it is often quoted in reviews of genetic influences on crime.

The Danish adoption study

Studies of family influences are always dogged by the fact that findings such as 'crime runs in families' can be interpreted in two very different ways; as evidence of the importance of either family environment or genetics. Studies of adopted children have been used in a number of contexts to clarify the relative influence of genetic and environmental factors in families. As adopted children share genetic material with their biological parents and then grow up in a different family environment, they offer the potential for observing the comparative effects of family environment and genetics. A major longitudinal study of the lives of adopted children in Denmark offered the chance of witnessing the relative influence of genetics or family environment on offending (Mednick *et al.* 1987). Data were gathered on all non-familial adoptions that took place in Denmark between 1924 and 1947. The fact that this period includes World War II is significant. Due to the social disruption of war, large numbers of adoptions took place in this period in Denmark, and there was a shortage of adoptive families. There was therefore relative leniency in deciding who was allowed to become an adoptive family – so long as they had no criminal conviction in the past 5 years, people were allowed to adopt. Data were obtained on 14,427 adoptees, which included information about the place of birth and who the parents were. The adoptees were then followed up to see who had a criminal record in adult life.

Table 4.6 Comparison of conviction rates for adopted boys with biological parents with criminal records, and those without such records; for those whose adopted parents had criminal records, and those without (from Mednick *et al.* 1987: 75)

	Have biological parents been convicted?	
	Yes	No
Have adopted parents been convicted?		
Yes	24.5% (of 143)	14.7% (of 204)
No	20.0% (of 1226)	13.5% (of 2492)

Table 4.6 shows that the group of adoptees who were most likely to have a criminal record were those whose biological and adoptive parents had criminal records (24.5 per cent of adoptees falling in this category had a criminal record themselves). The group with the next highest likelihood of committing an offence were those whose biological parents, but not adoptive parents, had a criminal record (20.0 per cent of these adoptees had a criminal record). The groups with the lowest rates of conviction were the two groups whose biological parents did not have any criminal convictions. Of those boys whose biological parents did not have a criminal record, those whose adoptive parents had criminal convictions had slightly higher rates of offending than those whose adoptive parents did not have convictions.

While at first look, this study seems to suggest that there is something significant being transmitted biologically, a number of caveats have to be made. It needs to be noted that much fewer adoptees had an adoptive parent with a criminal record than had a biological parent with a criminal record (347 versus 3818). Moreover, and even more significantly, none of the adoptive parents had a conviction within 5 years of the adoption (since they would have been ruled out as adoptive parents). It is reasonable to argue that, almost by definition, none of the adoptive parents were serious chronic offenders. Indeed, the adoptive parents' 'conviction rates are below those of the population averages for their age, sex and time period' (Brennan *et al*. 1996: 116). More starkly, just 0.8 per cent of the adoptive fathers had two or more convictions, while 10.2 per cent of the biological fathers had two or more convictions. As discussed in Chapter 3, there are very sound reasons for believing that there may be important differences in terms of criminality between those who have a single minor conviction and those that have a number of convictions. Those with a single conviction are very likely to be indistinguishable from non-offenders in terms of social and familial upbringing and psychological characteristics (particularly if the offence occurred in the teenage years). In this study, it is reasonable to assume that the direct influence of being brought up by an adoptive criminal parent was not really appearing here, perhaps leading to an exaggeration of the seeming genetic effect. A truer test would be to compare the conviction rates of those with biological parents who were chronic offenders (and then adopted into non-criminal households) with those of boys adopted away from non-criminal parents and then brought up by chronically offending parents. This would be a highly unethical study to carry out, however, since it would involve the deliberate placement of children with known chronic offenders (who, as we also know, are likely to be carrying with them other psychological and social difficulties). This point draws attention to the difficulty of using experimental methods in the real world. It needs to be understood that this study is not a robust comparison of genetic and environmental effects, although it is often presented as this (Eysenck 1987: 66; Feldman 1993: 50; Harrower 1998: 23). Table 4.6 does suggest an interaction between genetic effects and environment, but it cannot be claimed to be truly testing the difference between hereditary and environment.

Further analysis of the data available on the concordance rates for 'criminal conviction' among adopted siblings does suggest some genetic loading (Brennan *et al*. 1996). The concordance rate for convictions for boys who are not related, and who were reared apart, is 8.5 per cent. The conviction concordance rate for half-siblings raised apart is 12.9 per cent. For full siblings, it rises to 20 per cent (Brennan *et al*. 1996). Cloninger and Gottesman (1987) review twin studies and find significantly greater rates of concordance for monozygotic twins than for dizygotic twins for adult criminality (but not for juvenile crime).

So, overall, these figures suggest an element of genetic predisposition. However, even the strongest advocates of genetic explanations would not suggest that there is a 'criminal gene' that leads to criminal behaviour. Therefore, the question arises, if there is some predisposition being inherited by some people, what might that be? Clearly, there may be some connection with disorders such as ADHD or conduct disorder discussed in the previous chapter. While the nature of, and influences on, attention deficit remain to be fully explored, there is already research that points, at the very least, to interactions between biological dispositions such as ADHD and family characteristics (Clarke *et al.* 2002; Peris and Hinshaw 2003).

Poverty and diet

Theoretical links between diet and antisocial behaviour have been made for some time. Diet might provide a mechanism through which family types can directly affect children's behaviour. Schoenthaler and Bier (2000) carried out a randomised, double-blind trial among schoolchildren aged 6–12 in the USA. They found that those given vitamin and mineral supplements were significantly less likely to be disciplined for antisocial behaviour over a 4-month period. Gesch *et al.* (2002) carried out a similarly randomised, controlled trial among young adult prisoners in the UK. The experimental group were given a combination of vitamin, mineral and fatty acid supplements, and this group showed a significant reduction in recorded antisocial behaviour over the study period.

Certainly, one of the very practical tasks of families is to provide food. It is very likely that there are strong links between poverty, family difficulties and poor diet (Bennett *et al.* 1995). It is conceivable that poor diet is one factor through which social factors can operate through families to affect children's behaviour very directly. Healthy food is often less available in more socially deprived areas (Donkin *et al.* 2000).

Conclusion

Findings pointing to the significance of families as a causal factor in criminality have consistently been found throughout the history of criminological investigation. There seems to be good theoretical reasons to believe that parents can indeed have a profound influence on their children's development. The assumption that the influence that families have on the early years of life is in some way involved in the promotion of criminal behaviour has certainly been an explicit influence on government policy in the UK since the 1990s (some of the policy initiatives will be discussed in the concluding chapter).

The evidence that abuse and neglect are clearly related to various poor outcomes for the children involved is now very strong. Questions remain, however, as to the mechanism, and whether parents can have a significant impact on the moral behaviour of their children through more subtle means than overt abuse and neglect. Some of the work reviewed in this chapter has argued that the development of the 'moral emotions' is key to understanding the growth of moral behaviour in children. Some of the possible influences on the development of the 'moral emotions' are perhaps far more subtle and involve communication and interaction between parents and their children. Research in the future may be able to tease out the causal directions. However, as discussed in relation to the adoption studies, there are considerable ethical problems involved in setting up studies that can manipulate factors concerning the way children are brought up.

It also needs to be strongly acknowledged that families do not bring children up in isolation. Ceballo and McLoyd (2002), for example, found that parents who had more social support themselves were better able to use positive parenting techniques but that this effect was reduced in particularly severely deprived neighbourhoods. Dearing (2004) reports complex interactions between parenting styles, ethnicity, and the social characteristics of the community. The importance of wider social influences, perhaps working in interaction with family factors, will be explored further in the next chapter on youth crime. Work on the significance of the development of the moral emotions through adolescence will be examined there, as issues of autonomy and identity become more significant during adolescence.

Chapter 5

Youth crime

Introduction

This chapter explores the relationship between young people and criminal behaviour. There are two issues to be considered. The first is the question of how old people should be before they are held to be responsible for their criminal acts; the second is the broad question of why so much crime seems to be committed by young people. Taking into account all types of crime, there seems little doubt that the greatest volume of crime is committed by young people.

As observed in Chapter 2 'Mental Disorder: Madness, Personality Disorder and Criminal Responsibility', there has been a long history of leniency toward people who commit offences but who are considered to be not fully responsible for their actions. Some defendants are deemed to be somehow mentally disordered (as discussed fully in Chapter 2), and some children have been allowed to escape the force of law, on the assumption that they are too young to bear responsibility for their actions. Therefore, the first issue to be discussed in this chapter is that of the age at which children should be subject to special provision under the law. Just as there are still many arguments concerning the categories of mental disorder and how they might be defined, so there are unresolved debates about the age at which people become fully responsible for their criminal actions. However, it will be argued in this chapter that light can be thrown on this debate by considering the wider issue of why the relationship between youth and crime appears to be so strong. Examination of the question of why so many young people commit the vast majority of offences gives insight into the factors that are relevant to the issue of responsibility. It will be argued that moral understanding and behaviour can be understood in terms of developmental achievements that occur *through* adolescence. This would suggest that countries (such as the UK) that assume that children are criminally responsible before adolescence or become so in early adolescence are probably mistaken. Moreover, such developmental achievements need to be understood as occurring in psychological and social contexts; thus, there is inevitably a certain amount of variation in terms of when various stages of responsibility are reached. Evidence presented in the previous chapter (Chapter 4, 'Familial and Parental Influences' suggested that the quality of parent–child relationships is a significant factor in the development of the moral emotions in children – in particular, the process by which individuals become able to process shame into experiences of guilt that can lead to more 'moral' responses. Evidence will be presented in this chapter that there are also key developmental challenges during adolescence involving the moral emotions. Crucially, these challenges typically involve a renegotiation of familial relationships as the adolescent separates both socially and psychologically from parents and begins to establish a more autonomous identity. It can be argued that the establishment of a relatively autonomous identity is a prerequisite of certain kinds of moral behaviour. Such a view of the importance of autonomous identity to morality can almost be considered to be by definition, in that decisions that are made after the consideration of moral principles might well require people to ignore the immediate pressures and concerns that surround them. It can also be argued, however, that part of the shift toward that more autonomous sense of self occurs only through increasing engagement with relationships with others (notably peer groups) outside the family. The process of adolescent development is thus highly complex, involving processes of separation and individuation alongside the renegotiation of relationships with families and peers. Criminal behaviour can occur in two ways during this stage; a certain amount of deviant behaviour may be regarded as the inevitable result of processes of separation from parental authority and also might occur as individuals become reliant on delinquent groups for a sense of identity and belonging that is separate from their families.

Age and criminal responsibility

A 5-year-old boy, out shopping with his parents, picks up a toy car in a shop and after playing with it for a while, puts it into his pocket and leaves the shop with his parents.

Few people are likely to believe that this ought to be considered a criminal act. It would appear to be common sense that a child so young could not possibly understand enough about shops and money, let alone morality, to realise that he has done anything wrong. Indeed, there is no known legal system that would not share this view. If the child were age 9, then, perhaps, perceptions might change a little. It might be assumed that a 9-year-old does understand that goods in shops have a price and that money is needed to pay for those items. And yet, legally, that child is also highly unlikely to be seen as culpable for his acts. Most current legal systems would not prosecute a 9-year-old for such an offence. The assumption is perhaps that a 9-year-old is unlikely to grasp the full significance of what they have done, or perhaps the consequences. As Table 5.1 shows, however, the age at which children are considered to be legally responsible for their actions varies hugely across different nations.

The age of responsibility in England and Wales was subject to controversial change in the 1990s. In 1933, the Children and Young Persons Act raised the age of criminal responsibility to 10 in England and Wales (it had previously been as low as 7). In addition, the ancient notion (stemming from the fourteenth century) of *doli incapax* was

Table 5.1 International comparison of the age of criminal responsibility (from Urbas 2000)

	Age of criminal responsibility
England and Wales, Australia	10
Canada, Greece, Netherlands	12
France, Israel, New Zealand	13
Austria, Germany, Italy, many eastern European countries	14
Denmark, Finland, Iceland, Norway, Sweden	15
Japan, Portugal, Spain	16
Belgium, Luxembourg	18

accepted. According to the 1933 Act, this meant that it was assumed that children below the age of 14 are 'incapable of committing a crime because they lack the necessary criminal intent'. It was up to the prosecution to rebut this presumption and prove that children have 'mischievous discretion'; they may choose to act despite knowing that their actions are 'seriously wrong' (Walsh 1998: 2). The Crime and Disorder Act 1998 effectively abolished the principle of *doli incapax*, and so the true age of responsibility became 10. The home secretary argued in 1998: 'The presumption that children aged ten to thirteen do not know the difference between serious wrongdoing and simple naughtiness flies in the face of common-sense and is long overdue for reform (cited in Newburn, 2003: 215).

The issue of criminal responsibility and children was brought into sharp relief by the killing of 2-year-old Jamie Bulger in 1993 (Downing Stepney and Jordan 2000; McMahon and Payne 2001). Two 10-year-old boys were tried and convicted for murder at Preston Crown Court. They were tried as though they were adults in a Crown Court, as the principle of *doli incapax* was successfully rebutted by the prosecution. The prosecution argued that the boys knew the difference between right and wrong and were therefore fully culpable for their crimes. They were found guilty of murder and the then home secretary set a minimum sentence of 15 years. The UK government was taken to the European Court of Human Rights on the grounds that the children should not have been tried in an adult court and therefore did not receive a fair trial. The court also argued that the minimum sentence should not have been set by a politician. This allowed the minimum sentence of 15 years to be set aside. Despite great public controversy, the boys never served any part of their sentence in an adult prison. In the USA, with the continuing use of the death penalty, there are particular concerns about the issue of youth and criminal culpability for murder (Steinberg and Scott 2003).

Given that the age of responsibility is subject to such controversy and variation, is it possible to utilise knowledge about the social, emotional and psychological development of children to suggest an age at which children can be considered responsible? Rutter *et al.* (1998) argue that there is now a wealth of evidence that children and adolescents should be treated differently from adults. They point to findings from a range of developmental studies that demonstrate considerable maturation of cognitive and emotional capacities throughout adolescence. Developments occur in cognitive capacities for abstract thought and self-awareness:

> During early adolescence, young people's thinking tends to be become more abstract, multidimensional, self-reflective, and self aware, with a better understanding of relative concepts. They are better able to hold in mind several different dimensions of a topic at the same time and so generate more alternatives in their decisions making ... During adolescence, there is a marked increase in emotional introspection together with a tendency to look back with regret and to look forward with apprehension. That is, not only do young people become increasingly able to consider the long term consequences of their actions, they also tend to consider the long-term consequences more in terms of their own sense of responsibility and with increased awareness of the effects of their actions on other people.
>
> (Rutter *et al.* 1998: 28)

Rutter *et al.* (1998) also suggest that developing capacities to experience and understand guilt and shame might also be significant. The difficulty with many of these concepts is that they do not necessarily lend themselves to easy measurement and the provision of concrete answers. A number of these particular issues will be taken up in the next section, which seeks to explain why so many young people, rather than older adults, seem to commit offences. If we can begin to understand this, perhaps we can also begin to tease out the most significant developmental or social factors that underlie the association between age and crime.

Why do young people commit crime?

There is a strong association in the public's mind between 'youth' and 'crime'. A case can be made that this link has been made for a couple of centuries at least (Shore 2000). Indeed, the facts on the relationship between age and offending seem to be rather robust (e.g. Newburn 1997). As the longitudinal studies analysed in Chapter 3 demonstrate, there do seem to be strong correlations between age and offending. The peak age of occurrence of a first recorded offence is around 12–13 years of age (MORI (2004) suggest that the peak age for first time offending is 11–12). The most common age of offending is around 14–16 years (MORI (2004) suggest that it is as young as 14), offending behaviour slowly decreasing until there is quite a sharp fall from around 23 years of age.

It has been claimed that adolescence emerged as a notable period of life only alongside industrialisation and the extended education of young people (Aries 1962). In former times, children moved straight from childhood into adult roles and employment. However, this well-known quotation from William Shakespeare (*The Winter's Tale* (1611), act iii, scene 3) suggests that the perception of a link between young people and delinquency is not wholly new:

I would there were no age between ten and three and twenty, or that youth would sleep out the rest; for there is nothing in the between but the getting wenches with child, wronging the aged, stealing and fighting.

With no access to official statistics or crime surveys, Shakespeare, writing 400 years ago, appears to pinpoint the peak ages of offending (between 10 and 23) with remarkable accuracy. That Shakespeare was observing what was happening around him is supported by Beier (1978: 210), who uses Bridewell records to argue that 'London by 1600 was experiencing large scale juvenile delinquency. It would be no exaggeration to compare the situation to ghetto areas of Western cities today.' Rawson (1839), using figures that were only just becoming available on crime and population drew attention to a similar relationship between age and crime at the beginning of the nineteenth century.

The longitudinal research reviewed in Chapter 3 suggests that there are good reasons for viewing much youth offending as a particular phenomenon. Moffitt (1993) distinguished between 'life-course-persistent' (LCP) and 'adolescent-limited' (AL) offending, the former being characterised by the appearance of behavioural difficulties early in childhood, and offences occurring before adolescence and continuing through adolescence and well into adulthood. The offences committed are likely to be of a relatively serious nature. The life histories of those in the LCP category tend to be marked by quite serious social and family disadvantages. The AL group are less easily distinguished from the non-offending peers and restrict their offending to their adolescent years. It may be that in assessing the relationship between crime and youth we are really seeking to understand the AL group. Findings from crime surveys and self-report surveys confirm that a considerable volume of crime (albeit mainly minor crime) is committed by young people. MORI (2004) found that the most common offences committed by teenagers in mainstream education are fare dodging (50 per cent), hurting someone without the need of medical treatment (43 per cent), graffiti (35 per cent) and damaging property (34 per cent). While much of the criminological concern is with boys who offend, it should be noted that there is evidence that teenage girls are also likely to be involved in minor delinquency (Phillips 2003), and that the distinction between AL and LCP offenders can be meaningfully applied to girls as well (Moffitt and Caspi 2001).

As will be reviewed, there are a number of theoretical perspectives that effectively predict that all teenagers indulge in some form of delinquency. Indeed, data from a number of sources (the London and the Dunedin longitudinal studies, to mention two that have been explored in some detail in Chapter 3) suggest that complete abstinence is rare. The Dunedin study did identify such a group, and Moffitt *et al.* (1996) refer to the group of adolescents who did not seem to carry out any delinquent acts as 'the abstainers'. West (1982) had noted from the London study that this was in some ways a rather 'deviant' group. Early findings from the Dunedin study suggested that there might indeed be good reason for seeing the group of 'abstainers' as having their own problems. It seemed to be possible that the group were abstaining from crime because they were so socially isolated that they were removed from the influence of peers. At age 18, they were assessed to be 'over controlled, fearful, interpersonally timid, and socially inept' (Moffitt *et al.* 2002: 182). When they were followed up at age 26, a rather different picture emerged, however. They seemed to be relatively successful, educationally and financially. They were not the wealthiest group, but this was largely because they had spent their early adult years gaining qualifications and professional training, rather than earning money. They were generally free of mental health problems and were in stable relationships. While the findings at age 26 do not rule out the possibility that psychological impairments might arise later in life (Raine *et al.* 2005), their adult lives were undoubtedly looking optimistic.

Nevertheless, it does seem that it can be seen as 'normal' for most adolescents to indulge in some delinquent behaviour. A substantial minority become involved in more serious antisocial behaviour only during their adolescence. Moffitt (1993) suggests that 26 per cent of the Dunedin sample could be classified as AL offenders, and they are very different from the LCP offenders. In contrast to the LCP offenders, there is little continuity in their behaviour across time. Even within adolescence, the AL offenders may have periods of time when they do not offend. Their offending is far less likely to generalise to different contexts. They might well, for example indulge in drug taking and shoplifting, but at the same time be quite conforming in school, for example. They are often far removed from the antisocial syndrome that often marks the LCP offenders. Moffitt (1993: 686) asks the following questions:

> Why do youngsters with no history of behaviour problems in childhood suddenly become anti-social in adolescence? Why do they develop antisocial problems rather than other difficulties? Why is delinquency so common among teens? How are they able to spontaneously recover from an anti-social life-style within a few short years?

Moffitt (1993) suggests that the questions can be answered by supposing that young people in modern industrial societies are aware of a maturity gap as they reach their teenage years. They are sexually developed and yet are socially many years from being accepted as adults. One way they have of finding respect (and, to an extent, access to adult pleasures of material goods and sex) is through delinquency. A difficulty with this theory, and one that Moffitt raises herself, is that it over-predicts delinquency. That is, since nearly all adolescents in Western societies experience this maturity gap, surely most of them should follow the same pattern of offending. Moffitt's answer is to point to the self-report surveys that suggest that the overwhelming majority of teenagers do indulge in some antisocial behaviour. An important question, therefore, emerges from Moffitt's work on AL offenders – are they simply identical to the non-offending group, the only difference being that they have been convicted of some minor offending? It seems that the AL group were not distinguishable from the non-offenders as children. However, follow-up further into adulthood is suggesting that things are not quite as simple as that, as the AL group identified in the Dunedin study seem to be carrying on offending more than expected (Moffitt *et al.* 2002).

Follow-up of the Dunedin sample at age 26 years provided opportunity for further insight into the progress of both AL and LCP groups (Moffitt *et al.* 2002). As discussed in Chapter 3, this study certainly reinforces the validity of the definition of the LCP group as a particularly problematic group. The definition of the AL group predicts that by age 26 their offending should have greatly declined, if not ceased. The AL group were doing significantly better than the LCP group (as judged by rates of offending, seriousness of offending, and problems with relationships); they were, however, 'still in trouble'

(Moffitt *et al.* 2002: 199). Moffitt *et al.* (2002) suggest that the reason for the continuation of the offending of the AL group into adulthood is the extended adolescence now being experienced by many adults in Western countries (Valentine 2003). This comes about as crucial markers of adulthood get pushed later and later. Stable employment is often not achieved until the late twenties nor is marriage or the birth of the first child. Clearly, this is one feasible explanation. Another explanation is that although the AL group may not be as deviant as the LCP group, they may represent a group who have encountered developmental problems in adolescence that have longer-term implications. They may not be *that* different from their non-offending counterparts, but there may be some important differences. As the evidence suggests that they were not distinguishable as children, it may be that something happened to them during adolescence that needs to be understood. The rest of this chapter will be concerned with theories that seek to understand why so many people commit crime during their adolescent years.

A number of prominent criminological theories have been concerned with explanations of the phenomenon of youth crime. As outlined briefly in Chapter 1, 'strain and subcultural theory' and 'control theory' have both, at least implicitly, aimed at understanding youth crime. The implications of these theories will briefly be considered here.

Sociological theories

Strain and subcultural theory

As discussed in Chapter 1, Robert Merton (1938), the American criminologist, is credited with popularising 'strain theory'. This was a political analysis that saw the competitive capitalist system as being responsible for the growth of crime. Capitalism, it was argued, encouraged the idea of individual greed, and designated material wealth as a crucial mark of status and success. Cloward and Ohlin (1960) applied strain theory directly to youth crime. Certain groups of young people had inferior access to material goods and opportunities. One way of coping with this apparent lack of success was to develop a subculture where different values predominated.

A major problem for such theories that suggested that the chief motivation for youth crime is access to goods that were unavailable through legitimate means, is the fact that levels of crime seem to have risen in the post-war years – as prosperity has greatly increased.

It did not seem tenable that young people were being motivated to crime simply through poverty. Runciman (1966) sought to answer this criticism by suggesting that perhaps the experience of *relative deprivation* might be important. Runciman proposed that although prosperity was generally increasing, it was being distributed unequally. So, even though people were becoming generally better off than their parents' generation, they may still feel relatively deprived compared to others. Very simply, some young people who have less than others, see what opportunities others have and feel envious and hostile because they feel *relatively* deprived. They do not have the social and educational resources to get access to those commodities and so they rebel and steal. The question still remains as to why it might be young people in particular that are prone to experience and act upon this relative deprivation. Why should their parents not also act on these feelings?

Cohen (1965) is a key name with his book on British youth delinquency, *Delinquent Boys*. He described typical delinquents as working-class boys who rejected the middle-class values they found being presented to them at school. Being involved in crime was in a sense a normal part of growing up. Yet, again, the question of why it should be that young people are prone to such strong peer influences is raised, but left unanswered.

Youth crime and social control
As described in Chapter 1, an important strand in criminological thought in the past few decades has sought to understand the phenomena of crime not through an examination of the underlying *causes* of crime, but by analysing what factors make crime *less* likely. Hirschi's (1969) original thesis on the significance of social control could be argued to be particularly pertinent to understanding youth crime. Adolescents could be seen as a group in Western society who are relatively free of social control. As teenagers grow older, they spend increasing amounts of time free of direct family control and yet have some years to wait before they are more fully controlled by the typical burdens of adulthood: jobs, mortgages/rents and their own family commitments. In this gap between childhood and adulthood, individuals are free to act on their impulses and therefore tend to commit more crime than other age groups. This sociological explanation, which has been favoured by Terri Moffitt (1993), whose

work has emphasised the significance of the AL offenders, does go some way to explaining why large numbers of young people become involved in crime (albeit rather minor acts of criminality). Indeed, it is not incompatible with the psychological theories that will be discussed below.

The psychology of adolescent development

Psychological theories do appear to address, fairly directly, the issue of why young people commit more crime than other age groups. They generally stand in opposition to the sociological arguments by assuming that there is something about young people as individuals that makes them more likely than mature adults to commit offences. Two notable traditions of psychological theory have suggested that this is a crime-prone period due to either emotional or cognitive developmental processes, respectively. Each of these will be considered in turn, but an argument will be made that insight can be more usefully gained by considering the development of the 'moral emotions' in adolescence. This builds on ideas introduced in Chapter 4 concerning the development of the moral emotions during early childhood. Theories of 'moral emotions' usefully blend theories of cognitive and emotional development with factors of social influence such as peer groups. As discussed, there has been speculation about the significance of family context in the early years of life. The interest in families is also a theme that continues as the development of moral emotions in adolescence is explored. There seems to be evidence that at this stage the influence of peer groups and wider forces also need to be considered.

Cognition and moral development

Cognitive theories of moral development have sought to understand the intellectual development of the capacity for moral thought and behaviour (Palmer 2003). Lawrence Kohlberg's elaboration of Piaget's work has been used to link juvenile delinquency to stages of moral development (e.g. Campagna and Harter 1975). Piaget argued that children's intellectual development necessarily passed through a series of orderly stages as they built up a cognitive model of the world. Lawrence Kohlberg took this same analysis and applied it the development of moral thinking, and drew up a model that consisted of three levels of moral development (Table 5.2).

If Kohlberg's scheme is correct, many teenagers may simply be insufficiently morally developed to be able to make mature

Table 5.2   Kohlberg's stages of moral development (from Kohlberg 1963)

Level 1: Preconventional or premoral. At this level, there is no real differentiation between moral and self-serving values.

Stage 1: Punishment and obedience. At this stage of moral reasoning, a decision is made to carry out an act according to the immediate physical consequences. So even quite young children may avoid doing something knowing that they will be told off by their parents if they did carry out the act.

Stage 2: Instrumental relativism. At this stage, actions are judged by how well they achieve instrumental aims – directed by the concrete exchange of favours. So children may do something nice and helpful in order to please their parents, knowing that this might lead to a reward. So behaviour is still entirely instrumental; there is no real notion of doing good, but behaviour is planned somewhat.

Level 2: Conventional. The stage of law and order. Moral value is defined quite narrowly in terms of social conformity.
The age of transition to this stage is thought to be typically 10–13 years.

Stage 3: Interpersonal concordance. At this stage, people are guided by wanting to fit in with others, to be approved of. Very often this will lead to pro-social behaviour, but not if the immediate social peers are behaving antisocially.

Stage 4: Law and order. Here emphasis is given to duty and respect for authority. There has been an internalisation of rules, but they are simply adhered to – there is little understanding of the underlying principles.

Level 3: Post-conventional or principled.
This is the level where true moral thought can be seen to occur.

Stage 5: Social contract. There is an emphasis on judging the balance of individual rights and the consideration of social utility.

Stage 6: Universal ethical principles. This stage represents the most sophisticated understanding of moral issues. Moral judgement is determined by feelings of mutual respect, trust, and justice and equality that are informed by principles that appeal to logical universality. There is an awareness of the consistency and immutability of absolute moral value.

There has been difficulty in substantiating this latter stage: there are strong arguments that it is really culture specific and gender biased.

moral decisions. A number of studies have investigated whether there are detectable differences in moral development between delinquents and non-delinquents. If there were such differences they would be taken as evidence that cognitive development does have implications for moral behaviour. A typical example of such a study is that by Campagna and Harter (1975). They studied 21 boys whom they describe as 'sociopathic' (they claim to use the term 'sociopath' interchangeably with 'psychopath'), residents at a state-run centre (in the USA) who were being treated for a variety of psychological problems. The sociopath group were selected by the presence of antisocial behaviour and the kind of background that would be predictive of delinquency. They matched this group, by IQ scores, with a control group of ordinary schoolchildren. They used Kohlberg's moral reasoning interviews to compare the moral reasoning performance of the two groups. Boys were presented with various scenarios involving different moral dilemmas. They were asked for their solutions to the dilemmas in a series of questions and prompts. The interviews were recorded and the boys' responses were scored according to the kinds of moral reasoning being used. This work is described in some detail in Chapter 6 (in relation to gender differences in moral development). It is sufficient to say at the moment that those who are considered most moral would make decisions according to universal principles of right and wrong rather than by what brings benefit to the individuals involved or indeed what is deemed right by the law.

Campagna and Harter found that the sociopathic group were more likely to use cruder level 1 moral reasoning, a finding that might be used as evidence that the juvenile offenders were cognitively less well morally developed. Even within their study, they noted that although the groups were matched on crude IQ score, the sociopath group did significantly worse on verbal reasoning, and that, of course, might itself explain why they did not do as well in a quite difficult interview situations in which they had to explain their reasoning. There is also the major difficulty that here we have a group of known delinquents being interviewed about moral matters by someone in authority. It is conceivable that they would have wanted to give the conventional, most law-abiding answer rather than the most moral (which might imply breaking the law). Nevertheless, it is plausible that natural delays in cognitive development that occur in adolescence do help us to understand why youth crime is so widespread.

Some of the family factors discussed in previous chapters that have been associated with lower levels of delinquency might also be consistent with the promotion of cognitive development and thus moral reasoning. Discipline practices that involve parents explaining why behaviour is wrong (Speicher 1994) do correlate with higher levels of moral reasoning among adolescents and children. However, families that engage in those discussions also tend to be characterised by higher levels of cohesion, warmth and supervision (Palmer 2005), so it is difficult to conclude that the cognitive factors on their own are the most crucial. The significance of emotional development will be considered next.

Emotional development

A number of psychological theories of development have portrayed the period of adolescence as being a troubled one. The American psychologist G. Stanley Hall, at the beginning of the twentieth century, is often credited with 'discovering' adolescence as a period of great turmoil. He is known as the father of child psychology in the USA, publishing the first comprehensive study of adolescence in 1904. In this, he proposed a theory of development called 'recapitulation'. The idea of recapitulation during development originally emerged from study of how fetuses develop in the womb. Human fetal development is said to mimic the various stages of evolution. It goes through a period of being fish-like and then bird-like before becoming typically mammalian. Stanley Hall argued that the psychological development of the individual mirrors the social evolution of mankind (Stanley Hall 1904). The adolescent period of development was a time of great stress and change. Adolescence marked the period of transition from childhood to adulthood, mirroring a stage of transition in human evolution from prehistoric times, when social life was primitive and largely disorganised, to the beginnings of civilisation. To Stanley Hall, it was a time of great creative potential and yet a struggle for civilised behaviour. He listed several contradictory traits that he took as characterising adolescence: on the one hand, eagerness, zest, enthusiasm and intellectual curiosity, alternating with, on the other hand, apathy, inertia and indifference. The adolescent could be capable of notable sensitivity and altruism – or cruel selfishness. Delinquency and crime were a result of uncontrolled natural revolt against the system that was trying to restrain them (Stanley Hall 1912). Stanley Hall was involved in the opening of the Juvenile Psychopathic Institute in Chicago in 1909, a move that reflected anxiety about troubled youth in that rapidly growing city.

Psychoanalytic theory has been largely typical in following the idea that youth is a period of *Sturm und Drang*. Early psychoanalytic theory did not, however, have much to say about adolescence as a developmental period, since Freud and his immediate successors were much more focused on the psychological significance of early childhood up to age 5 or 6. His daughter Anna Freud was the first psychoanalyst to carry out significant theoretical work on adolescence. In *The Ego and the Mechanisms of Defence* (1936), she emphasised the period as involving change and oscillation:

> Adolescents are excessively egoistic, regarding themselves as the centre of the universe and the sole object of interest, and yet at no time later in life are they capable of so much self-sacrifice and devotion. They form passionate love-relations only to break them off as abruptly as they began them ... They oscillate between blind submission to some self-chosen leader and defiant rebellion against any and every authority.
>
> (Freud 1936: 137–8)

For Anna Freud, adolescence *should* be a difficult stage:

> I take it as normal for an adolescent to behave for a considerable length of time in an inconsistent and unpredictable manner ... Such fluctuations would be deemed highly abnormal at any other time of life.
>
> (Freud 1958: 260)

The British psychoanalyst Donald Winnicott, who wrote extensively about youth and delinquency (Winnicott 1984), saw delinquent theft as representing children's attempt to steal back what they felt had been lost to them. In this, he saw delinquency as sometimes a hopeful sign, as delinquent children at least had the unconscious belief that things could get better if they got back what they felt had been lost. To the psychoanalyst, this is a more positive situation than that facing people who has never felt their emotional needs being met. Winnicot also saw the apparent destructiveness in delinquency as the individual making an unconscious demand for boundaries and attention. In more general terms, Winnicott believed that there is an element of aggression inherent in adolescence and subscribed to the view of adolescence as being a necessary period of turmoil and change. To Winnicott, part of the psychological task of becoming an adult is to take over control from the previous generation. In the unconscious mind of the developing adolescent, this represents the overthrow and 'murder' of the parents. Such powerful feelings are likely to arouse conflicting feelings in terms of sorrow and guilt, a state of affairs that might help explain some of the strongly oscillating moods that can seem to characterise adolescence (Costello (2002) usefully reviews Winnicott's thinking on delinquency).

Erik Erikson is another psychoanalytic theorist who viewed adolescence as a period where conflicts over identity are prominent. Erikson has been influential, as he wrote on development throughout life and described eight ages of development from birth to death (Erikson 1965). Erikson envisaged adolescence as the fifth period of development, in which the task was to steer a path toward a secure identity through a period that might be marked by *role confusion*. Erikson focused on the need of adolescents to leave behind their childhood identity and forge a new adult identity. This can be a very worrying time, as adolescents might feel quite cut adrift and prone to panic, and so latch onto whatever roles or identities that might be available to them. They may, for example, seem to over-identify with some person or group of people. This is why, suggested Erikson, we witness in adolescents the powerful idealisations, the dramatic falling in love, and the strong identification with peer groups and subcultural groups in particular. Teenagers are prone to become intensely loyal to sets of beliefs or particular groups, such as (during different periods) 'goths', 'mods', 'rockers', 'punks' or 'skinheads'. To Erikson, such identifications are caused by adolescents feeling that they have to seize an identity from those they see around them. If there were problems at this stage, according to Erikson, they might come about by a premature foreclosure of this process, in which someone holds on to an identity, or a way of being too soon. Thus, the fluctuations, and the changeability are, to Erikson, signs of health. Erikson's ideas do not necessarily explain offending as such, but they do explain why teenagers might be prone to very powerful identifications with peer groups whose values might be in opposition to those in the mainstream. It may well be that this shift toward peer identifications in this age group is significant in opening up different avenues of social influence.

Autonomy, individuation and morality

All psychological theories of adolescence tend to portray the period as marked by increasing efforts of adolescents to separate from parents and establish themselves as viable autonomous individuals. It has been argued that the development of autonomy from parents is a necessary step toward adolescents building up their own resources, including the ability to make moral decisions (Blos 1979; Beyers and Goossens 1999). The argument is that until we have a clear sense of our own identity it is difficult for us to make autonomous moral judgements. Younger children, for example, tend to be influenced by the moral judgements of the people, particularly adults, around them (Dorr and Fey 1974).

The development of an autonomous identity is a demanding pathway, however, and it seems also beneficial if this process takes place while good relationships with parents are maintained. Frank *et al.* (2002: 431), for example, refer to adolescents who are unable to 'balance intrapsychic and social presses for greater autonomy with continuing needs for parental approval and support [and who] appear vulnerable not only to anxiety and depression ... but also negative peer influence, alcohol and drug problems, and involvement in antisocial activity'. Frank *et al.* (2002) emphasise the possible importance of recognising that there may be distinct processes that involve *mutuality* (where there is recognition of a balance between autonomy and connection in adolescent relationships) and *conflictual independence* (where adolescents must separate and rework their childhood identity). Fleming (2005) provides some empirical support for the notion that normal adolescent moral development requires conflict with parents, and he reports a questionnaire study of the attitudes and behaviour of Portuguese adolescents in relation to independence and autonomy. Fleming argues that the process of development is driven by desire for autonomy, and notes a move from this desire being expressed in concerns over the body in early adolescence (styles of dress becoming important, for example) toward greater concern with autonomy in terms of interpersonal relationships (choosing friends and romantic partners) in later adolescence. Fleming (2005: 13) argues that autonomy is a state that has to be fought for through challenges to the parents' authority, and by disobedience of parental rules. It is only through such conflict that an autonomous sense of self can develop. Steinberg (1999, quoted in Fleming 2005) has argued that a distinction is usefully made between independence and autonomy. While independence refers to adolescents' ability to act on their own, autonomy 'means more than behaving independently. It also means thinking, feeling, and making moral decisions that are truly your own, rather than following along with what others believe' (Fleming 2005: 2). Thus, according to Fleming, it is the development of autonomy during adolescence that is key to the development of truly moral behaviour. If there is independence from family without autonomy, the individual may well come under the influence of peers (who themselves have not developed more autonomous modes of behaving).

So, to all these psychological theorists, the volume of crime committed by young people might simply reflect the emotional turbulence of the period. There may be an acting out of the aggression and turmoil, and challenges made to parental authority, fuelled by the desire for autonomy being experienced at this time. An interesting paradox emerges, as perhaps it is only through conflict with parental authority that truly moral thinking and behaviour can emerge. This is certainly a complicated developmental pathway that is being envisaged here. Perhaps it is by considering cognitive development alongside emotional development that most insight can be gained. Indeed, Fonagy *et al.* (2004: 323) argue that it is cognitive development itself that generates new emotional challenges for adolescents, as cognitive advances create 'new ways of thinking about people's feelings', which can in themselves be challenging. The issue of the development of the 'moral emotions' in adolescence will be considered next.

The development of 'moral emotions' in adolescence

As discussed in the previous chapter on the importance of family relationships, efforts have been made to explore the significance of the development of the 'moral emotions' of guilt, shame and empathy in childhood (Eisenberg 2000). It was argued there that an important distinction might be made between guilt and shame, shame being a visceral and painful signal of disapproval or a fear of abandonment, while the experience of guilt results from a more developed and reflective processing of negative emotion, such as shame.

There is good reason to believe that matters concerning shame may become relatively prominent in the second year of life, when issues of individuation and attachment arise as the child can begin to be able to act independently in the world (Schore 1994) (as discussed in Chapter 4). It is arguable that shame also assumes considerable importance during adolescence, when conflicts around autonomy as well as sexuality, and bodily appearance come to the fore (Reimer 1996). Indeed, recent psychological work on shame points to its emerging in what might seem to be contradictory ways in adolescence – when there is a failure to develop autonomy and when there is a failure to fit in with loved ones' expectations (Reimer 1996; Schore 1998). Better family relationships during adolescence seem to be protective against delinquency. Robertson (1999), for example, using data from interviews with adolescents, argues that shared family leisure activities are important in avoiding delinquency (just as shared leisure activities when children are younger is protective, as discussed in Chapter 4). There is no doubt that the links between autonomy and individuals' relationships with families and psychological functioning are complex (Beyers and Goossens 1999). However, consideration of the distinction between guilt and shame may be helpful to our understanding.

The previous chapter drew attention to the difference between guilt and shame proneness (pp. 116–19). Tangney *et al.* (1996: 797) argue that '[A]cross all ages, shame proneness was clearly related to maladapted responses to anger, including malevolent intentions; direct, indirect, and displaced aggression; self directed hostility; and negative long-term consequences. In contrast guilt-proneness was associated with constructive means of handling anger.' Stuewig and McCloskey (2005) explored the relationship between parenting factors in adolescence and 'guilt proneness' or 'shame proneness'. They used their own longitudinal data to argue that adolescents who experience rejection by their parents are less likely to be 'guilt prone' and more likely to be 'shame prone', while those who experience 'parental warmth' are more likely to be 'guilt prone' and less 'shame prone' (Stuewig and McCloskey 2005: 332). They suggest that this is because

A warm, supportive family environment devoid of rejection and harsh criticism may encourage adolescents to take responsibility for transgressions without generalizing the negative feelings to the entire self.

(Stuewig and McCloskey 2005: 334)

Although lower scores on guilt proneness led to heightened delinquency, the authors did not find a direct relationship between shame proneness and general delinquency. This might not be surprising because shame-anger responses do not necessarily translate into higher rates of general delinquency, but might instead lead to possibly isolated outbreaks of aggression and violence. The relationship between shame and outbreaks of violence will be explored further in Chapter 7. There is also a strong inverse relationship between shame and empathy (Tangney 1995; cited in Reimer 1996), which might well lead ultimately to less moral behaviour. However, the negative relationship between guilt proneness and delinquency was clear. So it could be concluded that the more able people are to process negative feelings, such as shame, into guilt, the more likely they are to behave in pro-social ways.

While family relationships might have their place, it is also undeniable that peer relationships become more significant during the period of adolescence. This is due to the greater physical freedom that adolescents enjoy, but may also be a likely consequence of psychological development (as explored in the section on 'Emotional development' above).

Peer groups, reputation and delinquency

A commonly made observation about offences carried out by young people is that many of them are carried out when in the company of others (Agnew 1991). Emler and Reicher (1995) suggest that this is significant, and they argue that it implies that what young people are doing through indulging in delinquency is fashioning their public identities in ways that will see them accepted by their peers. On its own, like the sociological theories discussed earlier in this chapter, this would still beg the question of why young people in particular should be so concerned with their public identities.

One answer to this is that adolescence needs to be understood as a process that involves the shifting of emotional attachments away from families and toward other relationships. 'Delinquent' peer groups are thus doubly attractive, as they not only offer companionship and security but also a direct means of rebellion and separation from parental authority. Walker-Barnes and Mason (2001) provide some support for this in their study of the gang involvement of teenagers in a Miami (USA) high school. They found that superficial involvement in gangs (such as using gang hand signals and wearing gang colours) when young people made the transition to high school was very common, but this involvement fell away for most during the academic year. Walker-Barnes and Mason (2001: 1862) suggest that this may be because 'participation in these nominal gang activities may provide security and a sense of belonging during the transition' to high school. As they became more involved in school activities, their need for the security of the gang diminished. Those from families with higher levels of 'parental warmth' showed lower levels of this initial involvement in gang activity. They also found that those who were more seriously involved in gang activities (including more serious delinquent activities) stayed more consistently involved over time. Such findings would be predicted by the distinction between AL and LCP. While no analysis of the role of gender is made in this study, the question remains as to why adolescent boys in general, rather than girls, should be so concerned about and influenced by peer groups. It may be that some of the developmental issues that have been discussed in relation to adolescence, coupled with issues connected to masculinity (which will be discussed in detail in the next chapter on the significance of gender in crime), do go some way to explain this. There are good reasons to think that boys are more likely to experience their identity as 'uncertain' or perhaps 'fragile'. It can certainly be argued (this issue is discussed in Chapter 6) that many teenage boys are defensively covering up feelings of anxiety about weakness and fear of abandonment. Matza (1964), while critical of psychological theory, still argued that 'masculine anxiety' was a significant force in delinquent gang cultures. Therefore, the feeling of belonging to groups that place value on strength and aggression may well be very attractive.

Undoubtedly, there are strong relationships between delinquency and the presence of delinquent peers in social networks. In other words, a teenager who offends is very likely to have friends who also offend (Vitaro and Wanner 2005). This, of course, does not necessarily mean that having delinquent friends is the cause of the delinquency. It may well be that someone inclined to delinquency will seek out those with similar personalities and interests. Some support for the significance of prior experience is provided by Henry *et al.* (2001), who used longitudinal data (from the Chicago Youth Development Study) to show that youths who had been subject to less warmth and inferior parenting skills were more likely to develop relationships with delinquent peers. Conversely, those from families characterised by warm interpersonal relationships and 'effective parenting' were more likely to affiliate with non-delinquent and non-violent peers (Henry *et al.* 2001: 184). So, perhaps boys with less secure relationships with families, and thus who are less secure in their identities, might be more attracted to peer groups that offer the chance for association with a strong, powerful alternative to those families.

Beside peer groups and gangs, adolescents can also gravitate to more intimate relationships. Laub and Sampson (1993) argued that a young man adopting a delinquent lifestyle could be diverted from the pathway to long-term criminality by involvement in a successful intimate partnership and perhaps marriage. Meeus *et al.* (2004) confirmed this effect with their longitudinal data on adolescents and young adults in The Netherlands. Young people in long-term relationships are less likely to be involved in crime. The difficulty with these findings is that they do not rule out the possibility that those who are psychologically able to become involved in such long-term relationships are already endowed with sufficient psychological and social capital to make involvement in a criminal lifestyle less likely.

Questions of identity and threatened identity do emerge as significant factors in studies of violence (as will be explored in some detail in Chapter 7). Anderson (1998) and Fagan and Wilkinson (1998) describe the impact of the interaction of high levels of social deprivation and violence in US urban environments on the identities of the young people growing up in those areas. The attainment of a reputation for violence and, in the US context in particular, the acquisition of a gun appear to be an efficient way of shoring up a sense of a viable identity. The acquisition of a reputation for strength is perhaps one way of young men's establishing themselves as viable individuals in environments that both socially and psychologically offer little but fragility and uncertainty. Some of these issues concerning the significance of strength and reputation to young men are taken up further in the next chapter.

Sensation seeking and adolescence

Another feature of the behaviour of many adolescents (particularly boys) is risk taking (Bell and Bell 1993). Lyng (1990) has argued that through involvement in risky activities, such as sky diving and rock climbing, individuals are attempting to explore the boundaries or the edges of the self (he thus refers to such risky activities as 'edgework'):

> Participants in virtually all types of edgework claim that the experience produces a sense of 'self-realization,' 'self-actualization,' or 'self-determination'. In the pure form of edgework, individuals experience themselves as instinctively acting entities, which leaves them with a purified and magnified sense of self.
>
> (Lyng 1990: 860)

Through such physical excitement, individuals are not only experiencing a pure 'and magnified sense of self', but are avoiding the more complex and threatening task of engaging with the demands on the self posed by the wider social world:

The intensification of fear and the demands for immediate response obliterate the process of imaginative rehearsal and the sense of one's actions being directed by a social agenda of someone else's making. The responses of the individual engaged in edgework are self-interested, spontaneous, and fully intelligible. In contrast to the aims of normal, day-to-day behavior, the immediate goal of one's actions in edgework cannot be regarded as trivial. The point is to survive, and most people feel no ambivalence about the value of this goal.

(Lyng 1990: 881)

Lyng (2004) has applied this argument to criminal activity and argues that, by becoming involved in offending, people are attempting to achieve a sense of selfhood and fulfilment that transcends the bonds of modern social constraint. The vast preponderance of young men in these activities suggests a slightly different analysis. It would be in keeping with the theorisation of adolescent development presented here that these are adolescents who are exploring the boundaries of the self – in an effort to establish a coherent sense of themselves as autonomous selves. Taking risks is therefore an activity through which people can experience themselves as consisting of a sturdy and coherent self. For some social groups, street crime and drug taking may be outlets of a felt need to explore and construct a coherent sense of themselves.

Education and delinquency

Another observation that has been made frequently is the robust negative association between educational involvement and delinquency. Engagement with the education system would seem, on the face of it, to be a factor that is strongly protective against delinquency. For example in the UK, the Youth Justice Board has been commissioning surveys of young people's involvement in offending for a number of years. The data draw attention to the significance of involvement in education. Pupils excluded from school are more likely to be involved in more frequent and serious offending than their colleagues in school (MORI 2004). Those playing truant at a younger age are also more likely to offend at an early age. Those offending at an earlier age are more likely to be the LCP offenders described by Moffitt's categories (see Chapter 3).

Those excluded begin their offending at a younger age – it seems that school exclusion is at least a significant signal of real difficulties.

The issues of identity that have been discussed may throw some light on this. Young people who are able to find some validation and feeling of belonging within the education system may need a delinquent identity less than those who do not find such a sense of belonging within the official system.

Ethnicity, delinquency and exclusion

Figures on rates of exclusion among different ethnic groups draw attention to the importance of ethnicity in this area. Wright and Weekes (2003) argue that black pupils often behave in ways that resist the racism they experience in school, and can thus find themselves in greater conflict, leading to exclusion. Demie (2001) traces the complex relationship of ethnic group and school achievement in England and Wales. Children from Caribbean backgrounds do relatively poorly; children with African backgrounds do rather well. Gender has a considerable impact, girls outperforming boys in most ethnic groups. As Demie acknowledges, no measure of social class was taken with this data, and that may well explain many of the variations found. Brown and Evans' (2002) US study found that European-American high-school children are more likely to be involved in extracurricular activities than their Hispanic and African-American counterparts. Archer and Yamashita (2003) draw attention to the great paradox of the greater visibility of young black males in public discourse about crime, but their invisibility in academic debate. This is certainly a relatively unexplored avenue in criminology, although the significance of links between issues of identity and ethnicity are touched on by Katz (1988), Messerschmidt (1993) and Anderson (1998).

Hormonal/physiological development

Besides theories of cognitive and emotional development, other theories assume that the rates of delinquency can be explained by reference to the physical changes occurring in the young. Adolescence is known to be a period of greatly increased hormonal levels, notably the androgens ('male' hormones). Associations have been made between androgen levels and aggressiveness and antisocial behaviour. The relationship remains unclear and is certainly complex (Olweus *et al.* 1980; Olweus 1987; Rubinow and Schmidt 1996). Life events certainly have an impact on testosterone levels. This issue will be dealt with in more detail in Chapter 6 in relation to gender differences (pp. 157–9).

Conclusion

This chapter has focused on understanding why there seems to be such a strong relationship between adolescence and delinquency. Many adolescents commit minor offences; indeed, it is arguable that it is, at least statistically, normative for adolescent boys to commit offences. This chapter has reviewed a number of explanations for this. The capacity for moral behaviour can be argued to be a considerable developmental achievement. People not only have to develop the cognitive ability to think in terms of different points of view and apply rules across different contexts, but they also have to develop the capacity to process complex emotions such as shame. The experience of shame can provide threats to people's sense of identity. Indeed, through putting sociological and psychological findings and theories together, a case can be made that issues of identity are crucial to understanding the links between youth and delinquency. It can be argued that both the social and psychological tasks of adolescence are to separate from parents and family of origin and to form a viable autonomous identity. Behaviour based on moral decisions becomes possible only if an individual has a sufficiently secure sense of identity to permit autonomous decisions. Without a sense of identity and the concomitant senses of agency and purpose, people are likely simply to fit in with immediate group norms. Delinquent peer groups can be doubly attractive to young people in that they offer the opportunity of direct rebellion and independence alongside a sense of belonging that can reinforce an identity as a strong and viable person. Delinquency can also be understood in terms of risky behaviour, in which people can experiment with the limits or 'edges' of themselves (Lyng 2004). It will be argued in the next chapter that delinquent peers and risky behaviour can be particularly attractive to adolescent boys, who can feel their identities to be more tenuous than do girls; yet, boys may also feel that they need to live up to masculine ideals of strength and toughness.

This chapter began by raising the vexed issue of youth and criminal responsibility. The significance of viewing the moral emotions as development achievements is clear. That 10-year-olds know the difference between right and wrong in the abstract does not mean that they have achieved sufficient moral autonomy to behave morally when faced with social contexts that offer particular guidance. There are good reasons to believe that young people with a less secure sense of identity, born perhaps of less secure family environments, will be prone to be influenced by their peers.

In discussing the strong relationship between youth and crime in this chapter, it must be acknowledged that the relationship is most marked between young *men* and crime. The next chapter will explore the relationship between gender and crime. Masculinity is strongly associated with crime.

Chapter 6

Gender and crime

Introduction

Alongside awareness of the disproportionate numbers of young people offending is the widely accepted fact that men commit more crime than women. While the bald 'facts' of the over-representation of men in the crime statistics have been known for a long time, they have been largely 'taken for granted' (Messerschmidt 1986; Heidensohn 1996). Thus, the longitudinal studies, such as the London Study, reviewed in Chapter 3, studied only boys. The gender bias in criminality was not questioned, and there was little interest in studying gender as a significant variable that itself might shed light on the causes of crime. There has, however, been a recent growth in interest in exploring the implications of the gender bias in crime (Jefferson 1997). Can these gender differences tell us something interesting about the cause of crime, or about differences between men and women?

Table 6.1 demonstrates the extent of the gender bias in terms of the overall volume of crime in the UK (Social Trends 2004, using Home Office figures). If we look at the overall category of all indictable offences, there are roughly 4.4 convictions of men to every conviction of a woman. There are important differences when different categories of crime are considered. The gender ratio is at its lowest in the category of theft and handling (3:1), while there are, for example, 5.5 times more male convictions for violence than female, eight times more for robbery, and 14.5 times for burglary.

Table 6.1 Convictions for indictable offences (Social Trends 2004)

	1996 (1000s)		2002 (1000s)	
	M	F	M	F
All indictable offences	435.9	96.1	391.5	88.6
Theft and handling	152.6	56.8	131.5	50.1
Criminal damage	12.4	1.3	12.5	1.6
Drug offences	96.0	11.5	84.1	9.8
Violence	51.7	8.9	51.8	9.5
Robbery	5.6	0.6	7.2	0.9
Burglary	37.2	2.0	30.4	2.1

Explanations of the gender differences in criminal activity fall into three categories:

1. There are innate differences between men and women that lead to different rates of criminal behaviour.
2. Men and women are socialised into adopting different behaviours – some of which are more likely to be associated with criminal behaviour.
3. There are cultural differences in the constructions of masculinity and femininity that shape the behaviour of individuals, leading to differential crime rates.

However, two slightly different questions can be asked in respect of these different theories. First why do men commit so much *more* crime than women, and second, why do women commit so much *less* crime than men? The first part of this chapter will consider the first question, exploring explanations of why men commit more crime than women.

Men, masculinity and crime

The question of how the male propensity to criminal behaviour can be explained has most often been tackled in terms of the debate between nature and nurture. Do men tend to have biological tendencies to be more aggressive and antisocial than women, or are men being socialised to be more antisocial?

Biological explanations

One of the perennial debates in psychology has been whether the physical differences between men and women are reflected in psychological differences. One school of thought supposes that men are genetically driven to be more aggressive and risk taking, and that women are genetically programmed to be more social and caring. If such fundamental differences exist, they would go some way to explaining the differences in crime rates. Daly and Wilson (1988) drew together data from many cross-cultural studies to present a convincing argument that men have been much more likely than women to kill others throughout history and across cultures. They argue that this suggests there is a biological tendency to violence in men. Daly and Wilson (1988) present an argument, based on Darwinian ideas of natural selection, that male ancestors, for reason of sexual selection, would have been favoured if they were more aggressive toward others, particularly sexual rivals.

Conclusive evidence that particular inherited characteristics lead to consistent psychological differences has been hard to find, however. The difficulty has been that many differences in behaviour and attitudes that certainly do become apparent between males and females can usually be explained in terms of genetics or socialisation. Certainly, by the time children are 2–3 years of age, behavioural differences can clearly be observed. Dipietro (1981), for example, carried out an often-quoted study demonstrating differences in 'rough-and-tumble' play among boys and girls. Groups of boys or girls aged 2–3 years were observed playing in a room supplied with lots of toys and play equipment. The boys were judged to be indulging in far more rough and tumble than the girls. That is, the boys were seen to be pushing, shoving, mock wrestling and fighting. The girls appeared to be much more sedate in their play, even organising a form of queue to use the trampoline. While this finding of marked differences in play styles has been found consistently, it can still be, quite reasonably, argued that these children, by 2–3 years of age, are influenced by cultural pressures and processes of socialisation. Hence, efforts have been made to observe gender differences in the behaviour of very young babies, before processes of socialisation can have much impact. Pomerleau *et al.* (1992), for example, suggest that 5-month-old boys, in laboratory conditions, while being no more generally explorative, were less attentive to familiar objects than their female counterparts. It is possible to speculate that if boys are less likely to find the familiar interesting, they may acquire a greater interest in risk taking and hence criminal behaviour later in life. This is clearly a rather large speculative leap, however. In addition, if there were some inherited propensity to more risk taking or aggressive behaviour, there would need to be some physiological correlate. The physiological variable that has attracted most attention as an explanation for the male propensity to violence and criminality is the 'male hormone' (or androgen) testosterone.

Testosterone and crime

A couple of pieces of evidence have been drawn together to implicate testosterone as a cause of antisocial behaviour in young men. First, boys experience great increases in androgen levels throughout their adolescence (the period when antisocial behaviour also peaks). Second, in a number of mammal species, there does seem to be a direct relationship between testosterone levels and aggressive behaviour.

Since the years of peak testosterone levels match very well the peak years of male offending (females also experience increases in androgen levels during these years but on a much smaller scale), it has been suggested that it is those high levels of testosterone that is leading to more aggressive and antisocial behaviour. Testosterone has been implicated as a causal agent of aggression for a long time. Among some animal species, the effects of testosterone seem to be clear. For example, young male rhesus monkeys ordinarily exhibit more rough-and-tumble play than their female siblings. If testosterone is administered to pregnant rhesus monkeys, however, their female offspring exhibit more characteristically male behaviour. While for ethical reasons, such experimental data are lacking for human subjects, reports of human fetuses that, have been exposed to high levels of testosterone are consistent with this (Mazur and Booth 1998). This has led to the suggestion that fetal testosterone levels do have a role in shaping brain structures that may, in turn, be associated with more typically 'male' behaviour.

More immediate effects of testosterone have also been noted. In some species, the impact of testosterone on behaviour can be observed very directly. For example, castration of male red deer (which leads to a massive reduction in testosterone levels) reduces their aggression and fighting with other male deer. Administration of testosterone by injection reinstates the aggression. Such straightforward relationships between testosterone and behaviour have not been found among more socially sophisticated animals, however, as studies of various species of tamarin, rhesus or talapoin monkeys have found (Turner

1994). There are suggestions that hormone levels in man (and other primates) do not correlate in any simple way with aggression or violence, but might instead bear more relationship to 'dominance' behaviour (Mazur and Booth 1998). Dominance refers to the apparent social status of the individual. This status may be determined by various factors, and these might include overt aggression, but it more often involves more complex social interactions. While some studies comparing testosterone levels among offenders have shown higher levels among the more violent offenders, these findings have not been consistently replicated (Ramirez 2003). The significance of androgens as explanations of youth crime is briefly discussed in Chapter 5 and, in relation to sex crime, Chapter 8.

Another important factor that needs to be taken into account when considering the influence of testosterone on behaviour is the fact that hormone levels themselves are reactive to life events. Rats that have just 'won' a fight show increased testosterone levels (Schuurman 1980). People involved in competitive sport show raised testosterone level before the competition, which stay higher in the winners than the losers (Mazur and Booth 1998). Such effects have been found to occur even among football supporters. Bernhardt *et al.* (1998) found that supporters of the winning side show elevated testosterone levels, while the losers' levels go down, after the game. Klinesmith *et al.* (2006) found that the simple act of holding a gun can also increase testosterone levels.

Interactions between testosterone levels and more complex social conditions are suggested by data reviewed by Mazur and Booth (1998). They report studies from the USA showing no differences in testosterone levels between groups of black or white male children (6–18 years), but significantly higher testosterone levels among black male adults than white male adults. This difference is only sustained, however, among younger and less educated black males. Black and white college graduates have similar testosterone levels. Mazur and Booth (1998) suggest that these findings might be explained by the different challenging social conditions faced by black men who do not have the social benefit of college education. They are more likely, Mazur and Booth (1998) suggest, to have to face difficult social circumstances, including gang and honour cultures. Such findings suggest very strongly that biological factors need to be understood as interacting with culture.

The neurotransmitter serotonin has also been implicated as a cause of male antisocial behaviour; it is suggested that lower levels, perhaps more commonly found in men, are associated with irritability and aggression (Moir and Jessel 1995). Moffitt *et al.* (1998) report consistent differences in blood serotonin levels among violent men. As Moffitt *et al.* acknowledge, there are, however, obstacles to concluding that serotonin levels, or genetic predisposition to serotonin, significantly determines criminality. First, the details of how the neurotransmitter operates, what the interactions with other neurotransmitters are, and where the specific neurological sites of action might be, are extremely complex and are only just beginning to be explored (Rubin 1987; Berggård *et al.* 2003). Second, we know that serotonin levels can be affected by the environment. Rats given electric shocks or kept in isolation show reduced levels of serotonin. People who suffered losses and stressful events have also been shown to have reduced levels of serotonin (Gillespie *et al.* 2005). Clearly, the question can still be asked – are lower serotonin levels a cause of more impulsive aggressive behaviour, or the result of higher levels of stress? It might well be argued that offenders are people who have suffered deprivations (as suggested by longitudinal studies) and losses, and therefore have lower levels of serotonin.

Overall, there are grounds here to suggest some interesting interactions between biological factors and social experience, a subject that deserves further exploration. Morrell and Murray (2003), for example, present evidence of boy babies being more vulnerable to 'poor parenting', leading to less ability to regulate emotions (work on the significance of the ability to regulate and reflect on emotions is discussed in relation to the moral emotions in Chapter 4, and in relation to violence in Chapters 7 and 8).

Theories of socialisation

The apparent dominance of crime by men has been subject to some historical dispute. Feeley and Little (1991) used court records from the seventeenth to the twentieth centuries to argue that women were far more equally represented in the crime statistics during the seventeenth and early eighteenth centuries (in England at least), but that this involvement dwindled through the eighteenth and nineteenth centuries. Shoemaker (2001) argues that more modern forms of masculinity in which violence is discouraged by the law, were being propagated throughout the eighteenth century. Wiener (2004) argues that during the nineteenth century the criminal justice system in England became ever more concerned with crimes of violence and came to concentrate on men. The reasons may be complex, but they certainly suggest that general crime is not entirely the result of biological givens. There has indeed been a strong tradition of psychological research that has attempted to explain both violence and gender differences in behaviour in terms of theories of socialisation (Hoffmann *et al.* 1994). Bandura's (1973) classic work on mechanisms of social learning suggested three channels for socialisation: family, peer group, and the wider culture. There appears to be a reasonable amount of evidence to support the general thrust of the argument that people can learn behaviour from their environment. Children exhibit more aggressive behaviour after witnessing adults behaving aggressively. Bandura himself initiated the famous 'bobo doll' experiment, discussed in Chapter 1 (Bandura *et al.* 1961), in which young children were noted to be more likely to behave aggressively after witnessing an adult behave aggressively toward a large doll.

Children who grow up experiencing violence in their family are more likely to be violent themselves as adults (Widom 1989). Such findings, however, need to be understood within the context of the evidence about the significance of family influences explored thoroughly in Chapter 4. Fergusson *et al.* (2006), for example, found that although the childhood experience of witnessing parental violence is associated with later domestic violence, this statistical effect does not survive when other negative childhood factors are taken into account, suggesting that the simple observation of violence is not a sufficient cause of violence itself. It is also clear that teenagers and children who have delinquent peers are more likely to be delinquent themselves (see Chapter 5 for discussion of the influence of peer relationships on youth crime). It may well be that they are therefore learning the antisocial behaviour from their delinquent peers (Sutherland 1947). The difficulty is, of course, that these findings may be explained equally well by assuming that young people with an interest in delinquent activities are attracted to those with similar interests. Similarly, there is evidence that those who have histories of violent conduct are more likely to have watched more violent films (Newson 1994). This does not, of course, mean that the violent films cause the behaviour. It is also plausible that those who are attracted to violence are more likely to seek out media portrayals of violence as well. The evidence about the impact of exposure to portrayals of violence in the media is also difficult to disentangle from the other influences on people and individual differences (Pennell and Browne 1999). Overall, with particular respect to the question of gender differences, and theories of social learning, we would still need to ask how or why boys are exposed to greater pro-criminal social learning forces than girls.

In general, in view of the often heated debate between those who argue that the characteristics of men that lead them to be more antisocial are endowed by their biology and those who argue that men are simply socialised to be more antisocial, it seems unlikely that there will be a simple resolution. There are, however, a couple of important facts that may help us understand what is going on. First, the evidence that men present more of a problem in terms of crime, and crimes of violence in particular, throughout history and across civilisations, appears to be overwhelming. This would seem to be highly suggestive of some kind of constitutional, biological bias within men toward aggressive and antisocial behaviour. Second, however, it is very clear that the rate of criminality, and violence in particular, has varied greatly through time and currently varies considerably across cultures. Figures on homicide (a relatively robust statistic, as it is usually not controversial that a violent crime has been committed), suggest significant differences. In Norway, the homicide rate in 2001 was 0.95 per 100,000 of population, while, in the USA it was 5.56; in Estonia, 10.6, and in South Africa, 55.6 (Barclay and Tavares 2003). This suggests the important influence of culture. As Daly and Wilson conclude in their book, which is otherwise a highly polemical argument *for* the importance of the biological dimension of masculinity in determining violent behaviour: 'The enormous variability in national homicide rates should be grounds for optimism: there *are* social milieus where killing is extremely rare. With the elimination of social inequality and desperation, we may yet see homicide become an almost negligible source of human mortality' (1988: 297).

It will be argued that what is required is a turning away from the more simplistic explanations of gender and crime toward ones that can be more sensitive to issues of culture and individual psychology. Moves have been made toward analyses that examine the role of masculinity in more cultural contexts. These theories will now be discussed.

The problematisation of masculinity in criminology: the cultural dimension

Since the early 1990s, there has been an upsurge in interest in the cultural constructions of 'masculine identity', which itself may be a cause of crime (Jefferson 1997). Jefferson's description of three theoretical movements that began to explore masculinity itself as a part of the crime equation, provides a useful introduction to this area.

First, there was radical feminism, which argued that male violence (and sexual violence in particular) was a symptom of hostility between genders and of a patriarchal society that sought to keep women in their place. As Susan Brownmiller famously argued of rape, 'It is nothing more or less than a conscious process of intimidation by which *all men* keep *all women* in a state of fear' (Brownmiller 1975: 15). Thus, individual acts of violence could be seen as acts of power, and the assertion of status. The difficulty with this formulation is that it is not clear how men's greater involvement in crime generally, other than crimes of violence against women, can be explained by patriarchy. Nor is it clear that this helps us understand why crime seems to be carried out disproportionately by those of low social status. As the longitudinal studies (reviewed in Chapter 3) demonstrate, serious crime is more likely to be committed by those who come from families and circumstances that meant that they grew up in the face of multiple disadvantages.

Such observations gave rise to the second movement to which Jefferson (1997) points. This is another largely sociological perspective that aims to put masculinity within its different social and cultural contexts. It emphasises that there are a variety of masculinities that may seek various forms of expression within different circumstances (Connell 1995). Particularly offensive incidences of male violence might be understood as occurring within the cultural constraints of the participants. Jefferson refers to Messerschmidt (1993), who looks at crime in terms of its possible role in allowing men to believe themselves to be achieving a sense of fulfilled masculine identity. Messerschmidt suggests that we are asking the wrong question if we ask why masculinity leads to crime. He suggests that crime is a means through which masculinity is expressed and achieved. Messerschmidt uses the New York 'wilding' rape case as an example. A woman jogger was beaten and repeatedly raped in New York's Central Park. She was 'dragged unconscious to the bottom of a ravine some two hundred feet from the road, where she was left for dead. When she was eventually found, she had lost three-fourths of her blood; her body temperature had fallen to 80°F, she had sustained multiple skull fractures; there were cuts and bruises on her chest, arms, hands and feet' (Messerschmidt 1993: 114). Immediately after the offence, the attackers were described as 'exuberant – laughing and acting stupid, leaping and cavorting ... they were twirling and flinging the victim's clothes' (Messerschmidt 1993: 114). A group of young African-American and Hispanic youths (aged 15–17) were convicted of the crime. Messerschmidt argued that this horrible crime had to be understood within the context of class and ethnic disadvantage (see also Anderson 1998; Fagan and Wilkinson 1998). Such seemingly arbitrary abuse of physical power was one, however pathetic, way that those youths had of bolstering their sense of male identity. Other men may be able to express their need to be seen as strong and powerful by more legitimate routes – through having a well-paid job, big car, or social status. As Messerschmidt puts it:

> Because the immediate sensation of masculine power was seductive for these boys, group rape became a resource for accomplishing gender and constructing a particular type of masculinity, a collective, publicly aggressive form of masculinity. … Due to position in social divisions of labour and power, many young, marginalised, racial minority men bond to form violent street-group formations. They adapt to their economic and racial powerlessness by competing with rivals of their own class, race and gender for personal power. For these young men, the personal power struggle with other young, marginalised, racial minority men is a resource for constructing a specific type of masculinity – not masculinity in the context of a job or organisational dominance but in the context of 'street elite'.
>
> (Messerschmidt 1993: 116)

It is an interesting irony that this case has continued to be something of a political battleground in the USA (Hancock 2003). To add credence to initial claims that the teenagers were 'framed', a convicted rapist confessed 10 years later to being the sole offender. While the original convictions were overturned, the precise rights and wrongs of the case remain contested. Whether a particular miscarriage of justice took place in this specific case or not, is not relevant to the analysis here, in that, clearly, there are many incidences of young men behaving extremely badly. In the UK, a 14-strong gang apparently attacked and raped a 37-year-old woman on a canal towpath in west London in July 2000, although it is noteworthy that in addition to the two boys convicted of the offence, an 18-year-old girl was also convicted. In echoes of the New York case, police reported that in their investigation they were led to the gang because its members had been loudly boasting about the episode (BBC News 2001).

Jefferson argues that there are two problems with Messerschmidt's formulation. First, Messerschmidt places a strong emphasis on 'normative' notions of masculinity. In other words, the notion that 'masculinity' is somehow synonymous with power, strength and concern with status (as in the above paragraph from Messerschmidt) is left unquestioned. Why should young *men* be so concerned with these attributes? Second, nothing is really said about individual differences. Messerschmidt's ideas might be able to explain why certain groups of men are more likely than others to construct an apparently antisocial masculine identity hewn from acts of violence, but they do not explain why particular individuals turn to crime. Not all men who are similarly disadvantaged resort to the same kind of offending.

Jefferson's third stage of questioning 'masculinity' for the role that it may play in crime is therefore one that tries to incorporate the understanding of masculinity as being shaped within certain cultural constraints alongside more psychological perspectives that can perhaps throw light on individual differences and might help explain why masculine identities can often be so caught up with destructiveness. A very important strand, as far as Jefferson is concerned, is contemporary psychoanalysis, and this will require some discussion.

Traditional psychoanalytic accounts of masculinity

At first glance, psychoanalysis might seem an odd place to seek out psychological explanations of men's over-representation in criminal statistics. Traditional Freudian psychoanalysis portrays men as the more 'moral' gender. According to the psychoanalytic view of gender development, the key maturational moment for boys is the resolution of the Oedipus complex. The Freudian account suggests that infants ideally grow up with a feeling of happiness and security, as they feel little division between themselves and their mothers. As boys develop awareness of genital pleasure and genital differences, they become aware that their mothers do not have a penis. The unconscious belief forms that the consequence for staying in this state of unity with their mothers is to lose their penis (as logic suggests, their mothers have already). The solution to this dilemma is to separate from the mother ('dis-identify' – Greenson 1968) and become like (identify with) the father, as a way of being with their own wife/mother. Thus, according to Freud, the rules of society enter the world of boys in a very stark and powerful way. They experience strong anxiety about what might happen to them if they do not curb their desires.

Girls, on the other hand, are left in the supposedly more ambiguous situation of having to separate and then identify with their mother, and they do not have the same anxieties about the consequences of breaking rules. To Freud, this meant that feminine identity is not so clear-cut; the imposition of the external cultural rules is less marked since they do not have the fear of castration if they break the rules (Freud 1925). The obvious empirical difficulty that this theory runs into is that men and boys are far more likely to break the rules than their female counterparts (as crime statistics so clearly demonstrate). More contemporary psychoanalytic accounts, which have caught the attention of some criminological theorists, do address this conundrum, however.

Contemporary psychoanalytic accounts of masculinity

Some support for the original psychoanalytic view of moral development appeared to come from studies of moral development instigated by Lawrence Kohlberg, who was building on the work of Piaget in describing moral thought as emerging through a series of developmental stages. Kohlberg, as described in Chapter 5 ('Youth Crime'), argued that the most moral form of thinking is the abstraction of immutable rules that can be transferred from situation to situation.

Kohlberg created a set of tasks to study the development of moral thinking, and many of his findings suggested that when boys and girls are given various reasoning tasks that involve making moral decisions, boys are indeed more likely to demonstrate clearer moral reasoning (Caputo 2000). One of the best-known tests of moral reasoning is Heinz's dilemma. Children are given the following scenario:

> In Europe, a woman was near death from a special kind of cancer. There was one drug that the doctors thought might save her. It was a form of radium that a druggist in the same town had recently discovered. The drug was expensive to make, but the druggist was charging ten times what the drug cost him to make. He paid $200 for the radium and charged $2,000 for a small dose of the drug. The sick woman's husband, Heinz, went to everyone he knew to borrow the money, but he could only get together about $1,000 which is half of what it cost. He told the druggist that his wife was dying and asked him to sell it cheaper or let him pay later. But the druggist said: 'No, I

discovered the drug and I'm going to make money from it.' So Heinz got desperate and broke into the man's store to steal the drug for his wife. Should the husband have done that?

(Kohlberg 1963: 19)

While marks are awarded for the clarity of moral thinking, it was assumed that those with more 'superior' moral thinking would generally argue that Heinz would be right to steal the drug if they were in some way employing the reasoning that protection of human life is more important than adherence to a law that is merely protecting the profits of the 'druggist'.

This work was revisited by Carol Gilligan (1982), who was troubled that girls seemed consistently to score lower on these tests of moral reasoning. She argued that it was possible to listen to what the boys and girls were saying and hear that they were speaking from different perspectives. Boys were more likely to use the judicial reasoning – applying general principles (such as, in this case, that human life is worth more than money). Boys seemed to be more able to say, 'Yes, he should steal the drug – his wife is more important than the pharmacist's profit.' This example is from Gilligan's book (1982: 26) – here is an 11-year-old boy explaining why Heinz should steal the drug:

Jake (aged 11):
For one thing, a human life is worth more than money, and if the druggist only makes $1000, he is still going to live, but if Heinz doesn't steal the drug, his wife is going to die.
Why is life worth more than money?
Because the druggist can get a thousand dollars later on from rich people with cancer, but Heinz can't get his wife again.
Why not?
Because people are all different and so you couldn't get Heinz's wife again.

So this seems like a very clear-cut and moral response. Gilligan suggests that girls seemed, on the face of it, to be less sure. For example, here is an 11-year-old girl (Gilligan 1982: 28) addressing the same dilemma:

Amy (11):
Should Heinz steal the drug?
Well, I don't think so. I think there might be other ways besides stealing it, like if he could borrow the money or make a loan or

something, but he really shouldn't steal the drug – but his wife shouldn't die either.
Why shouldn't he steal the drug?
If he stole the drug, he might save his wife, but if he did, he might have to go to jail and then his wife might get sicker again, and he couldn't get more of the drug, and it might not be good. So they should really just talk it out and find some other way to make the money.

Amy's response seems not to point to a clear moral action, unlike Jake's. Clearly, any suggestion that such evidence points to boys possessing a higher form of morality would need also to explain the evidence on criminality and gender. Not all crimes could be explained away by suggesting that boys were making recourse to some higher moral reasoning, as in this dilemma. Carol Gilligan's approach was to suggest that it was necessary to listen again to what the girls were actually saying when they were answering this question. She argued that girls were, in some senses, actually showing more sophistication in their answers. While there might seem to be a less coherent moral response, Gilligan suggests that the girls' responses were, first, more grounded in reality and, second, more embedded in relationships. At first glance, Amy might seem less clear, and more ambivalent in her thinking: 'he really shouldn't steal the drug – but his wife shouldn't die either.' However, her responses can also be understood as being much more embedded in the reality of human relationships. She worries about the impact that Heinz's offending would have on his wife; she thinks there must be another way of solving this problem. Far from being less moral, Gilligan argues that girls could be seen as more realistic. So although it might seem like a good idea to steal the drug, in reality unless you happen to be an experienced burglar, breaking an entry to the pharmacist would be difficult to do. Girls also were seeing things in terms of the relationships involved: What effect would Heinz' committing a crime have on the wife? What use would he be to her, if he was in prison? Surely, it must be possible to sort something out with the pharmacist? Or maybe Heinz could borrow the money?

Gilligan uses contemporary psychoanalytic theory to explain these differences, utilising Nancy Chodorow's (1978) influential work on the implications of the psychoanalytic perspective on the developmental tasks of boys and girls. Chodorow does not argue at all with Freud's vision of the Oedipus complex, but she does take issue with its implications for adults. According to the Freudian account, the developmental path for the male child is to separate from the mother and then identify (through fear of punishment) with the father. For boys, the task is to become like their father, and to become different from, to separate themselves from, their initial love object, the mother. For girls, the task is rather different; yes, they must separate from the mother, but to reach mature adulthood, the girl can become like her mother, like her first love object. So women are left with a part of themselves as being that blissful early fusion. Men, however, must define themselves as being different from their mother, different from femininity and from all the positive feelings of nurturance and care that a small child would ordinarily associate with his mother. Chodorow points out that, in recent times in Western societies, fathers, and masculine figures in general, are far more likely to be absent and the mother present during childhood. This means that as girls grow up they can build a real relationship with their mother and then identify with her. Girls are therefore forming their identity through building a relationship with a real person,[1] whereas boys very often do not have masculine figures around them with whom they can build real affectionate relationships and build their identity around. Boys can however, seek to build their masculine identity, in two ways:

1. Through defining themselves as being different from femininity. In this way, masculine identity becomes something very negative, based on a denial of things that are felt to be feminine or maternal, such as care and intimacy.
2. By constructing a masculine identity through identifying with the cultural images of masculinity that they see around them. These are often images available through the mass media featuring fictional hypermasculinity, or the images of masculinity they find presented in peer groups (this perhaps might explain why men are more psychologically vulnerable to external influences and why boys seem more likely to form gangs than girls).

The general implications for adult men and women of all this are very different. Women have the capacity for contentment within them. The experience of blissful unity, that everyone once knew, is part of their adult identity. Men's identities are more 'fragile', and not based on the solid ground of real relationships with others. They define themselves through denial of femininity and by identification with an image of masculinity that emphasises strength and autonomy (Maguire 1995). Gilmour (1991) documents in detail how 'masculinity' across the world appears to be a far more 'ascribed' status than femininity. That is, it has to be won, and constantly proven. Men are thus more insecure, and contentment is always outside themselves, since they have had to deny it as part of their identity. Hence, men are left feeling that experiences of contentment are not to be found within themselves. So men are, on the one hand, more outward-looking, seeking pleasure outside themselves in an effort to achieve the kind of peace and contentment that is always beyond them. On the other hand, they are also angry and full of bitterness, feeling separated from the world of warmth and comfort. They are likely to feel particular anger toward women, from whom they have become isolated (Minsky 1998).

More recent psychoanalytic thought has questioned the idea that masculine development necessarily involves a repudiation of femininity through such a process of *dis-identification* from the mother. Diamond (2004) draws together theoretical work that suggests that the model that saw masculine identity as requiring dis-identification from femininity was actually describing a pathological process (however common that might be). It was a process occurring in families marked by conflict between parents and/or gender roles. Examples are mothers who may have strong negative feelings about masculinity and so may be unable to identify with the developing masculine identity of their son; and fathers who, if not entirely absent, are also hostile to women and femininity, and who would only discourage and ridicule any apparently feminine characteristics developing in the boy. The resulting masculine identity forged in such circumstances would be one that is rigidly 'hypermasculine', that sees value in aggression, autonomy and overt hostility to the softer world of connection and femininity. Diamond (2004) argues that there are 'healthier' processes of development, in which a more flexible masculine male identity can be nurtured. Among the conditions that would foster this development are 'mothers' who are able to identify with and relate positively to the masculine sides of their children, and 'fathers' who are able to relate positively to the more feminine sides of the boys. These conditions will help the boys cope with what Diamond refers to as the *inevitable* trauma of realising that they are different from their mothers. This trauma is often compounded by the way that 'very young boys are typically shamed into withdrawing from their mothers more than they naturally desire. Thus, the boy not only loses a large part of his primary dyadic connection and "ideal" state with his mother, but also simultaneously is forced to repudiate, renounce or deny what he has lost' (Diamond 2004: 371).

Further analysis of the relationship between masculinity and crime will necessarily take place in the following chapters when we look in more detail at violent crime and sex crime. The relative frequency with which women are the victims of male violence certainly raises questions about men's relationships with and feelings toward women.

Women and crime

The question of the relationship between women and crime, and women's relatively lowly contribution to the crime rates can also be raised. It has been suggested that women's contributions to crime are somehow being ignored. For while it is true that gender has not been considered as an important variable in understanding crime, it is also true that the great majority of studies of crime have focused on men. The classic longitudinal studies discussed in Chapter 3 were exclusively concerned with the development of boys into delinquents. The engagement of traditional criminology with female criminality is described very well by Heidensohn (1996).

Does female criminality go undetected?

Some rather diverse voices throughout the history of criminology have suggested that the figures suggesting an enormous gender bias in criminal behaviour are essentially false. This theory was put forward in a comprehensive fashion by Otto Pollack (1961) in his book, *The Criminality of Women*. He argued that female crime is masked by:

1. The under-reporting of female offences. Men may feel embarrassed to admit and report that they have fallen victim to female crime.
2. The lower detection rates of female offenders. When women do commit offences, they are often offences that are more difficult to detect, and they may be cleverer than men at disguising their offences.
3. The greater leniency shown to women by the police and courts. Even when women are caught, Pollack argues that the police and courts are more likely to treat them leniently, due to chivalrous attitudes.

Pollack had recourse to biology to argue that women are inherently more capable of deceit than men, because women can fake sexual arousal and orgasm, and hence they can, according to Pollack, easily manipulate men. Pollack suggests therefore that women are often the instigators and masterminds behind crime rather than the actual perpetrators. While Pollack's work, with its rather clear thread of misogyny, has been largely discarded the idea that an essentially masculine criminal justice system is somehow not engaging with female criminality has lingered. More recently, for example, Motz (2001), while not challenging the overall dominance of male criminality, still argues that female abuse of children often remains hidden. The idealisation of 'motherhood', Motz argues, leads to the failure to see the violence that women can do to their children. As will be explored in the next chapter, it does seem that the one type of homicide in which women do numerically rival men is in the killing of their own children. These numbers remain small, however, compared to all the other types of murder (such as killing sexual partners or male adversaries). Where Motz may have a very important argument is in pointing us toward understanding female violence as being directed inward, and toward themselves. This theorising clearly does fit the data indicating that levels of self-harm are very much higher among women than men (e.g. Hawton *et al.* 2003; Rodham *et al.* 2005). This work will be returned to later. Self-harm aside, it remains a fact that despite many years of speculation, we have yet to uncover any great amount of hidden female criminality. Steffensmeier and Allan (1996), using largely US data, argue that while there is a great difference in the volume of overall crime between the genders, there are also important differences in the pattern of offences. Female offences are more likely to be of a relatively minor nature. The following questions therefore need to be raised and what evidence there is evaluated:

- Are there theories that can help us explain why women seem to commit so much less crime?
- What do we know about the psychology of women who commit crime – are they like the men who commit crime, or are they more 'deviant'?
- Given the suggestions about men and their cultural roles leading to higher rates of criminality, as gender roles change, will we see increasing rates of female criminality?

Why do women commit less crime than men?

It may be that the answer to this question simply lies within the theories that seek to explain men's greater involvement in crime that

171

have already been discussed. The relevant question might still be, why do *men* commit so much crime? However, some have argued that understanding women's relatively meagre contribution to the crime figures might help us understand more about crime and the causes of crime.

Women are more honest

Is there any evidence that women are more generally honest than men? Ward and Beck (1990) report experimental findings suggesting that men are more likely to behave dishonestly than women. Farrington and Knight (1979) addressed this question in a series of experiments. They left addressed envelopes on the street containing different amounts of money, and the other variable was that the apparent recipient of the money was either a wealthy man or an old lady. They observed who picked up the letter and whether they eventually sent it on. Obviously, the honest thing to do is to post the letter. Generally women were no more honest than men, except where larger amounts of money were involved: then about half the men retained the money but only a quarter of the women.

Sung (2003) discusses findings suggesting a positive relationship between honesty in government practices and gender, less corruption being associated with larger numbers of women working in government. Sung notes that, Dollar *et al.* (2001) have proposed that this suggests that women are a good influence in that they are more likely to behave ethically, these findings might better be explained by assuming that more open, liberal systems of government also have more women working in them.

Heidensohn (1996) has argued that attention to women's roles in crime tells us a great deal about the social inhibitions that prevent people from committing crime. There are a couple of related ideas that connect with control theories in criminology. As discussed in Chapter 1, Hirschi (1969) argued that most criminologists are missing the point in asking, why do people commit crime? They should instead ask what stops people from offending? Therefore, it might be that women in general make useful case studies as a group of people who are subject to greater social control than men (Heidensohn 1996). There are two overlapping hypotheses to consider here: do women have more controls and restrictions placed upon them, or do they just have fewer opportunities to offend?

Less opportunity to commit crime

The argument here is that the gendered pattern of employment has presented men with greater opportunities for offending than women. Men are more likely to be employed in jobs that provide opportunities for theft – such as working on the docks, airport loading, van driving, the building trade and antique dealing – which all provide access to opportunities for crime. If women have been traditionally employed in the home, they will have more restricted opportunities. As women enter the labour market, their work-based opportunities for offending are more likely to lead to white-collar crime than other types. These offences are less likely to be detected, and it can be argued that at a petty level the line between criminal and non-criminal does become blurred.

Women are more controlled

In her book *Women and Crime*, Frances Heidensohn (1996) argues that women are far more controlled than men. Adolescent girls tend to be given less freedom by parents than their male siblings. Daughters are seen as more vulnerable – to the risk of pregnancy, for example – and are given less freedom than their brothers. As adults, women are still more likely to take on direct responsibility for child rearing. It is these responsibilities that keep a check on their behaviour. In addition, so much public space has traditionally been masculine. Pubs and clubs where men might gather and meet others involved in crime have been spaces from which women are excluded. So, overall, the argument here is a largely sociological one: women are more watched, controlled, and too busy to commit crime.

In addition to the questions of why women commit less crime than men and, perhaps, in what ways women differ from men, there is also the question of the women who do commit crime – how might they be different from other women?

Pathological women?

Whether we assume that the reason for women's lower offending rates is that they are more controlled, or, for some reason, they are more conforming, the question arises as to whether women who do commit offences are a more deviant group. If it is true that men often fulfil a masculine ideal by criminal behaviour (Messerschmidt 1993), then it cannot be said that women are fulfilling a feminine ideal. It has certainly been a long-standing belief of those involved in criminal justice that female offenders are more likely to be sick rather than simply criminal (Smart 1976). Recent work on female juvenile offenders has been informed by this assumption (Maden *et al.* 1992; Dixon *et al.* 2004). However, when comparisons have been made of the mental states of male and female offenders, differences do not seem very apparent. Fazel *et al.*'s (2002) meta-analysis of 62 surveys of prison populations has already been discussed in Chapter 3 (pp. 39–41) and indicates that women prisoners are not diagnosed with mental disorder any more frequently than men. In fact, when the, perhaps controversial, category of personality disorder is taken into account, male prisoners are more likely to exhibit mental disorder. The evidence of these surveys suggests that women who reach the prison end of the justice system are not more likely than men to be suffering from mental illness. It needs to be emphasised, however, that levels of mental disorder are high among both men and women in prison.

As already noted, the detailed longitudinal studies of what leads to criminality have tended to concern themselves with boys. Therefore, easy comparison between pathways to more everyday delinquency are hard to make. Caplan *et al.* (1980) carried out a study of referrals made to a psychiatric clinic for juveniles in Toronto, Canada, which sought to address the issue of gender differences. They used a large sample in an area not dogged by the high levels of social deprivation of the US ones. The sample was made up of offenders who had been recommended for treatment by a court (1050 boys and 383 girls; aged 7–16 years). They found that the girls had generally less serious offences (frequently less serious theft, truancy, and drinking under age).

They analysed a large number of variables to do with the history of the young offender, psychiatric symptoms, educational record, family history, social life, friendships, and history of offending. They found that for the majority of variables, there were no significant differences between the males and females. Girls tended to be referred later in their career, were more likely to have a history of separations from parents, more likely to be living apart from parents, and more likely to be in care. On the other hand, boys had more psychiatric symptoms and behaviour difficulties earlier. The authors conclude that they had found no confirmation that female offenders are more deviant than male offenders.

Pre-menstrual syndrome (PMS)

Just like the interest in male hormones as stimulants of criminality among men, there has been parallel interest in hormones as causes of female deviance. As women experience regular monthly changes in hormone levels, these have been associated with mood and behavioural

Table 6.2 Time of offences ($n = 156$)
(Dalton 1961)

Day of cycle	Number	%
1–4	41	26
5–8	13	8
9–12	20	13
13–16	21	13
17–20	19	12
21–24	7	5
25–28	35	22.4

changes. Both Freud and Pollack suggested that women became aggressive at times of menstruation because of the unfairness of it all. It has become common parlance for women to consider themselves as being emotional around menstrual times. Dalton (1961) examined the relationship between criminal behaviour and menstruation. She interviewed 156 female prisoners, asking them when in their monthly cycles they committed the offences (Table 6.2).

In Table 6.2, days 1–4 refers to actual menstruation, so days 25–28 is the premenstrual phase. It seems, on the face of it, to be quite striking that almost 50 per cent of offences occurred around menstruation. There are some problems with entirely accepting the findings. The data are based on retrospective self-reports. Arguably, the women may have felt that their behaviour would be seen in a better light if they had been affected by menstruation. However, since then this has become a controversial area with some arguing, and some data suggesting, that the experience of premenstrual mood changes is affected by social expectations that arise out of particular social conditions (Ussher 2006). Johnson (1987) took an anthropological perspective and argued that pre-menstrual syndrome (PMS) ought to be viewed as a culture-bound disorder, restricted to the West and that it came about through cultural conflict about the role of women.

PMS has, however, been used successfully in the courts. In 1980, a barmaid, Sandra Cradock, pleaded not guilty to the charge of murdering another woman, on the grounds of diminished responsibility: her plea of manslaughter was accepted. Sentencing was delayed while Cradock underwent progesterone treatment, which was seen as successful, and she received a probation order rather than a prison sentence (Easteal 1991). Easteal (1991: 8) concludes in her review of the use of PMS in courts that it 'should not be used frivolously but ought to be restricted to cases involving the small minority of women whose premenstrual symptoms are so incapacitating that they lack the necessary criminal intent'.

Female violence and the increase of female criminality?

If it were true that female criminality is relatively low due to pressures of socialisation, or of social control, we would expect to see levels of female criminality increasing as social roles shift. Anecdotal reports of levels of violence increasing among girls are becoming common. A report in *Newsweek* entitled 'Bad girls go wild' (Scelfo and Adams 2005) is typical of many popular reports that recount the salacious details of violence by girls, and point to seemingly alarming percentage increases. Leschied *et al.* (2001) provided a more sober review of the evidence, and their starting point is evidence of an increase in officially reported incidents of violence by girls in Canada. They are at pains to point out, however, that the base rates for such incidents is very low, and the overall rates are still very small compared to violence by boys.

Steffensmeier *et al.* (2005: 394) use detailed analyses of US data to argue that there is no real increase in female violent crime. They argue that the apparent rises are due to a number of policy shifts that have effectively widened the net so that more female violence is likely to be reported. These shifts include widening the definitions of violence so that more minor incidents are included, and less tolerance within families and schools of young people's behaviour. They conclude (2005: 397):

> The rise in girls' violence, it appears then, is more a social construction than an empirical reality. It is not so much that girls have become any more violent; it is that the avenues to prevent or punish violence have grown so enormously.

There has been sporadic interest in the involvement of girls in gangs, although the focus of much of the work on gangs has been on boys throughout most of the past century (Chesney-Lind and Hagedorn 1999). Girls have tended to be viewed either as bit part players in gangs (as providers of sexual services to the male gang members, for example) or, more recently, as forming gangs that emulate and rival male gangs (Joe Laidler and Hunt 2001). Overall, it is hard to find very hard evidence that female crime is becoming more significant.

One area where women do seem to hold their own against men in terms of numbers of violent incidents is in violence against their own children (Polk 1994). This issue will be discussed in the next chapter.

Conclusion

There is increasing interest in exploring gender as a key variable that might help us understand criminal behaviour. The vast majority of crime is committed by men. An important fact concerning the differential rates of crime is that the finding of relatively high levels of criminality among men compared to women appears to be quite a robust one across cultures. This might suggest that there is something constitutional in the differences between men and women. However, the different rates of serious crime across cultures and the evidence of some variation across time (Feeley and Little 1991) suggest that culture and environment have their parts to play as well. It may therefore be that we do need to use theories of gender that are both more culturally sensitive and more able to integrate issues of individual psychology.

The next two chapters will explore particular categories of offending – violence and crimes of intimacy (sexual and 'domestic' violence) – in which there is certainly a preponderance of male offenders, and there are perhaps good reasons to think that the masculinity of those offenders is significant.

Note

1 Motz (2001) makes the important suggestion that when the girl's identification with the mother is quite negative, this can have important psychological implications (to be discussed in the next section on women and crime).

Chapter 7

Understanding violence: learning from studies of homicide

Introduction

In looking more closely at crimes of violence, this chapter will begin by shifting the analysis away from a search for distal causes of crime (such as the backgrounds of the offenders) toward looking at what we can learn from examining the immediate circumstances of violent incidents. Katz (1988) was critical of criminological approaches that were too 'preoccupied with a search for background factors, usually defects in the offender's psychological backgrounds or social environments', and argued that more attention needed to be given to the immediate event of the criminal act itself, in particular 'the positive, often wonderful attractions within the lived experience of criminality' (Katz 1988: 3). There is a body of work that, while not quite following Katz' suggestion of exploring what it 'feels, sounds, tastes, or looks like to commit a particular crime' (1988: 3), has looked in detail at who harms whom in what particular circumstances. It will be argued that an examination of the detail of violent events can actually lead us to a better understanding of the wider context and give us fresh perspectives on the motivations for violent crime.

This chapter will be particularly concerned with 'homicide', that is, the killing of a human being by another. Although homicide is a comparatively rare act, it can be a very useful crime to study. This is so, first, because it is a violent event that is relatively easy to define. Someone has died, and this is a comparatively robust 'fact' – there is a corpse. Second, the details of the event tend to be recorded (very often in considerable detail). Although there may be occasions when the cause of death is uncertain – there might be doubt about whether a death had resulted from an act of suicide or murder, for example – these difficulties are infrequent compared to the great difficulties faced by those studying other forms of violence in which issues of definition become highly convoluted (Levi 1997). The point at which someone's aggression toward others can be considered a violent crime is open to great dispute and historical and cross-cultural variation. The likelihood of such acts of violence being reported and recorded is also subject to similar variation. Hence, studies of homicide, despite the comparative rarity of the incidences, have been fertile territory for studying crimes of violence.

Observations of the significance of interactions between victims of violence and the perpetrators have been made for some time (e.g. Wolfgang 1958; Luckenbill 1977; Polk 1994). There are important consistencies between the observations made in these studies (notably the prominence of male violence) that will be discussed in detail in this chapter. The consistencies have, however, been used in very different ways to argue, on the one hand, for the importance of cultural factors in determining behaviour in these scenarios, and, on the other hand, for the ultimate significance of biological imperatives in shaping violent incidents. It will be argued here that these data illustrate very directly how people must be understood as functioning within specific immediate circumstances, but also within their own histories and cultures. Close analysis of these acts reveals that they require a psychological analysis in order to become comprehendible, but that they are psychological events that are linked to wider social and cultural issues.

The first part of the chapter will review a number of studies that have examined in some detail the circumstances in which homicides occur. Several useful perspectives are suggested by analysis of these studies. One striking fact is that men are the perpetrators in the overwhelming majority of cases. Other important facts to emerge are that the largest categories of homicide are, first, those that occur within the context of either sexual or family relationships, and, second, those that involve 'confrontational' violence between men (that is disputes that 'flare up', often over seemingly minor matters). The significance of violence occurring within family and sexual relationships will be pursued further in the next chapter. The second part of this chapter will meanwhile focus on understanding the phenomenon of violence (and particularly murder) occurring in the context of confrontation and 'rage'. The third part of the chapter will explore the possibility that some individuals are more prone to these rage reactions, and that these reactions can be understood within the context of their life histories and personalities. The fourth part of the chapter will explore the circumstances of female violence. It is notable that not only are there far fewer such incidents involving female violence, but also the pattern of offences is rather different.

Scenarios of homicide

Luckenbill (1977) carried out a study of 71 homicides that were committed over a 10-year period in one county in California. Luckenbill's analysis was heavily influenced by Goffman's (1959) work on the importance of social scripts in understanding social behaviour, so the emphasis was on examining the event in terms of a 'situated transaction'. The relevance of analysis of the social meaning of the acts is certainly suggested by the fact that so many homicides took place in front of an audience (a finding confirmed by other studies, such as Polk 1994). Luckenbill identified the following stages in the interactions between offenders and their (eventual) victims:

1 The first move, often initiated by the (eventual) victim, was to act in a way that is perceived by the (eventual) offender as some kind of challenge. This might be a verbal insult directed at the offender, his family or his friends. It might be a refusal to comply with the wishes or requests of the offender, or it might involve some non-verbal or physical gesture.

2 The initial act of the victim is perceived as being a personal affront. Luckenbill is careful to point out that it is the offender's perception that is crucial here, and the perception might be far from rational.

3 The offender chooses to respond to the perceived insult by making some kind of 'retaliatory move aimed at restoring face and demonstrating strong character' (1977: 181). Other options might be to ignore, or find some reason to excuse, the insult. These options are not taken in the cases that lead to homicide. Luckenbill found that 14 per cent of the retaliations at this stage involved physical retribution that immediately led to the death of the victim. Most cases were an attempt to salvage face by verbal or physical means. Most often, there was some indication of contempt aimed at the victim.

4 Stage 4 involves the victims deciding how to respond to the dilemma that they have been presented with; they have now been issued with a challenge to their own strength of character. Like the offender in stage 3, they have a range of options, which might include apologising or leaving the situation. In the cases of homicide, these more benign options are not taken, and the challenge is returned – sometimes verbally, sometimes physically.

5 Luckenbill argues that once the victim has decided not to stand down from conflict, there is then, effectively, a 'working agreement' between the offender and victim that violence is the way to resolve the situation, and there is some kind of physical altercation. In the cases studied by Luckenbill, this led to the death of the victim.

6 As the victim falls, the transaction is ended either by the offender fleeing the scene or staying there, voluntarily or involuntarily, to be apprehended by the police.

Luckenbill concluded that 'murder is the outcome of a dynamic interchange between an offender, victim, and in many cases, bystanders. The offender and the victim develop lines of action shaped in part by the actions of the other and focused toward saving or maintaining face and reputation and demonstrating character' (Luckenbill 1977: 186–7).

A great deal of work on violence, and homicide in particular, confirms a number of these observations. A particularly thorough study of incidences of homicide was carried out by Kenneth Polk, who studied all the homicides that were known to have taken place between 1985 and 1989 in the Australian state of Victoria (Polk 1994). Polk's fine-grained analysis deserves further attention. Polk also found that frequent incidences of homicide occur in front of an audience (70 per cent of the cases of 'confrontational homicide', for example), a finding that certainly helps to substantiate Luckenbill's stance that such violence needs to be understood in terms of the social meaning of these acts. While Polk also found that an audience was often a significant factor, he made great theoretical use of the fact that the overwhelming majority of the offenders were male. Luckenbill had also found that men were in the great majority of the offenders, but had made little theoretical use of this in his analysis. Polk, using the often highly detailed case records, provides an analysis of 381 cases of homicide and breaks the killings down into categories, as shown in Table 7.1.

Table 7.1 Categories of homicide in Victoria, Australia (from Polk 1994)

Context of sexual intimacy	101	27%
Confrontational homicides	84	22%
Homicides originating in family intimacy	40	11%
Originating in other crime	61	16%
Conflict resolution	38	10%
Victims of mass killers	15	4%
Unsolved/unclassifiable	22	6%
Special cases	18	5%
Mercy killing	1	<1%
Total	380	100%

There was a clear preponderance of men among the offenders, just 43 of the offenders being female (11 per cent). This proportion is confirmed by official records on homicide in the UK, where, in a sample of over 2000 offenders, 89.7 per cent were male (Francis *et al.* 2004). The largest category of killing in Polk's study was 'homicides occurring in the context of sexual intimacy', (*n*=101), which will be discussed in more detail in Chapter 8. The related category of 'homicides originating in family intimacy' was also large. Most of these involved parents killing their children. This latter category is the one area where women hold their own in terms of numbers. Female familial violence is discussed in more detail in the next chapter. Fourteen of the child victims were killed by their mothers, and 14 were killed by their fathers (in two cases, both parents were deemed responsible, and in another, responsibility was not assigned). The second largest category of homicide is referred to as 'confrontational homicide' (*n*=84, 22 per cent of all homicides), which will be looked at in more detail here.

Confrontational homicide

The overwhelming majority of these incidents featured men as both victim and offender. Just four (5 per cent) of these confrontational homicides involved women as victims and offenders. While there are a number of slightly different scenarios included here, the typical confrontational homicide involved one man fatally attacking another after some dispute. Here is a typical case (Polk 1994: 60), the killing of Gabe W., a 32-year-old soldier:

Gabe W. boarded a train at Flinders Street station after an evening of drinking with his friends. When Gabe attempted to take a seat where Mike M. was sitting with his feet spread across 2 seats, Mike ordered him, 'offensively', to move onto another seat. Challenged, Gabe refused, and attempted to force his way onto the seat. Mike leaped up and struck Gabe, and the two fought. Although Gabe received a number of blows, and was kneed in the face, he finally managed to pin Mike down.

Witnesses relate that at this point Gabe said: 'If you don't stop now, I'll break your neck.' Then, believing that Mike would stop, Gabe released him. Mike instead produced a knife, stabbing Gabe three times in the chest. One of the blows penetrated the heart. Gabe collapsed and died in the aisle.

A number of themes can be picked out of this case; the killing occurs through two men confronting each other over a minor matter, the confrontation occurs in a public place, and the participants had both been drinking alcohol. Perhaps the very trivial nature of the precipitating events is the most striking point. In an earlier study of homicide in the US city of Philadelphia, Wolfgang (1958) had drawn attention to the size of this category. Fagan and Wilkinson (1998) also provide examples of fatal violence occurring in response to seemingly trivial slights. The encounter could be broken down into the kind of sequence outlined by Luckenbill:

1 challenge: 'Can you move?'
2 rebuttal: '*1?- off!'
3 escalating challenge (more physical – sits anyway)
4 recourse to physical violence
5 escalation of violence, including use of the weapon.

Archer (1994) compares this kind of sequence of events to an intraspecies animal fight and notes a number of differences, such as the use of alcohol and weapons (although some animal species can be 'armed' with teeth and claws). Archer also notes that in a conflict between two animals of the same species, 'Fights stop when one animal abruptly ceases fighting, leaving the other one victorious' (Archer 1994: 130). While other animals tend to get out of dangerous situations, where there is little to gain, as soon as possible – human males – of the most intelligent species on the planet, sometimes fight to the death over a trivial resource such as a seat (as Mike and Gabe demonstrate). Two possible explanations suggest themselves:

1 Men are actually very stupid, driven by primitive instincts over which they have no control.
2 Alternatively, the apparently trivial event must be understood in a different way. Perhaps it can be viewed as something that has great meaning to the participants. There is perhaps something at stake to the participants that is far more valuable than the chance to sit down on a train journey.

Daly and Wilson (1988: 128) argue that the explanation lies within the second alternative and that:

> the emphasis on 'triviality' obscures a still more important point. A seemingly minor affront is not merely a 'stimulus' to action, isolated in time and space. It must be understood within a larger social context of reputations, face, relative social status, and enduring relationships.
>
> (Daly and Wilson 1988: 128)

They suggest that it is helpful to understand that the men were not really fighting over a trivial object (such as a train seat) but were involved in a far more powerful symbolic battle over *reputation*. Thus, the fact that many of these events occur in public might well be of significance. The loss of face or reputation can occur only if there are witnesses. Perhaps the men are involved in a defence of their public identities. Gilligan (1997: 112) argues that the very triviality of some of these events is significant and points to understanding of the role of shame in these incidents. On one level, the participants may know that feeling so belittled by someone threatening to take a seat from them is 'pathetic', but that will only provoke further feelings of shame that in turn may make violence more likely. The significance of shame as one of the 'moral emotions' has been discussed in previous chapters, particularly in relation to the development of morality in families and in adolescence. Meanwhile, however, the question that needs to be answered, is why it is individual *men* rather than women who seem prone to violence in such confrontations.

Understanding masculine rage and violence

Two explanations for the association between violent rage and masculinity can be assessed. First, there is the evolutionary explanation of such behaviour as having evolved, so that it may now be in a sense programmed within male genes. Second, there are explanations that make links between the responses of individuals within particular cultural contexts to emotions such as shame. These responses are being mediated within masculine ways of being.

An evolutionary explanation

Daly and Wilson (1988) argue that confrontational violence like this can be understood as a product of the evolutionary history of human beings. They suggest that men in such situations are acting in accordance with their genetic inheritance. For men 'reputation' is very important because at least for male ancestors, it was reputation for strength and toughness that determined their place in the group hierarchy and their access to resources and sexual partners (the latter point being particularly pertinent to an evolutionary explanation). As Daly and Wilson (1988: 128) put it,

> A seemingly minor affront is not merely a 'stimulus' to action, isolated in time and space. It must be understood within the larger social context of reputations, face, relative social status and enduring relationships. Men are known by their fellows as the sort 'who can be pushed around' or 'the sort that won't take any shit', as people whose word means action and people who are full of hot air, as guys whose girlfriends you can chat up with impunity or guys you don't want to mess with. In most social milieus, a man's reputation depends in part upon the maintenance of a credible threat to violence.

Thus, Gabe and Mike (whose confrontation is described by Polk and summarised above) were perhaps defending their places in an imagined hierarchy. Any loss of face might have involved them in some fall in this imagined social hierarchy. Assuming that that social hierarchy also determined how likely an individual was to attract sexual partners, then such a fall would reduce the likelihood of their reproducing. According to Daly and Wilson, 'masculine' behaviour has evolved to be sensitive to such reductions in reproductive potential. As will be discussed in the next chapter, evidence of incidents of violence occurring within the context of sexual relationships might also be used to give credence to this evolutionary account of male violence (in particular, through discussions of jealousy). The challenges that the evolutionary accounts still face, at the moment, are to pin down behavioural differences between men and women in physiological differences between males and females (as discussed in relation to biological explanations in Chapter 6). Other theoretical attempts to understand the phenomenon of confrontational violence have taken a more psychological perspective, examining the experiences of the protagonists in terms of the emotional reactions involved and making links to their psychological history.

Shame, respect and violence

The last chapter on gender and crime examined theories that suggested that men are less likely than women to have a secure sense of identity. Masculinity has been argued to be a culturally more ascribed status, with men being required to prove their strength and independence (Gilmore 1991). More psychologically, it is also argued that boys' identities are less likely to be built on identifications they make with men as they grow up (as men may not be around during their childhoods), but is more dependent on identifications made with cultural images of masculinity. Such identifications are thus more fragile. Girls, it is argued, often have the advantage of being able to build their feminine identities through relationship with women who are present during their childhood. Previous chapters have also considered the significance of shame as a 'moral emotion'. It was suggested in Chapter 4 ('Familial and Parental Influences') that while shame does act as a powerful signal of social disapproval, its presence does not necessarily lead to pro-social behaviour, but instead it needs to be processed into the more reflective feeling of guilt before more reparative and constructive behaviour can follow. A case can be made that the bringing of these two theories together might well help us understand the phenomena of masculine rage. As discussed in Chapter 4, shame is a signal of disapproval that is invoked as people feel that they are failing to reach a required standard of behaviour. Men, it can be argued, are more prone to experience shame, as they are more likely to feel that their identities are flawed in some way, because their identities are perhaps more dependent upon constant external approval (as discussed in Chapter 6, 'Gender and Crime').

Katz (1988) has written in some detail on the significance of *humiliation* as a trigger for violence. Katz adopted a phenomenological approach in trying to understand the experiences of people who had become violent. In these cases, he refers to the way that the offenders convert feelings of humiliation, via feelings of righteousness, into rage. In focusing on the phenomenology of humiliation, Katz (1998: 25) draws attention to the emotion of shame:

In humiliation, the person is overcome with an intolerable discomfort. Humiliation forces him to feel himself as soul, to become intensely aware that his being is spiritual, not protected by physical barriers between the internal and the external. ... Humiliation takes over the soul by invading the whole body. The humiliated body is unbearably alive; one's very being is humiliated.

There is now a developing literature that seeks to link violent incidents, such as the confrontational homicides described by Polk (1994), with study of the emotion of shame. To recap very briefly the discussion of Chapter 4, while a precise definition of shame that satisfies everyone remains elusive (Pattison 2000), it may be roughly defined as the feeling that the self is somehow lacking. It is the powerful feeling of wanting to disappear, to be unseen. As in Katz's description of humiliation, shame involves an unpleasant awareness of the self.

Gilligan (2003: 1997) became interested in the connection between shame and violence through his clinical work with offenders. He noticed how frequently he heard them describe how they felt that being 'disrespected' was a justification for their violence. This rationale was used to justify incidents similar to the confrontational homicide events that have been discussed. Gilligan also noted that feelings of respect and pride came out as significant in the commission of crimes such as robbery as well. As one offender he spoke to put it, 'I never got so much *respect* before in my life as I did when I pointed a gun at some dude's face' (2003: 1149). Similar points about the significance of pride emerge from interviews with convicted robbers in the UK (discussed on pp. 193–4 of this chapter). Gilligan argues that

> the basic psychological motive, or cause, of violent behaviour is the wish to ward off or eliminate the feeling of shame and humiliation – a feeling that is painful and can even be intolerable and overwhelming – and replace it with its opposite, the feeling of pride.

> (Gilligan 2003: 1154)

This chimes well with Katz' description of rage being used to overcome feelings of humiliation, and is also consistent with the shame-rage cycles described by Lewis (1987; see also Nathan 1987). Gilligan argues that people may act violently as they experience degrees of shame so intense that it threatens the cohesion and viability of the self. Gilligan

(2003: 1168) uses contemporary psychoanalytic theory (as discussed in the previous chapter) to argue that shame is a powerful feeling, as it signals disapproval and alarm that social bonds are threatened and evokes feelings from infancy about the danger of being disapproved of and thus rejected and abandoned:

> The fear that underlies and stimulates feelings of shame is the fear that one will be abandoned, rejected, or ignored and will therefore die because one is so weak, helpless, dependent, unskilled, and incompetent that one cannot take care of oneself, because of which one is also so inferior, unlovable, and unworthy of love that one probably will be abandoned.

There might be two ways of overcoming such feelings. People could communicate how they feel to others, and thus seek reassurance that they are not being rejected and at risk of abandonment and isolation. This is potentially a precarious strategy for those who are already concerned with exposing weakness and vulnerability, as asking for help might evoke those feelings of dependency that will threaten their (fragile) sense of masculine strength and autonomy. Alternatively, people can simply seek to expel any feelings of weakness by demonstrating how strong and powerful they are, by acting with violence. This is an example of the 'bypassed shame' that Helen Block Lewis described (e.g. Lewis 1987) that can lead to shame-rage cycles (Scheff 1987, 2003). Ray *et al.* (2004) use a similar model to explain racist violence.

Of course, Gilligan has to acknowledge that while experiences of shame and humiliation are universal, they rarely lead directly to violence. Various theories have been put forward to suggest why some people might be prone to rage-type violence in terms of the personalities of the perpetrators, and these will first be reviewed, before returning to Gilligan's own ideas concerned with the role of self-esteem and masculinity.

Personality types and confrontational rage murder

The perpetrators of rage-type crimes have consistently been of interest to psychologists and psychiatrists because these people have often appeared to be psychologically 'normal' until they carry out the attack. Cartwright (2002) reviewed the work of various clinicians who have sought to understand the psychology of those committing acts of violence through rage. A number of strong themes emerge from a review of this work. The first observation is that, as Polk's study well demonstrates, many rage-type murders occur in the context of sexual intimacy. While crimes of violence that occur in the context of sexual relationships will be explored in more detail in the next chapter, Meloy (1992) argues that this fact should alert us to the significance of intimate attachments and the emotions that they involve in understanding rage violence in general. The second observation is that, although the offender will often have presented a quite normal personality to the world, up until the event, this has been disguising considerable inner turmoil. Wertham (1962) refers to the idea of 'catathymic' crisis to argue that rage murders might appear as sudden eruptions but have actually been prepared for a long time. Third, Cartwright argues that those prone to rage violence often have a poor capacity for mental representation of their own emotions. Each of these last two points will be discussed (the significance of sexual intimacy as a trigger for violence will be considered in more detail in the following chapter).

Putting on a front or 'false self'

Using psychoanalytic language, Cartwright (2002), suggests that rage murderers frequently exhibit a 'narcissistic exoskeleton'. This 'defensive organization [is] characterized by a rigid split between a constellation of idealized object relations and internalized bad objects, where the former assumes the position of an outer "holding" personality' (2002: 113). In other words, people develop a false self, meaning that they present an ideal version of themselves to the world. Underneath, there are very angry and unhappy feelings. The ideal, false self requires constant reinforcement and reassurance from other people, as it is not being reinforced from within. Relationships with other people are likely to remain superficial, as they are required only to play an admiring role at a distance. Too much intimacy would allow others to see beneath the false self. Difficulties arise when the ideal image presented to the world is threatened by the intrusion of reality, and the hidden angry feelings can no longer be contained by the exoskeleton. Lasch (1979) argued that this personality type was becoming ever more common as a result of cultures of superficiality and consumerism (discussed in the concluding chapter).

Cartwright uses the case study of 'Andrew' to illustrate this personality formation. Andrew grew up with little respect for his alcoholic father, who was often violent to his mother. While his mother looked after him materially, it was not an affectionate relationship. Perhaps not surprisingly Andrew quickly grew to put a great deal of store on 'independence'. His self-image as strong and independent was reinforced as he became a successful sportsman, gaining a certain amount of fame and popularity. Any emotional needs he had were apparently met by his own success and the company and support of admiring sporting friends. Material wealth and status symbols became important to his sense of well-being. As his sporting career came to a natural end, he went into sports-related business activities, in which he experienced some difficulties. His marriage broke down, with little apparent emotional impact on him. He was let down by a business partner, who suddenly left the country, leading to the business being liquidated. Andrew started another company that was more successful. The ex-partner who had previously left returned and demanded a job in the new company. Although Andrew refused this demand, he did agree to meet the man (who was known to be quite aggressive) to talk the situation through.

> However, the meeting escalated into a heated argument about their past business relationship. Moments later, without hesitation, Andrew shot his former partner several times, killing him instantly. Before the outburst he recalled trying to sit and calm himself but 'felt a deep pain that [he had] never felt before ... something very powerful.
>
> (2002: 115)

Cartwright's explanation for this is that Andrew had built a personality that was like an 'exoskeleton' around himself. The personality that Andrew presented to the world was cut off from his feelings and history. The very angry feelings, provoked mainly by the neglect from his father, were hidden away. The exoskeleton, rather fragile and disconnected from Andrew's own history, depended on constant reinforcement from people around him, who would play their part in supporting this image of the successful, popular sportsman and businessman. The ex-business partner by not playing the part, by treating him without respect, effectively fractured this outer shell and allowed the more aggressive feelings to come to the fore.

Failure of representational capacity

Cartwright (2002) argues that violence can also be understood as occurring in some individuals when there is failure of representational capacity. Cartwright describes the case of 'Philip', who killed a neighbour in a parking rage incident outside his house. This appears to be a classic example of confrontational homicide as described by Polk (1994). Philip had no history of violence, and he had a successful career for which he was much admired. The violence was directed at a neighbour, described as a friend, who had clearly admired Philip for his career success. They had an argument about a parking space, the neighbour insulted Philip, and this led to the violence. It seems that the lack of respect here is again crucial; it was experienced as 'a danger' to his life. As he himself describes it, in the face of this disrespect, thought seemed to stop:

> When he said 'fuck you', I lost it and felt there was no way out. It was like I had lost myself actually and become numb to everything around me. ... Something snapped and told me that it would never be the same again. ... He was my neighbour, a friend. We had never fought before, but at that moment it was like he was someone else, a kind of danger to my life who would not hear what I was saying.
>
> (Cartwright 2002: 168)

At this point, Philip hit the man several times, chased after him when he tried to run away, and then killed him by beating his head against the kerb several times. Cartwright (2002) suggests that there is significance in the fact that a few weeks before the incident Philip had made a mistake at work that had led to his being criticised. At the time, Philip had taken this badly and had contemplated leaving the job, but had carried on, and things had seemed to return to normal. However, his image of himself had been shaken by the episode, and this new incident in which his formerly respectful neighbour was showing him disrespect provided another threat to his identity that led to his being quite unable to think, and he could only act (with violence).

Fonagy *et al.* (2003) have argued that moments of failure of representational capacity, when thought seems to stop and simple feeling and action take over, can be linked to early familial relationships. This work has already been discussed in Chapter 3 in relation to theories of personality disorder. Fonagy *et al.* (2003) argue that the ability to represent (mentalise) one's own feelings and reflect on them is a developmental achievement that depends on close and empathic relationships in the early years of life. People who have not developed a strong ability to represent themselves mentally and emotionally may, particularly at times of stress, be unable to think about feeling at all. They are left simply to respond to those feelings. As discussed earlier, shame is a particularly powerful emotion that has been associated with violence, as it brings with it a threat to a person's self.

Gilligan (1997) argues that the following preconditions make violent response to shame more likely: the lack of capacity for guilt, the lack of alternative means of building esteem, and dependence on the traditional masculine gender role. Each of these will be briefly discussed, as they provide a useful way of summarising a number of issues that have been discussed previously in the book.

Individual has not developed capacity for guilt

Gilligan (1997, 2003) argues that most people, as they experience feelings of anger and wanting to harm others, usually also experience concomitant feelings of guilt, self-reproach, pity and even love. For violence to occur, it must be either that the particular conditions overwhelm any such feelings of guilt, or the individuals themselves have no, or only limited, capacity to feel guilt or other inhibitory emotions. Gilligan (1997: 113) observed that feelings of guilt seemed to be absent from the offenders he worked with: 'No-one feels as innocent as the criminals; their lack of guilt feelings, even over the most atrocious of crimes, is one of their most prominent characteristics.' As discussed previously (see Chapter 4, particularly in relation to the development of the moral emotions), the ability to process shame into more reflective feelings of guilt can be regarded as a developmental accomplishment. Fongay et al. (2003) argue that good, empathic relationships are needed in children's early life to help them develop an internal sense of themselves and their emotions, and hence the capacity to reflect on their own feelings. The development of the moral emotions was also traced in adolescence (see Chapter 5).

Lack of alternative means of restoring self-esteem

Most people who feel humiliated by a particular experience often feel they can restore a sense of pride by recourse to different means other than violence. In the face of a threat to esteem, most people will be aware of other factors in their lives of which they can feel proud. A man who is disrespected by someone else, perhaps over an argument over a parking space (like Philip above), may be relatively unaffected if he feels that he is respected in other ways. He may be able to shrug off the incident if he feels secure in being valued in other aspects of his life – in his family or career, for example. However, if he is humiliated and feels trapped, and feels that he has no alternative means of saving face, this is a potentially dangerous situation.

There are important parallels here with the work discussed in Chapter 6 'Gender and Crime', on how masculinity can be regarded as a fragile status. A masculine identity has been portrayed as one that often has to be reinforced and protected. Messerschmidt (1993) argued that crime and violence are often culturally sanctioned ways in which men who are marginalised from more legitimate forms of securing reputation can establish a masculine identity.

If the individual has been socialised into the male gender role

Gilligan argues that cultural norms of masculinity that surround males are important factors in explaining violence. Men are likely to resort to violence as a way of warding off feelings of shame if they have been socialised into a 'typical' male gender role, that places emphasis on physical strength and violence as a means to solve problems and from which men can derive esteem. This 'means he has been taught that there are many circumstances and situations in which one has to be violent in order to maintain one's masculinity or sense of masculine sexual identity and adequacy, and in which a non-violent man would be seen as impotent and emasculated, a coward, wimp, eunuch, boy, homosexual, or women, a man who has no balls'. Feelings of shame are often denied and repressed:

> Behind the mask of 'cool' or self assurance that many violent men clamp onto their faces – with a desperation born of the certain knowledge that they would 'lose face' if they ever let it slip – is a person who feels vulnerable not just to 'loss of face' but to the total loss of honor, prestige, respect and status – the disintegration of identity, especially their adult, masculine, heterosexual identity; their selfhood, personhood, rationality, and sanity.
>
> (Gilligan 1997: 112)

Thus, although factors of individual development may play their part, so do cultural images and constructions of masculinity.

Gangs, boys, street crime and masculinity

While the analysis of the significance of masculinity emerged from studies of homicide, it is one that has relevance for understanding

193

more common acts of violence. Wright *et al.* (2006) report on interviews with offenders serving sentences for robbery in the UK. They argue that previous studies have tended to accept the rational explanations of why people became robbers. Morrison and O'Donnell (1996), for example, argue that armed robbers made rational calculations involving the minimum amount they would expect to gain from committing a robbery, alongside their calculations about the likelihood of getting caught, and the possible sentences they might receive. Their explanations of their own behaviour are that they rob people because they need the money. Willott and Griffin (1999) give similar accounts of individual men presenting their motives for being involved in crime. Wright *et al.* (2006) take issue with this analysis and argue that, although the people that they interviewed did indeed often say that they robbed for money, analysis of why they needed the money was revealing. High on the agenda were the material trappings of success and status. Cars, jewellery and designer clothes were considered important because of the public statement they made. Some of the interview material reported by Wright *et al.* (2006) points very clearly to issues of masculinity and identity. Karl, for example, directly reports a lack of money as making him feel 'like shit', but when he has money he feels 'big':

> I just love money, it's like I feel big when I got money, like when I haven't got money, it feels like shit, do you know what I mean, 'cause I like to be able to do stuff. I like to have the money, it's like secure ... having money, I love, I love money, I love money.
> (Wright *et al.* 2006: 9)

Similarly, Fagan and Wilkinson (1998: 164) report that those involved in the violent world of drug gangs in the urban USA described themselves as being 'drawn into drug selling by the lure of "easy money" and having the means to acquire the "gear" (clothes, jewelry, sneakers, guns, and other accessories'. The money from the drugs business is spent on adorning the body, the outward marks of success. Jonathan (interviewed by Wright *et al.* 2006: 8) makes the link between cash, status and sexuality very clear:

> Lads always have the money. Always have the cash on 'em like. Even when we don't need it, got to have a ready supply. ... We all sit around and look at our piles, counting our stashes of cash, innit. ... Just to show off to the girls, like. The more money you had, the more status.

Perhaps a great deal of violence can therefore be understood in terms of men defending masculine identities. Male violence will be explored further in the next chapter that examines sexual violence and violence that occurs within intimate relationships. The next section looks at those relatively rare cases of homicide committed by women.

Women who kill

Despite the repeated claims that women's crimes often go undetected, data from studies of homicide (where the evidence that a crime has been committed and evidence about the circumstances of the crime tend to be kept in detail) strongly confirm that men commit far more murder than women. Francis *et al.* (2004), for example, present figures suggesting that less than 11 per cent of homicides in the UK are committed by women. Kenneth Polk's (1991, 1994) study confirms a similar rate of homicide by women. Polk also analyses the homicides that are carried out by women. They are not only smaller in number but also they are sufficiently different from male homicides in terms of the pattern of offences to merit a separate analysis. While 43 homicides, or 11 per cent of the sample he looked at, involved female perpetrators, just 9 per cent of the cases involved *only* female perpetrators acting without men. Women hardly feature at all in the category of confrontational homicide (only four out of 84 confrontational homicides involved female perpetrators). There were two main types that involved fatal female violence: killing sexual partners (often in response to being a victim of violence) and mothers killing their own children. The killing of sexual partners often seems to occur as a result of quite extreme provocation, and sometimes the killing was straightforwardly the result of actions taken in self-defence. The killing of children, however, does seem to be more psychologically complex.

Women killing sexual partners
Polk (1991) reports 15 cases in this category (12 men killed by female partners). Polk notes that although the murder of sexual partners is a significant category when men kill women, there were important differences when women were the killers. Women were more likely to kill in response to domestic violence (in 8 of the 12 cases). Polk (1991: 152–3) gives the following example of a case in which the provocation and direct trigger of self-defence was clear. G.C. had endured 6 years of violence at the hands of her husband, Bob C.

Things reached crisis point as she tried to get him to leave the home, and after a series of increasingly violent incidents,

> Bob filled up the bathtub and closed the doors to the bedrooms of the children's room. He then approached G., who was seated on the couch in the lounge room, and announced that he was going to kill her, but that she had to choose whether it was to be by being drowned, stabbed or strangled. Bob then went to the kitchen, returning with a knife. He then proceeded to poke and prod at G. with the knife, taunting her and repeating over and over that he was going to kill her. He kept this tormenting behaviour up for some time, dragging her from room to room.

> At one point, as Bob was attempting to try a shift to a new form of torment, he jabbed the knife point down into the floor. G. immediately grabbed it up, and they started to struggle over the knife. As she said later to the police: 'I realised that it was me or him'. G. gained control over the knife for a brief moment, and stabbed Bob once in the stomach. When Bob slumped back into a chair, G. was able to escape from the house and summon help.

> Bob was first conveyed to a local hospital, then transferred to Melbourne where he died one month later from complications resulting from his wounds. Before he died, Bob acknowledged that G.'s account of the events leading to his wounding was accurate, and the Coroner found that G. had caused her husband's death '… in lawful defence of herself'.
>
> (Case No. 3945-85).

It seemed to be entirely clear in this case that the killing was in self-defence, and the coroner was happy to agree with this. It is evident that Bob was the aggressor, and had G. not acted to defend herself, she would have been killed. There have been a number of cases in the last few decades in which women who have killed their husbands, alleged at trial years of abuse, but the defence of 'self-defence' proved more controversial because the killing appeared to have taken place after the immediate threat was over.

On 9 May 1989, Kiranjit Ahluwalia set fire to her husband's (Deepak) bedclothes while he slept (Young (1996), discusses this case). He died 10 days later in hospital from the severe burns he received. Kiranjit Ahluwalia was charged with murder. Her plea at the trial was one of manslaughter, on the grounds that she had suffered 10 years of provocation (violence, intimidation and abuse). Perhaps in part because of embarrassment, Kiranjit Ahluwalia did not present the details of the abuse she had suffered to the court. This led the judge to suggest that the violence she had suffered was 'not serious', and the prosecution claimed that she had merely been 'knocked about'. Her plea of manslaughter due to provocation was rejected, and the jury found her guilty of murder. At appeal in 1992, a retrial was granted on the grounds that expert evidence and psychiatric reports had not been presented at the original trial. At the retrial in September 1992, Kiranjit Ahluwalia was found guilty of the lesser charge of manslaughter on the grounds of diminished responsibility. She was sentenced to 3 years and 4 months, the time she had already served, and so was immediately released.

Despite the eventual outcome of this process, there was still controversy about the trial. It was felt that a key reason for the failure of Kiranjit Ahluwalia's plea of 'provocation' was the failure of the court to comprehend her behaviour. The time that had elapsed between the last attack on her and her retaliation (a few hours) was deemed to be a 'cooling down' period, and not a 'boiling over' period, as her defence suggested. The court seemed to struggle with the idea that provocation could be a mitigating factor if an individual had time to cool down between the provocation and the act.

A number of cases have a similar pattern within the criminal justice system. Donna Tinker and Sarah Thornton both became causes for feminist protest. The difficulty that occurs in the defence of these cases is that they seem to fit cleanly neither with the idea of self-defence nor with 'provocation'. Motz (2001) tackles this problem of how 'battered women who kill' can be dealt with in the criminal justice system. She argues that women who kill in these circumstances have to be understood as having being driven by 'a rational basis', and they come to kill, as it offers the 'only viable solution to an intractable and life-threatening problem' (Motz 2001: 243). Motz gives a detailed case description of a woman called 'Eve', who had suffered years of physical abuse by her partner. On the night of the killing, he had pushed and threatened their young children, and punched her in the face and then seven or eight times in the stomach. He then continued to drink what remained of a bottle of whiskey. Eve found that the children were terribly distressed, and this realisation triggered the thought that the situation was completely unbearable – that she had to do something to stop it immediately. She then went back downstairs, seeing her own face in the mirror:

she saw that her face was puffy and distorted, that her make-up had run all down her face making her look grotesque and mad. Her blouse, which had been washed and ironed for work that night, was covered with blood and foundation and several buttons had come off. She looked, she said, 'completely mad, like a crazy, slovenly woman'. ... She felt full of resolve and rage. On entering the living room she saw that her partner had fallen into what seemed like a heavy sleep, a half finished drink spilled on his lap and the glass on the floor by his feet. She felt a flash of elation when she saw him lying there, no longer capable of assaulting her. Her only thought had been to stop the misery and terror to which she and her family had been subjected and in order to do this she had to kill her partner, then, without hesitation, while he slept. The hysteria and fear had left her and she felt calm, determined and composed. She fetched a knife from the kitchen and stabbed her sleeping partner three times in the chest, puncturing his lungs and killing him almost instantly.

(Motz 2001: 241)

Motz goes on to describe how Eve, although initially charged with murder, was tried on the lesser charge of manslaughter, on the grounds of diminished responsibility due to untreated depression. Motz objects to this formulation, arguing that Eve's actions should certainly be 'excused', but not on the implied grounds of 'madness'. Instead, Motz argues, Eve's actions should be read as the rational manoeuvrings of a woman trying to protect herself and her children. She felt that she and her children were in danger and a way of protecting them all was to attack the husband. This she could only do when he was asleep. Thus, Eve was not acting through mental illness, but was responding to finding herself with no other means of escape. Similar reasoning about female crime is also found in feminist-inspired criminological work, such as that of Carlen (1988), who interviewed female offenders (generally convicted of less serious offences). She argues that the women had little choice but to turn to crime. Often coming from deprived, poverty-stricken backgrounds, they found crime to be the one way they had of manoeuvring in desperate economic circumstances. A good example is provided by Kim, age 28, who describes an apparently entirely rational process of career choice:

I knew I had to do this [commit crime] to survive and there were 4 things I could have done in Clapton. I could have become a prostitute, but I was shy with my body so I ruled that out. I could have become a pickpocket, but i can't go off and steal from a person, my conscience wouldn't let me. Shoplifting is fine, but it's a lot of work. Or I could do the cheques and chequebooks which were just nice for me because it wasn't interfering with anybody and to me it was the easiest thing in the world ... it was just like a job. The rewards are good and it's easy.

The argument that female offenders are simply acting rationally in economically distressed circumstances might be seen as somewhat undermined by material in other interviews in the same book that hint at lives marred by abuse and deprivation (rather like the boys and men in the longitudinal studies discussed in Chapter 3). However, Motz is surely correct in arguing that the criminal justice system has difficulties in excusing behaviour simply on the grounds of powerful irrational feelings. It might be argued that the criminal justice system demands control of those feelings. Rozelle (2005), for example, presents the very coherent case that courts should not allow the simple fact that someone has been provoked to extreme anger by the actions of another to be used as a defence against a charge of murder.

Children killed by parents

Eight per cent of all homicides studied by Polk were cases in which children had been the victims of parents (28 cases). This is the one area where women are holding their own in terms of numbers, half of the parental killers of children being their mothers. A number of these killings were of newborn children, killed by young mothers often scared and confused by what was happening.

Three of the cases of killings occurred in the context of the mother's suicide. Polk notes that these seem to take place, tragically, as a last desperate act of 'protection'. One case involved parents who both had psychiatric difficulties. They separated, and at the point where their relationship seemed to be irretrievably falling apart,

George came over to see the children. Connie asked him to spend the night, but he refused. A day or two later, he informed her that he intended to move into a flat with a fellow worker who was female. This was enough to tip Connie over the edge. She confided to the babysitter that she intended to commit suicide, and that she 'loved the children too much to leave them behind'. After the babysitter left, Connie wrote out several long suicide notes. She left extensive instructions regarding their funerals, stating she wanted her son buried to her left, the daughter to her right. She had purchased new clothes for the children's funerals, and laid them neatly on the couch. In the note to her parents, Connie wrote: 'I don't feel I am murdering my children, but saving them from sorrow and pain without their father ... it's the only way out ... all I ever wanted in life was a happy marriage and happy, healthy children ... I have tried very hard ... I cannot leave my children behind ... At least with God there will be peace and happiness and no pain, so I will take them where they will be happy, and I will be there to care for them' (Case No. 2886-85).

(1994: 142)

Other children seemed to die as a result of more overtly aggressive behaviour. Motz argues that the fact that women do kill their children tells us a great deal about the relationship between femininity and violence. She argues that female violence is just as real as male violence, but that it is manifested very differently. Male violence is aimed at others, while female violence is aimed at women themselves (and at their own children as extensions of themselves). Her argument is consistent with the contemporary psychoanalytic account of gender difference (that masculinity is based on a denial of femininity, while female identity is based on identification with the mother). If the identification with the mother is any way problematic (perhaps through a negative relationship with the actual mother), then women internalise a hated figure. When angry, their aggression will be aimed at themselves, attacking the internalised maternal object within.

Motz describes her therapeutic work with 'Dawn' after she had murdered her 11-month-old baby boy (Gabriel). Dawn herself had had a deprived childhood. Her mother had suffered from serious mental illness, and she had lived in children's homes as a result (where she had felt abandoned and suffered abuse). Dawn's marriage had fallen apart, and Gabriel had already been taken away from her and put in foster care, due to Dawn's inability to cope. She planned the killing on the day of having 'access' to her son when she had heard news that her husband was going to divorce her. She strangled Gabriel as he slept next to her, and then immediately told the foster carer, who called the police. Motz interprets what Dawn tells her about the killing:

At the moment of the killing Dawn had become enraged by her own abandonment, by her husband, son, and at a deeper level, her own mother. In fantasy she became the abandoned infant whose depressed mother had neglected and rejected her. She powerfully projected these feelings onto Gabriel, who became the embodiment of the unwanted, demanding and completely helpless child. She also saw him as absolutely hers, and felt that if she couldn't have him then neither could anyone else.

(Motz 2001: 120)

Motz suggests that Dawn kills her son because she identifies with him and hopes that, by destroying him, she is also getting rid of the vulnerable part of herself; at the same time, she punishes herself and those around her (her mother and her husband) who did not 'care enough'. Whether this is a good account of infanticide, it is certainly true that rates of recorded self-harm are very much higher among women than men (Rodham *et al.* 2005; Haw *et al.* 2006). This would be consistent with the argument that women internalise aggression while men externalise it (hence the complementary figures on male violence to others). The fact that young men are more likely to kill themselves (Men's Health Forum 2001) might seem to contradict this analysis. Nathan (2004: 170), however, argues that the 'psychodynamics of suicide and self-harm are quite different' in a way that would be consistent with the analysis of gender differences here. Self-harm, he suggests, is the result of people feeling that there is something bad inside themselves that needs to be cut or forced out. If that internal bad object can be removed, then the self would be left to live happily. Suicide is the result of people feeling that there is a good object somewhere inside themselves that could be released if only the bad self surrounding it could be destroyed. It is men with their flawed sense of identities or the narcissistic exoskeleton (Cartwright 2002) that would be more prone to suicide.

Polk's analysis of cases in which men kill their own children suggests a slightly different understanding, as the children's defiance was often a trigger for the male violence (Alder and Polk 1996).

Conclusion

This chapter has used data on homicides to gain insight into violence. Studies of homicide are a rich source of data, as the events tend to be reported in considerable detail. By examining the details of these violent events, we have been led back to some significant issues that have emerged in previous chapters.

Shame and masculinity emerge as significant factors in understanding violence. The second largest category of homicide (according to Polk's analysis) was that of 'confrontational homicide' typically taking place when two men confront each other, often unknown to each other and fighting over something that seems from the outside to be quite trivial. Such incidents are certainly consistent with the idea that men are fighting to protect an image of themselves as strong individuals. The triviality of the triggers for violence is also consistent with the idea that their identities are often experienced as fragile. This issue will be taken further in the next chapter when the most common category of homicide is explored – homicide within the context of sexual intimacy. These killings are typically carried out by men murdering the women that they are, or had been, in relationships with. The next chapter will also explore more generally the violence that occurs in family relationships and also crimes that directly involve sexual behaviour (rape and paedophilia in particular). Through that chapter the themes of men, masculinity and emotion emerge very strongly.

Chapter 8

Intimate violence and sexual crime

Introduction

This chapter is concerned with understanding the violence that occurs in the context of intimate and sexual relationships. This topic demands further understanding of the violence that occurs in relationships between people, and particularly how violence interacts with issues of gender. Studies reviewed in the last chapter (Chapter 7, 'Understanding Violence') suggest that the most frequent incidents of fatal violence are those occurring in the context of intimate and sexual relationships. There is good evidence that this is indicative of high levels of general violence occurring within sexual and family relationships. For a number of years, concern has been raised about the apparent regularity with which women meet violence at the hands of men (Tham *et al.* 1995), usually when the men are married to, or otherwise involved in a sexual relationship with, the victim (Dobash and Dobash 1979). For example, Walby and Allen (2004), using a British Crime Survey methodology, found that 21 per cent of women reported at least one incident of non-sexual domestic threat of, or use of, force since their sixteenth birthday. Walby and Allen (2004) also found that 7 per cent of women in their sample reported having suffered serious sexual assault at least once in their lifetime. These and other similar observations made over the years have led to political analyses of how such events need to be understood in terms of the power that men have traditionally held over women. Perhaps male violence and sexual violence in particular can be understood in terms of patriarchy; that is, a cultural order that suggests that it is acceptable for men to dominate and control women (Brownmiller 1975). It is certainly difficult to contradict those who argue that in many ways violence against women appears to have been culturally sanctioned. Historically, women have been viewed as the property of men; indeed, rape was considered to be impossible within marriage until 1991 in England and Wales.

Two particular topics will be explored in this chapter; first, crimes of violence that occur in the context of sexual or family intimacy, and, second, crimes involving sexual behaviour. The first topic includes incidents of 'domestic violence'; that is, crimes of violence that occur in the context of intimate relationships (people who are married or who are otherwise partners). The second topic includes crimes involving sexual behaviour; that is, rape, sexual assault and paedophilia (a topic that has been creating increasing public concern). The vast majority of these offences are committed by men; female sexual offending appears to be rare, despite increasing recognition that it does occur (Kemshall 2004; Robinson 2005).

Explanations of intimate and sexual violence can be placed in two broad categories. First, some seek to understand such behaviour in terms of the pathology of individual offenders; second, some assume that the causes lie within our cultural constructions of gender and sexuality. It will be argued that sex crimes and crimes of intimacy have to be understood in the context of both of these points of view. The phenomena of sex crimes demand the connection of social and cultural perspectives with the study of individual motivations and behaviour.

Domestic violence and violence in the context of sexual intimacy

Using British Crime Survey data, Walby and Allen (2004) estimate that 4 per cent of women have experienced some form of domestic violence (the definition here includes non-sexual threats or force used by a partner) in a 12-month period. This means that there were 12.5 million incidents of domestic violence directed at women in the 12 months prior to interview in the UK. In terms of sheer numbers of incidents alone, there is no doubt that domestic violence is a major criminal activity. The gendered pattern of offences (men being most commonly the perpetrators and women the victims) has led to a

Table 8.1 The source of conflict leading to the first episode of domestic violence (from Dobash and Dobash 1984)

	n	%
Expectations of domestic work	37	37
Possessiveness/sexual jealousy	31	31
Money	7	7
Status problems	3	3
Sexual refusal	6	6
Woman's effort to leave	5	5

plausible feminist analysis that focuses on male power and the subjugation of women.

There have been surprisingly few empirical investigations of specific incidents of violence and the motivations of individual perpetrators. In this respect, not only was Dobash and Dobash's (1984) study of domestic violence pioneering, but it also remains relevant. They carried out semi-structured interviews with women who had fled domestic violence to live in a women's refuge. They asked the women in detail about the first, the last, and the worst incident.

It is interesting to note that possessiveness and sexual jealousy feature prominently (31 per cent of these first-episode incidents falling into this category). The other large category is 'expectations of domestic work', suggesting that violence also occurs here in response to conflict about control. Dobash and Dobash (1984) also looked at what had been the specific trigger for violence:

- 37: arguing back
- 21: questioning the legitimacy of his argument
- 9: refusing to argue back
- 11: initiating argument herself
- 8: hitting him first
- 5: calling him names
- 4: threatening/attempting to leave.

It seems that many of these triggers are consistent with the idea that men are responding to perceived threats to their 'authority', just like those men involved in confrontational homicides discussed in the previous chapter.

Some doubt might be cast on a simple formulation of domestic violence as centring on patriarchy. Attention has been drawn to evidence about the number of offences occurring in which women are the perpetrators and men the victims. The BCS data, for example, also reveal that 2 per cent of men were victims of domestic violence in the year prior to interview (Walby and Allen 2004). Such figures might be used to suggest a shift away from seeing domestic violence as such a gendered issue (Straus 1992). Such an adjustment in perception is, however, not entirely warranted, as male victimhood only emerges as looser definitions of violence are used. In this study, the definition included self-reports of the experience of the 'threat of force'. Perhaps verbal threats such as 'I'll thump you if you do that again' are relatively common. It may be that the real meaning or intention behind the threat varies considerably in ways that may not be captured by the questionnaire that simply records incidents of the threat being made. Certainly, when more serious offences are considered, a clear gender imbalance is revealed. Of the more 'heavily abused' (defined by having been a victim four or more times at the hands of the 'worst perpetrator') 89 per cent of the victims are women.

Intimate and fatal violence

In order to avoid some of the difficulties encountered in the definition of violence, the previous chapter focused on homicide, as these are usually clearly defined acts of violence. It is apparent that studies of homicide strongly reinforce assertions concerning the gendered nature of domestic violence. These studies also provide a useful platform for the further analysis of 'intimate violence'. Wolfgang (1958), using data on homicide gathered in the US city of Philadelphia in the 1950s, pointed out that the bedroom appeared to be the most dangerous room in the house; for women, at any rate. In Polk's detailed study of homicide in the Australian State of Victoria (described in Chapter 7), the single largest category of homicide comprised deaths occurring in the context of sexual intimacy. Out of the 380 deaths studied, 101 (27 per cent) occurred in these circumstances. The overwhelming majority (73 per cent) of these involved male perpetrators and female victims, as Table 8.2 illustrates.

In Table 8.2, in the category 'Male victim/male offender', all those involved were sexual rivals. Overall, male violence in the context of sexual relationships looms very large, incidents that seem to be triggered by jealousy being salient. There has been considerable

Table 8.2 Crimes occurring in the context of sexual intimacy, $n=101$ (from Polk 1994)

	n	%
Female victim/male offender	73	72
Jealousy/control	58	58
Depression/suicide	15	15
Male victim/female offender	12	12
Provoked by violence	8	8
Control/other	4	4
Male victim/male offender	13	13
Female victim/female offender	3	3
Total	101	100%

interest in the psychology of male jealousy for some time (Yates 2000).

Male jealousy and violence

The largest category of homicide occurring in the context of sexual intimacy was that of fatal jealousy. Here is a typical example of what appears to be fatal jealousy from Polk's study:

Eileen (26, secretary) went out with Michael (25, bouncer) but then began to attempt to withdraw from the relationship. M. found this difficult to accept and began to utter threats (he had a history of violence with previous girlfriends). One night he broke into her flat suspecting that she was sleeping with someone else.

Crisis came Christmas day they were both at a party, M. became angry when E. was 'over-familiar' with a male guest. M. left, and E. went with him indicating that she would return shortly. They were heard to argue in a car. Police were summoned and E. was found strangled to death. When questioned M. said 'I strangled the bitch, that's all.' When told that she was dead, Michael stated that further: 'Fucking good, the bitch deserved it ... I wasn't going to let anyone hurt anyone again. I knew I had to do it ... I just lost it, she wasn't going to hurt me or anyone else again.'

(Polk 1994: 33)

How can we explain why Michael was motivated to kill Eileen? Certainly, in any rational terms, it is hard to understand the murder. Michael himself seems to have gained little. He appears to have made little attempt to get away with the crime. It might be, like many of the murders in this category, that Michael has been motivated by feelings of jealousy. Rather than tolerate Eileen's rejecting him, separating and perhaps being with another man, Michael killed her.

If these incidents of violence are motivated by jealousy, why do men seem to be more likely to act upon these feelings? Daly and Wilson (1988) argue that evolution has shaped the behaviour of men and women in different ways. Men's propensity to violent jealousy can be understood in terms of differential investment in sexual reproduction. It makes sense, the suggestion is, for men to be more anxious about sexual infidelity, since, ultimately, women know that any child they have is 'theirs' but men have to live with the knowledge that any child their partner bears could have another biological father. It is this anxiety, Daly and Wilson (1988) suggest, that leads to the disposition to jealousy and the control of sexual partners.

Such theorising is criticised by Harris (2003), who reviews a great deal of evidence on gender differences in jealousy. Harris suggests that the greater number of jealousy-inspired murders might simply be an artefact of the fact that men commit far more acts of violence than women anyway. This is consistent with the finding that self-reported feelings of jealousy do not vary between genders. Grice and Seely (2000), for example, failed to find that men had greater physiological responses to imagining scenes of infidelity than women. Perhaps, there is nothing special about the crimes of sexual jealousy; it may be that men are simply more violent and liable to act on those feelings. The difficulty with this argument is that it takes us back to the unquestioning view of men being more violent and crime prone than women, and appears to abandon any attempt to understand why this might be.

Pines and Friedman (1998) reported a series of studies comparing women's and men's experiences of jealousy. They reported largely similar experiences across the genders. Men and women were equally likely to report feelings of jealousy as being an issue in relationships, to be concerned about jealousy, and to have similar attitudes to jealousy. Women, however, reported more intense feelings of distress in association with jealousy: 'their distress was manifested more than the men's in feelings of sadness, vulnerability, and pain' (Pines and Friedman 1998: 66). Pines and Friedman (1998) suggest two alternative explanations for this – first, that male respondents are simply more inhibited about reporting their own emotions, or, second, that women do indeed experience higher levels of distress in response to threats to their relationship. Pines and Friedman favour this latter explanation, arguing that relationships are more central to women's lives. As relationships are more central, they will experience greater distress when these relationships are threatened. The authors refer to contemporary psychoanalytic theory, as discussed in Chapter 6, to argue that there are psychological reasons that women have greater investment in relationships than men (Chodorow 1978; Gilligan 1982).

It could be argued, however, that the idea that relationships are more central to women's lives is contradicted by the data on jealousy and violence. The rates of jealous homicide seem to suggest that at least some men are acting on considerable feelings as they face the loss of a relationship. At least some aspect of the relationship, or its loss, seemed to be sufficiently significant to these men to inspire violence. Brown (2004) argues that male perpetrators of violence against women are often responding to feelings of abandonment. Brown also makes use of contemporary psychoanalytic accounts, but this time focusing on the self psychology of Kohut (e.g. 1971) to make an analogous argument to that made in Chapters 6 and 7, that men's sense of identity may be quite fragile and their feelings of worth may depend on the unquestioning and unconditional support of a partner. Any withdrawal of this support is experienced as a shameful threat to their identity. As discussed previously, shame itself, as the signal of the threat of abandonment, may be an intolerable experience for some men to experience. Men with only a limited ability to process emotion may be prone to act on these feelings (Gilligan 1997; Cartwright 2002). Thus, shame is quickly converted into rage and violence.

Jukes (1993) argues that men are psychologically predisposed to hate women. He uses a Freudian framework to argue that men often harbour feelings of envy and hatred of women, who represent the things in life they have become alienated from – feelings of warmth, security and love associated with femininity. The difficulty with such a sweeping analysis is that it does not properly address why only some men act in these violent ways toward women.

It could be argued that sexual infidelity offers a potential threat not simply to men's relationship, but perhaps also in some cases to their identity. This would fit with the line of argument in Chapter 7, particularly in relation to confrontational homicides. It was argued that the fatalities occurring in conflicts over what seem to be relatively trivial matters might be understood in terms of the men fighting to protect their reputation or their identity. In a similar way, perhaps real or imagined rejection by women poses a substantial threat to the identity of these men. Such a threat would have two effects – first, it would motivate them to protect their identity by attacking what threatened it; second, as they experience their identity as less coherent, their feelings of agency and responsibility would become dissipated (as discussed in Chapter 7, 'Understanding Violence'). As their ability to process and think about emotion is reduced, they become more prone to act in response to the feelings they experience.

Providing further support for the notion that the ability to process information is crucial to the inhibition of violence is a study by Umberson *et al.* (2003), who explored the emotional responses of violent men (who had a history of domestic violence) and compared them to non-violent men by asking both groups to keep structured diaries over a 14-day period. They found that the non-violent men reported that their own emotion state deteriorated when they suffered stress in their relationships and they felt that their personal control was reduced. The violent men, however, reported no emotional changes or alterations to their own feelings of control in response to stress and conflict in their relationships. They argue that these men were effectively denying and repressing their feelings and were thus far more likely simply to act on them. To talk about emotion (and possibly even to think about emotion) was itself threatening. As one man in the study put it in describing how he responded when his partner demanded to know how he felt – 'I kicked her off the couch and said "this is how I feel" ' (Umberson *et al.* 2003: 244). Men who were aware of their feelings might be able to reflect and think about those feelings rather than simply acting on them.

Fonagy (1999) traces the roots of domestic violence in disordered early attachments. Fonagy *et al.*'s (2003) work on the significance of the capacity to process and reflect on emotion was described in Chapter 4. To briefly summarise; in the context of poor caregiving experiences, children who have not been helped to process their early experiences of distress will fail to develop a coherent sense of themselves as thinking and feeling beings who can reflect and make decisions about their actions. Fonagy argues: 'When confronted with a frightened or frightening caregiver, the infant takes in as part of himself or herself the mother's feeling of rage, hatred, or fear, and her image of the child as frightening or unmanageable' (1999: 13). As such children mature, the one way of avoiding overwhelming feelings of distress is to make the outside world a manageable place.

They can experience themselves as integrated and viable people by finding situations and relationships in which they can play the role of strong and dependable person. They need to feel needed, that there are weaker people whom they can dominate:

> In adulthood, disorganized self-representation still manifests as an overwhelming need to control the other. Violent men have to establish a relationship in which their partner acts as a vehicle for intolerable self states.
>
> (Fonagy 1999: 14)

Fonagy (1999: 14) suggests that the specific trigger for violence is often some further evidence that the man does not have full control of the woman; it is 'almost inevitably ... a further indicator of the women's psychological separateness. Examples might be a new hairstyle, a passing remark that expresses concern about someone other than the perpetrator.' Feelings of rage follow, prompting the man to act out violence, to act on the body of the person he feels angry with. He lacks the sense of himself as a reflective individual with a mind who can think, and communicate and influence the mind of another, and so he must control the body of the other in a very direct way. Some empirical support for the notion that perpetrators of domestic violence had early attachment problems comes from a study by Worley *et al.* (2004), who found that all seven perpetrators that they investigated had experiences of 'unloving, rejecting and dangerous parenting' (2004: 35). The difficulty with this study is that it is retrospective – it relies on the self-reports of the perpetrators, and has no control group. Analysis of the longitudinal data from the Dunedin study suggests that there was evidence that the perpetrators of domestic violence were more likely to have come from lower a social class, and to have exhibited conduct problems and poor educational attainment during early childhood. They did not, however, necessarily have the more extreme difficulties stretching back into early childhood (as found in the life-course-persistent offenders, for example). Instead, difficulties emerged in adolescence when family relationships were poorer and educational achievement was low, and they were far more likely to be involved in aggressive delinquency and substance abuse as teenagers and to have poor mental health as adults (Moffitt and Caspi 1999). In some ways, the perpetrators of domestic violence were rather similar to the adolescent-limited offenders. However, more serious abuse was also found to be more strongly associated with the life-course-persistent offenders (Moffitt *et al.* 2002: 194).

Perhaps some of the ideas discussed in relation to male violence can shed light on why Michael should have killed his ex-girlfriend Eileen, as described at the beginning of this section on male jealousy. Perhaps Eileen's rejection of him provided such a threat to his identity that he felt her removal would somehow be more likely to preserve his identity. Those with a less secure sense of identity, with difficulties emerging in childhood or adolescence, may be more prone to these feelings. That issues of identity might somehow be linked to intimate violence is lent some support by the finding that 21 per cent of the homicides (involving a male perpetrator and female victim) identified by Polk as taking place within the context of sexual intimacy were also portrayed as involving depression, with suicide following the homicide.

Depression: murder and suicide

On 6 June 2004, Stuart Horgan clambered over the fence around the house in Oxfordshire where his wife, Vicky Horgan, was hosting a Sunday afternoon barbecue. They were separated, and there was a history of Stuart being violent toward Vicky. He carried a single- barrell shotgun and used it to shoot his wife, her mother and her sister. Only Vicky Horgan's mother survived. Stuart Horgan was arrested the next day. Two weeks later, he slit his own throat in a prison cell.

This dismal case was one of a long line of similar stories of men killing those they were currently, or had been, intimately involved with, followed by their own suicide, often more immediately than Stuart Horgan's (Brett 2002). 'Homicide-suicide' is a category of killing to which Marvin Wolfgang (1958) drew attention through his study of homicide in Philadelphia in the 1950s. He found 26 victims slain by 24 killers who went on to kill themselves. Twenty-two of the killers were men. Twenty of the homicide-suicides occurred in the home, with the most frequent room being the bedroom (8 cases) or the living room (8 cases). The motives for the homicide were judged to be as follows: family quarrel (10), jealousy (6), revenge (3), accidental (1), altercation (1), ill health (1), and unknown (4). So again, the significance of male violence in the context of family intimacy is raised.

Fifteen of the homicides documented by Polk (1994) fitted into the category of homicide-suicide. In some of the cases described by Polk (1994) the men who went on to kill themselves did not have histories of violence, and the murder/homicide/suicide seemed to be more linked to their own depression. One example follows:

DL (42) had been a highly successful owner of a car dealership, but had been out of business for several months. Late 1987 he bought a new dealership, but ran into the consequences of the economic downturn. Instead of making money, the losses began to mount rapidly and gradually built up to debts totalling hundreds of thousands of dollars. Friends noted physical and mental deterioration. Arguments broke out between him and his wife (age 42, homemaker).

On 11 February, DL. attempted to enter several hospitals, finally being assessed as having a major depression. Hospital agreed to admit the next day. Instead DL shot and killed his wife, shot and wounded his mother-in-law and then turned the gun on himself.

(Polk 1994: 3)

The presence of suicide does strongly suggest that the homicide occurred amidst a crisis of the self. Gilligan (1997) suggests that homicidal violence does indeed occur in the midst of a kind of death of 'the self', and certainly the occurrence of suicide alongside homicide would support this (Chan *et al.* 2004; Falk *et al.* 2004).

The following section will look at other crimes of violence that involve sexuality and intimacy – the sexual crimes of rape and paedophilia. Again these are crimes in which men dominate the statistics, and issues of masculinity do appear to be relevant to understanding the crimes.

Sexual crimes: rape

A wide range of offences can be included in the category of sexual offences, including rape, sexual assault, paedophilia, indecent exposure, voyeurism, bestiality and having sex in public places. Since the mid-1990s, there has been growing public and police interest in sexual crime that is associated with the Internet – most notably child abuse and pornography. Crimes such as exhibitionism (in which men inappropriately expose their genitals in public) are often regarded as less serious, although some argue that such an assumption is misleading as such offenders might also be involved in more serious crime (Fisher and Beech 2004).

This section will address the issues of rape and the next section addresses paedophilia. Both of these have been subject to both considerable academic debate and public concern. Both subjects are highly relevant to this book since both topics require the combined exploration of cultural and psychological issues. Traditionally, there have been two very different ways of understanding the crime of rape.

First, it has been argued that such crimes themselves are symptoms of widespread and deep difficulties in the relationship between the genders. Rape in particular has been argued, by a number of feminist scholars, to be both a symptom and a tool of men's dominance over women. Research that has looked at the significance of cognitions and attitudes (e.g. Malamuth 1981), and peer groups, such as that of Kanin (1985), provides some support for this idea. Attitudes that might be seen as being likely to be associated with or to encourage rape behaviour have been found to be alarmingly common among the 'normal' male population (see McDonald and Klein 2004 for review).

Second, and alternatively, it has been argued that sex crimes are problems of individual psychopathology. Early research work tended to focus on physical (particularly hormonal) factors. The evidence about direct biological causes of such crimes is not strong, however (Raboch *et al.* 1987). Psychological work has focused on inherent personality factors (Blackburn 1993), distorted attitudes or psychodynamic factors (Stoller 1976).

A fundamental question can be asked about rape that may be relevant to any judgement about which of the above the scenarios is the most relevant. Is rape a relatively rare crime committed by a few individuals, or is it actually such a common problem that we need to think of as symptomatic of a considerable problem between the genders?

The extent of the problem of rape

Given that rape is such an intimate crime, it is perhaps not surprising that there has been controversy over the frequency of its occurrence. Official figures on rape have been assumed to have been an underestimate for many years, the argument being that large numbers of rapes are not reported to the police. Many victims have felt reluctant to come forward for various reasons, including fear and shame, feelings which have been exacerbated by the often hostile or ambivalent response of the police and courts (Heidensohn 1996). Data from victim surveys have suggested that rape is a not an uncommon experience. Hall (1985) conducted a survey in London which found that 17 per cent of the women surveyed reported having been raped. Surveys of undergraduates have also revealed high proportions reporting the experience. Mary Koss, who has carried out surveys across the USA has concluded that 15 per cent of women had been raped. Hall Smith *et al.* (2003) report that 21.1 per cent of their sample of US college women reported having had the experience of 'forcible rape' by the end of their college lives.

It is important to note that many incidents of sexual assault are carried out by men who are known to the victims. Walby and Allen (2004), using British Crime Survey data, report that the offender was an 'intimate' of the victim in 47 per cent of serious sexual assaults. This category included husband, partner, ex-husband and ex-partner. In 18 per cent of cases, the attacker was a stranger. The frequency of pre-existing intimacy between the attacker and the victim suggests that there is some conceptual continuity in the violence occurring within intimate relationships, as has already been discussed.

Taxonomies of rape offenders

It would seem that for a long time those who have worked with sex offenders have believed there are different types of offender. This belief is reflected in a number of attempts to draw up taxonomies (categories) of rapists. An early approach was that of Guttmacher (1951), who based the following taxonomy on clinical experience of working with rapists:

1 *the true sex offender*: offender has a sexual motive, to obtain sex
2 *the sadistic sex offender*: violence and brutality are part of the attraction
3 *the aggressive offender*: someone for whom rape is simply one part of a violent criminal lifestyle.

Similar typologies have been based on clinical experience (e.g. Groth *et et al.* 1977). Using a more sociological framework, Scully and Marolla (1984) produced a not entirely dissimilar five-category taxonomy based on interviews with convicted rapists:

1 *Revenge and punishment* – the men said that following some perceived betrayal by their partner, they raped someone in order to get even.
2 *Opportunistic* – they saw rape as an 'added bonus' while committing another crime.

3 *Sexual motivation* - getting what was not otherwise available. The phenomenon of 'date rape' features here.
4 *Power and dominance* – this group seemed to be motivated by particular aspects of rape: the feeling of power and dominance, the impersonal aspect of rape.
5 *Recreation and adventure* – usually young men in groups. The 'reward' here seemed to be in terms of group acceptance, being accepted as one of the gang.

If we assume there is some truth in the range of motivations here, then it is safe to make a couple of general conclusions:

1 There is a considerable range of motivations for men committing rape.
2 There are some complicated attitudes to sex, sexuality and violence being demonstrated here. Some of the reasons for rape seem to be about sex itself – the sex could almost be seen as a commodity which the men are taking. For others, the rape appears to be an act of violence, and the sex seems incidental to the achievement of a perceived status or the expression of aggression.

There are a number of reviews of theories about the motivations for this kind of sexual violence (Craissati 2005). One early theory of rape supposed that it was carried out by men who were simply sexually frustrated (Kanin 1983). For one reason or another, these men perhaps had difficulty in forming relationships and indulging in normal sexual relationships. This theory can be largely discounted. For one thing, rapists often have quite extensive, non-coercive sexual histories and have in general not been found to lack social skills.

The following section will explore some of the key theories. Theories that take a biological and then a psychological perspective will be examined. The influence of culture, and in particular the roles of masculinity and culture, will then be examined.

Individual biological predisposition

A number of theories have sought to explore the roots of sexual violence in biological predisposition. This is not surprising given that perhaps it is easy to associate sexual violence with primitive animalistic instincts. This was certainly the view of Lombroso (discussed in Chapter 1). There are now two specific biological theories of rape. One is that rape is the result of hormonal imbalance, particularly an excess of androgens ('male' hormones). In support of this theory is evidence from animal studies that does demonstrate clear links between hormone levels and sexual activity and aggressive behaviour. As described in Chapter 6, 'Gender and Crime' it is in reality rather difficult to pin down the behavioural effects of hormonal differences. Hormone levels themselves are also influenced by events around the individual. In addition there are recorded cases of sexually aggressive violence being carried out by men with very low levels of androgens (e.g. Raboch *et al.* 1987).

The idea that men might be sexually aggressive in response to a genetically determined programme was advanced by Thornhill and Palmer (2001). They argued that from a biological perspective rape 'makes sense'. That is, men who rape might well make women pregnant meaning that their genes are propagated. In support of this theory, they argue that the majority of rape victims are women of childbearing age. Their theory has difficulties in explaining why many victims of rape do not fit into that category (girls, older women or men), nor does it explain why particular men might rape. It does little to explain cultural variations in rape (explored below), and has faced trenchant criticism that it appears to normalise, and thus comes perilously close to justifying rape (e.g. Travis Brown 2003).

Pathological attraction? Studies of arousal

Other theories of rape assume that at least some offenders are particularly attracted to the combination of sexual feelings with violence and aggression, leading them to commit violent sexual acts. This might be due to some predisposition or could have been learnt through abusive experiences, childhood experimentation, or exposure to pornography that features the combination of violence and sex (McGuire *et al.* 1965). MacCulloch *et al.* (2000) made use of learning theory to propose that a learnt association between sexual feelings and violence can be built up in a child experiencing abuse. The association can then be reinforced through fantasy. This could explain the link between experience of childhood abuse and the relative likelihood of sexual aggression later in life (as discussed in Chapter 4). Psychologists have been carrying out research for a number of years to assess whether particular individuals are more susceptible to different sexual stimuli. A typical study involves showing film depicting sex scenes involving rape and violence to a group of convicted rapists and to a group of non-rapists. Both groups might then be shown film of consensual, non-violent sex, the hypothesis being that the rapists would be more aroused by the violence than the non-violent scenes while the non-rapists would be aroused only by the non-violent scenes. In order to assess how aroused individuals are by these different stimuli, we might simply ask people how aroused they feel. There is an obvious problem in how truthful offenders would be in admitting their violent interests. Lie detectors (polygraphs) of various forms have therefore been employed to identify deceit. Different kinds of polygraphs that measure general symptoms of anxiety such as heart rate and palm sweating have been used in these cases (assuming that lying is an anxiety-provoking exercise). There are general difficulties with the validity of polygraphs, many doubts being cast on how effective they are in identifying lying (Memon *et al.* 1998). For more direct assessment of sexual arousal, psychologists have designed various devices, generally called penile plethysmographs, that, measure changes in penis volume or diameter. The operative belief here is that there is one part of the male anatomy that cannot lie.

The early studies, such as that by Barbaree *et al.* (1979), suggested greater arousal in rapists to rape stimuli than non-rapists. They found greater arousal to consenting sexual scenes among non-rapists than rapists. This led to the straightforward suggestion that rapists are motivated by an interest in the combination of violence and sex. Other studies have suggested a more complicated picture. Abel *et al.* (1977), for example, reported that rapists found portrayals of consenting sex just as arousing as non-rapists, but that non-rapists found depictions of non-consenting sex less arousing than non-rapists. This led to the hypothesis that it was not that rapists had greater motivation but that they had less inhibition. Perhaps the non-rapists were being put off by the coercion in the depictions. It was perhaps not so much that the rapists were being aroused by the non-consenting and coercive aspects of the depictions, but that they were not 'turned off' by it. In partial support of this idea, Quinsey and Earls (1990) found that the negative responses of the non-rapists could be ameliorated by suggestion. If they were reassured that it was common for men to be aroused by depictions of rape, then they were also aroused. Baxter *et al.* (1986), however, found that both rapists and non-rapists were less aroused by the rape depictions than depictions of consenting sexual activity. They argued that theirs was a more accurate finding, as they had used a larger sample.

Conclusions are difficult to draw from these studies of arousal. There are a number of methodological problems with them. First, the studies generally put rapists together in one group, whereas clinical evidence and the more sociological research by others, such as Scully and Marolla (1984) referred to previously, suggest that men convicted of rape may be very different from each other and have committed rape for very different reasons (there is also the issue of the exclusion of 'acquaintance rapists', who are far less likely to be convicted and thus be included in samples of sex offender). Perhaps we need more research on subgroups of rapists. Second, there is the difficulty of the peculiarity of the experimental situation here. These studies on arousal involve the wiring of a strange apparatus around the penis of the research participant, who is then shown pornographic images while a team of researchers around the corner monitor physiological changes. The subject of the experiment knows that every movement of his penis is being monitored. This seems a fairly 'perverse' situation, arguably a long way from 'real' life. Third, there are objections that some men can control their responses anyway and can certainly learn to fake their responses despite some effort being make to control for this (Howitt 2006: 142). Fourth, it has been found that although there are correlations between known offending behaviour and susceptibility to arousal to sexual violence, those correlations are relatively low (Hall *et al.* 1993). Looman and Marshall (2005) suggest that the difficulties with phallometric assessment mean that this is no longer a valid avenue for research, although Lalumière and Rice (2007) dispute this sweeping conclusion.

The notion that sexual proclivities have somehow been learnt has led to treatments that assume that they can be unlearnt. These have been used more often with paedophile offenders (see Quinsey and Earls (1990) for a review of the use of learning theory techniques to modify the behaviour of sexual offenders).

Psychoanalytic theories of sadism

Contemporary psychoanalytic contributions to understanding violence, and male violence in particular, have already been explored in some detail. While there are no psychoanalytic theories of rape itself, psychoanalysis has a lot to say about sexual development and how perversions of 'normal' sexual behaviour can develop. Of likely relevance here might well be the development of sadism (that is, the sexual pleasure gained by harming others). Broadly speaking, psychoanalysis sees human sexual development beginning at birth, and as consisting of the gradual imposition of various barriers and taboos. We start out, in Freud's famous phrase, as 'polymorphously perverse'. For the young child, 'anything goes' if it feels good. Only with time do people become inhibited and their desires directed along culturally accepted channels. Perversions can then be understood as failure to develop these inhibitions, or misdirection along an inappropriate channel, or perhaps return to a more regressed infantile state of functioning.

Perhaps it is in the theories of sadomasochistic perversion that psychoanalysis might have something to offer in terms of understanding individual motivation for sexual violence and rape. Robert Stoller (1976) has written about the development of such theories as formalised in the 'core complex' (Glasser 1992, 1988). The core complex model of sadomasochism assumes that such behaviour stems from anxiety provoked by people's poor sense of their own identity in the face of the desire for intimacy. These ideas overlap with those on the relationship between certain notions of fragile masculinity and violence (explored in Chapters 6 and 7). It is assumed that enjoying intimacy, particularly sexual intimacy with someone is desirable – the sensation of closeness, of 'being in love', perhaps giving someone the feeling of being 'as one' with another. The paradox is that to enjoy this kind of experience – falling in love – we assume that people require a sense of themselves as a strong, viable individual. People who do not feel secure in their identities are vulnerable to feeling that if they get too close to someone they will be engulfed and will disappear. So, people with a weak sense of identity want to feel close, and to experience unity with someone, but they are also terrified of the experience. A solution to this paradox is 'sadomasochism'; that is, to act sadistically toward those that one feels love for, so that one can both love someone and at the same time literally attack them, maintaining distance and boundary. Glasser (1992) gives the example of one of his male psychoanalytic patients reflecting on a sexual encounter with his girlfriend that appears to illustrate this ambivalence directly:

> When she put her tongue into his mouth he had a sense of her possessing him intrusively; and when he put his tongue in her mouth, he had a slight feeling of her engulfing him. Sometimes he would want to bite her ... on one or two occasions he had an image of strangling her. Glasser (1992: 496)

The development of this kind of ambivalence would be seen, not unexpectedly for psychoanalytic theory, to relate to people's early experience of mothering. Perhaps a man experienced his mother as being very overpowering, and that his needs as an individual were not considered. Brittain (1970) had earlier developed a theory of sexual sadism that assumed that male sadists have insecure attachments, created by overprotective, overwhelming mothers and hostile aggressive fathers. Other psychoanalytic theories have emphasised the feelings of envy and hostility that men may hold toward women (e.g. Jukes 1993), which would certainly explain the volume of violence directed by men toward women. What Glasser and others are adding here is some explanation of why quite a lot of that violence might be sexual in nature. It is often through sexual relationships that people seek comfort and a shoring up of a fragile sense of themselves as loveable. The paradoxical difficulty is that intimacy can also threaten the exposure of that very sense of fragility. Hence, perhaps, so much male aggression is aimed at women with whom those men are, or have been involved with in sexual relationships. Women simultaneously offer the hope of connection and love, and the threat of abandonment and humiliation. Retaliatory humiliation is suggested by the well-documented incidences of the humiliation of the victims of sexual assault (Darke 1990). Scheff and Retzinger (1997) argue that sexual assault and rape can be understood in terms of shame-rage cycles. Thus, links can be made with more general explanations of the violence that men use against women, as men may feel the need to assert themselves as stronger and more capable than those that they also need. Fonagy's (1999: 16) reports of the explanation of one man who had repeatedly raped his partner, 'to take the smirk off her face', is strongly suggestive of the need to assert power and to humiliate. Fonagy argues that this is ultimately about the defence of a precarious sense of selfhood, and that it is only at such moments of violence 'that such individuals feel coherent and real' (1999: 16). We will be drawn back to issues of masculinity and the ability to process and make sense of emotion when the relation between culture and sexual violence is considered.

Cognitive theories of sexual offending

The cognitive schools of psychological thought have taken a very different approach to understanding sexual violence. As explored in Chapter 1, cognitive theories assume that offenders are making a rational decision to commit a particular offence. Analysis of the rationale for a particular crime might well reveal distorted thinking about the crime. The implicit assumption here is that 'sex' is a desirable commodity that someone might want to take from others. It is assumed that offenders have distorted thinking about their victims' willingness to have sex, or about the acceptability of using force and coercion. Cognitive behaviour therapy has been a popular treatment for sex offenders for many years (Beckett 1994; Beech and Fisher 2004), the treatment rationale being that sex offenders have developed distorted beliefs about their victims and the impact of their offences on them. A rapist might, for example, argue that the women he raped had wanted to have sex really, or that it was acceptable to coerce women.

Despite the volume of work and the fashionability of cognitive treatment of sex offenders, research in this area has found that it is generally not possible to distinguish between the attitudes of offenders and non-offenders. In fact, it has been found, perhaps disturbingly, that many of the attitudes that it was assumed would distinguish offenders from non-offenders and might lead someone to become a rapist are commonly found in the 'normal' population of men (Polaschek and Ward (2002), provide a review). There are two ways of understanding these findings – it may be that attitudes do not relate to behaviour very well, and we must look elsewhere for the causes of sexual offending, or, alternatively perhaps many men are indeed potential rapists and the cognitive distortions might be wide spread among men. This latter argument is, of course, in keeping with radical feminist theories (Brownmiller 1975).

Studies by Malamuth (1981), for example, have tried to assess the likelihood of, or the proclivity to, rape by asking people about their attitudes to sexual coercion, and whether such behaviour might be acceptable. Malamuth found that around 35 per cent of men had attitudes that suggested a high LR (likelihood to rape). Similarly high proportions have been found in a number of studies (e.g. Chiroro *et al.* 2004). Such findings need to be interpreted with some caution, however. It may be that such attitudes do not necessarily lead to such behaviour. Indeed, Briere and Malamuth (1983) discovered no relationship between likelihood to rape and a series of actual behaviours:

1 current sex life and relationships with the opposite sex
2 importance and pleasantness of sex, and knowledge about sex
3 sexual conservatism or inhibitions
4 the use of and reaction to pornography.

The attitude of apparent likelihood to rape, therefore, did not seem necessarily to correlate with a set of behaviours which might also be consistent. This might suggest that either the measure LR is meaningless or that behaviour (and maybe rape) is about something else – it is not driven by attitudes. Baker *et al.* (2006) argue that despite the fashion for cognitive treatment programmes there may be real difficulties in engaging the majority of sex offenders. Cognitive treatment programmes depend on the ability to reflect and think about conscious thought processes, whereas there is evidence that sex offenders may have difficulty in reflective thought (as discussed in relation to domestic violence and male violence in particular), and that sex offending is symptomatic of disturbances at emotional and relational levels (Scheff and Retzinger 1997). It can be argued, however, that the study of attitudes does lead us to important cultural issues.

Cultural attitudes and rape

The study of individual differences in attitudes to rape has been used to explore cultural differences. Burt (1980) developed the Rape-Myth Acceptance Scale (RMA) in order to study cultural differences in social attitudes to rape. The RMA contains such items as 'all women want to be raped', 'no woman is raped unless she wants it', and 'she was asking for it'. Respondents are asked how much they agree with the statements. Burt (1980) found that the RMA seems to distinguish reliably between men and women when tested on US college students (Jones *et al.* 1998). Since then, various scales have been devised to measure individual differences in attitudes that might encourage rape (e.g. Acceptance of Interpersonal Violence (AIV) and Adversarial Sexual Beliefs (ASB)). These all correlate together, and males generally hold these views more than women. It has been argued that higher acceptance does go along with higher incidences of rape in cross-national comparisons (Pollard (1994) reviews some of these findings).

Sanday (1981) advanced anthropological evidence that 'rape-free' societies do exist (she included societies that had very low rates of rape in this category). She argued that the important characteristics of such societies are that women's contributions to the society are considered important and the sexes are considered to be of equal general value. Watson-Franke (2002) also marshalled evidence from various anthropological studies of cultures in which rape, if not quite non-existent, is considered extremely rare. She argues that cultures that have very low rates of rape are those that have a matrilineal order (in which family belonging is determined by the mother) and in which women's material and economic contribution to the society

223

is recognised and valued. As far as men's role is concerned, Watson-Franke (2002) suggests the key issue is that the biological reality of paternity is of little significance compared to the task of bringing up children. The men do 'usually carry major responsibilities with regard to the upbringing of the next generation, although their role in creating life is downplayed' (2002: 603). So men are valued, but not for the biological role they play in procreation. Watson-Franke (2002) argues that it is the notion that boys should separate themselves from women and be autonomous that can cause difficulties (see also Diamond 2004).

Culture, masculinity and sexual violence

Kersten (1996) considered cross-cultural issues in sexual violence by comparing Japan, Germany and Australia. According to official records, the Australian rate of rape is 20 times that of Japan, and three times the German rate. While accurate cross-cultural figures on crime are notoriously difficult, Kersten goes to some some lengths to put official records into context.

At first glance, the low visibility or rate of rape in Japan seems to defy common sense and some major sociological theories. Sanday, for example, suggests that frequent rape goes with clearly marked traditional gender roles, the subordination of women and an acceptance of male violence. On the first two counts, certainly Japan ought to have a high rate of rape. On the face of it, the status of Japanese women is lower than that of Australian women. In Japan, women certainly do not have anything approaching equality of opportunity in the workplace. The derogation of women, with portrayal of sexual violence in pornography (the Japanese phenomenon of pornographic comics called *manga*), would seem to be at least as common as in the West.

Kersten explores other cultural factors that might explain the low rate of sex crime. Japan is arguably a society where people's work and school lives are highly organised and time-consuming. There seems not to be the same leisure time available in which sexual attacks might take place. There is less emphasis on romantic love and dating in Japan, and this might also mean that the opportunities for 'date rape' are reduced. Marriages, although not exactly arranged, seem to be distinctly pragmatic affairs to Western eyes. Privacy is relatively rare, certainly for young people, as families tend to live in small apartments. This would present few opportunities for date rape to occur. And, although women do have a subordinate position in the workplace, they are perhaps very much in charge at home.

Perhaps it is in Japan's images of masculinity that the differences between the West (and Australia in particular) become most marked and suggestive. In the life worlds of the ordinary Japanese man, as Kersten (1996: 391) says, 'public displays of toughness, independence, and potency as indicators of masculinity defined as social and cultural achievement are rather frowned upon. The group of males in the workplace and in the pub after work exhibits patterns of "maternal values": understanding, an emphasis on caring for others and on reliability and displays of emotion.' This is in contrast to the hypermasculine ideal that permeates a great deal of Australian culture. According to Kersten, attacks on male homosexuals are unknown in Japan. Kersten argues that in Australia the ideal of masculinity that has predominated in Australia is in crisis – the availability of well-paid masculine jobs diminishes as women become more powerful. The loss of traditional avenues for masculine power and identity might well lead to the use of other means such as direct attacks on women.

It should be noted, however, that Konishi (2000) argues that much of the rape crime in Japan goes unreported, and reports that a community sample of women in Tokyo suggests that 8.5 per cent of the women had been raped at least once. This does not necessarily undermine Kersten's argument, as it may be that the under-reporting is in terms of 'acquaintance rapes', which Kersten acknowledges may well be significantly under-reported in Japan. Kersten still argues that there is something about the cultural manifestations of masculinity making 'public' stranger rape more likely in the West.

Another dimension of culture argued to be of significance in determining rates of rape is the availability of and attitudes to pornography. It would seem to be a matter of common sense that pornography (particularly that which features sexual violence) is likely to cause rape. By watching such material, men might perhaps learn to associate sexual pleasure with violence and want to act upon their desires. It is certainly arguable that pornography demeans and objectifies women. In partial support of this theory are the reports of sex offenders themselves, who commonly report 'using' pornography (often of a violent nature) prior to committing offences. Despite the seeming logic of this relationship, it has actually been hard to establish a causal relationship between pornography and sexual violence. Studies of the impact of the greater availability of pornography on rates of sex crime have been made in a number of countries. Diamond and Uchiyama (1999) report that the liberalisation of censorship laws in Japan and the increasing availability of pornography since the early

1970s has been associated with a decrease in the levels of recorded sex crime. Similarly, Kutchinsky (1991) summarises the findings of studies that suggest that the increasing availability of pornography in a number of European countries has been associated with decreases in the rate of sex crimes. It might be argued that the greater availability of pornography allows greater discussion, less repression of sexual desires, and reduction of the feelings of shame associated with sex.

Scheff and Retzinger (1997) imply that social attitudes that connect sexual feelings with shame might well play a causal role. They suggest that the combination of feelings of shame about sex with certain masculine ways of being can be a cause of sex crime. They argue that sexual offences can be triggered as perpetrators try to ward off feelings of shame, in much the same way as violence can be caused by someone seeking to avoid shame (described in some detail in Chapter 7). Scheff and Retzinger (1997) argue that sexual feelings and sexual encounters are often beset with shame, as they involve the exposure of the body, intimacy and vulnerability. Hence, situations involving sexual feelings are likely to trigger feelings of shame. People (usually male) who are unable to tolerate and therefore process shame are prone to act out aggressively. In order to ward off those feelings of vulnerability and fear of abandonment, men may well be led to defensive 'boldness, anger and aggression' (Scheff and Retzinger 1997: 15). Women, on the other hand, are more likely to withdraw in the face of shame and are hence perhaps less likely to be sexual offenders (Scheff and Retzinger 1997).

In support of their theory, Scheff and Retzinger (1997) argue that rapists are likely to have low self-esteem. Scheff and Retzinger (1997) refer to studies that suggest that rapists tend to score either low or high on measures of self-esteem. They argue that the high scorers do not really have high self-esteem at all, but they are actually highly defended against experiencing those negative feelings about themselves. That is, they do have powerful feelings of inadequacy but are covering them up with a false, hypermasculine front. They point to a study by Lawson (1979; cited by Scheff and Retzinger 1997) that seems to confirm this. Lawson asked prison staff about the self-esteem of rapists who had obtained high scores on self-report measures of self-esteem. They were seen by the prison staff as actually having low self-esteem, but they compensated for this with an exaggerated masculinity. By the penile response method, Proulx et al. (1994) found that convicted rapists were not more aroused than 'normal' men by depictions of violent sexual coercion, but were aroused by scenes that involved the victim being humiliated. The suggestion of the involvement of shame here relates to the idea, explored in the previous chapter, that male violence could occur as men feel that their image as a strong and autonomous being is threatened. In some men, the experience of shame leads directly to action and violence rather than thought.

Difficulties in reflecting on feeling were explored in a study by Senn *et al.* (2000), who looked at self-reported-sexually coercive behaviour (ranging from rape to sex play with arguments/reassurance) in a community sample of Canadian men. They found that the men's 'inability to feel the full range of emotions and to express them freely was an important predictor of coercion' (2000: 109). This inability was a better predictor of coercion than attitudes to rape. This is highly consistent with some of the work on domestic violence discussed in the previous section. Men able to reflect and think about negative feelings may be less likely simply to act on them. Scully (1988) tried to examine the emotions that were involved as the convicted rapists that she had interviewed actually carried out their offences. In addition to asking about their feelings after the attack, she also asked the men she was interviewing to imagine themselves in the position of their victims; what had they felt and how had they perceived their attackers? This is quite a sophisticated task, requiring not only that the offenders have a good representation of themselves and their emotional states but also of their victims. If these men found this difficult, it would entirely fit with Fonagy *et al.*'s (2004) theorisation of the relationship between violence and the inability to mentalise emotional states. They did indeed find aspects of these tasks difficult. Examining the responses of the men when asked about their feelings after the offence, Scully comments that 'the overwhelming majority of these men did not experience guilt or shame'. Indeed, from 'the emotionally flat perspective of almost half these men nothing much had happened' (1998: 206). As one rapist reported, 'I felt like I got what I wanted and had to get on with my business. She was of no more concern. I went to pick up my girlfriend.' Scully divided the men into those that admitted having forced someone to have sex ('admitters'), and those who acknowledged that they had sex with someone but denied that they had really forced their victim ('deniers'). Three-quarters of the 'admitters' could provide a description, and most of them used negative language to describe themselves (from their victim's point of view). For example, 'Like an animal, like you would describe someone you hated that was foul and disgusting – hideous is a good way to put it' (Scully 1998: 205). It is certainly plausible that being seen as powerful, strong, and scary was part of the motivation. However, 45 per cent of the deniers were completely unable to say how their victim would describe them, and another 45 per cent used positive language such as 'Not as mean or violent, just OK friendly' (1988: 205). The suggestion that these offenders have distorted memory seems the most probable explanation of these unlikely judgements, in most cases. In contrast to their seeming inability to reflect back on their own actions and feelings, however, the same group of deniers were able to describe their victims and their feelings. The victims were typically described as terrified, or perhaps initially resistant but then becoming passive in terror. The most common descriptions of the victims' feelings were those featuring 'powerlessness – humiliation and degradation' (1998: 207). While it is important to acknowledge important variations (some men did express considerable guilt, for example), in general these startlingly brazen accounts help paint a picture of men unable to reflect on their own feelings, but acting out feelings of anger, and inflicting humiliation and degradation on their victims in order to make themselves feel strong and powerful.

It might be argued that there are good reasons to believe that the motivations of male sexual violence against women are in many ways quite continuous with the motivations of general violence. Men who are violent are perhaps trying to ward off feelings of vulnerability and insecurity. Women may often be the target because they not only offer particular threats to esteem, but might also offer the vision of security and love that is unattainable and envied. Indeed, there is good evidence that those who offend against women in this way also commit other types of offences; they are likely to be generalists (Soothill *et al.* 2000). Like the more serious persistent offenders, sexual offenders are likely to have diagnoses of personality disorder (Rice and Harris 1997; Bogaerts *et al.* 2005).

The next topic is again one in which men dominate the statistics – sexual offences against children. Why should children also be so often the target of male sexual violence?

Paedophilia and sexual offences against children

The word *paedophile* literally means those who love children, but has come to mean in psychiatric terms adults who are sexually attracted to prepubescent children (Hall and Hall 2007). This attraction might be manifested in fantasies, use of child pornography, and sexual acts with children. In reality, sexual offences against children also involve offences against post-pubertal children who are under the age of consent (which varies considerably country to country (Seto 2004)).

Crimes involving sexual offences against children have drawn increasing public concern. Kemshall and McIvor (2004: 7) argue that by the 1990s the 'spectre of the predatory paedophile, had come to dominate the penal agenda'. There have been a series of legislative initiatives in the UK, such as, most notably, the 'Sex Offender Act' (Home Office 1997) which set up the 'Sex Offenders Register'. This required that all those convicted of any kind of sex offence register their name, address and National Insurance number with the police. They are then duty bound to inform the police if they move. Offenders have to comply with these instructions for 5 years if they are sentenced to less than 6 months in custody (or 7 years if there is a hospital order), or indefinitely if sentenced to longer than 30 months. Schools and other relevant bodies who employ people to work with children can check whether job applicants are on the register. Legislation concerning the register was updated in 2003 (Home Office 2003). Offenders have to inform the police of a new address within 3 days. If they stay temporarily at another address for 7 days or travel abroad, they must inform the police. Failure to comply with any of the above is a criminal offence that carries a prison sentence of up to 5 years. This exceptional provision, although it covers all sexual offenders, was largely inspired by anxiety about those who offend against children. It powerfully illustrates the degree of anxiety that has been provoked by sexual crimes against children. Clearly, it suggests that there is a belief that sex offenders continue to pose a serious threat to the public long after they have served their sentences.

Despite some awareness of and interest in women who commit offences against children (Kemshall 2004; Bunting 2005; Robinson 2005), there is little doubt that the overwhelming majority of sexual offences involving children are committed by males. For example, in the year 2000, only 1 per cent of recorded sexual offences in England and Wales were committed by females (Home Office 2001).

There are a number of issues to take into account when analysing the motivations of those who are convicted of sexual offences against children. There is first the range of offences, including rape and violent sexual assault; the non-contact offences, including exhibitionism; and, more recently, offences involving pornography and the Internet (Home Office 2003). The second important issue to be aware of is the fact that many offenders against children are actually young people themselves (Calder 2005). Technically, a 16-year-old boy who has sex with a 15-year-old girl is considered to be a sex offender.

Adult 'child sex' offenders

Just as with those who sexually offend against adults it is probably important to recognise that there are probably different types of child sex offender. An influential typology was drawn up by Groth and Birnbaum (1978), who suggested that there are two important categories of child sex offenders: first 'fixated offenders', who are thought to have their sexual interests fixed upon children, and second, 'regressed offenders', who are thought to have their main sexual interests focused on adults, but who, in times of psychological stress, might find their sexual attention turning to children as a regression to a more primitive, childish psychological state. In a similar fashion, Glasser (1988) distinguished between 'secondary paedophilia', in which the offending occurs in the context of some other pathology or breakdown, and 'primary paedophilia', in which the offending is carried out by someone who is functioning apparently 'normally' in other ways. This latter category can also be subdivided into the 'invariant paedophile' whose sexual interests are consistently directed toward children, and the 'pseudo-neurotic', who might be generally attracted to adults but at times of stress becomes involved with children. Glasser (1998) argues that all are 'profoundly disturbed individuals'. De Masi (2007) describes a simple distinction between the 'structured' (consistent interest in children) and the 'occasional' paedophiles, but agrees with Glasser that the 'occasional' paedophiles are covering up more profound disturbance.

Glasser (1998) argues that incestuous offenders are very different from non-incestuous paedophiles. Incest offenders are defined as those who offend against members of their own family, and Glasser suggests there may be slightly different motives. It has certainly been argued that the frequency of such incestuous offences means that the public should be more concerned with the danger posed by ordinary men in families than the danger from attack by a stranger. However, the distinction is open to dispute. Itzin (2001), for example, argues that there is now good evidence that those who abuse their own children are also likely to abuse children sexually outside the family. Victims of incestuous assault are prominent in the statistics on sexual abuse, simply because they live in proximity and are therefore vulnerable to those particular offenders.

The lack of systematic studies of child abusers is notable (Seto 2004). Those studies available are often subject to a number of methodological flaws, studies commonly having small and undefined samples (groups of offenders that happen to be in treatment, for example). The vast majority of the research has taken place on known offenders, with the extent of sexual attraction to children among men who either do not get caught or who do not act on these desires being largely unknown. There have been studies of non-offenders, but these have been self-selected groups. Even studies of offenders are often limited to those in various forms of treatment (Seto 2004). A study by Craissati and McClurg (1996) is notable in that they report a comprehensive study of all those convicted of sexual offences against children in southeast London over a 2-year period. It should at least give an inclusive picture of the full range of offenders who are convicted of a crime. They later report on the treatment of these offenders (Craissati and McClurg 1997). For comparison, they recruited a control group of violent or property offenders (who had no history of sexual offences). Their child offender group consisted of 80 individuals, and they reported on crimes against 122 victims. The average age of the victims was 10.5 years; 45 (37 per cent) of the victims were male and 77 (63 per cent) were females. Only 7 (6 per cent) of the victims were male strangers and 6 (5 per cent) were female strangers. Twenty-seven (22 per cent) of the victims were male acquaintances and 27 (22 per cent) were female acquaintances. Fifty-five (45 per cent) of the victims were related to the offender. In terms of the nature of the offences, they reported on 150 individual offences: 14 (9 per cent) involved anal intercourse; 10 (6.5 per cent) rape; 101 (68 per cent) indecent assault; 16 (11 per cent) gross indecency; 2 (1 per cent) unlawful sexual intercourse; 1 (0.5 per cent) exposure; and 6 (4 per cent) other.

The child sex offenders appeared to be an intellectually deprived group of men. Intelligence was measured on the Weschler Adult Intelligence Scale (WAIS), and the average IQ score was 90. Only four men scored above average and three men scored below 70 (and so would be regarded as 'mentally handicapped'). Although equivalent measures were not taken among the control group, the data suggest that this is an intellectually deprived group (in support of this is the fact that the child offender group were more likely to have attended a special school). Indeed, low intelligence has been consistently found among child sex offenders (Seto 2004). There were no differences from the control groups (violent and theft offenders), in ethnicity, marital status, number of adult sexual relationships, contact with family, parental divorce, emotional neglect as children, or contact with psychological services.

The child offenders were significantly older (with a mean age of 41 compared to 31 and 32 for violent and property offenders). The child sex offenders were significantly more likely to report no adult social contacts – that is, they were more likely to be socially isolated. They were significantly more likely to report histories of having been sexually abused than both violent and theft offenders. Both violent offenders and child offenders were significantly more likely to report histories of physical abuse compared to the theft offenders. The child offenders were more likely to have been bullied in school, but were actually more likely to be in stable employment (but no details were given about the nature or status of this employment). The finding that sex offenders are likely to have histories of childhood physical and emotional abuse and family dysfunction has been confirmed by many studies (e.g. Lee *et al.* 2002).

Overall, Craissati and McClurg (1997: 1075) conclude that, although their data point to a range of types of offenders they 'are strongly suggestive of a cluster of childhood experiences differentiating these sex offenders from other types of offender'. Some caution might be required, however, as this study, like many others, depends on the self-report of offenders themselves. Lee *et al.* (2002) cite Hindman's (1988) study that suggests that offenders are likely to 'over report' histories of abuse. Lee *et al.* (2002: 88) used a retrospective methodology, but included measures of 'social desirability' that aimed to give a picture of how likely the offenders would be to present themselves in a good light. They found that the paedophile group did not score more highly on the 'social desirability' measures;   therefore, they argue that a history of child abuse is a specific predictor of paedophilic offending. The social desirability measure does not, of course, entirely remove the possibility that the child offenders were embellishing their accounts.

To avoid the difficulties created by relying on retrospective accounts, longitudinal studies are required. Longitudinal studies of victims of child abuse are, however, relatively rare, and this makes the study reported by Salter *et al.* (2003) significant. They report on a longitudinal study of the impact of sexual abuse. They found of 224 male victims, of whom 26 went on to commit sexual offences (mainly against children outside the home). So while it should be noted that such figures make it clear that sexual abuse does not inevitably lead to a victim's becoming an offender, there is still a marked association. Salter *et al.* (2003) also compared the group who went on to become abusers themselves with those who did not. They did not find that the abusers had been subject to more severe sexual abuse, or more physical abuse. The abusers were significantly more likely to have been physically neglected, and to have been abused by a woman.

The presence of such strong indicators of early experiences of deprivation and abuse is, of course, consistent with many observations made about the backgrounds of those who might be described as life-course-persistent offenders and also those who come to be labelled as suffering from personality disorder (discussed in some detail in Chapter 3). It is interesting to observe that those who sexually offend against children are less likely to be versatile in their offending (Lussier *et al.* 2005), in contrast to those who offend against adults, who tend to commit other offences (Soothill *et al.* 2000). In other words, they are less likely to be generalist offenders, in contrast to those who offend sexually against adults. So, although a background marked by deprivation is common, there is something particular about paedophilic offending. There is good reason to believe that this extra factor is commonly the presence of sexual abuse or physical abuse when a child.

The possibility that paedophiles might suffer from personality disorder was investigated by Cohen *et al.* (2002). They tested the hypothesis that paedophiles can be characterised as suffering from impulsive aggressive personality disorder, and they found, that while this was not necessarily true, they could conclude that there was evidence of 'severe and pervasive personality impairments' in the paedophiles (2002: 132). Tardif and Van Gijseghem (2001) argue that paedophiles have a 'more fragile and vulnerable body image' (2001: 1390) than non-sex offenders and 'present a less solid ego identity compared with [non-sex offenders] on various aspects of their relationship with others'.

Glasser (1988) has argued that paedophilia is a symptom of profound psychological disturbances of identity due to difficulties in processes of internalisation that should normally take place as an individual develops. According to psychoanalytic theory, individuals develop and mature by identifying with and internalising objects (people) around then. So, typically, a young boy would identify with and then internalise a version of his father, becoming more like an adult male through development. People mature by copying and becoming like adults around them. The paedophile as a child is unable to identify with adults in the same way. This might well be because of some traumatic abusive relationship with an adult that leaves the child fearful of adults. Being unable to identify with adults, they are left unable to mature, and so are left internally childlike. Thus, as adults, they are still fearful of adults and see themselves as childlike. Because they experience themselves as childlike it is easy for them to identify with children, but at the same time to assume that children have the same sexual feelings that they have as adults.

233

This would fit the observations of those, like Kegan (1986), who observe the childlike responses of many of those with 'psychopathy'. According to Glasser, the paedophile can represent an extreme form of the narcissistic personality or false self that was linked to violence in Chapter 7. The fragile outer shell that might present as a strong adult image to the world is covering up a very immature and undeveloped personality. As discussed in Chapters 6 and 7, there are good reasons to think that such character formations are more likely to be associated with masculinity, with boys more likely to be unable to identify with adults around them. The notion that childhood trauma is significantly associated with the development of paedophilia is certainly backed up by empirical study. The study by Craissati and McClurg (1996), already referred to, found that 51.5 per cent of their sample of male paedophiles had been sexually abused as children; 63 per cent reported emotional neglect, and 40 per cent reported physical abuse. Overall, only 23.7 per cent of the sample had no experiences of physical, sexual or emotional neglect. It would be interesting to know more about this latter group.

It is striking how little research there is on the lives of paedophile offenders. This may well reflect what a complex and sensitive area this is (Glasgow 1993), or perhaps the stigma attached to their behaviour. What we do know of them suggests they are a particularly deprived group – often intellectually deprived and having experience of emotional and sexual abuse. One quite rare study of what child abusers have to say is that by Colton and Vanston (1996), whose book mainly consists of interview extracts with men who had been convicted of abuse and who were enrolled in a therapeutic programme. They were all professional men of some kind and so were perhaps not typical (compared to the sample reported by Craissati and McClurg 1996). Colton and Vanstone argue that 'the theme of masculinity clearly threads through all of the extracts in this book' (1996: 150) but that the issue was often not raised explicitly, although 'David', one of the abusing men, did bring this up:

> I can identify the need to fulfil an image, a macho image and a role which I could no longer do. I mean, with the stress and the strain of maintaining that image, it was finally giving in. I think [I had] the need to find some sort of 'love' or emotional outlet and contact, which I hadn't got.
>
> (Colton and Vanstone 1996: 151)

Overall, the evidence available seems generally to fit well with theoretical models that suggest that paedophile offenders are profoundly psychologically disturbed and that this disturbance has its roots in childhood. However, more work needs to be done in this area, perhaps particularly focusing on understanding offenders who do not have obvious histories of abuse themselves.

Adolescent sex offenders

It is being increasingly acknowledged that a significant proportion of those who offend against children are actually young people themselves (Calder 2005). Veneziano and Veneziano (2002) report estimates that 30–50 per cent of child sexual abuse offences are perpetrated by adolescents. This might well be an underestimate due to some reluctance to report such offences (NCH 1992). The fact that a considerable proportion of offences are committed by young people is entirely consistent with the pattern of general criminal activity. As explored in Chapter 3 ('Criminal Careers Research') and Chapter 5 ('Youth Crime'), in terms of general criminal activity, young people commit the overwhelming majority of offences. However, the case has been made very convincingly that a large proportion of those young offenders fit into the category of 'adolescent-limited' offenders (Moffitt 1993). This group, as described in Chapters 3 and 5, tend to commit relatively minor offences and restrict their offending to the adolescent years. It can be argued that in some ways adolescent-limited offenders are not so different from their non-offending peers.

Therefore, a number of questions arise in relation to adolescent sex offenders. Can they be understood in the same terms as adult offenders? Or is at least a subgroup of such offenders substantially different from adult offenders? Attempts to categorise adolescent sexual offenders are not advanced, despite widespread recognition that they are undoubtedly a heterogeneous group (Veneziano and Veneziano 2002). It does seem clear that adolescent sex offenders are likely to have backgrounds marked by social and emotional deprivation (Veneziano and Veneziano 2002). Such backgrounds are found in common with both adult sex offenders and relatively serious general offenders. Gretton *et al.* (2005) report on a 10-year longitudinal study of adolescent sex offenders who were referred by courts in Canada for treatment. Those with 'psychopathic' characteristics (or features of antisocial personality disorder) were less likely to complete treatment, and were more likely to go on to commit more serious sexual and other violent offences.

Masson (2004) reports evidence that the majority of adolescent offenders do not continue to offend when adults. Perhaps there is a similar division between the more serious offenders and those, like the general adolescent-limited offenders, who may desist from offending as they mature. In this, the sex offending is perhaps similar to the non-sexual offending patterns of the adolescent-limited offenders. Detailed longitudinal work will be necessary before these issues can be fully teased out.

Female sexual offenders

Statistically speaking, female sexual offenders are certainly in the minority as far as official records are concerned. Some figures suggest that less than 1 per cent of all offenders against children are female (Kemshall 2004). A number of writers suggest that such figures significantly underestimate the numbers of such offences and that female abusers are an important, neglected group. Various reasons are put forward for this state of affairs. It is argued that male victims may be less likely to complain, and the powerful cultural idealisation of motherhood makes it very hard to see that women do harm and abuse children. Studies of female abusers are certainly based on small numbers.

As discussed in Chapter 6 ('Gender and Crime', in relation to female violence p. 171), Motz (2001) is one of those that suggest that female crime and offences against children in particular have been largely neglected, and she argues that women are psychologically often predisposed to offend against children as a continuation of a propensity to self-harm. She also argues that women are more likely to identify with children and thus see them as extensions of themselves. She describes working with 'Allison', a woman in her late thirties who was accused of sexually abusing her daughter. Allison had experienced sexual abuse by her sister as a young child and her own daughter made very plausible allegations when taken into care. Motz (2001: 55) argues, 'In her mind Jennifer stood for her, and was the repository of her self-hatred and the target for her murderous impulses. The sexual sadism she directed towards her represented a kind of psychic murder.' Other studies also suggest that female abusers come from disturbed families (where incestuous abuse is common) and have suffered abuse themselves (Kemshall 2004). It would seem that histories of abuse and abuse at younger ages are even more common among female than male abusers (Robinson 2005). Poor relationships with mothers have also been noted, fitting well with Motz' formulation. The relative apparent scarcity of female offenders does mean that studies are based on small samples and are often impressionistic.

Conclusion

This chapter has explored the issue of violence in the context of intimate relationships. In terms of volume and impact, these crimes are perhaps the most significant that society faces. A number of themes emerged in analysis of violence in the previous chapter that pointed to the significance of the role of masculinity in violence. These themes have continued to be of relevance here.

Sex crime is an area of criminal activity that is not well understood. There are difficulties in the study of such crimes. The crimes themselves are often hidden, with victims often unwilling, or perhaps unable, to report them. Offenders in this area of crime, even more than others, are unwilling to admit and to talk about their offences. Sex crimes are shrouded by shame; perhaps, as Scheff and Retzinger (1997) argue, it is this very shame that may provoke sexual violence. Researchers themselves may be reluctant to study in such a fraught area (Glasgow 1993).

It is clear that sex crimes are far more likely to be committed by men than women. Many of the factors that lead men to become serious 'generalist' offenders are also present in the backgrounds of sex offenders. They are more likely than non-offenders to come from emotionally deprived backgrounds; from families where life is marked by neglect and erratic, harsh discipline. There do seem to be significant overlaps between violent offenders and those who offend sexually against adults. We also know that men who have been victims of sexual abuse themselves as children are more likely to become sex offenders themselves.

Those who offend against children are likely also to have backgrounds marked by similar factors, but are more likely themselves to have experienced sexual abuse. Of course, not all those so abused become offenders, and not all offenders have been victims as children. Research on paedophilia is particularly undeveloped; abhorrence at the offences has perhaps meant that few have wanted to enter this area with much curiosity. Nevertheless the model put

237

forward by Mervin Glasser, who suggests that the internal world of the paedophile is peopled with children rather than adults, is certainly consistent with much of the empirical evidence about the frequency with which perpetrators have themselves been abused by adults when children. Small wonder that they are be reluctant to identify with the adults around them.

Chapter 9

Conclusions

This chapter will review some of the material and ideas presented in the book, first, by providing an overview of the important themes; second, by reflecting on how they present a challenge to contemporary criminology; and third, by considering some of the implications of those findings for possible intervention strategies.

Overview

The book has presented the case for the closer integration of psychological approaches with mainstream criminological investigations of the causes of criminal behaviour; in particular, a psychosocial approach has been proposed that enables the consideration of the internal and emotional worlds of individuals alongside the social dynamics more traditionally studied by mainstream criminology. As discussed in Chapter 1, psychological perspectives on crime for many years have been pursued separately from mainstream criminology, which, as it developed in the second half of the twentieth century, became a discipline dominated by sociological thinking. It has been argued that this is now an untenable division. This book has explored a number of ways in which psychological approaches that are sensitive to issues of emotions are particularly useful at bridging the gaps between disciplinary approaches.

Chapter 2, 'Mental Disorder: Madness, Personality Disorder and Criminal Responsibility', looked at a number of ways in which questions about the mental state or sanity of offenders has presented problems for the criminal justice system. It is apparent that for many centuries those accused of serious offences have been treated more leniently if they were seen to be 'mad'. Yet, the detail of how mental disorders and illnesses can be conceptualised in relation to offending remains controversial. For almost 200 years, there has been debate over offenders who seem to have normal cognitions and perceptions but who have abnormal emotional responses. The English doctor Prichard (1835) talked about such offenders in terms of 'moral insanity'. He argued that such people should be understood to be suffering from a mental disorder. Prichard was unsuccessful in this argument, and a clearly cognitive version of insanity and the insanity defence was established. This is well represented by the M'Naghten rules that defined when the 'insanity defence' might be accepted in court. These rules put great stress on the defendant's ability to reason, so that only defendants who exhibited clearly disordered perceptions or delusions could be considered insane. Despite this, there are continuing debates and difficulties over the status of the mental health of many offenders. In particular, it seems that over 60 per cent of the prison population is made up of people suffering from 'personality disorders', notably 'antisocial personality disorder'. While there are disagreements over definitions and the medical status of such disorders, these are people who have demonstrable difficulties in either understanding emotions or controlling them. They are also apparently clear thinking and not deluded, but their behaviour and their relationships with others can be highly abnormal and problematic. It is apparent that the criminal justice system is highly ambivalent about how such emotional disorders might be handled. The UK government has been pressing for personality disorders to be generally taken much more seriously by the health service (DOH 2003), and the concern about the danger posed by individuals who are described as dangerous and suffering from personality disorder appears high and is manifest in various policy initiatives (DoH 2003; Cabinet Office 2006). The numbers of people in prison who can be identified as suffering from such disorders is certainly high. Their presence raises questions about the boundary between mental health and criminal justice issues. Whether the identification of personality disorders as mental disorders is helpful, there does seem to be strong evidence that those with such difficulties tend to have experienced negative life events (Pagano *et al.* 2004) and deprived childhoods in particular (Bandelow *et al.* 2005).

The significance of the life history of the individual is explored in greater detail in Chapter 3, 'The Contribution of Criminal Career

Research'. This chapter examined the findings of longitudinal studies that make very clear the link between accumulations of deprivation, including the social and familial, and later offending activity. That is, the more social, and familial disadvantages people face, the more likely they are to lead difficult and troublesome lives. There do appear to be real overlaps between issues of mental health, with their roots in social conditions, and the behaviour of the most serious offenders. Another, very important, lesson of the longitudinal studies is that studies based on understanding distinctions between those who offend and those who do not are far too simplistic. Offenders and non-offenders need to be understood as heterogeneous groups. The distinction made by Moffitt (1993) between adolescent-limited (AL) offenders and life-course-persistent (LCP) offenders has stimulated considerable interest. There are clear parallels between the characteristics and life histories of the LCP group and those who might be deemed to suffer from 'personality disorders'. These are individuals who are identifiable early in life (often it is claimed by 5 years of age), as having emotional and behavioural problems. They are more likely to come from 'problem' families, to have disrupted school careers, and, as adults, to have turbulent relationships with others. The area of overlap with those suffering from mental health problems appears to be strong.

While the LCP offenders are undoubtedly the perpetrators of the offences that cause most public anxiety about crime, it is youth offenders who commit the greatest volume of crime. The findings of the longitudinal studies suggest that there is considerable overlap between the AL offenders and normal adolescents, the majority of whom seem to be involved in minor offending. The issue of why so many young people become involved in minor offending is taken up in Chapter 5, 'Youth Crime', which explored how the well-known age and crime relationship can be understood. Why is it that such a high proportion of criminal activity is committed by young people? The findings from the longitudinal research on AL offenders might be seen as being quite comforting on one level, as they suggest that this group, although quite large (perhaps around 25 per cent of the male population), tend to restrict themselves to committing more minor offences and are apt to grow out of offending altogether in their adult years. Such findings certainly suggest that more resources should be spent on intervening with the LCP offenders, although questions might still be asked about whether more psychological perspectives on adolescent behaviour might be helpful in understanding a phenomenon that causes fairly considerable social problems. A number of theories suggest that adolescence is a period of life in which individuals attempt to construct identities for themselves. In order to make moral decisions, people need to have a sufficient sense of themselves as autonomous beings to be able to think and act with some independence of immediate pressures and concerns (such as peer pressures, for example). Some implications for this will be discussed later, but it is certainly important to recognise that the development of 'moral emotions' during adolescence needs to be understood as a developmental achievement. The capacity to process moral emotions is generally not present at the beginning of adolescence; it develops alongside people's sense of themselves as autonomous individuals who exist in relation to others. This is a psychologically complex developmental process that occurs throughout the adolescent years and into adulthood. Criminal justice systems that assume that children as young as 10 can be held entirely responsible for their criminal actions need to be far more aware of this work on moral emotions.

One obvious criticism of the model proposed here that stresses the need of individuals to be able to process emotion such as shame, is that it is, again, simply privileging abstract reason (guilt) over the more primitive world of feeling (shame). This criticism is analogous to that made by Carol Gilligan (1982) of Lawrence Kohlberg's work on moral development (discussed in Chapter 5). However, the formulation proposed here suggests that the opposition proposed by Gilligan between abstract reason and autonomy (typically associated with masculinity) and the ethic of care (associated with femininity) is not necessary. It may be better to understand that the capacity for moral thought and behaviour does entail the ability to process and reflect upon feelings and to act autonomously. The ability to process emotions and act autonomously, however, can develop only through relationship with others. As discussed in previous chapters, there is evidence that the relationships between children and parents (Chapter 4) and adolescents and parents (Chapter 5) can be significant in allowing the individual to develop the ability to process emotions. The end result is relatively autonomous and reflective thinking. But this can be achieved only through relationship to others.

The overlap between those who might be diagnosed as suffering from personality disorders (most notably antisocial personality disorder) and those identified as LCP offenders is also notable. Governments in the UK and elsewhere have certainly become interested in the possibility that the most serious offenders, both in volume and seriousness, might be identifiable very early in their lives. Those who fit Moffitt's description of LCP offender often have exhibited behavioural difficulties very early in life (as young as 3 or 5 years of age) and have educational, social and family histories that are marked by difficulties.

Longitudinal research seems repeatedly to point to the significance of family life and parenting in the lives of those identified as LCP offenders. Chapter 4, 'Familial and Parental Influences', examined the evidence of the association between family factors and criminal offending. The more serious offenders do seem to come from backgrounds marked by difficulties and typically low levels of supervision, poor parenting factors and even abuse. Such findings have stimulated the interest of governments, as they provide a potential rationale for intervention strategies aimed at young children and their families who may be vulnerable to such difficulties. What emerges from review of the research on families is how little is definitely known about the significant points of parenting. Work on the 'moral emotions' suggests ways forward for research in the area, but also implies that adequate parenting is not likely to be conveyed by a few parenting classes. Work on the significance of shame and its power to shape and constrain behaviour points to the importance of emotional attunement between parents and children. Such a condition is hard to create for adults with few emotional resources themselves and little social support, and living in stressful circumstances.

Another important fact about crime, which seems to be resilient across time and culture, is that the overwhelming majority of it is committed by men. This issue was explored in Chapter 6, 'Gender and Crime'. The question of whether this is simply a state of affairs that needs to be accepted, or whether it is a product of particular forms of masculinity that are created in various cultural circumstances, is an issue that can be explored. Closer analysis of some of the crimes committed by men certainly reveals a host of psychological issues that might well be relevant to understanding why men do what they do. Chapter 7, 'Understanding Violence: Learning from Studies of Homicide', and Chapter 8, 'Intimate Violence and Sex Crime', both explored the relationship between men, masculinity and violence further. The fact that men dominate the figures on crime, particularly the more violent crimes across the world and throughout history, might point us to biological explanations of gender differences. However, the extent of cultural differences in rates of violence (data on homicide, as discussed in Chapter 7, are considered to be reliable indicators of national variations) suggests that cultural factors need to be taken into account. A striking trigger for male violence appears to be the emotion of shame, and this links with earlier material about the significance of the moral emotions. Perhaps men that have not developed the capacity to regulate feelings of shame are prone to violence. Examination of the more serious violent offenders points us back toward the issues of mental disorders raised at the beginning of the book. Theoretical work suggesting that paedophiles suffer from very profound disorders of identity is supported by empirical evidence on the likelihood of their having very damaged childhoods.

Psychosocial understanding of criminal behaviour: the significance of emotion and personality in conditions of 'high modernity'

It will be argued here that the approach taken in this book is increasingly relevant to understanding and thus reducing crime. The proper integration of the emotional aspects of people's experiences within criminological theory can lead to a much needed reinvigoration of criminological theory.

As discussed in Chapter 1, criminology became a largely sociological discipline, taking the view that crime can be understood in terms of the social forces creating it. While the idea that poverty directly creates crime was easily refuted, the notion that there is some link between social deprivation and crime has persisted. What has been termed the 'aetiological crisis' (Young 1986) arose in criminology as crime levels soared in the West during the second half of the twentieth century, just as general levels of wealth, and the provision of better standards of health, housing and education also increased dramatically. Young (1986) argued that this crisis led to paralysis in criminological theory, so that 'talk of theory, causality and justice has all but disappeared' (Young 1986: 30). A few years later, Young (1999) revisited this work by arguing that criminology needs to engage with the changing character of crime in the face of changes brought about by late modernity and the social exclusion of many working-class men created by the dissolution of the traditional industries of mass employment. More recently, Young (2003) has argued that this changing economic climate requires theoretical models that bring together the study of structure and agency: 'Merton with energy, Katz with structure'. Young argues that the order of late modernity creates ontological insecurity – among both the apparent winners and the losers in these new economic arrangements. Both groups, the so-called socially excluded and the included, feel the same threats to security; the forces of globalisation, the seeming randomness of market forces, and 'the widespread discontinuities of personal biography both in the world of work and within the family, coupled with the undermining of a sense of locality', are experienced by all (Young 2003: 399–400). Envy and resentment are not a one-way street between the included and the excluded. The 'included' are often working longer hours, and they are ever more likely to be on temporary contracts, and living in mounting debt. They may well be prone to 'look down' with some resentment at those living in social housing, with apparently many hours more leisure time and regular access to recreational drugs (legal or otherwise). The excluded meanwhile can still angrily 'look up' at the included, with easier access to the material spoils of modernity and more of the conventional markers of achievement. While there is nothing new about class resentments, the pain of these was ameliorated in the past, Young suggests, by the experience of solidarity, but 'now this fixed infantry of conflict is substituted by the loose cannons of discontent' (1999: 7), and we are left to make sense of these feelings, or just react to them on our own.

A number of theorists have argued that the social and cultural changes being wrought under the name of high modernity are having significant impact at the level of personality. Elias (1994), writing in the 1930s, argued that in trying to understand 'the civilizing process' it is necessary 'to investigate ... the transformation of both the personality structure and the entire social structure' (1994: 411). It is the former dimension that has been lacking in criminological theory. The first chapter of the book mapped the very different routes taken by sociological criminology and psychological approaches to criminal behaviour. There is still a strong reluctance among criminologists to engage with the psychological aspects of criminal behaviour. In particular, there are four areas that criminological theory has not explored, to the great detriment of our understanding of crime:

1 Theorising the inner experiences of the emotional lives of individuals.
2 Theorising the inner experience and psychological roots of masculine modes of experience and behaviour.
3 The significance of family and intimate relationships in shaping people's interactions with the wider world.
4 The overlaps between issues of criminal behaviour and mental health.

It can be argued that the incorporation of these perspectives within criminological theory is ever more urgent, because they are becoming more relevant to understanding crime.

Emotional experience, morality and modernity

Cas Wouters (1999) has argued directly that the rising crime rate over the latter half of the twentieth century can be explained by the social changes that have required rather different forms of consciousness. He also assumes that the second half of the twentieth century has ushered in a new world of a rather different moral order that requires that individuals have a different psychological make-up. Up until the first half of the twentieth century, he argued, Western societies were fairly rigidly hierarchical. People largely 'knew their place'; it was mainly accepted that authority flowed downward. Wouters argues that this social hierarchy was mirrored in the psychic structures of individuals. Moral behaviour was largely governed by the superego. That is, individuals internalised a self-monitor that would punish the individual for wrongdoing. The individual was brought up to have an automatic sense of right and wrong. It became 'second nature' to know that wrongdoing is not acceptable. People essentially learnt this by being punished for doing wrong as children. Thus far, the view of the necessity of controlling emotion and impulses is consistent with that of Elias (1994). Since then, Wouters argues, an increasingly fluid society has emerged that requires that those emotions and impulses become available to consciousness. The traditional structures of authority are questioned while the boundaries between social classes and groups are relatively unstable. These changes require different forms of consciousness. We have moved, in Wouters' terms, from 'second nature' to 'third nature', that is, from a situation where doing the right thing is largely automatic and unquestioned, and individual drives and impulses are largely buried, to one where we are expected to be aware of our own impulses and drives. He suggests that 'conscience has lost automatic ascendancy. Internalized controls of a rather fixed kind ... changed from being an advantage to being a handicap; they became too rigid and stiff' (1999: 424). The idea of 'personality' has thus become more important as a crucial capacitor of authority and action. We are expected to reflect on our circumstances and choose how to behave, selecting from a range of options. In Anthony Giddens' terms, we are now required to be managers of a reflexive project (Giddens 1991), constantly choosing how to act and how 'to be'.

Wouters implies there was a period of transition roughly between the 1950s and the late 1980s. Individuals were liberated as traditional boundaries around class, authority and sexuality began to fall away. People were encouraged to be more aware of, and allowed to act upon, the range of emotions and impulses inside themselves. As an illustration, Wouters quotes from a Dutch comedian describing a visit to a petrol station:

> It is a self service station and when I walk inside to pay (after a habitual quick look to see how I could avoid paying by tearing away unnoticed from the place) I receive a Free Drinking Glass.
>
> (Wouters 1999: 421)

Wouters suggests that the joke in parentheses is notable for its assumption that such criminal thoughts are now quite casual and commonplace. Wouters goes as far as to argue that

> this collective transition, from rather rigid discipline to reflexive and flexible calculation, was so drastic and risky that it may largely explain the *overall* rise in crime rates.
>
> (1999: 427)

Wouters suggests that different types of family behaviour and child rearing have become required to create individuals who are less controlled by a repressive conscience but are instead more conscious of their impulses and emotions. Wouters does not explore this issue of what family practices might be required, but some of the material reviewed in this book does give some pointers in terms of how the development of the 'moral emotions' has emerged as an important theme and the way that an individual's responses to the 'moral emotions' are to an extent forged within early relationships.

John Braithwaite's ideas about the significance of shaming techniques and restorative justice (Braithwaite 1989) drew the attention of criminology to the moral emotions. The notion of 'restorative justice' has been influential in justice practice in different parts of the world. Braithwaite's premise is that cultures that properly utilise the power of shame tend to be more effective in reducing crime than those that rely on stigmatisation and guilt. He argues that the typical Western practice of imprisonment results in stigmatisation and exclusion. These result in the offender's being estranged from the distress they have caused, as they do not have to face that distress. They will be yet more alienated from the community they have offended against. They will thus be more likely to offend again. Braithwaite proposes that it is more effective to get offenders to come face to face with the distress they have caused – they need truly to experience shame, which can only be done through relationship to others. Offenders who thus experience shame can then make some reparation and so be reintegrated into their communities. Braithwaite argues that the community makes clear that it is the criminal act that is disapproved of, not the offenders themselves.

Although restorative justice practices have their critics (e.g. Bennett 2006), in many ways Braithwaite's message is consistent with some of the themes of this book. Braithwaite argues that the emotional worlds of offenders are more significant determinants of behaviour than the rational models often assumed by the criminal justice system (whereby people are supposed to be deterred from offending if they are presented with clear enough consequences), or criminological theory (in which people are often portrayed as manoeuvring in difficult circumstances). The explorations in this book of the significance of shame as a 'moral emotion', however, render elements of Braithwaite's ideas problematic. Braithwaite argues that shame is the more significant moral emotion. The analysis within this book suggests that shame is indeed fundamental, but it needs to be understood not only in terms of the relations in which it arises, but also in terms of the individual's capacity to process and make sense of shame. On its own, the experience of shame can directly lead to highly antisocial behaviour. If shame means anything, it is the feeling people have as they experience themselves as being somehow not good enough. It represents a sense of threat to an individual's identity, triggering fears of uselessness and abandonment. Shame itself can be a significant trigger for violence, as explored in Chapter 7 in looking at confrontational violence between men, and as a trigger for male violence against women in Chapter 8. The idea that the provocation of shame itself will necessarily lead to more pro-social behaviour is certainly doubtful. Instead, it has been argued in this book that there may well be an important developmental achievement in an individual learning to process shame, rather than simply experience it. It is very important to note, however, that there is good evidence that the developmental achievement is one that occurs within relationship to others.

Shame, identity and personality disorder

While Braithwaite berates the modern world for eschewing shame, other social theorists have argued quite the reverse. Giddens argues that under conditions of high modernity 'shame rather than guilt tends to come to the fore as a feature of psychic organisation' (1991: 69). Shame is the signal of alarm about the danger of abandonment and isolation. It is the feeling that judgement is being made that the self is lacking, not viable and worthless. In the conditions of high modernity, when we are set free of the certainty of the bonds of class, religion, community and family solidarity, we are constantly in danger of exposure and isolation. Far from needing to provoke shame, we are at risk of drowning in it. The problem has become increasingly how to manage shame.

The difficulty is that shame has become something that we increasingly have to manage at an individual level. In conditions where the self is more embedded and the individual is less exposed, shaming depends to an extent on the manipulation of social bonds. In these conditions of disembedded high modernity, we have to manage ourselves, manage our attachments – choose how to live and how to be. Far greater internal resources are now required to maintain the narrative of ourselves, which is 'a struggle at best won only provisionally and always entailing expenditure of considerable amounts of psychological energy' (Frosh 1991: 187).

While acknowledging the shift toward the individual in terms of the agency required in the construction of selfhood in the conditions of high modernity, Giddens (1991) has been relatively optimistic about the changes being wrought by these conditions. Freed from the snares and burdens of tradition and repression, we become free to explore different, and better, kinds of social relations. Traditional, and oppressive, gender roles can be shaken off. We have the possibility of the 'democratic pure relationships', negotiated to the satisfaction of all parties. Different family forms and lifestyles can be tried out – from single parenthood, gay parenthood, and 'living apart together'. Writing some years earlier, Lasch (1979) had also observed the changes being wrought by these social conditions on the psyche. He was far less optimistic, however, and argued that the 'personality disorders' were coming to be the characteristic personality formations of our times. He argued that we had entered an 'age of narcissism'. While in common usage narcissism has come to mean 'self-love', its use in the clinical world carries anything but this meaning. The narcissistic personality is one that has few inner resources, that feels empty, worthless and unlovable. The only way such a personality can maintain esteem and identity is by searching for constant external reassurance and validation. Lasch emphasised three aspects of modern culture that are responsible for reproducing this personality on a large scale:

- The dissolution of community and the subsequent encouragement of transient and superficial relationships. Individuals are not given the opportunity of consistent relationships that can develop over time, allowing an inner sense of worth to be built.

- A world of media and advertising that provokes desires and can satisfy those desires through the purchase of easily available goods. Thus, desires are not met through the achievement of goals that might involve long-term work or commitment, but by the acquisition of material goods.

- Parents who themselves have little sense of inner worth have children to meet their own emotional needs. They love their children only when they are 'good' and meet the needs of the parents. The children are not loved for who they are. Thus, such children grow up feeling that they are loved only when they are performing for others.

While Lasch (1979) has been accused of harking back to a patriarchal golden age when people knew their place, men were the head of the household, and their womenfolk looked after them, his psychological analysis deserves some attention (Barrett and McIntosh 1982; Frosh 1987). It can certainly be plausibly argued that it is men who are going to be most vulnerable to these trends. On an individual level, it has been argued that they do face a more problematic developmental pathway, boys being required to develop masculine identities often in environments where men are not around, and in cultures where masculinity can be very strongly associated simply with rather two-dimensional images of strength, autonomy, violence and not a little misogyny. In terms of the social roles then on offer, men who might be looking for the traditional well-paid, non-skilled or semi-skilled employment have found that it is not there. They do not have the option of the domestic role to fall back on, as women do. Men can be caught in a trap of ever increasing reliance on an image of toughness and strength that is covering up feelings of weakness and shame. As Connor (2001: 212) puts it, in explaining why men are so beset with shame: 'Men are spent up: masculinity is a category of ruin, a crashed category. It's a bust.'

Hayward (2004: 5) has written on the significance of consumer culture in contemporary criminality. He applauds Lasch for 'brilliantly' pointing out the significance of the impact of consumer culture on identity. However, in a familiar move for criminological theory, the psychoanalytic foundations of Lasch's analysis are entirely ignored. To Lasch, consumerism is indeed part of the problem, but the attraction of consumerism relies on sufficient numbers of people depending on the quick fix of consumption to feel whole. For Lasch, far too many people are growing up in families and communities without any real sense of worth.

It is within men that this emptiness has the most significance. It is within the topic of masculinity that the failure to explore the psychological roots of emotional conditions has now become most stark. Young (1999) has picked up the argument that the changes of late modernity have impacted most harshly on men. As their relatively well-paid jobs in heavy industry have disappeared, so have their roles as breadwinners and heads of households. While women have the option of taking on the role of motherhood for respect and esteem, men are more likely to suffer the full consequences of this disembedded experience, being left without roles and sources of respect:

> Young men facing such denial of recognition turn, everywhere in the world, in what must be almost a universal criminological law, to the creation of cultures of machismo, to the mobilization of one of their only resources, physical strength, to the formation of gangs, and to the defence of their own 'turf'. Being denied the respect of others they create a subculture that revolves around masculine powers and 'respect'.
>
> (Young 1999: 12)

The difficulty here is that the association of 'masculinity' with physical strength, gang cultures and respect remains entirely unquestioned (a common stance within criminology, as explored in Chapter 6). Instead it is suggested that this is something akin to a natural law. The discussion of the relation between masculinity and crime in Chapter 6 suggests that investigating masculinity itself is extremely worthwhile. There seems little evidence to suggest that we should see aggressive behaviour by men as simply natural and biologically derived. It has been argued in this book that there may be much to gain by understanding the links between cultural factors and individual psychology. It can plausibly be argued that men do find themselves in a different position in relation to these new conditions of high modernity, not simply because they do not have a domestic role to fall back on (which itself needs to be opened to reflection and question), but because they often stand in a different relation to others, and this can leave them more exposed to the ravages of modernity.

Young (2004) makes good use of Nightingale's (1993) compelling ethnographic account of life in a poor black community in Philadelphia. Nightingale makes the important point that despite the economic exclusion, this is a community that is thoroughly culturally 'included'. It has been drenched in the mainstream values of consumerism and ethics of violence:

> New pairs of sneakers every month, Mickey-Mouse T-shirts, glorified caricatures, 'racial-obsession', 'patriotism' and 'law and order' ideas, and long lines of African-American people outside showings of *Terminator* or *Nightmare on Elm Street* are all important to the inner city story.
>
> (Nightingale 1993: 11)

Another aspect of the lives of the delinquent and often violent young people is also prominent in Nightingale's story, but is left alone by Young – their desperately bleak family lives. Their mothers are young, and they have had babies in an attempt to find 'affection they thought they could expect from an infant and from the aura of adulthood they hoped could come from being a mother'. They have no physical or psychological resources for the real needs of a baby and child. Parents who only have children for their own needs are the essential ingredient of Lasch's narcissistic personality. The real needs of children cannot be met, so even 'crying babies in the neighbourhood are often told simply to "shut up" or are sometimes even slapped' (1993: 101). By the time they are toddlers, the children are spending most of their time on the street among their peers. Parenting, when it happens, is usually 'forceful'. Physical punishments are often brutal, the 'parents ... taking out their own pain on their kids' (1993: 104). Boys are particularly at the sharp end. Girls are more likely to spend time with mothers and are spared the more violent treatment of their brothers. Nightingale reports strong beliefs about the need to beat boys, partly as a way of controlling them, but also in order to 'harden them up'. Almost no affection is shown to them in the home. He describes plaintive scenes of young children seeking affection:

Infants, toddlers and kids under about eight or nine usually have not yet shed universal, nonaggressive expressions of emotional vulnerability, like crying and open calls for hugs, ... Whole groups of little kids who are playing together in [the] neighbourhood will drop whatever they are doing whenever an adult who has a reputation for being affectionate drives up the street, and they will race each other to be the one to open the car door, or be the first to be picked up or given a hug.

(1993: 47)

Beliefs that boys should not show feelings, vulnerability or any signs of femininity are all pervasive. A particularly rigid view of masculinity is enforced. Nightingale describes how 'Omar', one of the young people he came to know well, was very affected by being severely whipped with a belt by his father when he put a pillow under his jumper pretending to be pregnant. The accompanying lecture on the evils of 'acting gay' he could still recite 'many years later' (1993: 103).

The boys are left alone among their peers to don the mask and attire of masculinity, so readily available from the imagery of Hollywood, hip hop and gangsta rap:

Even at age two or three, before male restrictions on emotional expression begin to constrict their behaviour, boys already begin to practice many of the basic poses and rules of masculine self-expression they will later perfect in adolescence. By the fifth or sixth grade [age 9–11], inner-city elementary schoolteachers regularly report, the bright eyes of their boy students start to glaze over in preparation for assuming a 'tough look'. And at about the same age, boys ... start to control crying or even smiling in public as they begin to spurn affection.

(1993: 47)

If there is to be a refreshed criminology that is fit to engage with the reality of the multi dimensional aspects of people's lives, it needs to include the emotional and internal worlds of children like these.

Reducing crime

The rest of the chapter will briefly outline some possible implications of the issues discussed in the previous chapters. Four particular topics will be considered. First, there is the issue of the significance of family relationships and what might be done to intervene. Second, there is the issue of youth crime. Third, there is the large difficulty of the relationship between gender, masculinity and crime. Fourth, can the associations between issues of mental health and crime lead to useful interventions?

Families and early intervention strategies

In thinking about crime reduction policies, one obvious route is to consider the fact that the so-called LCP offenders seem to be often identifiable early in their lives. The question arises as to what strategies might be developed to intervene early and prevent the problems from becoming long-standing ones. There is also evidence of the significance of families and crime, and the UK government has undoubtedly been strongly influenced by such findings. One notable policy initiative was 'Sure Start', an ambitious policy that aimed to channel resources to families of the 0–3-year age group. A government review of services for children in 1998 concluded that provision for pre-school children was very patchy, some areas having little or no provision. The review also considered evidence of the significance of early experience (Utting *et al.* 1993) as a cause of social exclusion that makes people vulnerable to delinquency. Sure Start aimed to create comprehensive, locally based services for young people and their families. In order to avoid the stigma that might be created if services were targeted at particular families, the early schemes were targeted at areas of relative deprivation, but aimed to provide for all families of young children in that area. The format of the schemes was to be decided locally but generally included nursery/day-care provision, health advice and education, as well as community and leisure activities. It is interesting to note the scope of this policy, emphasis being put on resources to build community networks as well as on the provision of parenting and health classes. In this latter respect, Sure Start was influenced by ideas about the significance of social bonds and social capital. By 2004, the government had spent more than £1 bn on 500 Sure Start schemes providing support for one-third of disadvantaged children under 4 years old across England – some 400,000 in all (Sure Start).

In part, the rationale for Sure Start came from schemes such as Early Head Start in the USA, a highly intensive scheme aimed at providing educational support for deprived families. Evaluation was built into the development of Sure Start (studies being carried out locally on all the individual projects, and surveyed by the National Evaluation of Sure Start based at Birkbeck College, University of London). Early findings of the national evaluation caused some concern (NESS 2005). These findings indicated that less deprived families living in Sure Start areas seemed to be benefiting from those services. They were more positive about their communities and used more positive parenting techniques, and their children exhibited fewer behavioural problems. More deprived families living in the Sure Start areas seemed to be doing less well than comparable families in non-Sure Start areas. The authors conclude that 'among the disadvantaged families living in the deprived Sure Start Local Programme (SSLP) areas, parents/families with greater human capital were better able to take advantage of SSLP services and resources than those with less human capital (i.e. teen parents, lone parents, workless households)' (NESS 2005: 8). Given that one of the major aims was to improve the life chances of the more deprived children, this seemed a perplexing finding. Although the researchers were at pains to point out that the findings are very early, and that many of the expected benefits of Sure Start would be long-term, this has caused some concern.

The findings of this book suggest that the advantages provided by schemes such as Sure Start would very likely take time to develop. In the first place, it is clear that 'good parenting' is not simply a set of techniques that can be easily learnt. Moreover, the findings reviewed in Chapter 4, 'Familial and Parental Influences', suggest that families that are clearly associated with poor outcomes are those that are abusive and highly neglectful, and so may well prove to be a highly challenging group with which to engage. Further initiatives have been heralded by the government document *Reaching Out* (Cabinet Office 2006), which perhaps points to policies that may target those seen as in most need of support in the future.

The UK government has also sought to pressurise families to take more responsibility for their children's behaviour by various 'parenting orders'. The Criminal Justice Act 1991 (Section 58) required that the parent of an offender aged 10–16 years accompany that child to the court and pay any fine or costs. The courts were given the power to 'bind over' parents insisting that they stop their child from offending, on pain of being fined. The clearly punitive nature of this received considerable criticism (Arthur 2005). The subsequent Crime and Disorder Act 1998 gave courts the power to direct parents to compulsory parenting classes, the belief being that while some parents needed to be confronted with their responsibilities, other parents of delinquent teenagers wanted to be able to control their children but did not know how.

The Anti-Social Behaviour Act 2003 continued the trend of the government pushing responsibility for youth crime onto parents. This gave power to Youth Offending Teams (YOTs) to apply to the courts for parenting orders. They might do this if they were working with a young offender but felt that the difficulty lay with the parents. Such initiatives have been heavily criticised by criminologists for shifting the blame for many social problems onto parents (Day-Sclater 2000).

In reality, parenting orders have not been widely used (Arthur 2005). The material reviewed in this book suggests that there might well be many families that would benefit from such training. A meta-analysis of evaluations of parenting classes suggests that they can be effective (Reyno and McGrath 2006). However, a common finding has been those families facing the greatest social difficulties tend to be poor attenders and are more likely to drop out (Reyno and McGrath 2006).

Lyons-Ruth (1996: 69) argues that difficulties in emotional attachments between mothers and their infants 'occurred predominantly in the context of maternal childhood experiences of family violence or abuse'. In other words, the difficulties very likely go back several generations. Pinderhughes *et al.* (2000) found that stress appeared to have a significant impact on parents' ability to use more thoughtful discipline techniques. The more stressed parents are, the more likely they are to use inconsistent and harsh discipline. Weissman *et al.* (2006) report that helping mothers come out of depression can quickly reduce psychological distress (including behavioral problems) in their children. All this suggests that good parenting, although a significant factor, cannot be regarded as simply a set of techniques that can be taught and learnt. The particular circumstances in which families live can play a part, but so also can the psychological lives and histories of the parents. Ceballo and McLoyd (2002) show how improving the social support available to parents can have beneficial effects on parenting, but that this is far more difficult in poorer, higher-crime neighbourhoods. At the very least, these caveats suggest the harm in simplistically blaming parents and making their lives more difficult that they already are.

Young people and crime

Besides the LCP offenders, the other significant group of offenders to emerge from the longitudinal studies are the adolescent-limited (AL) offenders. As already discussed, the point that emerges very strongly from Chapter 5 'Youth Crime' is that there are strong psychosocial reasons for the involvement of young people in crime. In some respects, a certain amount of rebelliousness and sensation seeking can be regarded as psychologically normal. The capacity for moral decision-making and behaviour can be regarded as a developmental achievement that will often become more fully developed only during adolescence. The adolescent needs to develop not only cognitive abilities but also the ability to process complex emotions such as, and notably, shame. How shame is processed and experienced is connected to people's sense of identity. For people to be able to behave in moral ways, they must reflect on their emotional experiences, rather than simply acting in response to feelings, and this implies a secure sense of self. Such a secure sense of identity develops in relation to others. Adolescence is a time when peer groups become very important, but if these groups are the only real source of friendship and sense of connection, the situation may be potentially problematic.

The apparently increasing use of knives and even guns by young people in the UK has been causing anxiety. Fagan and Wilkinson (1994) point out that it would probably be very helpful to understand adolescent gun crime in terms of the social interactions in which it actually takes place. They outline a number of potential perspectives for understanding the phenomenon, and issues of identity are very prominent. Writing in the US context, they argue that the ready availability of guns is no doubt one aspect of their increasing use by young people. However, they suggest that there is also an increasing *demand* for guns among 'ghetto' youth, for whom the gun takes on huge symbolic value of strength and respect. Paul Kassman (2007: 2) described London teenage gang cultures as centring on the manufacture of respect ('rep'):

Most urban street crime is committed by under 18s on other under 18s, the main prize being an enhanced rep', rather than the odd £10 or mobile phones and MP3 players taken from the victims.

The rules and codes for most gang members are clearly understood and accepted. For most teenagers full of adolescent insecurities, the idea of losing face is hard to accept. Grafted on to a gang lifestyle, where your rep' and your gang's rep' are at stake, the idea of losing face or backing down is unthinkable. A trivial disagreement or conflict at school or in college will usually degenerate into an all-out gang confrontation.

An important policy initiative directed at youth crime in the UK are the YOTs. The Crime and Disorder Act 1998 required all local authorities in England and Wales to set up such multiagency teams, to whom are referred all young people entering the youth justice system. Although the shape of YOTs is under local control, they are required to include the police, social services, probation services, health services and education. The rationale of such a multiagency approach is that these young people often have social, educational and health needs, although Paylor and Simmill-Binning (2004) suggest that the integration of services has not always been easy.

One concern has been whether the YOTs are targeting the right group. Clearly, the evidence presented in Chapter 3 suggests that there are large numbers of youth offenders who do not necessarily go on to to present major problems (the AL offenders) and that resources might be better focused on the serious offenders. In response to this, YOTs are required to target 'prolific offenders' (Youth Justice Board 2004a).

The findings of this book also point us toward the difficulties faced by young in people in terms of their struggles for identities. In current social conditions, constructing an identity is difficult and uncertain work. Perhaps too many young people, boys in particular, find themselves isolated in this task. They are simply left to identify with many of the culturally sanctioned images of masculinity.

Young people spend a great deal of their time in the education system. As discussed in Chapter 5, engagement in education is an important protective factor against delinquency. There is a great deal of evidence on the associations between school disaffection, truancy, exclusion, unemployment and offending (Ball and Connolly 2000; Flood-Page *et al*. 2000; Payne 2000; Stone *et al*. 2000). Engaging the many boys who are apparently alienated from education remains a key task.

It will be hard to 'turn the clock back' on the consumer society and the images of masculinity that are promulgated in the mass media, but perhaps more could be done to ensure that competing versions of masculinity are more readily available.

Gender, masculinity and crime

The considerable preponderance of men in statistics on crime is now one of the great undisputed facts about crime. As discussed in Chapter 6, there has been increasing interest in exploring masculinity as an important factor or cause of crime, particularly in relation to more serious and violent crime. The apparent cross-cultural and historical continuities of the gender and crime relation do lend some support to those who argue that we must look to the biological differences between men and women to understand this state of affairs. On the other hand, the cultural variations in levels of violence still point to the very significant influence of culture. The analyses of masculine violence in Chapters 7 and 8 suggest that a great deal of violence stems from men's concerns about their own identity and their relationship with others. The cultural dimensions of sexual violence seem to be particularly clear.

Gilligan (1997) has argued that we must look closely at the conditions in society that encourage and foster shame and humiliation if we want to reduce levels of violence. One notable source of humiliation is economic inequality. Those who feel themselves to be judged as failures in a society that values wealth as a mark of success will, Gilligan argues, be prone to shame and rage. More even distribution of wealth is therefore one way of reducing levels of shame and therefore violence, suggests Gilligan. It is important to note that if economic inequality has an impact, it is disproportionately affecting men. Gilligan argues that here we must look at gender roles, and in particular how men and women stand in relation to 'honour'. Women are shamed for being too active, particularly in relation to sexual activity, whereas men are shamed for being too passive and weak. To change male behaviour, we need to examine and change gender roles, Gilligan argues. Men should not be encouraged to base their identities on strength and aggression. The difficulty with such a cultural analysis is that it does not address the issue of the apparent near universality of those gender differences. It is here that the more psychological dimensions of gender differences that were discussed in Chapter 6 might be useful. Masculine identities are forged in relation not only to cultural constructions of gender but also amidst family and kinship relationships. A number of writers have followed a Freudian line of argument that the developmental tasks of boys and girls are fundamentally different. Boys are required to separate themselves from their mothers and to identify with their fathers. Girls need to separate but can then build an identity through relationship with their mothers. If the boy's relationship with his father is not close (as will be the case if the father is not around very much), the boy is left 'knowing' that he must 'dis-identify' with his mother and perhaps identify with the cultural images of masculinity around him. Through this process of 'dis-identification', boys distance themselves from femininity and associated positives such as nurturance and care.

Diamond (2004) has argued that this process of dis-identification, although very common, is not inevitable. He argues that healthier kinds of gender distinctions can emerge given the right kind of parenting. That means mothers who are happy to embrace masculine traits and fathers who are not fearful of feminine traits. Nightingale's descriptions of the brutal enforcement of homophobia among the community he lived in is striking. There is no doubt that homophobia is widespread, and certainly endemic in schools (Warwick *et al.* 2004). The impact of this on those who are gay is bad enough, but the question of what this says about our conceptions of gender is also highly significant. It is arguably symptomatic of a deeply held fear of tainting masculinity with femininity. Such rigid views of masculinity can leave men and boys stranded with a very desiccated version of what it is to be human.

Mental health, change and crime

A strong theme of this book has been the stress on the overlaps between mental health issues and criminality – particularly more serious criminality. While there is a clear logic for early intervention strategies, there is a danger of neglecting intervention in the lives of adults who have already developed problems. Besides the misery being borne by and directly caused by this group, there is also the likelihood of the continuing intergenerational transmission of the psychological sources of such misery. Is it possible that a mental-health orientated strategy might be effective here? The overlap between mental health issues and crime is most visible when prison populations are surveyed. Clearly, the current most likely intervention is prison, which appears to offer little serious hope of rehabilitation.

Horne (2004) notes the irony that as the fashion in criminology came to focus more and more on the social conditions causing crime, and the view that any conception of offenders' difficulties in psychological terms is stigmatising was propagated, offenders became more likely to be diverted away from psychological help and toward the criminal justice system.

Of course, however, it needs to be noted that, by far the biggest category of mental disorder among the prison population is that of 'personality disorder'. Real controversy exists over whether these disorders should be recognised as mental health syndromes, an argument that has been occurring for almost 200 years (as discussed in Chapter 2). It is certainly plausible to argue that disorders of personality are simply descriptions of difficult and often 'bad' people. Therefore, this would render their presence among the prison population unsurprising. Against this view is the fact the people with such diagnoses do often have similar, and very negative, social and familial background characteristics. They have backgrounds suggestive of people with mental health problems.

The UK government remains concerned to do something about those deemed to be offering from 'personality disorders', arguing that personality disorder should be treated by the National Health Service. The government is convinced that personality disorder is now a significant cause of social exclusion (Cabinet Office 2006), and also that people with personality disorders may be a significant threat to public safety, and it has promoted the idea that particular attention needs to be given to those with dangerous and severe personality disorder (DSPD). Government concern that professionals should engage to a much greater degree with personality disorder has caused major problems in the revision of the Mental Health Act.

Further difficulties arise when the question of whether such difficulties can be treated is considered. Fiona Warren and colleagues (2003) provided a comprehensive review of the evidence on the tractability of 'severe personality disorders'. Their report strongly makes the point that a great deal more work needs to be done. As they bluntly conclude, 'there is no evidence that "DSPD" can or cannot be treated' (2003: 120). They do say that there is at least 'promising evidence' that therapeutic communities offer a hope of positive change. This is interesting because the treatment rationale of therapeutic communities is that people learn about themselves through having to relate to other people in an intensive environment (Campling and Haigh 1999). Therapeutic communities have certainly worked with extremely difficult people. At various points in the book, attention has been drawn to the importance of individuals being able to process and reflect upon powerful feelings rather than simply acting on them. The capacity seems crucially to develop in relation to other people. This is certainly what therapeutic communities seek to offer. Parker (2003) describes some of the work of HM Prison Grendon, which deals with serious, violent and sexual offenders as a therapeutic community. He points out how most of the prison system works to exacerbate the personality difficulties of most inmates. Prisons tend to be highly 'masculine' environments in which reflecting on emotion is distinctly discouraged:

Prison inmate culture tends to generate a powerfully defensive barrier to therapeutic work and promote the adoption of bravado, aggressive displays and of externalizing personally felt difficulties outwards on to any available other.

(Parker 2003: 170).

The evidence that therapeutic efforts in prison will have difficulties in making up for the negative effects of prison remains strong (Ortmann 2000; Merrington and Stanley 2004).

Further work

This book has set out the case for the closer integration of psychological perspectives and criminological theory on criminal behaviour. What emerges from this dialogue is a psychosocial perspective that is rather different from a traditional psychological one. It is clear that the psychosocial perspective adopted in this book has been far more methodologically and theoretically eclectic than conventional psychological approaches. By bringing together models built in the clinical world, work on the intimate world of emotions – for example, on the significance of shame – we are brought back to the significance of the social conditions in which such emotional worlds are embedded.

The rift between criminology and more psychological theorisation of the individual is no longer tenable. The changes wrought by changing social conditions have shifted 'personality' toward the centre of the analysis. If criminology is to be able to grasp the significance of these changes and contribute to debate and policy, it needs to take up the tools that will enable investigation of the social, emotional and moral worlds of individuals.

References

Abel, G.G., Barlow, D.H., Blanchard, E.B. and Guild, D. (1977) 'The Components of Rapists' Sexual Arousal', *Archives of General Psychiatry*, 34: 895–903.

Agnew, R. (1991) 'The Interactive Effect of Peer Variables on Delinquency', *Criminology*, 29: 41–72.

Ahmed, E., Harris, N., Braithwaite, J., and Braithwaite, V. (2002) *Shame Management Through Reintegration*. Cambridge: Cambridge University Press.

Aichorn, A. (1925) *Wayward Youth*. London: Imago Publishing.

Alder, C. and Polk, K. (1996) 'Masculinity and Child Homicide', *British Journal of Criminology* 36(3): 396–411.

Anderson, E. (1998) 'The Social Ecology of Youth Violence', in M. Tonry and M. Moore, *Youth Violence*. Chicago: University of Chicago Press.

APA (American Psychiatric Association) (1983) *The Insanity Defense Position Statement*. Washington, DC: APA.

APA (American Psychiatric Association) (1994) *Diagnostic and Statistical Manual of Mental Disorders* (4th edn) (DSM-IV). Washington, DC: APA.

Archer, J. (1994) 'Violence Between Men', in J. Archer (ed.) *Male Violence*. London: Routledge.

Archer, L. and Yamashita, H. (2003) 'Theorising Inner-City Masculinities: "Race", Class, Gender and Education', *Gender and Education*, 15(2): 115–32.

Aries, P. (1962) *Centuries of Childhood*. London: Jonathan Cape.

Arthur, R. (2005) 'Punishing Parents for the Crimes of Their Children', *Howard Journal*, 44(3): 233–53.

Augstein, H.F. (1996) 'J C Prichard's Concept of Moral Insanity – a Medical Theory of the Corruption of Human Nature', *Medical History*, 40: 311–43.

Baker, E., Beech, A. and Tyson, M. (2006) 'Attachment Disorganization and Its Relevance to Sexual Offending', *Journal of Family Violence*, 21(3): 221–31.

Ball, C. and Connolly, J. (2000) 'Educationally Disaffected Young Offenders', *British Journal of Criminology*, 40: 594–616.

Bandelow, B., Krause, J., Wedekind, D., Broocks, A., Hajak, G. and Ruther, E. (2005) 'Early Traumatic Life Events, Parental Attitudes, Family History, and Birth Risk Factors in Patients with Borderline Personality Disorder and Healthy Controls', *Psychiatry Research*, 134: 169–79.

Bandura, A. (1973) *Aggression: A Social Learning Analysis*. Englewood Cliffs, NJ: Prentice-Hall.

Bandura, A., Ross, D. and Ross, S. (1961) 'Transmission of Aggression Through Imitation of Aggressive Models', *Journal of Abnormal and Social Psychology*, 63: 575–82.

Barak, G. (1994) *Varieties of Criminology*. Westport, CT: Praeger.

Barbaree, H.E., Marshall, W.L. and Lanthier, R.D. (1979) 'Deviant Sexual Arousal in rapists', *Behaviour Research and Therapy*, 17(3): 215–22.

Barclay, G. and Tavares, C. (2003) *International Comparisons of Criminal Justice Statistics 2001*. London: Home Office.

Barrett, M. and McIntosh, M. (1982) *The Anti-Social Family*. London: Verso.

Baumrind, D. (1971) 'Current patterns of parental authority', *Developmental Psychology Monographs*, 4: 1–102.

Baumrind, D. (1978) 'Parental Disciplinary Patterns and Social Competence in Children', *Youth and Society*, 9: 238–76.

Baxter, D.J., Barbaree, H.E. and Marshall, W.L. (1986) 'Sexual Responses to Consenting and Forced Sex in a Large Sample of Rapists and Nonrapists', *Behaviour Research and Therapy*, 24(5): 513–20.

BBC News (2001) 'Girl, 18, convicted of canal rape', http://news.bbc.co.uk/1/hi/uk/1225124.stm.

Beccaria, C. (1819) *An Essay on Crimes and Punishments* (2nd American edn). Philadelphia: Philip H. Nicklin.

Beck, A.T. (1967). *Depression: Causes and Treatment*. Philadelphia: University of Pennsylvania Press.

Becker, H. (1963) *Outsiders: Studies in the Sociology of Deviance*. New York: Free Press.

Beckett, R. (1994) 'Cognitive-Behavioural Treatment of Sex Offenders', in T. Morrison, M. Erooga and R.C. Beckett (eds) *Sexual Offending Against Children: Assessment and Treatment of Male Abusers*. London: Routledge.

Beech, A. and Fisher, D. (2004) 'Treatment of Sex Offenders in the UK in Prison and Probation Settings', in H. Kemshall and G. McIvor (eds) *Managing Sex Offender Risk*. London: Jessica Kingsley.

Beier, A.L. (1978) 'Social Problems in Elizabethan London', *Journal of Interdisciplinary History*, 9(2): 203–21.

Belfrage, H. (1998) 'A Ten-Year Follow-up of Criminality in Stockholm Mental Patients: New Evidence for a Relation between Mental Disorder and Crime', *British Journal of Criminology*, 38(1): 145–55.

Bell, N. and Bell, R. (1993) *Adolescent Risk Taking*. Newbury Park, CA: Sage.

Benedict, R. (1946) *The Chrysanthemum and the Sword: Pattern of Japanese Culture*. Boston: Houghton Mifflin.

Bennett, C. (2006) 'Taking the Sincerity Out of Saying Sorry: Restorative Justice as Ritual', *Journal of Applied Philosophy*, 23(2): 127–43.

Bennett, N., Dodd, T., Flatley, J., Freeth, S. and Bolling, K. (1995) *Health Survey for England 1993*. London: HMSO.

Berggård, C., Damberg, M., Longo-Stadler, M., Hallman, J., Oreland, L. and Garpenstrand, H. (2003) 'The Serotonin 2A–1438 G/A Receptor Polymorphism in a Group of Swedish Male Criminals', *Neuroscience Newsletters*, 347: 196–8.

Bernhardt, P.C., Dabbs, J.M., Jr, Fielden, J. and Lutter, C. (1998) 'Changes in Testosterone Levels During Vicarious Experiences of Winning and Losing Among Fans at Sporting Events', *Physiology and Behavior*, 65: 59–62.

Beyers, W. and Goossens, L. (1999) 'Emotional Autonomy, Psychosocial Adjustment and Parenting: Interactions, Moderating and Mediating Effects', *Journal of Adolescence*, 22: 753–69.

Blackburn, R. (1993) *The Psychology of Criminal Conduct: Theory, Research and Practice*. Chichester: Wiley.

Blackburn, R. (2000) 'Treatment or Incapacitation? Implications of Research on Personality Disorders for the Management of Dangerous Offenders', *Legal and Criminological Psychology*, 5: 1–21.

Blackburn, R., Logan, C., Donnelly, D. and Renwick, S. (2003) 'Personality Disorders, Psychopathy and Other Mental Disorders: Co-morbidity Among Patients at English and Scottish High-Security Hospitals', *Journal of Forensic Psychiatry and Psychology*, 14(1): 111–37.

Blair, J. and Frith, U. (2000) 'Neurocognitive Explanations of the Anti-social Personality Disorders', *Criminal Behaviour and Mental Health*, 10: S66–S81.

Blair R.J. (1995) 'A Cognitive Developmental Approach to Morality: Investigating the Psychopath', *Cognition*, 57: 1–29.

Blos, P. (1979) *The Adolescent Passage*. Madison, CT: International Universities Press.

Bogaerts, S., Vanheule, S. and Declercq, F. (2005) 'Recalled Parental Bonding, Adult Attachment Style, and Personality Disorders in Child Molesters: A Comparative Study', *Journal of Forensic Psychiatry and Psychology*, 16(3): 445–58.

Bohner, G., Reinhard, A., Rutz, S., Sturm, S. and Effler, D. (1998) 'Rape Myths as Neutralising Cognitions: Evidence for a Causal Impact of Anti-victim Attitudes on Men's Self-Reported Likelihood of Raping', *European Journal of Social Psychology*, 28: 257–69.

Bonger, W. (1969) *Criminality and Economic Conditions*. Bloomington, IN: Indiana University Press. [Originally published 1916, by Little, Brown and Co.]

Braithwaite, J. (1989) *Crime, Shame and Integration*. Cambridge University Press: Cambridge.

Brame, B., Nagin, D.S. and Tremblay, R.E. (2001) 'Developmental Trajectories of Physical Aggression from Secondary School Entry to Late Adolescence', *Journal of Child Psychology and Psychiatry and Allied Disciplines*, 42(4): 503–12.

Brennan, P.A., Mednick, S.A. and Jacobsen, B. (1996) 'Assessing the Role of Genetics in Crime Using Adoption Cohorts', in CIBA Foundation, *Genetics of Criminal and Anti-social Behaviour.* Chichester: Wiley.

Brett, A. (2002) 'Murder-Parasuicide: A Case Series in Western Australia', *Psychiatry, Psychology and Law*, 9(1): 96–9.

Brittain, R.P. (1970) 'The Sadistic Murderer', *Science and the Law*, 10: 198–207.

Brookman, F. and Maguire, M. (2003) *Reducing Homicide: A Review of the Possibilities.* London: Home Office.

Brown, J. (2004) 'Shame and Domestic Violence: Treatment Perspectives for Perpetrators from Self Psychology and Affect Theory', *Sexual and Relationship Therapy*, 19(11): 39–56.

Brown, R. and Evans, W. (2002) 'Extracurricular activity and ethnicity: Creating Greater School Connection Among Diverse Student Populations', *Urban Education*, 37(1): 41–58.

Brownmiller, S. (1975) *Against Our Will: Men, Women, and Rape.* New York: Simon and Schuster.

Buchanan, A. and Leese, M. (2001) 'Detention of People with Dangerous Severe Personality Disorders: A Systematic Review', *Lancet* 358: 1955–9.

Bunting, L. (2005) *Females Who Sexually Offend Against Children: Responses of the Child Protection and Criminal Justice Systems.* London: NSPCC.

Burn, G. (1984) *Somebody's Husband, Somebody's Son.* London: Heineman.

Burt, C. (1925) *The Young Delinquent.* London: University of London Press.

Burt, M. (1980) 'Cultural Myths and Support for Rape', *Journal of Personality and Social Psychology*, 38: 217–30.

Cabinet Office (2006) *Reaching Out: An Action Plan on Social Exclusion.* London: HM Government Cabinet Office.

Calder, M.C. (2005) *Children and Young People Who Sexually Abuse: New Theory, Research and Practice Developments.* Lyme Regis: Russell House.

Campagna, A.F. and Harter, S. (1975) 'Moral Judgement in Sociopathic and Normal Children', *Journal of Personality and Social Psychology*, 31: 199–205.

Campbell, J. (2006) 'Homelessness and Containment – A Psychotherapy Project with Homeless People and Workers in the Homeless Field', *Psychoanalytic Psychotherapy*, 20(3): 157–74.

Campling, P. and Haigh, R. (1999) *Therapeutic Communities: Past, Present, and Future.* London: Jessica Kingsley.

Caplan, P., Awad, G.A., Wilks, C. and White, G. (1980) 'Sex Differences in a Delinquent Clinic Population', *British Journal of Criminology*, 20(4): 311.

Caputo, G. (2000) 'The "Voice of justice" vs. the "Voice of Care": The Assignment of Criminal Sanctions', *Current Psychology*, 19(1): 70–81.

Carlen, P. (1986) 'Psychiatry in Prisons: Promises, Premises, Practices and Politics', in P. Miller and N. Rose (eds) *The Power of Psychiatry*. Cambridge: Polity.

Carlen, P. (1988) *Women, Crime and Poverty*. Milton Keynes: Open University Press.

Cartwright, D. (2002) *Psychoanalysis, Violence and Rage-Type Murder*. Hove: Brunner Routledge.

Ceballo, R. and McLoyd, C.C. (2002) 'Social Support and Parenting in Poor, Dangerous Neighbourhoods', *Child Development*, 73(4): 1310–21.

Cerezo, M.A. (1997) 'Abusive Family Interaction: A Review', *Aggression and Violent Behaviour*, 2(3) 215–40.

Chan, C.Y., Beh, S.L. and Broadhurst, R.G. (2004) 'Homicide-Suicide in Hong Kong, 1989–1998', *Forensic Science International*, 140: 261–7.

Chesney-Lind, M. and Hagedorn, J.H. (1999) *Female Gangs in America: Essays on Girls, Gangs, and Gender*. Chicago: Lakeview Press.

Chiroro, P., Bohner, G., Tendayi, V.G. and Jarvis, C. (2004) 'Rape Myth Acceptance and Rape Proclivity Expected Dominance Versus Expected Arousal as Mediators in Acquaintance-Rape Situations', *Journal of Interpersonal Violence*, 19(4): 427–42.

Chodorow, N. (1978) *The Reproduction of Mothering: Psychoanalysis and the Sociology of Gender*. Berkely, CA: University of California Press.

Christoffersen, M.N., Frances, B. and Soothill, K. (2003) 'An Upbringing to Violence? Identifying the Liklelihood of Violent Crime Among the 1966 Birth Cohort in Denmark', *Journal of Forensic Psychiatry and Psychology*, 14(2): 367–81.

Clarke, L., Ungerer, J., Chahoud, K., Johnson, S. and Stiefel, I. (2002) 'Attention Deficit Hyperactivity Disorder is associated with Attachment Insecurity', *Clinical Child Psychology and Psychiatry*, 7(2): 179–98.

Clarke, R.V. and Cornish, D.B. (1985) 'Modelling Offenders' Decisions: A Framework for Research and Policy', in M. Tonry and N. Morris, *Crime and Justice*, 6: 147–85.

Cleckley, H. (1941) *The Mask of Sanity: An Attempt to Re-interpret the Social Psychopathic Personality*. London: Henry Kimpton.

Cloninger, C.R. and Gottesman, I.I. (1987) 'Genetic and Environmental Factors in Antisocial Behaviour Disorders', in S.A. Mednick, T.E. Moffitt and S.A. Stack (eds) *The Causes of Crime: New Biological Approaches*. Cambridge: Cambridge University Press.

Cloward, R.A. and Ohlin, L.E. (1960) *Delinquency and Opportunity: A Theory of Delinquent Gangs*. New York: Free Press.

Cohen, A.K. (1965) *Delinquent Boys*. New York: Free Press.

Cohen, L., Gans, S., McGeoch, P. *et al.* (2002) 'Impulsive Personality Traits in Male Pedophiles Versus Healthy Controls: Is Pedophilia an Impulsive-Aggressive Disorder?', *Comprehensive Psychiatry*, 43(2): 127–34.

Cohen, L.E. and Felson, M. (1979) 'Social Change and Crime Rate Trends: A Routine Activity Approach', *American Sociological Review*, 44: 588–608.

Cohen, N. (2005) We All Have Personality Disorders Now', *New Statesman*, 11 July.

Coleman, J.C. (1988) 'Social Capital in the Creation of Human Capital', *American Journal of Sociology*, 94: S95–S120.

Colton, M. and Vanstone, M. (1996) *Betrayal of Trust: Sexual Abuse by Men Who Work with Children*. London: Free Association Books.

Connell, R.W. (1995) *Masculinities*. Cambridge: Polity Press.

Connor, S. (2001) 'The Shame of Being a Man', *Textual Practice*, 15(2): 211–30.

Conrad, S. and Morrow, R. (2000) 'Borderline Personality Organization, Dissociation, and Willingness to Use Force in Intimate Relationships', *Psychology of Men and Masculinity*, 1(1): 37–48.

Conseur, A., Rivara, F.P. and Barnoski, R.E.I. (1997) 'Maternal and Perinatal Risk Factors for Later Delinquency', *Pediatrics*, 99: 785–90.

Costello, S.J. (2002) *The Pale Criminal: Psychoanalytic Perspectives*. London: Karnac.

Craissati, J. (2005) 'Sexual Violence Against Women: A Psychological Approach to the Assessment and Management of Rapists in the Community', *Probation Journal: The Journal of Community and Criminal Justice*, 52(4): 401–22.

Craissati, J. and McClurg, G. (1996) 'The Challenge Project: Perpetrators of Child Sexual Abuse in South East London', *Child Abuse and Neglect*, 20(11): 1067–77.

Craissati, J. and McClurg, G. (1997) 'The Challenge Project: A Treatment Programme Evaluation for Perpetrators of Child Sexual Abuse', *Child Abuse and Neglect*, 21(7): 637–48.

Croty, H. (1924) 'The History of the Insanity Defence to Crime in English Law', *California Law Review*, 12(2): 105–23.

Crowe, M. (2004) 'Never Good Enough. I. Shame or Borderline Personality Disorder?', *Journal of Psychiatric and Mental Health Nursing*, 11: 327–34.

Dalton, K. (1961) 'Menstruation and Crime', *British Medical Journal*, 2: 152–3.

Dalton, K. (1986) 'Premenstrual Syndrome', *Hamline Law Review*, 9(1): 143–54.

Daly, M. and Wilson, M. (1988) *Homicide*. New York: Aldine De Gruyter.

Damasio, A.R. (1994) *Descartes' Error: Emotion, Reason and the Human Brain*. London: Picador.

Darke, J. (1990) 'Sexual Aggression: Achieving Power Through Humiliation,' in W.L. Marshal, D. Laws, and H. Barbaree (eds) *Handbook of Sexual Assault*. New York: Plenum.

Day-Sclater, S. (2000) 'Re-moralising the Family? Family Policy, Family Law and Youth Justice', *Child and Family Law Quarterly*, 12(2): 135–58.

Dearing, E. (2004) 'The Developmental Implications of Restrictive and Supportive Parenting Across Neighbourhoods and Ethnicities: Exceptions Are the Rule', *Applied Developmental Psychology*, 25: 555–75.

Decker, S., Wright, R. and Logie, R. (1993) 'Perceptual Deterrence Among Active Residential Burglars: A Research Note', *Criminology*, 31(1): 135–47.

De Masi, F. (2007) 'The Paedophile and His Inner World: Theoretical and Clinical Observations on the Analysis of a Patient', *International Journal of Psychoanalysis*, 88: 147–65.

Demie, F. (2001) 'Ethnic and Gender Differences in Educational Achievement and implications for school improvement strategies', *Educational Research*, 43(1): 91–106.

DfES (2001) *Schools: Achieving Success*. London: DfES.

Diamond, J. (2004) 'The Shaping of Masculinity: Re-visioning Boys Turning Away from Their Mothers to Construct Male Gender Identity', *International Journal of Psychoanalysis*, 85: 359–80.

Diamond, M. and Uchiyama, A. (1999) 'Pornography, Rape and Sex Crimes in Japan', *International Journal of Law and Psychiatry*, 22(1): 1–22.

Dinn, W.M. and Harris, C.L. (2000) 'Neurocognitive Function in Antisocial Personality Disorder', *Psychiatry Research*, 97: 173–90.

Dipietro, J. (1981) 'Rough and Tumble Play: A Function of Gender', *Developmental Psychology*, 17: 50–8.

Dixon, A., Howie, P. and Starling, J. (2004) 'Psychopathology in Female Juvenile Offenders', *Journal of Child Psychology and Psychiatry*, 45(6): 1150–8.

Dobash, R.E and Dobash, R.P. (1979) *Violence Against Wives*. London: Open Books.

Dobash, R.E. and Dobash, R.P. (1984) 'The Nature and Antecedents of Violent Events', *British Journal of Criminology*, 24(3): 269–8.

Dodge, K.A. and Schwartz, D. (1997). 'Social Information Processing Mechanisms in Aggressive Behavior', in J. Breiling and J. Maser (eds) *Handbook of Antisocial Behavior*. New York: Wiley.

DOH (2003) *Personality Disorder: No Longer a Diagnosis of Exclusion*. London: Department of Health.

DOH (2006) *The Mental Health Bill: Plans to Amend the Mental Health Act 1983*. London: Department of Health.

Dolan, M. and Fullam, R. (2004) 'Theory of Mind and Mentalizing Ability in Antisocial Personality Disorders with and without Psychopathy', *Psychological Medicine*, 34(6): 1093–1102.

Dolan, M. and Smith, C. (2001) 'Juvenile Homicide Offenders: 10 Years' Experience of an Adolescent Forensic Psychiatry Service', *Journal of Forensic Psychiatry*, 12(2): 313–29.

Dollar, D., Fisman, S. and Gatti, R. (2001) 'Are Women Really the Fairer Sex? Corruption and Women in Government', *Journal of Economic Behaviour and Organization*, 46: 423–9.

Donkin, A.J., Dowler, E.A., Stevenson, S.J. and Turner, S.A. (2000) 'Mapping Access to Food in a Deprived Area: The Development of Price and Availability Indices', *Public Health Nutrition*, 3: 31–8.

Donnellan, M.D., Ge, X. and Wenk, E. (2000) 'Cognitive Abilities in Adolescent-Limited and Life-Course Persistent Criminal Offenders', *Journal of Abnormal Psychology*, 109(3): 396–402.

Dorr, D. and Fey, S. (1974) 'Relative Power of Symbolic Adult and Peer Models in the Modification of Children's Moral Choice Behaviour', *Journal of Personality and Social Psychology*, 29(3): 335–41.

Downing, K., Stepney, P. and Jordan, B. (2000) 'Violent Youth Crime: The Rhetoric, Research and the Responsibilities of Government', *Educational Studies*, 26(1): 67–82.

DSS (Department of Social Security) (1975) *Report of the Committee on Mentally Abnormal Offenders*. London: HMSO.

Easteal, P. (1991) 'Premenstrual Syndrome (PMS) in the courtroom', *Proceedings of Women and the Law*, Australian Institute of Criminology, 24–26 September. Canberra: AIC.

Eichner, E. (1982) 'The Rise of Modern Science and the Genesis of Romanticism', *Publications of the Modern Language Association*, 97(1): 8–30.

Eigen, J.P. (1991) 'Delusion in the Courtroom: The Role of Partial Insanity in Early Forensic Testimony', *Medical History*, 35 25–49.

Eisenberg, N. (2000) 'Emotion, Regulation, and Moral Development', *Annual Review of Psychology*, 51: 665–97.

Elias, N. ([1939] 1994) *The Civilizing Process: Sociogenetic and Psychogenetic Investigation*. Jephcott (trans), Oxford: Blackwell.

Elkins, I., Iacono, W.G., Doyle, A. and McGue, M. (1997) 'Characteristics Associated with the Persistence of Antisocial Behaviour: Results from Recent Longitudinal Research', *Aggression and Violent Behaviour*, 2(2): 101–24.

Elliott, C. and Gillett, G. (1992) 'Moral Insanity and Practical Reason', *Philosophical Psychology*, 5(1): 53–64.

Ellis, L. and Walsh, A. (1997) 'Gene-Based Evolutionary Theories in Criminology', *Criminology*, 35: 229–76.

Emler, N. and Reicher, S. (1995) *Adolescence and Delinquency*. Oxford: Blackwell.

Erikson, E. (1965) *Childhood and Society*. Harmondsworth: Pelican.

Eysenck, H. (1987) 'Personality Theory and the Problem of Crime', originally published in B.J. McGurk, D.M. Thornton and J.M.G. Williams (eds) *Applying Psychology to Imprisonment*. London: HMSO. Reprinted in Farrington, D. (1994) *Psychological Explanations of Crime*. Aldershot: Dartmouth.

Eysenck, S.B.G. and Eysenck, H.J. (1970) 'Crime and Personality: An Empirical Study of the Three Factor Theory', *British Journal of Criminology*, 11: 49–62.

Fabricius, D. (2004) 'Guilt, Shame, Disobedience: Social Regulatory Mechanisms and the "Inner Normative System"', *Psychoanalytic Inquiry*, 24(2): 309–27.

Fagan, J. and Wilkinson, D.L. (1998) 'Guns, Youth Violence, and Social Identity', in M. Tonry and M. Moore (eds) *Youth Violence*. Chicago: University of Chicago Press.

Falk, J., Riepert, T. and Rothschild, M. (2004) 'Suicide by Cop: A Case Study', *Legal Medicine*, 6(3): 194–6.

Farrall, S. and Bowling, B. (1999) 'Structuration, Human Development and Desistance from Crime', *British Journal of Criminology*, 39(2): 253–68.

Farrington, D., Gallagher, B., Morley, L., St Ledger, R.J. and West, D. (1988) 'Are There Any Successful Men from Crimogenic Backgrounds', *Psychiatry*, 51: 116–30.

Farrington, D. (1994) *Psychological Explanations of Crime.* Dartmouth: Aldershot.

Farrington, D. (2002) 'Developmental Criminology', in M. Maguire, M. Morgan and R. Reiner (eds.) *The Oxford Handbook of Criminology.* Oxford: Oxford University Press.

Farrington, D. (2004) 'Criminological Psychology in the Twenty-First Century', *Criminal Behaviour and Mental Health*, 14: 152–66.

Farrington, D.P. and Knight, B.J. (1979) 'Two Nonreactive Field Experiments on Stealing from a "Lost" Letter', *British Journal of Social and Clinical Psychology*, 18(2): 77–84.

Farrington, D.P. and Hawkins, J.D. (1991) 'Predicting Participation, Early Onset, and Later Persistence in Officially Recorded Offending', *Criminal Behaviour and Mental Health*, 1: 1–33.

Farrington, D.P., Loeber, R. and Kammen, W.B. (1990) 'Long-term criminal outcomes of hyperactivity-impulsivity-attention deficit and conduct problems in childhood', in L. Robins and M. Rutter (eds) *Straight and Devious Pathways from Childhood to Adulthood.* Cambridge: Cambridge University Press.

Fattah, E.A. (1997) *Criminology: Past Present and Future: A Critical Overview.* Basingstoke: Macmillan.

Fazel, S. and Danesh, J. (2002) 'Serious Mental Disorder in 23,000 Prisoners: A Systematic Review of 62 Surveys', *Lancet*, 359: 545–50.

Feeley, M. and Little, D.L. (1991) 'The Vanishing Female: The Decline of Women in the Criminal Justice Process, 168: 1912', *Law and Society Review* 25(4): 739–78.

Feldman, P. (1993) *The Psychology of Crime: A Social Science Textbook.* Cambridge: Cambridge University Press.

Fergusson, D. Swain-Campbell, N. and Horwood, J. (2004) 'How Does Childhood Economic Disadvantage Lead to Crime?', *Journal of Child Psychology and Psychiatry*, 45(5): 956–966.

Fergusson, D.M. and Woodward, L.J. (1999) 'Maternal Age and Educational and Psychosocial Outcomes in Early Adulthood', *Journal of Child Psychology and Psychiatry*, 43(3): 479–89.

Fergusson, D.M., Boden, J.M. and Horwood, L.J. (2006) 'Examining the Intergenerational Transmission of Violence in a New Zealand Birth Cohort', *Child Abuse and Neglect*, 30(2): 89–108.

Fisher, D. and Beech, A. (2004) 'Adult Male Sex Offenders', in H. Kemshall and G. McIvor (eds) *Managing Sex Offender Risk.* London: Jessica Kingsley.

Fleming, M. (2005) 'Adolescent Autonomy: Desire, Achievement and Disobeying Parents Between Early and Late Adolescence', *Australian Journal of Education and Developmental Psychology*, 5: 1–16.

Flood-Page, C. Campbell, S., Harrington, V. and Miller, J. (2000) *Youth Crime: Findings from the 1998/99 Youth Lifestyle Survey: Home Office Research Study 209*. Home Office Research, Development and Statistics Directorate. London: Home Office.

Fonagy, P. (1999) 'Male Perpetrators of Violence Against Women: An Attachment Theory Perspective', *Journal of Applied Psychoanalytic Studies*, 1: 7–27.

Fonagy, P., Target, M., Gergely, G., Allen, J. and Batemen, A. (2003) 'The Developmental Roots of Borderline Personality Disorder in Early Attachment Relationships: A Theory and Some Evidence', *Psychoanalytic Enquiry*, 23(3): 412–59.

Fonagy, P., Gergely, G., Jurist, E.L. and Target, M. (2004) *Affect Regulation, Mentalization, and the Development of the Self*. London: Karnac.

Francis, B., Barry, J., Bowater, R., Miller, N., Soothill, K. and Ackerley (2004) *Using Homicide Data to Assist Murder Investigations*. Home Office Online report 26/04. London: Home Office.

Frank, S.J., Schettini, A.M. and Lower, R.L (2002) 'The Role of Separation-Individuation Experiences and Personality in Predicting Externalising and Internalising Dimensions of Functional Impairment in a Rural Preadolescent and Adolescent Sample', *Journal of Clinical Child and Adolescent Psychology* 31(4): 431–42.

Freud, A. (1936) *The Ego and Some Mechanisms of Defence*. London: Hogarth Press.

Freud, A. (1958) 'Adolescence', in *Psychoanalytic Study of the Child*, 13: 255–78.

Freud, S. (1925) *Some Psychical Consequences of the Anatomical Distinction Between the Sexes*. Pelican Freud Library, vol 7. Harmondsworth: Penguin.

Frosh, S. (1987) *The Politics of Psychoanalysis: An Introductin to Freudian and Post-Freudian Theory*. Basingstoke: Macmillan/Palgrave.

Frosh, S. (1991) *Identity Crisis: Modernity, Psychoanalysis and the Self*. Basingstoke: Macmillan.

Gadd, D. (2000) 'Masculinities, Violence and Defended Psychosocial Subjects', *Theoretical Criminology*, 44(4): 429–49.

Garland, D. (1997) 'Of Crimes and Criminals: The Development of Criminology in Britain', in M. Maguire, M. Morgan and R. Reiner (eds) *The Oxford Handbook of Criminology* (2nd edn). Oxford: Oxford University Press.

Garland, D. (2002) 'Of Crimes and Criminals: The Development of Criminology in Britain', in M. Maguire, M. Morgan and R. Reiner (eds) *The Oxford Handbook of Criminology* (3rd edn). Oxford: Oxford University Press.

Gesch, B., Hammond, S., Hampson, S., Eves, A. and Crowder, M. (2002) 'Influence of Supplementary Vitamins, Minerals and Fatty Acids on the Antisocial Behaviour of Young Adult Prisoners', *British Journal of Psychiatry*, 182: 22–8.

Giddens, A. (1991) *Modernity and Self-Identity: Self and Society in the Late Modern Age*. Cambridge: Polity Press.

Gillespie, N.A., Whitfield J.B., Williams, B., Heath, A.C. and Martin, N.G. (2005) 'The Relationship Between Stressful Life Events, the Serotonin Transporter (5-HTTLPR) Genotype and Major Depression', *Psychological Medicine*, 35(1): 101–11.

Gilligan, C. (1982) *In a Different Voice: Psychological Theory and Women's Development*. Cambridge, MA: Harvard University Press.

Gilligan, J. (1997) *Violence: Reflections on a National Epidemic*. New York: Vintage Books.

Gilligan, J. (2003) 'Shame, Guilt, and Violence', *Social Research*, 70(4): 1149–80.

Gilmour, D. (1991) *Manhood in the Making: Cultural Concepts of Masculinity*. New Haven: Yale University Press.

Glannon, W. (1997) 'Psychopathy and Responsibility', *Journal of Applied Philosophy*, 14(3): 263–75.

Glasgow, D. (1993) 'The Origins of Exploitative Sexuality: The Challenge of Conducting Useful Research', in L. Waterhouse, *Child Abuse and Child Abusers*. London: Jessica Kingsley.

Glasser, M. (1988) 'Psychodynamic Aspects of Paedophilia', *Psychoanalytic Psychotherapy*, 3(2): 121–35.

Glasser, M. (1992) 'Problems in the Psychoanalysis of Certain Narcissistic Disorders', *International Journal of Psychoanalysis*, 73: 493–503.

Glueck, S. and Glueck, E. (1968) *Delinquents and Non-delinquents in Perspective*. Cambridge, MA: Harvard University Press.

Goffman, E. (1959) *The Presentation of Self in Everyday Life*. Harmondsworth: Penguin Books.

Goring, C. (1913). *The English Convict: A Statistical Study*. London: HMSO.

Gottfredson, M.R. and Hirshi, T. (1990) *A General Theory of Crime*. Stanford, CA: Stanford University Press.

Grafman, J. (1996) 'Frontal Lobe Injuries, Violence and Aggression: A Report of the Vietnam Head Injury Study', *Neurology*, 46: 1231–8.

Graybar, S. and Boutilier, L. (2002) 'Nontraumatic Pathways to Borderline Personality Disorder', *Psychotherapy: Theory, Research, Practice, Training*, 39 (2): 152–62.

Greene, J. and Haidt, J. (2002) 'How (and Where) Does Judgment Work?', *Trends in Cognitive Science*, 6(12): 517–23.

Greenson, R. (1968) 'Disidentifying from Its Mother – Its Special Importance for the Boy', *International Journal of Psychoanalysis*, 49: 370–4.

Gretton, H., Catchpole, R., McBride, M., Hare, R., O'Saughnessy, R. and Regan, K.V. (2005) 'The Relationship Between Psychopathy, Treatment Completion and Criminal Outcome over 10 Years: A Study of Adolescent Sex Offenders', in M. Calder (ed.) *Children and Young People Who Sexually Abuse: New Theory, Research and Practice Developments*. Lyme Regis: Russell House.

Grice, J.W. and Seely, E. (2000) 'The Evolution of Sex Differences in Jealousy: Failure to Replicate Previous Results', *Journal of Research in Personality*, 34 348–56.

Groth, A.N. and Birnbaum, H.J. (1978) 'Adult Sexual Orientation and Attraction to Underage Persons', *Archives of Sexual Behaviour*, 7(3): 175–81.

Groth, A.N., Burgess, A.W. and Holmstrom, L.L. (1977) 'Rape: Power, Anger and Sexuality', *American Journal of Psychiatry*, 134: 1239–43.

Gudjonsson, G. (2003) *The Psychology of Interrogations and Confessions*. Chichester: Wiley.

Guerry, A. ([1883]/2002) *Essay on the Moral Statistics of France: A Sociological Report to the French Academy of Science*. H. Whitt, and V. Reinking (trans.) Lampeter, New York: Edward Mellon.

Guttmacher, M.S. (1951) *Sex Offences: The Problem, Causes and Prevention*. New York: W.W. Norton.

Haapasalo, J. and Pokela, E. (1998) 'Child Rearing and Child Abuse Antecedents of Criminality', *Aggression and Violent Behaviour*, 4(1): 107–27.

Hagan, J. (1990) 'The Pleasures of Predation and Disrepute', *Law and Society Review*, 24(1): 165–78.

Haji, I. (1998) 'On Psychopaths and Culpability', *Law and Philosophy*, 17: 117–40.

Hall, G.C., Shondrick, D.D. and Hirschman, R. (1993) 'The Role of Sexual Arousal in Sexually Aggressive Behaviour: A Meta-Analysis', *Journal of Consulting and Clinical Psychology*, 61(6): 1091–5.

Hall, R. (1985) *Ask Any Woman: A London Inquiry into Rape and Sexual Assault*. Bristol: Falling Wall Press.

Hall, R.C.W. and Hall, R.C. (2007) 'A Profile of Paedophilia: Definition, Characteristics of Offenders, Recidivism, Treatment Outcomes, and Forensic Issues', *Mayo Clinical Proceedings*, 82(4): 457–71.

Hall Smith, P., White, J.W. and Hollands, L.J. (2003) 'A Longitudinal Perspective on Dating Violence Amongst Adolescent and College-Age Women', *American Journal of Public Health*, 93(7): 1104–9.

Hancock, L. (2003) ' "Wolf Pack": The Press and the Central Park Jogger', *Columbia Journalism Review*, 1 Jan/Feb Online Journal.

Hare, R. (1993) *Without Conscience: The Disturbing World of the Psychopaths Amongst Us*. New York: Guilford Press.

Hare, R.D. (1991). 'The Hare Psychopathy Checklist – Revised', in D.J. Cooke and C. Michie (1997) 'An Item Response Theory Analysis of the Hare Psychopathy Checklist–Revised', *Psychological Assessment*, 9(1): 3–14.

Hare, R.D., Strachan, C. and Froth, A. (1993) 'Psychopathy and Crime: A Review', in K. Howells and C.R. Hollin, *Clinical Approaches to the Mentally Disordered Offender*. Chichester: John Wiley and Sons.

Harris, C.R. (2003) 'The Evolution of Jealousy: Did Women and Men, Facing Different Selective Pressures, Evolve Different 'Brands' of Jealousy? Recent Evidence Suggests Not', *American Scientist*, 92(1): 62–72.

Harris, N. (2001) 'Shame and Shaming: Regulating Drink Driving', in E. Ahmed, N. Harris, J. Braithwaite and V. Braithwaite (eds) *Shame Management Through Reintegration*. Cambridge: Cambridge University Press.

Harris, N. (2003) 'Reassessing the Dimensionality of the Moral Emotions', *British Journal of Psychology*, 94: 457–73.

Harrower, J. (1998) *Applying Psychology to Crime*. Abingdon: Hodder and Stoughton.

Haw, C., Hawton, K. and Casey, D. (2006) 'Deliberate Self-Harm Patients of No Fixed Abode: A Study of Characteristics and Subsequent Deaths in Patients Presenting to a General Hospital', *Social Psychiatry Epidemiology* 41: 918–25.

Hawton, K. (1989) *Cognitive Behaviour Therapy for Psychiatric Problems: A Practical Guide*. Oxford: Oxford University Press.

Hawton, K., Hall, S., Simkin, S., Bales, L., Bond, A., Codd, S. and Stewart, A. (2003) 'Deliberate Self-Harm in Adolescents: A Study of Characteristics and Trends in Oxford, 1990–2000', *Journal of Child Psychology and Psychiatry*, 44(8): 1191–8.

Hayes, S. (1996) 'Recent Research on Offenders with Learning Disabilities', *Tizard Learning Disability Review*, 1: 7–15.

Hayward, K.J. (2004) *City Limits: Crime, Consumer Culture and the Urban Experience*. London: Glasshouse Press.

Hayward, K.J. and Young, J. (2004) 'Cultural Criminology: Some Notes on the Script', *Theoretical Criminology*, 8(3): 259–73.

Heidensohn, F. (1996) *Women and Crime*. Basingstoke: Palgrave.

Henderson, D.K. (1939) *Psychopathic States*. London: Chapman and Hall.

Henry, D.B., Tolan, P.B. and Gorman-Smith, D. (2001) 'Longitudinal Family and Peer Group Effects on Violence and Nonviolent Delinquency', *Journal of Clinical Child Psychology*, 30(1): 172–86.

Hindman, J. (1988) 'Research Disputes Assumptions About Child Molesters', *National District Attorneys Association Bulletin*, 7: 1–3.

Hipwell, A., Loeber, R., Stouthamer-Loeber, M., Keenan, K., White, H. and Kroneman, L. (2002) 'Characteristics of Girls with Early Onset Disruptive and Antisocial Behaviour', *Criminal Behaviour and Mental Health*, 12: 99–112.

Hirschi, T. (1969) *Causes of Delinquency.* Berkley, CA: University of California Press.

Hirschi, T. and Hindelgang, M. (1977) 'Intelligence and Delinquency: A Revisionist Review', *American Sociological Review*, 42: 571–87.

Hirschi, T. and Gottfredson, M. (1990) *A General Theory of Crime.* Stanford: Stanford University Press.

Hodges, S. (2003) 'Borderline Personality Disorder and Post-Traumatic Stress Disorder: Time for Integration', *Journal of Counselling and Development*, 81: 409–17.

Hoffmann, J.P., Ireland, T.O. and Spatz-Widom, C.S. (1994) 'Traditional Socialization Theories of Violence: A Critical Examination', in J. Archer, (ed.) *Male Violence.* London: Routledge.

Holland, T., Clare, I.C.H and Mukhopadhyay, T. (2002) 'Prevalence of "criminal offending" by Men and Women with Intellectual Disability and the Characteristics of "Offenders": Implications for Research and Service Development', *Journal of Intellectual Disability Research*, 46(1): 6–20.

Hollin, C. (1990) *Cognitive-Behavioural Interventions with Young Offenders.* Elmsford, NY: Pergamon Press.

Hollin, C. (2002) 'Criminological Psychology', in M. Maguire, M. Morgan and R. Reiner (eds) *The Oxford Handbook of Criminology* (3rd edn). Oxford: Oxford University Press.

Holmes, S., Slaughter, J. and Kashani, J. (2001) 'Risk Factors in Childhood That Lead to the Development of Conduct Disorder and Antisocial Personality Disorder', *Child Psychiatry and Human Development*, 31(3): 183–93.

Holtzworth-Munroe, A. and Stuart, G.L. (1994) 'Typologies of Male Batterers: Three Subtypes and the Differences Among Them', *Psychological Bulletin*, 116(3): 476–97.

Home Office (1991) *The Criminal Justice Act 1991.* London: HMSO.

Home Office (1997) *The Sex Offenders Act.* London: HMSO.

Home Office (2001) *Criminal Statistics for England and Wales 2000.* London: Home Office.

Home Office (2003) *The Sexual Offences Act.* London: Home Office.

Hopkins Burke, R. (2005) *An Introduction to Criminological Theory.* Cullompton: Willan.

Horne, A. (2004) ' "Gonnae No' Dae That!" The Internal and External Worlds of the Delinquent Adolescent', *Journal of Child Psychotherapy*, 30(3): 330–46.

Howitt, D. (2006) *Introduction to Forensic and Criminal Psychology.* Harlow: Pearson.

Itzin, C. (2001) 'Incest, Paedophilia, Pornography and Prostitution: Making Familial Males More Visible as the Abusers', *Child Abuse Review*, 10: 35–48.

Jaffee, S.R., Caspi, A., Moffitt, T., Polo-Tomas, M., Price, T. and Taylor, A. (2004) 'The Limits of Child Effects: Evidence for Genetically Mediated

Child Effects on Corporal Punishment But Not Physical Maltreatment', *Developmental Psychology*, 40(6): 1047–58.

Jefferson, T. (1997) 'Masculinities and Crimes', in M. Maguire, M. Morgan and R. Reiner (eds) *Oxford Handbook of Criminology* (2nd edn). Oxford: Clarendon Press.

Joe Laidler, K.J. and Hunt, J. (2001) 'Accomplishing Femininity Amongst the Girls in the Gang', *British Journal of Criminology*, 41: 656–78.

Johnson, T. (1987) 'Pre-menstrual Syndrome as a Western Culture-Specific Disorder', *Culture, Medicine and Psychiatry*, 11: 337–56.

Jones, K. (1972) *A History of the Mental Health Services*. London: Routledge and Kegan Paul.

Jones, M.E., Russell, R.L. and Bryant, F.B. (1998) 'The Structure of Rape Attitudes for Men and Women: A Three-Factor Model', *Journal of Research in Personality*, 32: 331–50.

Juby, H. and Farrington, D.P. (2001) 'Disentangling the Link Between Disrupted Families and Delinquency', *British Journal of Criminology*, 41: 22–40.

Jukes, A. (1993) *Why Men Hate Women*. London: Free Association Books.

Kandel, D. and Wu, P. (1995) 'Disentangling Mother–Child Effects in the Development of Antisocial Behaviour', in J. McCord (ed.) *Coercion and Development of Anti-social Behaviour*. Cambridge: Cambridge University Press.

Kanin, L. (1983) 'Rape as a Function of Relative Sexual Frustration', *Psychological Reports*, 52(1): 133–4.

Karstedt, S. (2002) 'Emotions and Criminal Justice', *Theoretical Criminology*, 63(3): 299–317.

Kassman, P. (2007) *Guardian*, Society Section, 23 May.

Katz, J. (1988) *Seductions of Crime: Moral and Sensual Attractions in Doing Evil*. New York: Basic Books.

Kebbell, M. and Davies, G. (2003) 'People with Intellectual Disabilities in the Investigation and Prosecution of Crime', *Legal and Criminological Psychology*, 8: 219–22.

Kegan, R.G. (1986) 'The Child Behind the Mask: Sociopathy as Developmental Delay', in W.H. Reid, D. Dorr, J. Walker and J. Bonner (eds) *Unmasking the Psychopath: Antisocial Personality and Related Syndromes*. New York: W.W. Norton.

Kemshall, H. (2004) 'Female Sex Offenders', in H. Kemshall and G. McIvor (eds) *Managing Sex Offender Risk*. London: Jessica Kingsley.

Kemshall, H. and McIvor, G. (2004) *Managing Sex Offender Risk*. London: Jessica Kingsley.

Kernberg, O.F. (1992) *Aggression in Personality Disorders and Perversions*. New Haven, CT: Yale University Press.

Kersten, J. (1996) 'Culture, Masculinities and Violence Against Women', *British Journal of Criminology*, 36(3): 381–95.

Kjelsberg, E. (1999) 'Adolescent-Limited Versus Life-Course Persistent Criminal Behaviour in Adolescent Psychiatric Inpatients', *European Child and Adolescent Psychiatry*, 8: 276–82.

Klinesmith, J., Kasser, T. and McAndrew, F.T. (2006) 'Guns, Testosterone, and Aggression: An Experimental Test of a Mediational Hypothesis', *Psychological Science*, 17(7): 568–71.

Kochanska, G. (1990) 'Maternal Beliefs as Long-Term Predictors of Mother–Child Interaction and Report', *Child Development*, 61(6): 1934–43.

Kochanska, G., Forman, D., Aksan, N. and Dunbar, S. (2005) 'Pathways to Conscience: Early Mother–Child Mutually Responsive Orientation and Children's Moral Emotion, Conduct, and Cognition', *Journal of Child Psychology and Psychiatry*, 46(1): 19–34.

Kohlberg, L. (1963) 'The Development of Children's Orientation Toward a Moral Order, I: Sequence in the Development of Moral Thought', *Vita Humana*, 6: 11–33.

Kohut, H. (1971) *The Analysis of the Self: A Systematic Approach to the Psychoanalytic Treatment of Narcissistic Personality Disorders*. London: Hogarth.

Kolvin, I. Miller, F., Fleeting, M. and Kolvin, P.A. (1988) 'Social and Parenting Factors Affecting Criminal-Offence Rates: Findings from the Newcastle Thousand Family Study (1947–1980)', *British Journal of Psychiatry*, 152: 80–90.

Konishi, T. (2000) 'Cultural aspects of violence against women in Japan', *Lancet*, 355: 1810.

Kramar, J.K and Watson, W.D. (2006) 'Medico-Legal Knowledge and the Development of Infanticide Law', *Social and Legal Studies*, 15(2): 237–55.

Kratzer, L. and Hodgins, S. (1997) 'Adult Outcomes of Child Conduct Problems: A Cohort Study', *Journal of Abnormal Child Psychology*, 25(1): 65–81.

Kutchinsky, B. (1991) 'Pornography and Rape: Theory and Practice? Evidence from Crime Data in Four Countries Where Pornography Is Easily Available', *International Journal of Law and Psychiatry*, 14: 47–64.

Laible, D. and Thompson, R. (2000) 'Mother–Child Discourse, Attachment Security, Shared Positive Affect, and Early Conscience Development', *Child Development*, 71: 1424–40.

Lalumière, M.L. and Rice, M. (2007) 'The Validity of Phallometric Assessment with Rapists: Comments on Looman & Marshall (2005)', *Sexual Abuse: A Journal of Research and Treatment*, 19(1): 61–8.

Lang, S. Klinteberg, B. and Alm, P.O. (2002) 'Adult Psychopathy and Violent Behaviour in Males with Early Neglect and Abuse', *Acta Psychiatrica Scandinavica*, 106 (suppl 412): 93–100.

Lansky, M.R. (2003) 'Discussion of Peter Fonagy et al's. "The developmental roots of BDP" ', *Psychoanalytic Enquiry*, 23(3): 460–72.

Lasch, C. (1979) *The Culture of Narcissism*. London: Abacus.

Laub, J. and Sampson, R.J. (1993) 'Turning Points in the Life Course: Why Change Matters to the Study of Crime', *Criminology*, 31(3): 301–25.

Lawson, J.S., Marshall, W.L. and McGrath, P. (1979) 'The Social Self-Esteem Inventory', *Educational and Psychological Measurement*, 39: 803–11.

Lee, J.K.P., Jackson, H.J., Pattison, P. and Ward, T. (2002) 'Developmental Risk Factors for Sexual Offending', *Child Abuse and Neglect*, 26: 73–92.

Lee, R. and Coccaro, E. (2001) 'The Neuropsychopharmacology of Criminality and Aggression', *Canadian Journal of Psychiatry*, 46(1): 35–44.

Leichsenring, F., Kunst, H. and Hoyer, J. (2003) 'Borderline Personality Organization in Violent Offenders: Correlations of Identity Diffusion and Primitive Defense Mechanisms with Anti-social Features, Neuroticism, and Interpersonal Problems', *Bulletin of the Menninger Clinic*, 67(4): 314–27.

Lemert, E. (1951) *Social Pathology: A Systematic Approach to the Theory of Sociopathic Behaviour*. New York: McGraw Hill.

Leschied, A., Cummings, A., Van Brunschot, M., Cuningham, A. and Saunders, A. (2001) 'Aggression in Adolescent Girls: Implications for Policy, Prevention and Treatment', *Canadian Psychology*, 42(3): 200–15.

Levi, M. (1997) 'Violent Crime', in M. Maguire, M. Morgan and R. Reiner (eds) *Oxford Handbook of Criminology* (2nd edn). Oxford: Clarendon Press.

Levy, F. (2002) 'Project for a Scientific Psychiatry in the 21st Century', *Australian and New Zealand Journal of Psychiatry*, 36(5): 595–603.

Lewis, H.E. (1987) *The Role of Shame in Symptom Formation*. Hillsdale, NJ: Lawrence Erlbaum Press.

Lindsay, W.R. (2002) 'Integration of Recent Reviews on Offenders with Intellectual Abilities', *Journal of Applied Research in Intellectual Disabilities*, 15: 111–19.

Livaditis, M., Fotiadou, M., Kouloubardou, F., Samakouri, M. and Gizari, F. (2000) 'Greek Adolescents in Custody: Psychological Morbidity, Family Characteristics and Minority Groups', *Journal of Forensic Psychiatry*, 11(3): 597–607.

Loeber, R. and Hay, D. (1997) 'Key Issues in the Development of Aggression and Violence from Childhood to Early Adulthood', *Annual Review of Psychology*, 48: 371–410.

Lombroso, C. ([1876] 2006) *The Criminal Man*. M. Gibson and N. Hahn Rafter (trans.) Chesham: Duke University Press.

Looman, J. and Marshall, W.L. (2005) 'Sexual Arousal in Rapists', *Criminal Justice and Behavior*, 32(4): 367–89.

Lösel, F. and Schmuker, M. (2004) 'Psychopathy, Risk Taking and Attention: A Differentiated Test of the Somatic Maker Hypothesis', *Journal of Abnormal Psychology*, 113(4): 522–9.

Luckenbill, D.F. (1977) 'Criminal Homicide as a Situated Transaction', *Social Problems*, 26: 176–86.

Lussier, P., LeBlanc, M. and Proulx, J. (2005) 'The Generality of Criminal Behaviour: A Confirmatory Factor Analysis of the Criminal Activity of Sex Offenders in Adulthood', *Journal of Criminal Justice*, 33: 177–89.

Lykken, D. (2000) 'The Causes and Costs of Crime and a Controversial Cure', *Journal of Personality*, 68(3): 559–605.

Lyng, S. (1990) 'Edgework: A Social Psychological Analysis of Voluntary Risk Taking', *American Journal of Sociology*, 95(4): 851–86.

Lyng, S. (2004) 'Crime, Edgework and Corporeal Transaction', *Theoretical Criminology*, 8(3): 359–75.

Lyons-Ruth, K. (1996) 'Attachment Relationships Among Children with Aggressive Behavior Problems: The Role of Disorganized Early Attachment Patterns', *Journal of Consulting and Clinical Psychology*, 64: 64–73.

Maden, A., Swinton, M. and Gunn, J. (1994) 'A Criminological and Psychiatric Survey of Women Serving a Prison Sentence', *British Journal of Criminology*, 34(2): 172–91.

MacCulloch, M., Gray, N. and Watt, A. (2000) 'Britain's Sadistic Murderer Syndrome Reconsidered: An Associative Account of the Aetiology of Sadistic Sexual Fantasy', *Journal of Forensic Psychiatry and Psychology*, 11(2): 401–18.

Maguire, M. (1995) *Men, Women, Passion and Power*. Hove: Brunner-Routledge.

Maguire, M. (2004) *Understanding Psychology and Crime*. Maidenhead: Open University Press.

Maguire, M., Morgan, M. and Reiner, R. (1997) *The Oxford Handbook of Criminology* (2nd edn). Oxford: Oxford University Press.

Maguire, M., Morgan, M. and Reiner, R. (2002) *The Oxford Handbook of Criminology* (3rd edn). Oxford: Oxford University Press.

Malamuth, N.M. (1981) 'Rape Proclivity Among Males', *Journal of Social Issues*, 37(4): 138–57.

Mannheim, H. (1960) *Pioneers in Criminology*. London: Stevens and Son.

Marshall, W.L. Anderson, D. and Fernandez, Y. (1999) *Cognitive Behavioural Treatment of Sexual Offenders*. Chichester: Wiley.

Masson, H. (2004) 'Young Sex Offenders', in H. Kemshall and G. McIvor, *Managing Sex Offender Risk*. London: Jessica Kingsley.

Matza, D. (1969) *Becoming Deviant*. New York: Prentice-Hall.

Matza, D. (1964) *Delinquency and Drift*. New York: Wiley.

Mazur, A. and Booth, A. (1998) 'Testosterone and Dominance in Men', *Behavioural and Brain Sciences*, 21: 353–97.

McBrien, J. (2003) 'The Intellectually Disabled Offender: Methodological Problems in Identification,' *Journal of Applied Research in Intellectual Disabilities*, 16: 95–105.

McCallum, D. (2001) *Personality and Dangerousness: Genealogies of Anti-social Personality*. Cambridge: Cambridge University Press.

McCord, J. (1979) 'Some Child-Rearing Antecedents of Criminal Behaviour in Adult Men', *Journal of Personality and Social Psychology*, 37: 1477–86.

McCord, J. (1990) 'Long Term Perspective on Parental Absence', in L. Robins and M. Rutter, *Straight and Devious Pathways from Childhood to Adulthood*. Cambridge: Cambridge University Press.

McDonald, T.W. and Kline, L.M. (2004) 'Perceptions of Appropriate Punishment for Committing Date Rape: Male College Students Recommend Lenient Punishments', *College Student Journal*, 38(1): 44–57.

McGuire, R.J., Carlisle, J.M, and Young, B.G. (1965) 'Sexual Deviations as Conditioned Behaviour', *Behavior Research Therapy*, 2: 185–90.

McMahon, W. and Payne, L. (2001) 'Lessons from the Bulger Case', *Children and Society*, 15: 272–4.

Mednick, S., Gabrielli, W. and Hutchings, B. (1987) 'Genetic Factors in the Etiology of Criminal Behaviour', in S.A. Mednick, T.E. Moffitt and S.A. Stack, *The Causes of Crime: New Biological Approaches*. Cambridge: Cambridge University Press.

Meeus, W., Branje, S. and Overbeek, G.J. (2004) 'Parents and Partners in Crime: A Six Year Old Longitudinal Study on Changes in Supportive Relationships and Delinquency in Adolescence and Young Adulthood', *Journal of Child Psychology and Psychiatry*, 45(7): 1288–98.

Meloy, J.R. (1992) *Violent Attachments*. London: Aronson.

Memon, A., Vrij, A. and Bull, R. (1998) *Psychology and Law: Truthfulness, Accuracy and Credibility*. London: McGraw Hill.

Men's Health Forum (2001) *Young Men and Suicide*. London: Men's Health Forum.

Merrington, S. and Stanley, S. (2004) ' "What works?": Revisiting the Evidence in England and Wales', *Journal of Community and Criminal Justice*, 51(1): 7–20.

Merton, R.K. (1957) *Social Theory and Social Structure*. New York: Free Press.

Merton, R.K. (1938) 'Social Structure and Anomie', *American Sociological Review*, 3(5): 672–82.

Messerschmidt, J.W. (1986) *Capitalism, Patriarchy, and Crime: Towards a Feminist Criminology*. Lanham, MD: Rowman & Littlefield.

Messerschmidt, J.W. (1993) *Masculinities and Crime: A Critique and Reconceptualization of Theory*. Maryland: Rowman and Littlefield.

Mills, R.S.L. (2003) 'Possible Antecedents and Developmental Implications of Shame in Young Girls', *Infant and Child Development*, 12: 329–49.

Minsky, R. (1998) *Psychoanalysis and Culture: Contemporary States of Mind*. Cambridge: Polity.

Moffitt, T. (1993) 'Adolescence-Limited and Life Course Persistent Antisocial Behaviour: A Developmental Taxonomy', *Psychological Review*, 100(4): 674–701.

Moffitt, T., Brammer, G., Caspi, A., Fawcett, J., Raleigh, M., Yuwiler, A. and Silva, P. (1998) 'Whole Blood Serotonin Relates to Violence in an Epidemiological Study', *Biological Psychiatry*, 43(6): 446–57.

Moffit, T.E. and Caspi, A. (1999) 'Findings About Partner Violence from the Dunedin Multidisciplinary Health and Development Study', *National Institute of Justice: Research in Brief* (July). Washington, DC: US Department of Justice.

Moffit, T.E. and Caspi, A. (2001) 'Childhood Predictors Differentiate Life-Course Persistent and Adolescence-Limited Antisocial Pathways Among Males and Females', *Development and Psychopathology*, 13: 355–75.

Moffitt, T.E. Lynman, D. and Silva, P.A. (1994) 'Neuropsychological Tests Predict Persistent Male Delinquency', *Criminology*, 32: 101–34.

Moffitt, T.E., Caspi, A., Dickson, N., Silva, P. and Stanton, W. (1996) 'Childhood-Onset Versus Adolescent-Onset Antisocial Conduct Problems in Males: Natural History from Ages 3 to 18 years', *Development and Psychopathology*, 8(2): 399–424.

Moffitt, T.E., Caspi, A., Harrington, H. and Milne, B. (2002) 'Males on the Life-Course Persistent Pathways: Follow-up at Age 26 Years', *Development and Psychopathology*, 4: 179–207.

Moir, A. and Jessel, D. (1995) *A Mind to Crime.* New York: Signet Books.

Molan, M. and Douglas, G. (2004) *Questions and Answers: Criminal Law 2005-6.* Oxford: Oxford University Press.

Monachesi, E. (1955) 'Pioneers in Criminology. IX. Cesare Beccaria (1738-1794)', *Journal of Criminal Law, Criminology, and Police Science*, 46(4): 439–49.

Moran, P. (1999) 'The Epidemiology of Antisocial Personality Disorder', *Social Psychiatry and Psychiatric Epidemiology*, 34(5): 231–42.

Moran, P. and Hagell, A. (2001) *Intervening to Prevent Antisocial Personality Disorder: A Scoping Review.* London: Home Office Research, Development and Statistics Directorate.

MORI (2004) *Youth Justice Board: Youth Survey 2004.* London: Youth justice Board.

Morrell, J. and Murray, L. (2003) 'Parenting and the Development of Conduct Disorder and Hyperactive Symptoms in Childhood: A Prospective Longitudinal Study from 2 Months to 8 Years', *Journal of Child Psychology and Psychiatry*, 44(4): 489–508.

Morrison, D. and Gilbert, P. (2001) 'Social Rank, Shame and Anger in Primary and Secondary Psychopaths', *Journal of Forensic Psychiatry*, 12(2): 330–56.

Morrison, S. and O'Donnell, I. (1996) 'An Analysis of the Decision Making Practices of Armed Robbers', in R. Homel (eds) *The Politics and Practices of Situational Crime Prevention.* Monsey, NY: Criminal Justice Press.

Morrison, T., Erooga, M. and Beckett, R.C. (1994) 'Sexual Offending Against Children', London: Routledge.

Motz, A. (2001) *The Psychology of Female Violence: Crimes Against the Body.* London: Routledge.

Murdoch, D. and Barker, P. (1991) 'Basic Behaviour Therapy', Oxford: Blackwell.

Nathan, D.L. (1987) *The Many Faces of Shame*. New York: Guilford Press.

Nathan, J. (2004) 'In-Depth Work with Patients Who Self-Harm: Doing the Impossible', *Psychoanalytic Psychotherapy*, 18(2): 167–81.

NCH (National Children's Home) (1992) *The Report of the Committee of Enquiry into Young People and Children Who Sexually Abuse Other Children*. London: NCH.

Neisser, U. (1976) *Cognition and Reality: Principles and Implications of Cognitive Psychology*. San Francisco, CA: W.H.Freeman.

Nelken, D. (1994) *The Futures of Criminology*. London: Sage.

Nelken, D. (2002) 'White Collar Crime', in M. Maguire, M. Morgan and R. Reiner (eds) *The Oxford Handbook of Criminology*. Oxford: Oxford University Press.

Nemeth, A.J. (1995) 'Ambiguities Caused by Forensic Psychology's Dual Identity: How to Deal with the Prevailing Quantitative Bias and Scientistic Posture', *American Journal of Forensic Psychology*, 13(4): 47–66.

NESS (National Evaluation of Sure Start) (2005) *Early Impacts of Sure Start Local Programmes on Children and Families*. London: DfES.

Neubauer, P.B. (1960) 'The One-Parent Child and His Oedipal Development', in *Psychoanalytic Studies of the Child*, 15: 286–309.

Newburn, T. (1997) 'Youth, Crime and Justice', in M. Maguire, M. Morgan and R. Reiner (eds) *The Oxford Handbook of Criminolgy* (2nd edn). Oxford: Oxford University Press.

Newburn, T. (2003) *Crime and Criminal Justice Policy* (2nd edn). Harlow: Longman.

Newson, E. (1994) 'Video violence and the protection of children', *The Psychologist: Bulletin of the British Psychological Association*, 7(6): 272–4.

Nightingale, C.H. (1993) *On the edge: A History of Poor Black Children and Their American Dreams*. New York: Basic Books.

O'Brien, M., Mortimer, L., Singleton, N. and Meltzer, H. (2003) 'Psychiatric Morbidity Among Women Prisoners', *International Review of Psychiatry*, 15: 153–7.

O'Connor, T.G. (2002) 'Annotation: The "effects" of Parenting Reconsidered: Findings, Challenges, and Applications', *Journal of Child Psychology and Psychiatry*, 43(5): 555–72.

Olthof, T., Schouten, A., Kuper, H., Stegge, H. and Jennekens-Schinkel, A. (2000) 'Shame and Guilt in Children: Differential Situational Antecedents and Experiential Correlates', *British Journal of Developmental Psychology*, 18: 51–64.

Olweus, D. (1987) 'Testosterone and Adrenaline: Aggressive Antisocial Behaviour in Normal and Adolescent Males', in S.A. Mednick, S.A. Moffitt and S.A. Stacks (eds) *The Causes of Crime: New Biological Approaches*. Cambridge: Cambridge University Press.

Olweus, D., Mattesson, A., Schalling, D. and Low, H. (1980) 'Testosterone, Aggression, Physical, and Personality Dimensions in Normal Adolescent Males', *Psychosomatic Medicine*, 42(2): 253–69.

O'Malley, P. and Mugford, S. (1994) 'Crime, Excitement, and Modernity', in G. Barak (ed.) *Varieties of Criminology*. Westport, CT: Praeger.

Ortmann, R. (2000) 'The Effectiveness of Social Therapy in Prison', *Crime and Delinquency*, 46(2): 214–32.

Pagano, M.E., Skodol, A.E., and Stout, R.L. (2004) 'Stressful Life Events as Predictors of Functioning: Findings from the Collaborative Longitudinal Personality Disorders Study', *Acta Psychiaticra Scandanavica*, 110: 421–9.

Palmer, E. (2003) *Offending Behaviour: Moral Reasoning, Criminal Conduct and the Rehabilitation of Offenders*. Cullompton: Willan.

Palmer, E. (2005) 'The relationship Between Moral Reasoning and Aggression, and the Implications for Practice', *Psychology, Crime and Law*, 11(4): 353–61.

Parker, M. (2003) 'Doing Time: A Group Analytic Perspective on the Emotional Experience of Time in a Men's Prison', *Group Analysis*, 36(2): 169–81.

Patterson, G.R., DeBaryshe, B.D. and Ramsey, E. (1989) 'A Developmental Perspective on Anti-social Behaviour', *American Psychologist*, 44(2): 329–35.

Pattison, S. (2000) *Shame: Theory, Therapy, Theology*. Cambridge: Cambridge University Press.

Paylor, I. and Simmill-Binning, C. (2004) 'Evaluating Youth Justice in the UK', *American Journal of Evaluation*, 25(3): 335–49.

Payne, J. (2000) 'Young People Not in Education, Employment or Training', *Research Brief 201*. London: Department for Education and Employment.

Pease, K. (2002) 'Crime Reduction', in M. Maguire, M. Morgan and R. Reiner (eds) *The Oxford Handbook of Criminology* (3rd edn). Oxford University Press: Oxford.

Peay, J. (1997) 'Mentally Disordered Offenders', in M. Maguire, M. Morgan and R. Reiner (eds) *The Oxford Handbook of Criminology* (2nd edn). Oxford: Oxford University Press.

Pennell, A. and Browne, K.D. (1999) 'Film Violence and Young Offenders', *Aggression and Violent Behaviour*, 4(16): 13–28.

Pennell, H., West, A. and Hind, A. (2006) *Secondary School Admissions in London*. Clare Market Papers 19. London: London School of Economics.

Peris, T. and Hinshaw, S.P. (2003) 'Family Dynamics and Pre-adolescent Girls with ADHD: The Relationship Between Expressed Emotion, ADHD Symptomatology, and Comorbid Disruptive Behaviour', *Journal of Child Psychology and Psychiatry*, 44(8): 1177–90.

Phillips, C. (2003) 'Who's Who in the Pecking Order? Aggression and 'Normal' Violence in the Lives of Girls and Boys', *British Journal of Criminology*, 43: 710–28.

Piers, G. and Singer, M.B. (1953) *Shame and Guilt: A Psychoanalytic and Cultural Study*. Springfield, IL: W.W. North.

Pilgrim, D. (2001) 'Disordered Personalities and Disordered Concepts', *Journal of Mental Health*, 10(3): 253–65.

Pinderhughes, E.E., Dodge, K.A., Bates, J.E., Pettit, G.S., and Zelli, A. (2000) 'Discipline Responses: Influences of Parents' Socioeconomic Status, Ethnicity, and Beliefs About Parenting, Stress, and Cognitive-Emotional Processes', *Journal of Family Psychology*, 14: 380–400.

Pinel, P.H. (1806) *A Treatise on Insanity*. D.D. Davis (trans.). London: W. Todd for Calwell and Davis.

Pines, A. and Friedman, A. (1998) 'Gender Differences in Romantic Jealousy', *The Journal of Social Psychology*, 138(1): 54–71.

Piquero, N.L. and Benson, M.L. (2004) 'White Collar Crime and Criminal Careers', *Journal of Contemporary Criminal Justice*, 20(2): 148–65.

Polaschek, D.L. and Ward, T. (2002) 'The Implicit Theories of Potential Rapists: What Our Questionnaires Tell Us', *Aggression and Violent Behaviour*, 7: 385–406.

Polk, K. (1991) 'A Scenario of Masculine Violence: Confrontational Homicide', in P.W. Easteal and S. McKillop (eds) *AIC Conference Proceedings: 24–26 September 1991*. Canberra: Australian Institute of Criminology, 1993. Available at *www.aic.gov.au/publications/proceedings/17/*.

Polk, K. (1991) 'Homicide: Women as Offenders', in P.W. Easteal and S. McKillop (eds) *AIC Conference Proceedings: 24–26 September, 1991*. Canberra: Australian Institute of Criminology, 1993. Available at *www.aic.gov.au/publications/proceedings/16/*.

Polk, K. (1994) *When Men Kill: Scenarios of Masculine Violence*. Cambridge: Cambridge University Press.

Pollack, O. (1961) *The Criminality of Women*. New York: A.S. Barnes and Co.

Pollard, P. (1994) 'Sexual Violence Against Women: Characteristics of typical perpetrators', in J. Archer (ed.) *Male Violence*. London: Routledge.

Pomerleau, A., Malcuit, G. and Seguin, R. (1992) 'Five month old girls' and boys' exploratory behaviour in the presence of familiar and unfamiliar toys', *Journal of Genetic Psychology*, 153(1): 47–61.

Pratt, T. and Cullen, F. (2000) 'The Empirical Status of Gottfredson and Hirschi's General Theory of Crime: A Meta-analysis', *Criminology*, 38(3): 931–61.

Prichard, J.C. (1835) *A Treatise on Insanity and Other Disorders Affecting the Mind*. London: Sherwood, Gilbert and Piper.

Proulx, J., Aubut, J., McKibben, A. and Cote, M. (1994) 'Penile Responses of Rapists and Nonrapists to Rape Stimuli Involving Physical Violence or Humiliation', *Archives of Sexual Behavior*, 23(3): 295–310.

Putnam, R.D. (2000) *Bowling Alone. The Collapse and Revival of American Community*. New York: Simon and Schuster.

Quetelet, A. (1842) *A Treatise on Man and the Development of His Faculties*. Gainsville, FL: Scholars Facsimilies & Reprint.

Quinney, R. (1970) *The Social Reality of Crime*. Boston: Little Brown.

2222

2222222222222

Quinsey, V.L. and Earls, C.M. (1990) 'The Modification of Sexual Preferences', in W.L. Marshall, D.R. Laws and H.E. Barbaree (eds). *Handbook of Sexual Assault*. New York: Plenum Press.

Raboch, J., Charles, U., Cerna, H. and Zemek, P. (1987) 'Sexual Aggressivity and Androgens', *British Journal of Psychiatry*, 151: 398–400.

Rafter, N. (2004) 'The Unrepentant Horse-Slasher: Moral Insanity and the Origins of Criminological Thought', *Criminology*, 42(4): 979–1008.

Raine, A., Moffitt, T., Caspi, A., Loeber, R., Stouthamer-Loeber, M. and Lynam, D. (2005) 'Neurocognitive Impairments in Boys on the Life-Course Persistent Antisocial Path', *Journal of Abnormal Psychology*, 114(1): 38–49.

Raine, R. (1993) *The Psychopathology of Crime*. San Diego, CA: Academic Press.

Ramirez, J.M. (2003) 'Hormones and Aggression in Childhood and Adolescence', *Aggression and Violent Behavior*, 8(6): 621–44.

Ramon, S. (1986) 'Psychopathy: Its Professional and Social Context in Britain', in P. Miller and N. Rose (eds) *The Power of Psychiatry*. Cambridge: Polity.

Rankin, J.H. and Wells, L.E. (1994) 'Social Control, Broken Homes, and Delinquency', in Barak, G. (ed.) *Varieties of Criminology: Readings from a Dynamic Discipline*. Westport, CT: Praeger.

Rawson W.R. (1839) 'An Inquiry into the Statistics of Crime in England and Wales', *Journal of the Statistical Society of London*, 2(5): 316–44.

Ray, I. (1838) *A Treatise on the Medical Jurisprudence of Insanity*. Boston: Charles, Little and Brown.

Ray, L., Smith, D. and Wastell, L. (2004) 'Shame, Rage and Racist Violence', *British Journal of Criminology*, 44: 350–68.

Reimer, M. (1996) 'Sinking into the Ground': The Development and Consequences of Shame in Adolescence', *Developmental Review*, 16: 321–63.

Reyno, S.M. and McGrath, P. (2006) 'Predictors of Parent Training Efficacy for Child Externalizing Behavior Problems – A Meta-analytic Review', *Journal of Child Psychology and Psychiatry*, 47(1): 99–111.

Reznek, L. (1997) *Evil or Ill? Justifying the Insanity Defence*. London: Routledge.

Rice, M. and Harris, G. (1997) 'Cross-Validation and Extension of the Violence Risk Appraisal Guide for Child Molesters and Rapists', *Law and Human Behaviour*, 21(2): 231–41.

Rich Harris, J. (2000) 'The Outcome of Parenting: What Do We Really Know?' *Journal of Personality*, 68(3): 625–37.

Ritchie, J.H., Dick, D. and Lingham, R. (1994) *The Report into the Care and Treatment of Christopher Clunis*. London: HMSO.

Robertson, B. (1999) 'Leisure and Family: Perspectives of Male Adolescents Who Engage in Delinquent Activity as Leisure', *Journal of Leisure Research*, 31(4): 335–58.

Robinson, C.L. (1999) 'Observations on Cognition and Insanity', *American Journal of Forensic Psychology*, 17(4): 63–75.

Robinson, S.L. (2005) 'Considerations for the Assessment of Female Sexually Abusive Youth', in M. Calder (ed.) *Children and Young People who Sexually Abuse: New Theory, Research and Practice Developments*. Lyme Regis: Russell House.

Rodham, K., Hawton, K. and Evans, E. (2005) 'Deliberate Self-Harm in Adolescents: The Importance of Gender', *Psychiatric Times*, 22(1): 36–41.

Rönkä, A. and Pulkkinen, L. (1995) 'Accumulation of Problems in Social Functioning in Young Adulthood: A Developmental Approach', *Journal of Personality and Social Psychology*, 69(2): 381–91.

Rose, N. (1989) *Governing the Soul: The Shaping of the Private Self*. London: Routledge.

Rosenhan, D.L. (1973) 'On Being Sane in Insane Places', *Science*, 179: 250–8.

Ross, R.R. and Fabiano, E.A. (1985) *Time to Think: A Cognitive Model of Delinquency, Prevention and Offender Rehabilitation*. Johnson City, TN: Institute of Social Sciences and Arts, Inc.

Rozelle, S.R. (2005) 'Controlling Passions: Adultery and the Provocation Defence', *Rutgers Law Journal*, 37: 197–232.

Rubin, R.T. (1987) 'Neuroendocrinology of Antisocial Behaviour', in S.A. Mednick, T.E. Moffitt and S.A. Stack (eds) *The Causes of Crime: New Biological Approaches*. Cambridge: Cambridge University Press.

Rubinow, D.R. and Schmidt, P.J. (1996) 'Androgens, Brain and Behaviour', *American Journal of Psychiatry*, 153: 974–84.

Runciman, W.G. (1966) *Relative Deprivation and Social Jusitce*. London: Routledge.

Rustin, M. (2000) ' "Cruelty, Violence and Murder: Understanding the Criminal Mind" by A.H. Williams. Book Review', *British Journal of Criminology*, 40(1): 165–8.

Rutter, M., Giller, H. and Hagel, A. (1998) *Antisocial Behaviour by Young People*. Cambridge: University Press.

Salter, D., McMillan, D., Richards, M. *et al.* (2003) 'Development of Sexually Abusive Behaviour in Sexually Victimized Males: A Longitudinal Study', *Lancet*, 361: 471–6.

Sampson, R. and Laub, J. (1993) *Crime in the Making: Pathways and Turning Points Through Life*. Cambridge, MA: Harvard University Press.

Sanday, P.R. (1981) 'The Socio-cultural Context of Rape: A Cross-cultural Study', *Journal of Social Issues*, 37: 5–27.

Sankey, M. and Huon, G.F. (1999) 'Offence Seriousness in Adolescent Delinquent Behaviour', *Legal and Criminological Psychology*, 4: 253–64.

Sass, H. and Jünemann, K. (2003) 'Affective Disorders, Personality and Personality Disorders', *Acta Psychiatrica Scandinavica*, 108 (Supp 418): 34–40.

Sauvola, A., Koskinen, O., Jokekainen, J., Hakko, H., Jravelin, M. and Räsänen, P. (2002) 'Family Type and Criminal Behaviour of Male Offspring: The

Northern Finland 1966 Birth Cohort Study', *International Journal of Social Psychiatry*, 48(2): 115–21.

Scelfo, J. and Adams, W. (2005) 'Bad Girls Go Wild', *Newsweek*, 145(24).

Scheff, T. (1987) 'The Shame-Rage Spiral: A Case Study of an Interminable Quarrel', in H.E. Lewis (ed.) *The Role of Shame in Symptom Formation*. Hillsdale, NJ: Lawrence Erlbaum.

Scheff, T. (2003) 'Male Emotions/Relationships and Violence: A Case Study', *Human Relations*, 56(6): 727–49.

Scheff, T. and Retzinger, S. (1997) 'Shame, Anger and the Social Bond: A Theory of Sexual Offenders and Treatment', *Electronic Journal of Sociology*, 3(1).

Schoenthaler, S.J. and Bier, I.D. (2000) 'The Effect of Vitamin-Mineral Supplementation on Juvenile Delinquency Among American Schoolchildren: A Randomised, Double-blind Placebo-Controlled Trial', *Journal of Alternative and Complementary Medicine*, 6(1): 7–17.

Schore, A. (1994) *Affect Regulation and the Origin of Self: The Neurobiology of Emotional Development*. Hillsdale, NJ: Lawrence Erlbaum Associates.

Schore, A. (1998) 'Early Shame Experiences and Infant Brain Development', in P. Gilbert and B. Andrews (eds) *Shame: Interpersonal Behaviour, Psychopathology, and Culture*. Oxford: Oxford University Press.

Schutz, A. (1967) *The Phenomenology of the Social World* (G. Walsh and F. Leuchart, trans.) London: Heinemann.

Schuurman, T. (1980) 'Hormonal Correlates of Agonistic Behaviour in Adulthood in Adult Male Rats', *Progress in Brain Research*, 53: 415–20.

Scull, A. (1979) *Museums of Madness*. London: Allen Lane.

Scully, D. (1990) *Understanding Sexual Violence: A Study of Convicted Rapists*. London: Routledge.

Scully, D. (1988) 'Convicted Rapists' Perceptions of Self and Victim: Role Taking and Emotions', *Gender and Society*, 2(2): 200–13.

Scully, D. and Marolla, J. (1984) 'Convicted Rapists' Vocabulary of Motive: Excuses and Justifications', *Social Problems*, 31: 530–44.

Senn, C.Y., Desmarais, S., Verberg, N. and Wood, E. (2000) 'Predicting Coercive Sexual Behaviour Across the Lifespan in a Random Sample of Canadian Men', *Journal of Social and Personal Relationships*, 17(1): 95–1133.

Serran. G. and Firestone, P. (2004) 'Intimate Partner Homicide: A Review of the Male Proprietariness and the Self Defense Theories', *Aggression and Violent Behaviour*, 9: 1–15.

Seto, M. (2004) 'Pedophilia and Sex Offences Against Children', *Annual Review of Sex Research*, 15: 321–61.

Shaw, C. and McKay, H. (1942) *Juvenile Delinquency and Urban Areas*. Chicago: University of Chicago Press.

Shoemaker, R. (2001) 'Male Honour and the Decline of Public Violence in Eighteenth-Century London', *Social History*, 26(2): 190–208.

Shore, H. (2000) 'The Idea of Juvenile Delinquency in 19th Century England', *History Today*, June 21–7.

Silva, E.B. and Smart, C. (1999) *The New Family?* London: Sage.

Simons, R., Johnson, C., Conger, R.D. and Elder, G. (1998) 'A Test of Latent Trait Versus Life-Course Perspectives on the Stability of Adolescent Antisocial Behaviour', *Criminology*, 36(2): 217–43.

Simpson, M.K. and Hogg, J. (2001) 'Patterns of Offending Among People with Intellectual Disability: A Systematic Review. 1. Methodology and Prevalence Data', *Journal of Intellectual Disability Research*, 45: 384–96.

Singh, I. (2002) 'Biology in Context: Social and Cultural Perspectives on ADHD', *Children and Society*, 16: 360–67.

Slawson, J. (1923) 'Marital Relations of Parents and Juvenile Delinquency', *Journal of Delinquency*, 8: 280–83.

Smalley, S., Kustanovich, V., Minassian, S.L. *et al.* (2002) 'Genetic Linkage of Attention-Deficit/Hyperactivity Disorder on Chromosome 16p13, in a Region Implicated in Autism', *American Journal of Human Genetics*, 71: 959–63.

Smart, C. (1976) *Women, Crime and Criminology: A Feminist Critique*. London: Routledge, Kegan and Paul.

Smith, D. (2002) 'Crime and the Life Course', in M. Maguire, M. Morgan and R. Reiner (eds) *Oxford Handbook of Criminology* (2nd edn). Oxford: Oxford University Press.

Social Trends (2004) *Social Trends 34*. C. Summerfield and P. Babb (eds). London: HMSO.

Soothill, K., Francis, B. Sanderson, B. and Ackerley, E. (2000) 'Sex Offenders: Specialists, Generalists – or Both', *British Journal of Criminology*, 40: 56–7.

Soothill, K., Francis, B., Ackerley, E. and Fligelstone, R. (2002a) 'Murder and Serious Sexual Assault: What Criminal Histories Can Reveal About Future Serious Offending', Police Research Series 144. London: Home Office.

Soothill, K., Francis, B. and Fligelstone, R. (2002b) *Patterns of Offending Behaviour: A New Approach*. Home Office Findings 171. London: Home Office.

Soothill, K., Peelo, M. and Taylor, C. (2002c) *Making Sense of Criminology*. Cambridge: Polity Press.

Speicher, B. (1994) 'Family Patterns of Moral Judgment During Adolescence and Early Adulthood', *Developmental Psychology*, 30: 624–32.

Spinard, T.L., Losoya, S.H., Eisenberg, N. *et al.* (1999) 'The Relation of Parental Affect and Encouragement to Children's Moral Emotions and Behaviour', *Journal of Moral Education*, 28(3): 323–37.

Stanley Hall, G. (1904) *Adolescence: Its Psychology and Its Relations to Physiology, Anthropology, Sociology, Sex, Crime, Religion and Education*. New York: D. Appleton and Co.

Stanley Hall, G. (1912) 'Social Phases of Psychology', *Proceedings of the American Sociological Society*, 7: 38–46.

Steffensmeier, D. and Allan, E. (1996) 'Gender and Crime: Toward a Gendered Theory of Female Offending', *Annual Review of Sociology*, 22: 459–87.

Steffensmeier, D., Schwartz, J., Zhong, H. and Ackerman, J. (2005) 'An Assessment of Recent Trends in Girls' Violence Using Diverse Longitudinal Sources: Is the Gender Gap Closing?', *Criminology*, 43(2): 355–405.

Steinberg, L. and Scott, E. (2003) 'Less Guilty by Reason of Adolescence: Developmental Immaturity, Diminished Responsibility, and the Juvenile Death Penalty', *American Psychologist*, 58(12): 1009–18.

Stern, D. (1985) *The Interpersonal World of the Infant: A View from Psychoanalysis and Developmental Psychology*. London: Karnac Books.

Stern, S. and Smith, C. (1999) 'Reciprocal Relationships Between Antisocial Behaviour and Parenting: Implications for Delinquency intervention', *Families in Society*, 80(2): 169–81.

Stoller. R. (1976) *Perversion: The Erotic Form of Hatred*. Brighton: Harvester Press.

Stone, V., Cotton, D. and Thomas, A. (2000) 'Mapping Troubled Lives: Young People Not in Education, Employment or Training', *Research Brief 181*. London: Department of Education and Employment.

Straus, M. (1992) 'Sociological Research and Social Policy: The Case for Family Violence', *Sociological Forum*, 7(2): 211–37.

Stuewig, J. and McCloskey, L. (2005) 'The Relation of Child Maltreatment to Shame and Guilt Among Adolescents: Psychological Routes to Depression and Delinquency', *Child Maltreatment*, 10(4): 324–36.

Sung, H.-E. (2003) 'Fairer Sex or Fairer System? Gender and Corruption Revisited?', *Social Forces*, 82(2): 703–23.

Sure Start. Many reports available at www.surestart.gov.uk.

Sutherland, E.H. (1947) *Principles of Criminology*. Philadelphia: Lipppincott. Reprinted in *The Sutherland Papers* A. Cohen, A. Lindesmith and K. Schuessler (eds). Bloomington, IN: Indiana University Press.

Swanston, H., Parkinson, P., O'Toole, B., Plunkett, A., Shrimpton, S. and Oates, R. (2003) 'Juvenile Crime, Aggression and Delinquency after Sexual Abuse', *British Journal of Criminology*, 43: 729–49.

Tangney, J,P., Wagner, P.E., Hill-Barlow, D., Marschsall, D.E. and Richard, G. (1996) 'Relation of Shame and Guilt to Constructive Versus Destructive Responses to Anger Across the Lifespan', *Journal of Personality and Social Psychology*, 70(4): 797–809.

Tardif, M. and Van Gijseghem, H. (2001) 'Do Pedophiles have a Weaker Identity Structure Compared with Non-sexual Offenders', *Child Abuse and Neglect*, 25: 1381–94.

Taylor, C. (2001) 'The Relation Between Social and Self Control: Tracing Hirschi's Criminal Career', *Theoretical Criminology*, 5(3): 369–88.

Taylor, I., Walton, P. and Young, J. (1973) *The New Criminology: For a Social Theory of Deviance*. London: Routledge, Kegan and Paul.

Taylor, P. (1993) 'Schizophrenia and Crime: Distinctive Patterns in Association', in S. Hodgins (ed.) *Mental Disorder and Crime*. London: Sage.

Tham, S.W., Ford, T.J. and Wilkinson, D.G. (1995) 'A Survey of Domestic Violence and Other Forms of Abuse', *Journal of Mental Health*, 4: 317–21.

Thornhill, R. and Palmer, C. (2001) *A Natural History of Rape: Biological Bases of Sexual Coercion*. Cambridge, MA: MIT Press.

Timimi, S. (2004) 'ADHD Is Best Understood as a Cultural Construct', *British Journal of Psychiatry*, 8(9): 184.

Travis Brown, C. (2003) *Evolution, Gender, and Rape*. Cambridge, MA: MIT Press.

Tredget, J.E. (2001) 'The Aetiology, Presentation and Treatment of Personality Disorders', *Journal of Psychiatric and Mental Health Nursing*, 8: 347–56.

Trevarthen, C. (2001) 'Intrinsic Motives for Companionship in Understanding: Their Origin, Development, and Significance for Infant Mental Health', *Infant Mental Health Journal*, 22(1–2): 95–131.

Turner, A. (1994) 'Genetic and Hormonal Influences on Male Violence', in J. Archer (ed.) *Male Violence*. London: Routledge.

Umberson, D., Anderson, K., Williams, K. and Chen, M. (2003) 'Relationship Dynamics, Emotion State and Domestic Violence', *Journal of Marriage and Family*, 65: 233–47.

Urbas, G. (2000) 'The Age of Criminal Responsibility', *Trends and Issues in Crime and Criminal Justice No. 181*. Australian Institute of Crimnology, www.aic.gov.au.

Ussher, J (2006) *Managing the Monstrous Feminine: Regulating the Reproductive Body*. London: Routledge.

Utting, D., Bright, J. and Henricson, C. (1993) *Crime and the Family: Improving Child-Rearing and Preventing Delinquency*. London: Family Policy Studies Centre.

Valentine, G. (2003) 'Boundary Crossings: Transitions from Childhood to Adulthood', *Children's Geographies*, 1(1): 37–52.

Valiér, C. (1998) 'Psychoanalysis and Crime in Britain During the Interwar Years', *British Criminology Conferences*, vol. 1, J. Vagg and T. Newburn (eds).

Venables, P.H. (1987) 'Autonomic Nervous System Factors in Criminal Behaviour', in S.A. Mednick, T.E. Moffitt and S.A. Stack (eds) *The Causes of Crime: New Biological Approaches*. Cambridge: Cambridge University Press.

Veneziano, C. and Veneziano, L. (2002) 'Adolescent Sex Offenders: A Review of the Literature', *Trauma, Violence, and Abuse*, 3(4): 247–60.

Vitaro, F. and Wanner, B. (2005) 'Patterns of Affiliation with Delinquent Friends During Late Childhood and Early Adolescence: Correlates and Consequences', *Social Development*, 14(1): 82–108.

Vitelli, R.M. (1998) 'Childhood Disruptive Behaviour Disorders and Adult Psychopathy', *American Journal of Forensic Psychology*, 16(4): 29–37.

Vizard, E., French, L., Hickey, N. and Bladon, E. (2004) 'Severe Personality Disorder Emerging in Childhood: A Proposal for a New Developmental Disorder', *Criminal Behaviour and Mental Health*, 14: 17–28.

Volavka, J. (1987) 'Electroencephalogram Among Criminals', in S.A. Mednick, T.E. Moffitt and S.A. Stack (eds) *The Causes of Crime: New Biological Approaches*. Cambridge: Cambridge University Press.

Wadsworth, J., Burnell, I., Taylor, B. and Butler, N. (1985), 'The Influence of Family Type on Children's Behaviour and Development at Five Years', *Journal of Child Psychology and Psychiatry*, 26: 245–54.

Wagenaar, W.A., van Koppen, P.J. and Crombag, H.F.M. (1993) *Anchored Narratives: The Psychology of Criminal Conduct*. New York: Harvester Wheatsheaf.

Walby, S. and Allen, J. (2004) *Domestic Violence, Sexual Assault and Stalking: Findings from the British Crime Survey*. Home Office Research Study 276. London: Home Office.

Walker, N. (1968) *Crime and Insanity in England: Volume One: The Historical Perspectives*. Edinburgh: Edinburgh University Press.

Walker, N. and McCabe, S. (1973) *Crime and Insanity in England: Volume Two: New Solutions and New Problems*. Edinburgh: Edinburgh University Press.

Walker-Barnes, C. and Mason, C.A. (2001) 'Ethnic Differences in the Effect of Parenting on Gang Involvement and Gang Delinquency: A Longitudinal, Hierarchical Linear Modelling Perspective', *Child Development*, 72(6): 1814–31.

Wallace, C., Mullen, P., Burgess, P., Palmer, S., Ruschena, D. and Browne, C. (1998) 'Case Linkage Study', *British Journal of Psychiatry*, 172: 477–84.

Walsh, C. (1998) 'Irrational Presumptions of Rationality and Comprehension', *Web Journal of Current Legal Issues*, 3: http://webjcli.ncl.ac.uk/1998/issue3/walsh3.html.

Walsh, E., Buchanan, A. and Fahy, T. (2002). 'Violence and Schizophrenia: Examining the Evidence', *British Journal of Psychiatry*, 180: 490–95.

Walters, G. (2004) 'The Trouble with Psychopathy as a General Theory of Crime', *International Journal of Offender Therapy and Comparative Criminology*, 48(2): 133–48.

Walters, G. and Geyer, M.D. (2004) 'Criminal Thinking and Identity in Male White-Collar Offenders', *Criminal Justice and Behaviour*, 13(3): 263–81.

Ward D.A. and Beck, W.L. (1990) 'Gender and Dishonesty', *Journal of Social Psychology*, 130(3): 333–39.

Ward, T. (1999) 'The Sad Subject of Infanticide: Law, Medicine and Child Murder', *Social and Legal Studies*, 8(2): 163–80.

Warr, M. (1998) 'Life-Course Transitions and Desistance from Crime', *Criminology*, 36(2): 183–215.

Warren, F., McGauley, G., Norton, K. *et al.* (2003) *Review of Treatments for Severe Personality Disorder*. London: Home Office.

Warwick, I., Chase, E. and Aggleton, P. (2004) *Homophobia, Sexual Orientation and Schools: A Review and Investigation for Action*. London: Department for Education and Skills.

Watson-Franke, M.-B. (2002) 'A World in Which Women Move Freely Without Fear of Men: An Anthropological Perspective on Rape', *Women's Studies International Forum*, 25(6): 599–606.

Weisburd, D., Waring, E. and Chayet, E.F. (2001) *White Collar Crime and Criminal Careers*. New York: Cambridge University Press.

Weisser, M.R. (1982) *Crime and Punishment in Early Modern Europe*. Brighton: Harvester Press.

Weissman, M., Pilowsky, D. and Wickramaratne, P. (2006) 'Remissions in Maternal Depression and Child Psychopathology', *Journal of the American Medical Association*, 295: 1389–98.

Wertham, F. (1962) *A Sign for Caine: An Exploration of Human Violence*. New York: Macmillan.

West, D.J. (1982) *Delinquency: Its Roots, Careers, and Prospects*. London: Heinemann.

White, J.L., Moffitt, T.E., Earls, F., Robins, L. and Silva, P.A. (1990) 'How Early Can We Tell? Predictors of Childhood Conduct Disorder and Adolescent Delinquency', *Criminology*, 29(4): 507–33.

Whitely, J.S. (1996) 'The Anti-Social Personality Disorder: Strategies for Psychotherapy', in C. Cordess and M. Cox (eds) *Forensic Psychotherapy: Crime Psychodynamics and the Offender Patient*. London: Jessica Kingsley.

WHO (World Health Organisation) (1992) *International Statistical Classification of Diseases and Related Health Problems* (10th Revision) (ICD-10). Geneva: WHO.

Widom, C.S. (1989) 'The Cycle of Violence', *Science*, 244: 160–66.

Wiener, M.J. (2004) *Men of Blood: Violence, Manliness and Criminal Justice in Victorian England*. Cambridge: Cambridge University Press.

Wilkins, T.M. and Warner, S. (2001) 'Women in Special Hospitals: Understanding the Presenting Behaviour of Women Diagnosed with Borderline Personality Disorder', *Journal of Psychiatric and Mental Health Nursing*, 8: 289–97.

Williams, K.S. (1991) *Textbook on Criminology*. London: Blackstone.

Willott, S. and Griffin, C. (1999) 'Building Your Own Lifeboat: Working Class Male Offenders Talk About Economic Crime', *British Journal of Social Psychology*, 38: 445–60.

Wilson, H. (1980) 'Parental Supervision: A Neglected Aspect of Delinquency', *British Journal of Criminology*, 20: 203–35.

Wilson, J.Q. (1975) *Thinking About Crime*. New York: Basic Books.

Winnicott, D.W. (1984) *Deprivation and Delinquency*. London: Tavistock.

Wolfgang, M.E. (1958) *Patterns in Criminal Homicide*. Philadelphia: University of Pennsylvania Press.

Wolfgang, M.E. (1961) 'Pioneers in Criminology: Cesare Lombroso (1835–1909)', *Journal of Criminal Law, Criminology, and Police Science*, 52(4): 361–91.

Worley, K., Walsh, S. and Lewis, K. (2004) 'An Examination of Parenting Experiences in Male Perpetrators of Domestic Violence: A Qualitative Study', *Psychology and Psychotherapy: Theory, Research and Practice*, 77: 35–54.

Wouters, C. (1999) 'Changing Patterns of Social Controls and Self-Controls', *British Journal of Criminology*, 39(3): 416–32.

Wright, C. and Weekes, D. (2003) 'Race and Gender in the Contestation and Resistance of Teacher Authority and School Sanctions: The Case of African Caribbean Pupils in England, *Comparative Education Review*, 47(1): 3–20.

Wright, R., Brookman, F. and Bennett, T. (2006) 'The Foreground Dynamics of Street Robbery in Britain', *British Journal of Criminology*, 46: 1–15.

Yates, C. (2000) 'Masculinity and Good Enough Jealousy', *Psychoanalytic Studies*, 2(1): 77–88.

Yochelson, S. and Samenow, S. (1976) *The Criminal Personality* (vol. 1). New York: J. Aronson.

Young, A. (1996) *Imagining Crime*. London: Sage.

Young, J. (1986) 'The Failure of Criminology: The Need for a Radical Realism', in R. Mathews and J. Young (eds) *Confronting Crime*. London: Sage.

Young, J. (1999) *The Exclusive Society: Social Exclusion, Crime and Difference in Late Modernity*. London: Sage.

Young, J. (2003) 'Merton with Energy, Katz with Structure: The Sociology of Vindictiveness and the Criminology of Transgression', *Theoretical Criminology*, 7(3): 389–414.

Young, J. and Mathews, R. (1992) *Rethinking Criminology: The Realist Debate*. London: Sage.

Youth Justice Board (2004a) *Joint Inspection of Youth Offending Teams: The First Phase Annual Report*. London: Youth Justice Board.

Youth Justice Board (2004a) *Prolific and Other Priority Offenders Strategy: Guide for YOTs*. London: Youth Justice Board.

Zedner, L. (1991) *Women, Crime and Custody*. Oxford: Clarendon.

Author Index

Kemshall, H. 204, 229, 236, 237, 277
Kernberg, O.F. 68, 277
Kersten, J. 224, 225, 277
Kjelsberg, E. 104, 277
Kline, L.M. 214, 280
Klinesmith, J. 158, 277
Klinteberg, B. 114, 278
Knight, B.J. 172
Kochanska, G. 116, 120, 277
Kohlberg, L. 27, 30, 138, 139, 140, 165, 166, 242, 277
Kohut, H. 209, 278
Kolvin, I. 104, 278
Kolvin, P.A. 104, 278
Konishi, T. 225, 278
Kramar, J.K. 44, 278
Kratzer, L. 99, 278
Krause, J. 68, 240, 264
Kroneman, L. 102, 275
Kunst, H. 63, 68, 278
Kustanovich, V. 99, 287
Kutchinsky, B. 226, 278

Laible, D. 121, 278
Lalumière, M.L. 219, 278
Lang, S. 114, 278
Lansky, M.R. 69, 278
Lanthier, R.D. 218, 264
Lasch, C. 189, 249, 250, 251, 252, 278
Laub, J. 82, 95, 96, 97, 100, 114, 148, 278
Lawson, J.S. 226, 278
LeBlanc, M. 233, 279
Lee, J.K.P. 232, 278
Lee, R. 98, 278
Leese, M. 266
Leichsenring, F. 63, 68, 278
Lemert, E. 13, 278
Leschied, A. 176, 278
Levi, M. 179, 279
Levy, F. 99, 279
Lewis, H.E. 118, 187, 188, 279
Lewis, K. 211, 292
Lindsay, W.R. 50, 279
Lingham, R. 40, 286

Little, D.L. 159, 177, 271
Livaditis, M. 104, 279
Loeber, R. 88, 89, 99, 102, 134, 271, 275, 279, 285
Logan, C. 41, 70, 265
Logie, R. 28, 268
Lombroso, C. 2, 8–10, 21, 22, 23, 50, 58, 216, 279
Longo-Stadler, M. 159, 265
Looman, J. 219, 279
Lösel, F. 67, 279
Losoya, S.H. 120, 289
Low, H. 151, 253
Lower, R.L. 144, 272
Luckenbill, D.F. 179, 180–181, 183, 279
Lussier, P. 233, 279
Lutter, C. 158, 265
Lykken, D. 24, 105, 279
Lyng, S. 19, 149, 150, 152, 279
Lynman, D. 74, 88, 89, 90, 134, 281, 285
Lyons-Ruth, K. 120, 256, 279

MacCulloch, M. 217, 279
McGrath, P. 226, 278
Maden, A. 173, 279
Maguire, M. xv, 169, 266, 279
Malamuth, N.M. 214, 222, 280
Malcuit, G. 156, 285
Mannheim, H. 3, 280
Marschsall, D.E. 118, 146, 190
Marshall, W.L. 31, 218, 219, 226, 264, 278, 279, 280
Mason, C.A. 147, 291
Masson, H. 236, 280
Mattesson, A. 151, 283
Matza, D. 12, 28, 148, 280
Mazur, A. 157, 158, 280
McAndrew, F.T. 158, 277
McBride, M. 236, 273
McBrien, J. 50, 280
McCabe, S. 58, 291
McCallum, D. 61, 280
McCloskey, L. 146, 289

Urbas, G. 130, 290
Ussher, J 175, 290
Utting, D. 254, 290

Valentine, G. 136, 290
Valiér, C. 32, 290
Van Brunschot, M. 176, 278
Van Gijseghem, H. 233, 290
Vanheule, S. 228, 265
van Koppen, P.J. 62, 291
Vanstone, M. 234, 268
Veneziano, C. 235, 291
Veneziano, L. 235, 291
Verberg, N. 227, 287
Vitaro, F. 95, 148, 291
Vitelli, R.M. 66, 99, 291
Vizard, E. 91, 291
Vrij, A. 218, 281

Wadsworth, J. 107, 291
Wagenaar, W.A. 62, 291
Wagner, P.E. 118, 146, 190
Walby, S. 203, 204, 206, 215, 291
Walker, N. 42, 43, 44, 45, 46, 47, 58, 291
Walker-Barnes, C. 147, 291
Wallace, C. 51, 291
Walsh, A. 22, 270
Walsh, C. 131, 291
Walsh, E. 40, 51, 291
Walsh, S. 211, 293
Walters, G. 59, 100, 291, 292
Walton, P. xvi, 5, 14, 34, 93, 290
Wanner, B. 95, 148, 291
Ward D.A. 172, 292
Ward, T. 222, 232, 278, 284
Ward, T. 44, 292
Waring, E. 100, 101, 292
Warner, S. 63, 292
Warr, M. 97, 292
Warren, F. 70, 261, 292
Warwick, I. 260, 292
Wastell, L. 188, 285
Watson, W.D. 44, 278
Watson-Franke, M.-B. 223, 224, 292

Watt, A. 217, 279
Wedekind, D. 68, 240, 264
Weekes, D. 151, 292
Weisburd, D. 100, 101, 292
Weisser, M.R. 4, 292
Weissman, M. 256, 292
Wenk, E. 78, 269
Wertham, F. 189, 292
West, A. 94, 284
West, D.J. 74–86, 87, 89, 94, 115, 134, 270, 292
White, G. 174, 266
White, H. 102, 275
White, J.L. 91, 292
White, J.W. 215, 274
Whitfield J.B. 159, 272
Widom, C.S. 112–113, 160, 292
Wiener, M.J. 159, 292
Wilkins, T.M. 63, 292
Wilkinson, D.G. 203, 290
Wilkinson, D.L. 148, 163, 183, 194, 257
Wilks, C. 174, 266
Williams, B. 159, 272
Williams, K.S. xvi, xviii, 11, 93, 220, 290
Wilson, M. 22, 156, 161, 184, 185, 208, 268
Willott, S. 194, 293
Wilson, H. 105, 114, 293
Wilson, J.Q. xvii, 292
Winnicott, D.W. 142, 143, 292
Wolfgang, M.E. 9, 179, 183, 206, 210, 293
Wood, E. 227, 287
Woodward, L.J. 111, 271
Worley, K. 211, 293
Wouters, C. 246–247, 293
Wright, C. 151, 293
Wright, R. 194, 293
Wright, R. 28, 268
Wu, P. 122, 277

Yamashita, H. 151, 263
Yochelson, S. 31, 293

Subject Index